ANGLOPHILIA

Anglophilia
Deference, Devotion, and Antebellum America

ELISA TAMARKIN

THE UNIVERSITY OF CHICAGO PRESS
CHICAGO AND LONDON

ELISA TAMARKIN is associate professor of English at the University of
California, Irvine.

The University of Chicago Press, Chicago 60637
The University of Chicago Press, Ltd., London
© 2008 by The University of Chicago
All rights reserved. Published 2008
Printed in the United States of America

16 15 14 13 12 11 10 09 08   1 2 3 4 5

ISBN-13: 978-0-226-78944-6 (cloth)
ISBN-10: 0-226-78944-6 (cloth)

The University of Chicago Press gratefully acknowledges the generous
contribution of the University of California, Irvine, toward the publication
of this book.

Library of Congress Cataloging-in-Publication Data

Tamarkin, Elisa.
Anglophilia : deference, devotion, and antebellum America /
Elisa Tamarkin.
p. cm.
Includes bibliographical references and index.
ISBN-13: 978-0-226-78944-6 (cloth : alk. paper)
ISBN-10: 0-226-78944-6 (cloth : alk. paper)
1. United States—Civilization—1783–1865.   2. United States—
Civilization—British influences.   3. United States—History—Revolution,
1775–1783—Influence.   4. United States—Relations—Great Britain.
5. Great Britain—Relations—United States.   6. Great Britain—Foreign
public opinion, American.   7. Public opinion—United States—History—
19th century.   8. Popular culture—United States—History—
19th century.   9. Democracy—Social aspects—United States—History—
19th century.   10. Political culture—United States—History—
19th century.   I. Title.
E165.T17 2008
973.3—dc22

2007020556

For Mark Goble

Contents

Illustrations

Acknowledgments

One of the premises of this book is that acts of deference, when given freely, are the greatest privilege because they show faith in a world that is filled with worthiness and, so, worth deferring to. The book also suggests that being able to take pleasure in someone else's value confers value on ourselves, which is one way of saying that *Anglophilia*'s worth is in its acknowledgments.

This project took shape under the direction of Jay Fliegelman, who raised graduate advising to a high art and for whose virtuosity I owe my first, best thanks. He gave me the gift of my field and, much more, a relation to my field that is intimate, palpable, and filled with meaning and something like knowing what it's all about. His lessons are rightly legendary and, for this student (who is no exception), lifelong. Others at Stanford were generous: George Dekker taught me that the most imaginative histories can also be true; Arnold Rampersad taught me to think gracefully about class; John Bender made me responsible for what I say; and Terry Castle made me care more than anyone how I say it. The year Bryan Wolf visited, in 1995–96, was the year I began looking at paintings while understanding how devious my looking can be; for him, the pictures here are the stories in disguise.

For two years the English Department at the University of California, Santa Barbara (UCSB), showed me that intellectual courtesy is the complement to integrity and engagement; I am especially grateful for the continued warmth of Patricia Fumerton, Giles Gunn, Alan Liu, Mark Maslan, Candace Waid, and William Warner. Richard Helgerson had faith in the manuscript before it deserved anything of the kind, and I owe him most of my efforts to compensate since. At the University of California, Irvine, I benefited from the attentive and spirited advice of Richard Kroll, Rodrigo Lazo, Jayne Lewis, Michael Szalay, and Brook Thomas, all of whom read parts of the manuscript; from the ready support of Steven Mailloux, James McMichael, and especially Irene Tucker; and from both the material and needless indulgence of the department chair, Jerome Christensen.

This work was generously funded by the American Council of Learned Societies and by a University of California President's Research Fellowship, which allowed me to devote a full year to the manuscript. It was also made possible by fellowships from the American Antiquarian Society and the Library Company of Philadelphia, by the assistance of the wonderful staffs at both places, and by the staffs at the Massachusetts Historical Society, the Houghton Library, the New York Public Library, and the Huntington Library. I am particularly glad for the help of Joanne Chaison and John Hench at the American Antiquarian Society and of Connie King and James Green at the Library Company. I owe much to Karen Lawrence, Humanities Dean at the University of California, Irvine, and to Michael Szalay and Irvine's Humanities Center for publication subsidies toward the costs of production and the book's illustrations.

My fond thanks to Ross Posnock for reading so much and sympathetically and for contributing more to the book than I've let him know; to Helen Deutsch for her exuberance, intelligence, and getting involved; and to Dana Nelson for her generous and forbearing responses to the manuscript. I'm grateful to the late Michael Rogin for the hope that his confidence gave me to write a book in earnest. The following colleagues and friends talked with me about the book, provided occasions for sharing parts of it, or otherwise helped me think through my work and past it: Rachel Adams, Caroline Bicks, Helen Blythe, Amanda Claybaugh, Peter Coviello, Barbara Fuchs, Paul Gilmore, Teresa Goddu, Philip Gould, Eric Hayot, Cathy Jurca, Robert Levine, Chris Looby, Mark McGurl, Alex Nemerov, Sianne Ngai, Diana Paulin, Julie Rottenberg, Roger Stein, and Diane Simon. I received valuable suggestions from members of the Early American Research Focus Group at UCSB, the Americanist Research Colloquium at UCLA, and the Southern California Americanist Group, whom I especially thank for years of collegiality, continuity, and reading well. Without the support of Esther Levin, Ira Levin, Michelle Levin, Michael Cohen, and especially Civia Tamarkin, I would not have had the wherewithal to complete this project or to enjoy the fact of writing it.

I'm immensely grateful for the editorial care of Alan Thomas at the University of Chicago Press, for Randolph Petilos and the editorial team who saw the manuscript into print, and for Yvonne Zipter's expert and thoughtful copyediting. The three anonymous readers for the press offered detailed and searching responses to the manuscript and the best challenges in returning to it.

Portions of chapters 2 and 3 were first published in, respectively, *Modern Language Quarterly* 67, no. 2 (Spring 2006) and *American Literary History* 14, no. 3 (Fall 2002). My thanks to Marshall Brown at *MLQ* and Gordon Hutner at *ALH*, both exemplary editors, and to the anonymous readers whose suggestions strengthened my work in those pages and these.

This book is in memory of Bob Tamarkin, who taught me that a life of reading can be the point and not the excuse and who showed me that the best people are the very few who remember how to play. I adored him with all the privilege and sadness that involved.

For Mark Goble, who still seems willing to "stake his future on his faith" in me—all that follows is thanks to him. Learning to love the sincerity with which he lives and thinks has been the greatest sign for me of my self-worth. How lucky I am to know how smart he is.

Preface

Paying Respects

"Let him learn to hear the disappearance of things he was wont to reverence, without losing his reverence."
—RALPH WALDO EMERSON, *"Montaigne"*

Samuel F. B. Morse's *The House of Representatives* (1822) includes portraits of sixty-eight congressmen, six justices of the Supreme Court, a sergeant-at-arms, two doorkeepers, two servants, two editors of a local paper, a Yale professor, a Pawnee chief, and Morse's father, but the painting feels empty (fig. 1). The figures operate against the hall they fill. The entablature, sweeping upward to the right, encloses the viewer in the illusionistic space of the rotunda and from where we are—as if in the gallery—Congress appears small. The painting is set before an evening session (the clock above the doorway says 6:13), and the congressmen are reading, reclining, or talking in the dark hall that overwhelms them. The impulse to abundance in the scale of the building, and in the drapes, columns, and desks, does not argue against the picture's emptiness by granting us so much for such a minimalist effect. As a painting about the business of democracy, it is striking because the institution is too imperious, while its government is too casual and quiet.

Morse painted the scene after seeing John Trumbull's *The Declaration of Independence* (fig. 2), which toured in 1818 to the kind of commercial success that Morse never had, especially with *The House of Representatives*. In Trumbull's work, Congress watches the main event: Thomas Jefferson submits the declaration to Congress, with John Hancock presiding. The picture is committed to the proposition that something happens at the site of politics; the declaration is ready to be signed, and

FIGURE 1. Samuel F. B. Morse, *The House of Representatives*, 1822–23. In the Collection of the Corcoran Gallery of Art.

FIGURE 2. John Trumbull, *The Declaration of Independence*, 1787–1820. Yale University Art Gallery; Trumbull Collection.

its authority, as we know, is "self-evident" in the democratic will and feeling of the British colonists whose challenge to traditionary power produces, in Hannah Arendt's words, "one of the rare moments in history when the power of action is great enough to erect its own monument."[1] The declaration is illuminated on Hancock's desk against the dark cloth of Jefferson's sleeve—a vital object of attention, like the painting that bears its name. The drama consists in how republicans assemble around it. The central group stands shoulder to shoulder and, along with Hancock, effectively encircles the declaration, while Congress contains them all. The viewer completes the last circle and presumably emulates the absorbed attention of the figure at the far left leaning to get a better look or any of the men pitched forward in their seats. If the revolutionary event "does not possess any ontological guarantee"—a revolution, after all, creates a state "out of nothing"—Trumbull commemorates the moment of signing onto something, for *now* we understand that history happens when men of purpose come together and choose to make it.[2] The audience in Philadelphia is there to witness what Trumbull's audience looks to remember: the singular, contingent act that tells them who they are.

Half a century after the event, Morse painted a picture of Congress doing nothing much. Since politics is not the point of the painting at least we can say that this is not a democracy, in Tocqueville's sense, "given up to its own propensities."[3] There is no vital event before the House convenes or the lights are lit, so the representatives are given over to everyday exchanges or daily preparing and are scattered to fill a scene of Congress that remains constituitively unfulfilled. It is, to paraphrase Ernesto Laclau, an emptiness that we can signify in the hollowness at the center of the room that hangs at eye level or in the figures down below, materially bound to their idleness insofar as they need to be indifferently oriented for us to see their faces, which Morse took from life.[4] They answer to Trumbull's semicircle of portraits, which would be the alternative. In Trumbull, Hancock signals the event in a chair at the center of it; but here, the Speaker's chair is empty at the far left. There are no Founding Fathers, only Morse's father at a distance in the balcony. The declaration is not compelling at the heart of government but framed as a principle behind it—in this case, quite literally, on the back wall. The impossibility of saying in Morse's painting just what democracy might be for is how its representatives seem to name it: a society of individuals experiencing a structure of abandonment, and an absence of shared interests, together.

The hall that Morse painted was the new hall that Benjamin Henry Latrobe designed after the English burned the Capitol in the War of 1812. Morse spent the War of 1812 in England, studying at the Royal Academy, so one could say that his painting is a redemptive gesture of national service—not that Morse had said so. He was a strident democrat and nativist who ran political campaigns against "foreign influence" and "foreign importations" of the Irish especially; in art, he founded the National Academy of Design to encourage an American vernacular and cultural independence. In England in 1812, Morse endorsed the war, in opposition to his father's "infatuated" Federalism; the English, he wrote home, are "haughty . . . imperious . . . tyrannical."[5] Still, his letters from England indulge in a boyish tourist's blindness to the "extravagant abuse" he records; not feeling "any of those disagreeable feelings" that his politics demand, Morse comes to love the exertions of the British state apart from the power they represent. The queen's drawing room is "a singular sight to see" and so is the prince regent in his "splendid state carriage," and the "great many splendid equipages" at St. James and elsewhere. War brought its own garniture and array, and nothing compared, for example, to the "splendid *entrée*" of Louis

XVIII into London, when he was received at court by the "king's splendid band" and the queen of England, blowing kisses from the balcony
of the palace. Morse would "never forget" seeing the French king, who
had been exiled during Napoleon's rule, raised up before the adoration
of the British public "as if by magic . . . in an instant to his throne." ("In
the heat of my enthusiasm," writes Morse, "I joined with heart and soul
in the cries of '*Vive le roi!*'"[6]). There were other moments, too, when
he was "quite in love," during the celebrations of peace in 1814, following princes around London or attending Covent Garden to watch the
princes in the prince's box while *they* watched the entertainment. With
Morse always intent on getting a "better and nearer view," he wonders
if the king should die so he might "witness . . . a coronation."[7] Why else
would one put down a king?

    "Ritual is not technological," Edward Shils writes, to suggest that it is
not part of a chain of means or ends or useful "in any empirical sense,"
which is perhaps why the democrat at war reveres the pageantry of royalty since it is so useless to the position he takes.[8] "It is, perhaps, well I
am here," Morse says, "for, with my present opinions, if I were at home,
I should most certainly be in the army or navy."[9] It is a good thing he
is in England because otherwise he would fight it—a logic that reflects
an experience of enchantment that is indifferent to its cause. Morse's
devotion to the aesthetic forms of an iconic England is pitched against
the full seriousness of his antagonism; it is a conservative position but
also, in Laclau's sense, a "radical investment" because it is not determin-
able by any political ideas or commitments that Morse could normally
withstand.[10] It is, in fact, not normal at all for a democrat in England
at a time of war with England to find his affinities so opposed to his
beliefs; but I am interested in what it means—for Morse, and for other
Americans thinking through their loyalties and estrangements—to feel
the deepest reality of attachment without the reality behind it. Morse's
fascination with the symbolic rituals of England is made anachronistic
at the moment of war that occasions them; his responsiveness is exhil-
arated by a play of emotions that are unburdened by any content. England does not divert Morse from his politics, but at those times when
he decides, on the advice of his parents, to "be the artist wholly"—that
is, to lead a life as an artist in England that is irresponsible as such—he
is as positive in his devotions as if they carried the weight of his politics. Everything that Morse embraces while abroad suggests the need, as
Shils describes, to affirm rituals in the midst of crisis, only here they are

the enemy's rituals. Still, they have the quality to move you. "England," says Morse reciting a bit of verse, " 'with all thy faults, I love thee still.' " [11]

While in London, Morse anticipated painting an epic picture and purchased a "great canvas" to carry home. That canvas became *The House of Representatives*. It is a major history painting with little history in it. Morse's father and the Pawnee chief tell us this is 1822, because that year (the year Morse was in the House taking portraits), his father submitted a long report to Congress on Indian affairs east of the Mississippi; it argued for a policy of education and assimilation but was dead on arrival in a Congress that was moving toward Indian removal—a useless relic of an earlier commission. Nothing else is topical, unless one counts three architects of the Missouri Compromise, impalpably glowing in the center of the middle ground—their faces in the half-light are hard to distinguish. [12] Mostly, as I say, the picture seems unoccupied, a well of space without much doing at the site of democracy as Morse depicted it on his expansive canvas from England. He shows a diffused scene where each representative is at once distinctly realized and curiously lost; this is a massive assembly of portraits, but Morse blends their features, cloaks, and collars by a subtle concatenation of light, and by restricting the hue. There is little pattern to the distribution of the figures, which is appropriate since the House has not yet come to order and the representatives are left to talk casually among themselves or sit alone as they like in postures of conversation and reflection. In this scene, before the dramas of politics begin, we see an aestheticized accommodation to a diversity of interests. The outcome looks more like refinement than randomness. Congress had debated the Missouri Compromise and new members of the western states were clashing with eastern elites—the floor was a scene of outcry and "confusion"—but everything urges acceptance. [13] *The House of Representatives* doesn't argue. The culture of government underwrites its own significance in the easy light and atmosphere of the institution where the total effect contains the moment at which its elements might spin apart. This is government *as* an effect and culture, and not a proposition.

I want to suggest not that Morse's idling, melancholy *House of Representatives* pictures democracy at risk but, rather, democracy as it is most thoroughly at home. If democracy, as Claude Lefort observes, means that the "locus of power becomes an *empty place*," bereft of the embodiments of political authority, we see in Morse's painting an attempt to register this emptiness and to understand the energies that circulate within it. For Morse, they are markedly centrifugal—the farther away from the central recesses of the chamber we go, the more people we find spun out to the edges of the painting. Traditional models of authority are set aside; the scene of politics is emptied of what Kant describes as "pathological" content.[14] "Fathers," like Indian chiefs, are set aside and look like the material remains of an older order. In a variation on the logic of totemic fantasy, they are exalted in this picture (above us) precisely because they are diminished and derealized as figures of authority.[15] They stand behind the clock marking time.

Into this evacuated space, Morse raises up a doorkeeper to light the chandelier. The figure is magnificent: his silhouetted form against the Argand lamp seems to resurrect the attitude of *The Dying Hercules* (fig. 3) that Morse exhibited in London—the triumph of his years

FIGURE 3. Samuel F. B. Morse, *The Dying Hercules,* 1812–13. Yale University Art Gallery (gift of Samuel F. B. Morse).

there. The doorkeeper ascends on the ladder to reach the top and now the hall is fully luminous with candlelight: "I shall have it a candle-light effect," says Morse, "when the room, already very splendid, will appear ten times more so."[16] The spectacles of monarchy were "splendid" for him too, and Morse wants the chandelier to provide a comparable aesthetic for his image of democracy. The brilliant object at the center of the room has all the "incandescence" that Shils attributes to the effects of charismatic authority. As the focal point of a democracy in action, it is technically nonsensical; but if it has meaning in the picture, it is the same kind of meaning that the symbols and rituals of such authority make at the center of monarchical life. The representatives encircle the silhouette (itself a void in the middle of the scene) with the sort of compulsion that Slavoj Žižek finds in democracies, "to *encircle* again and again the site of the lost Thing" by means of "some 'empty' symbolic gesture."[17]

The picture of politics it produces for the viewer demands an awe that is distinctly unfamiliar as a feeling about democracy. The declaration hangs on the far wall much like a painting, and in its place Morse raises up a figure who has nothing to declare but has all the sense of "Mystery" that Morse also attributes to the sublime appeal of art.[18] The figure gestures to produce a moment of pure illumination, a positive expression in an empty hall that works with epiphanic power, but no ideas. Like the telegraph Morse invented later, the picture communicates in a flash. The painting, staged before the debates begin, says democracies come together not through language and abstract principles (the declaration works differently here) but through the prepolitical feelings we experience toward symbols and works of art.

How do democracies constitute themselves? In Horace Bonham's *Nearing the Issue at the Cockpit* (1878), a heterogeneous group of Americans unite around a common fascination (fig. 4). Ethnically and racially diverse, the crowd—gentleman and laborer, white and black—presses against the rail and rope that marks off the circle where the action is, which means they press against the picture plane as well. We need not turn to Clifford Geertz to understand the symbolic stakes behind a cockfight, but it does help to remember that such events are where experience is made "comprehensible by presenting it in terms of acts and objects which have had their practical consequences removed." Or more to the point, "the cockfight is 'really real' only to the cocks," and

FIGURE 4. Horace Bonham, *Nearing the Issue at the Cockpit,* 1878. In the Collection of the Corcoran Gallery of Art.

in Bonham's painting, it certainly is not real for us: the "issue" at hand, however vivid and dramatic it may be within the fiction of the image, is irrelevant to the spectacle of social feeling it so powerfully compels.[19] We see right through it to the belonging it occasions. The painting offers a visual correlative to Laclau's sense that there is always "something that the totality expels from itself in order to constitute itself," for in the painting, the symbolic event that frames the crowd is, quite simply, out of the frame.[20] For Bonham, what is at "issue" *is* what is absent for us but what we nonetheless try to look into when we want to understand the pleasures and forms that bring a diversified people together. It is a painting of democracy in which an absence is all there is to see.

This book is about absences and about the value of the symbolic forms and rituals that Americans excluded as they shaped their democratic culture in the years after independence from England. *Anglophilia* is about paying respects to the symbolic value of England. We might track this pattern of belief back to the first years following the Revolution and consider it a legacy of independence itself.[21] If England remained a compelling object of attention, it was because it mattered that much less to a nation that had successfully thrown it off. A profound reinvestment in the symbolic authority of England thus served as an index to the loss of real authority for an empire and monarchy that could at best influence the imagination of the colonies it no longer ruled. Antebellum Americans staged their deference toward England in elaborate rituals of fascination, but their deference was insignificant, except that it allowed for an experience of belonging that was made possible because they had no one to belong to but themselves.

This book traces the phenomenon of American Anglophilia as a devotion that provided not so much a place where antebellum Americans found release from the burdens of their own nationality, but where their "Americanness" was lived in other languages of national expression. The England that was especially attractive to Americans was also especially mysterious, and its effects were almost entirely the product of the dedication it inspired. I say this not to qualify the historical significance of American Anglophilia but to suggest that this significance resides largely with those aspects of American life we see illuminated in the image of "England" it brings forth. Anglophilia—as a fetish and nostalgia that is just as much a politics and aspiration—tells a story of English culture and society that is rooted in the character of English life but, finally, an expression of the anxieties and wishes of someplace else.

At times, Anglophilia may look like the perversity of a guilty conscience that will not own what it has fought to gain. "Come here, little boy, and show me your extraordinary jacket!": thus Henry James remembers being summoned at seven years old before the "great" William Thackeray, whose presence in New York represents, for him, a literary world that was "overwhelmingly and irresistibly English."[22] If this is a primal scene of anxiety in the face of English culture, James also produced this account of his "exposure" long after being recognized as the "Master" of a literary style that marks the modern, transatlantic world that succeeded Thackeray's. For even as Thackeray jokes about James's jacket and its big buttons—he calls him "Buttons"—James flaunts his vulnerability at least in part to indulge in the "extraordinary" expression of the moment he has managed to outlive. Such scenes both sustain the image of England's paternalistic presence in America and memorialize that presence as a tribute to America's feeling for it. The "benevolence" that James at last associates with Thackeray is the opposite of the dread that he inspires; and where James is elsewhere anxious about the influence of his own father (and his older brother, too) the influence of England is considerably more benign because it is more available for use.

"Come here, little boy": the appeal of England is always historically, if not personally, regressive. This does not mean that American Anglophila works only when employed as a language of conservatism and tradition. There are times when a pronounced attachment to England registers a critical sense of disaffection with American society, including its politics of slavery and its anti-intellectualism. Still, Anglophilia owes even its progressive energy to a backward belief in what might be called the "aura" of British Empire, with an emphasis on the "phenomenon of a distance, however close" that is, for Walter Benjamin, the singular experience of the aesthetic object.[23] We might say that Anglophilia makes an art out of colonial vicariousness: the fantasy that England still functions as an imperial metropolis for Americans patterns a devotion to a mythology of British sovereign power that sees it grow in strength the more that it recedes. "It has often been observed," writes Giorgio Agamben, "that the juridico-political order has the structure of an inclusion of what is simultaneously pushed outside." A parallel to this kind of logic seems to draw Americans back to Britain's monarchy—and especially the *"arcana imperii"* that represents the state's "communal life" in its most exceptional symbolic form—as a consequence of their revolt against it.[24] The allure of England's pageantry of state for Americans who consume it readily and sincerely is admittedly nostalgic but too far past the Revolution to attribute to the aftershocks of British rule in any convincing way. This is to suggest that an American love of monarchy—which is a fact of nineteenth-century culture that has largely been ignored—emerges from within the psychology of democratic life itself.

Thus while American Anglophilia trades in an iconography of (imperial) Englishness that has been variously explored among British subjects by Perry Anderson, Arjun Appadurai, David Cannadine, C. L. R. James, Tom Nairn, and others, it also remains an index to a particular experience of being American.[25] For while it is the case that Anglophilia's story takes us to some places where we might well expect to find it—in the character of American society and class, in the practices and pretensions of American taste, and in the vexed notions of American intellectualism—I am also interested in a far more pervasive network of affects and attachments that pattern a popular devotion across class, region, and even race. This book, then, is not about borrowings from abroad so much as an effort to work past narratives of British influence toward a more intricate culture of American response that included Whig elites, Boston Brahmins, radical democrats, urban immigrants, and the classes of students in Harvard Yard. We will see African Americans participating in the affiliating rituals and languages of Anglophilia, including some who laid claim to versions of an Anglo-Saxonism that seemed to be the exclusive province of white Americans in both the North and South. Indeed, the Anglophila I examine does not depend on prior ties or ethnic sympathies with Britain but, rather, exploits a complex of American attitudes toward history, sociability, and the emotional terrain of nationalism itself.

To this end, the book's dedication to an extensive archive is a central feature of its argument. I return to nineteenth-century America with a historicism that is less deductive than demonstrative: there are aspects of Anglophilia that are best understood from close attention to the works of famous figures from the period (Emerson, Hawthorne, and Lowell), while there are others that are most visible only when what travels under the ungainly name of cultural production, at its most ephemeral and anonymous, is allowed to occupy the foreground. I look at genteel society, where we might find the appropriative logic of class that Adorno, for one, associates with European Anglophiles (they draw on England, he says, for the "artificial preservation of a style").[26] But I also consider a much broader fascination with English society and its traditions that is resolutely popular, not simply because there is so much of it but because it allows for relations between a diverse cast of Americans who share little with one another save for the way that Englishness appeals to them. It should be obvious that American Anglophilia was not felt universally; by the same token, the rhetorics of nativism, and the frequent claims by many in the period that cultural nationalism is predicated on separation from Europe, should not be discounted. But I want to suggest that alongside such discourses we find a desire for more far-flung relations and for an exceptional American culture that is distinguished by its relish for these other, more superbly foreign ways. We need better to examine how nationalism, as a form of feeling, an ideology, and a set of practices, works every bit as seriously at bringing some aspects of the outside in, as it does at keeping others out. And to overlook this canny aspect of American culture—which says

that Americans adore England as a part of their national character—
is to risk forgetting just what it is about the nation that inspires reverence for its forms. "We are who we are," suggests David Harlan, by virtue
of who we care about.[27]

Chapter 1 traces the democratic fascination with both the sacred rituals of state and the personalized authority of the British monarchy,
while attempting to make sense of the symbolic value of such prepolitical attachments. I am interested not only in the comparative aesthetics
of governmental power but also in how such psychic projections onto
the forms and practices of a monarchy elsewhere helped to address the
political moment at home. Why, I ask, was a nation mystified by a queen
who wasn't theirs? In the decades leading up to the Civil War, Americans indulged in a cult of reverence toward Britain's monarchy not to
express their loyalty to Queen Victoria but to experience a compensatory and archaic sense of attachment to the idea of a state unlike their
own. Redefining allegiance as a felt response to dignity and grandeur
(as embodied in a queen), Americans who loved Victoria found new
ways to love America: they conceived of a different sort of patriotism
than that enacted by the rational bonds of democratic ideology. That
these political emotions were distinctly un-American was the point: if a
Revolutionary rhetoric seemed to admit the possibility, or inevitability,
of civil war, then perhaps a renewed commitment to belonging could
be learned from feelings for Britain and its objects of devotion.

    I take as my defining event the visit of Victoria's son, the Prince of
Wales, to America in the fall of 1860, when a "universal" and "democratic" love of British royalty, and the rapturous response on his behalf,
made for a surprising national experience and ritual of consensus at
the start of the Civil War. The prince's popularity speaks to a desire for
community—figured as the impulse of a people toward its symbols—
that is also a turn away from the clash of principles to the tangible exemplifications of social feeling. Recalling Victoria's own iconic status
in America from her ascension to the throne in 1837, I consider the
implications of such an enfranchising love for royalty but also how the
monarchophilia of the masses, amid the threats of political disunion,
became the basis of a new patriotism that linked national preservation to the sentiments of obedience and reverence that a monarchy inspires. The public fascination, then, did not mark a turn away from the
national crisis but, rather, a fantastic, impossible endgame for a certain

political culture of citizenship that saw American attachments to "Old England" as a pedagogical ground for the bonds of Union themselves.

The nostalgia for Britain's iconic power patterns an aesthetics of return to colonial structures of feeling. Looking back from beyond independence, Americans remembered their experience of empire as an elegiac fantasy of rank, stability, and paternal authority, where the life of the metropolis was reproduced in the society of Britons overseas. There are times, in other words, when the nineteenth century hesitated to leave behind the settled, hierarchized order against which the colonies rebelled. Instead, the pleasurable identifications with the social world of Britain—imagined always as a reliquary of tradition, ornament, and ritual—gave rise to a retrospective love of its imperial forms. Why, I ask, did the nineteenth century hope to recover, from the other side of independence, what it felt like to be a subject? Chapter 2 charts the melancholy return to "dependence" in the nation's memory of the Revolutionary War where separation from Britain was also a last, valedictory moment with Britain. New historiographical practices of the nineteenth century opened the way for alternative accounts of the Revolution that did not express a sense of national destiny but registered independence as a phenomenon of loss. As historical societies, documentary projects, and Congressional preservation acts made available a far more complete record of the Revolutionary War, historians discovered anecdotes of loyalists and monarchists, of love affairs across enemy lines, and of all the uninterrupted amenities and celebrations (the fetes, processions, dances, and meals) that gave character to the culture of the British campaign. A devotion to the archive permitted chroniclers of independence to indulge the full anachronism of an early American moment that may have had too much love for Britain to be of use for narratives of national progress; this same methodology allowed for sentiment itself to operate as a logic of historical engagement—as a feeling for the particularity of a past that remains most resonant in its most fragmented and anecdotal forms.

Whether or not a more traditional social order persisted in the midst of war and independence, antebellum Americans appeared intent on suggesting that it did. Their interest in anomalous gestures of affection—at least anomalous to romantic narratives of the Revolution—goes at least some way toward establishing, as Shils does, that deference in a democracy thrives as a "furtively admitted thing." From the perspective of Shils's sociology of interaction, the rituals and forms of civil conduct that we recognize as acts of deference speak to a desire "to live in a social world implanted with worthiness"—a world, that is, worth deferring to.[28] If we defer when we are obligated to do it (say, as subjects to a queen), then it is not deference at all. While power demands submission, Shils sees deference as a desire to submit that is compatible with democratic practice—an affect that says, I am free enough to admit your worth and to take my pleasure in it. So when General Schuyler extended a dinner invitation to General Burgoyne (asking humbly for the honor of his company)—though Burgoyne had, without cause, ordered his "splendid country-seat near Saratoga to be burnt"—what Schuyler admits is that there, in the midst of war, he was independent enough to defer to the general he admired.[29] The dinner was an exchange of respect and affability that had no consequence save to make such respect an end in itself, relieving war of its content for a play of social forms in which there was no real value but sociability. This was not an act of diplomacy or the life of war but an abstract play of forms that stood in relation to that life and gave it meaning (gave it worth) by preserving formal acts where real acts failed. "What does that prove?" to ask what the fool asks for Georg Simmel, when confronted with sociability. Nothing, maybe: but the "pure interaction," in which the "burdens" and "inequalities" of life were renounced in order to have satisfaction in the company of others, seems at least to suggest that there was nothing to prove. "It is a game," writes Simmel, "in which one 'acts' as though all were equal, as though he especially esteemed everyone."[30]

Nowhere does deference operate with more symbolic meaning than in the writings of black abolitionists on Britain. Acts of deference, Shils writes, finally dramatize "the problem of who is entitled to what," and for Frederick Douglass, William Wells Brown, Alexander Crummell, or Samuel Ringgold Ward, deference could express a certain will to entitlement in a vocabulary of civility and reverence. Britain offered at least some provisional satisfaction for the "allocative problem" facing African Americans who toured the British Isles as "loyal subjects" to the queen—paying homage to royalty and aristocrats—while staking their claims to worth, status, and even emotions that were socially denied them in America.[31] Chapter 3 looks at the Anglicization of antislavery and how black abolitionists refashioned themselves as "Englishmen," touring Britain with copies of *Jane Eyre*, queen-spotting in London, playing the connoisseurs of tea and tartans, Carlyle and

Macaulay, while seeking out the very spot, for example, where Mary Queen of Scots married Bothell. Embracing a contained life of sociability abroad, black abolitionists deferred to the gentility that best enacted it, and sometimes their deference served some point of antislavery and often it did not. What exactly does it mean for ex-slaves to defer? Whether tactical or sincere, the rituals and performances of deference served to include blacks within a model of British society that many Americans revered. But I am also interested in the moments when the esteem they showed and the functional play of sociability they sought were not perhaps the lies that would make such acts only instrumental to something else.

Thus while black abolitionists never fail to remind Americans that Britain had ended slavery and deserved regard for its better attitude toward race, there is a quality of excess in the expression of this regard that suggests a more complex projection onto the forms of Englishness. Britain's importance to the politics of antislavery was effectively assumed, but aspects of its culture and society were also indulged on their own terms, as if they were not as eccentric to the politics of the movement as they appeared. The attractions of an underdetermined Englishness are rarely disregarded by blacks abroad: the ease and range of English conversation, the manners of its aristocrats, and how they know instinctively to use them, the customs that maintain a sense of duty and decorum—a whole idiom of ritual and class, simply put, that seems decidedly conservative. Descriptions of a traditionary Englishness no doubt played well to white abolitionists and Anglophiles such as Wendell Phillips and Charles Sumner, whose own investment in a chivalric ideal treated ethical and benevolent behavior as the sign of status. Drawing on a model of the "gentleman" that saw style as the proof of moral character, the politics of American reform made its case on the appeal of class, where the example of England seemed to prove the analogy between gentility and virtue. The shared abolitionist attachment to England—with blacks celebrating their "fatherland" in the *Anglo-African Magazine* and white antislavery "cavaliers" fantasizing the nobility of the cause—also suggests a more accommodating Anglophilia that is not yet about race alone, and not yet about the supremacist Anglo-Saxonism of the late nineteenth century.

Still, there are moments when the eccentricities of Englishness, which Anglophilia registers, are more difficult to reconcile to an agenda even as self-consciously involved as that which abolitionists pursued in Britain. What finally is the point of an Anglophilia without qualities? The larger logic of intellectualism that we find in the writings of African Americans abroad suggests that it is exactly a cast of mind that need not attribute any purpose to the world in which it lives that marks the best practice of knowledge. That this cast of mind is conventionally associated with an English intellectual tradition makes it even more desirable for Douglass and other antislavery figures who style themselves as the first black intellectuals. In refusing to subordinate what they take in to what antislavery demands, African Americans in Britain reproduce the sensibility that American intellectuals more generally admire and define as English: from Emerson's approval of their "unconditional surrender" to the variety of experience, to Lionel Trilling's understanding of their "sincerity" as a disavowal of systems and abstractions, American intellectualism has looked to its English counterpart for its deference, we might say, to the complexity of reality itself.[32]

My final chapter takes up this model of intellectualism and considers the importance of Anglophilia to college life in the nineteenth century and to the academic mystique that it sustains. Why has intellectual and university culture historically assumed pretensions toward Britain? Where do the English accents come from? We see such figures as George Ticknor, Edward T. Channing, James Russell Lowell, and Henry Wadsworth Longfellow shaping a philosophy of intellectualism in America that patterns not only the content and pedagogic practices of higher education but also the daily routines and social pleasures of academic life. The book concludes, then, by looking at the emergence of an academic style in the nineteenth century and at how individual expressions of its character figure within a series of broader transformations that aimed to make schools (and Harvard especially) into more complete, and socially elaborate, institutions. My understanding draws on accounts of classroom practice—Channing or Lowell at the lectern—as well as student periodicals, college humor, burlesques, class day poems, slang dictionaries, guides to undergraduate life, and more, on the daily experience of being a student at Harvard, Yale, Princeton, Dartmouth, Williams, Amherst, or Bowdoin. A new emphasis on extracurricular diversions asked students increasingly to locate the significance of college in its social forms: from literary societies, fraternities, and intramural sports, to rituals of celebration and dress, the life of college came to reflect an appreciation for the bonds that students forged to each other through attachments to their institutions. The rise of student clubs and societies indicated just some of the ways that college sentiment was first organized and codified in antebellum America. The period gave us the first yearbooks, college reunions, college songs, and college novels. Commencement and other annual rituals took on new status as ceremonial performances of college feeling toward alma mater— all of which also served to distinguish a "Harvard man" or a "Princetonian" by reminding students that they owed their identities to the local culture of their respective colleges. From the broader anthropology of these identities, we discover how the social rituals made it possible for college in America to function as an institution of social identity in the first place; for the expectation that college life should have a distinctive character at all is a lasting consequence of this period. To say that this character is English is to suggest that behind the sense of college as an institution that we sentimentalize and love is an English understanding of how individuals belong to society, and it to them.

But Anglophilia in the academy also speaks to how particular styles of reading, writing, and thinking are associated with how knowledge is both acquired and performed in a social world. Professors such as Lowell and Channing are remembered as much for the affect of their intellectualism as for its content, always at ease with the widest range of materials and wary of ideas that might condition their responsiveness. Their style lent itself well to the humanities and literary study, where the goal of instruction was not to explain a text systematically but to demonstrate by anecdote and example how the experience of reading was subject to (and reflective of) contingency and feeling. The influence of this specific form of literary intellectualism continues to resonate in contemporary debates about the role of the humanities in the modern university; and while less strenuously challenged in the nineteenth century, it was still the case that faculty and students were forced to defend those styles of knowledge most associated with the liberal arts and the social values they implied. For Longfellow, Lowell, and other professors, this meant challenging the prestige of discipline and method, while renewing commitment to the felt realities of humanistic thought. For students, this meant championing an intellectual style that was known best as "Harvard Indifference": a casualness toward learning that rejected the pursuits of disciplinary knowledge for the sentimental education of dilettantes. At once an aesthetic and an epistemology, "Harvard Indifference" expressed a distrust of rigor, abstraction, and utility; intellectualism was a natural extension of how one lived at college, within a society of "chums" and amid the variety of things to do and know. The proper judgment of what they gained was finally indistinguishable from their feeling for it.

There are times, I should make clear, when these chapters breeze quite easily over political distinctions that are internal to Britain. The question of whether Scotland or Ireland figures differently in American Anglophilia is a complex one, particularly in matters of class or, in the case of abolitionism, when the relationship to a specifically Irish radicalism is at stake. I address these issues as they arise, and certainly when the fantasy of England is reckoned against Anglo-American foreign affairs before and during the Civil War. But if Anglophilia functions as an imaginary geopolitics—a desire by Americans to claim a transatlantic affiliation—it also speaks materially to a life closer at hand. So what passes as international is more often an attraction to Englishness for the way it articulates the idiom of a traditionary, local culture over and against the abstract interests that internationalism demands. Anglophilia is sometimes a cosmopolitan impulse and at other times a displaced and phantasmatic provincialism: the charms of England are trapped in amber and preserved, "this little world, / This precious stone set in the silver sea," that was already nostalgic for Shakespeare, much less for America. What Ian Baucom calls the "localist ideology" of Englishness is often what Americans are after, idealizing a familiar sense of place so that a return to England becomes of way of feeling firmly and emotionally at home. That said, the Englishness that is the object of Anglophilia can also seem like the culture that Baucom and other postcolonial critics describe as the extension of the romance of a site-specific national identity across the terrain of global empire, where the Englishness that results is analogous to, but never a substitute for, England itself.[33] In America, the Englishness that survives outside of the place, nation, or empire for which it is named may be nothing more than what Homi Bhabha describes as a belated "effect" of Britain's contact with other cultures.[34] In Britain, the Englishness that Americans love, like the "issue" at the heart of Bonham's society, may not exist at all.

But if the love is a fantasy its effects are real, political and historically apt, and my interests are finally not with Britain but with the United States. In suggesting that Anglophilia matters to antebellum America, I trace a willingness not only to acknowledge and accept Britain's place in the nation's history but also to define America itself in response to this acceptance. *Anglophilia* describes a condition of our national experience centered not around a revolutionary rejection, or a project of exclusion, but around a common focal point of our endearments—the sort of collective feeling Benedict Anderson calls to our attention when he writes that "it is useful to remind ourselves that nations inspire love." [35] The politics of what nations love—of what *other nations* nations love—is the abiding concern of what follows.

CHAPTER ONE

Monarch-Love; or, How the Prince of Wales Saved the Union

—"How'd'you? Haven't seen you these ten years. Where *have* you been?"—"To London."—"When did you return?"—"Yesterday."—"What news do you bring?"—"Nothing."—"How's cotton?"—"Don't know—don't deal in the article."—"How are consols?"—"Don't know; never had any."—"Indigo, sugar, and tobacco? on the rise, eh?"—"Really I don't know anything about them."—"When did the steamship leave?"—"Can't tell."—"Heard anything of our distresses abroad?"—"Not a word."—"Strange—very strange; we are a ruined nation."
—*New York Mirror* (May 5, 1838)

For Elias Canetti, "It all depends on this: *with whom we confuse ourselves.*" I am concerned in this chapter with a diverse cast of antebellum Americans for whom the figures of England provided exactly this opportunity to define themselves and their nation by means of an immense confusion. This is not the way we are used to defining America, particularly during a period remembered for its strong sense of national distinction. Few decades are better known for the energies spent fashioning resonant forms and native languages of national feeling, for a culture so determined, like Emerson's ideal scholar, "to be reckoned one character." But this is not the experience of definition Canetti suggests. His remark highlights the importance of not knowing just who it is we aren't, and it is this condition of productive vertigo that patterns the devotions I consider below. For nations inspire us—or conspire against us—not only to observe the limits of national culture but also to engage in all kinds of emulations and rituals of association, even, at times, to be most national while lost in fantasies of belonging elsewhere. There is, I want to argue, a sense of national experience that depends very much on the willingness to be disoriented, unable to distinguish fully between the cultures that are our own and those that we assign to others, yet at the same time, to feel no less "ourselves."[1]

The historical terrain this chapter covers is a familiar one that I will be describing in an unfamiliar fashion. We recognize the grand scale of this period's cultural ambitions in Whitman's 1855 preface to *Leaves of Grass,* or Melville's "Young America in Literature" from *Pierre,* texts determined to assume a certain magnitude in response to the nation, whether in ecstatic endorsement or inscrutable critique. What has long defined cultural life for the "American Renaissance" is a belief that the nation was the most influential expressive form, that whatever America was at the time—an experiment in language, a prophecy, an occasion for protest—it was, above all, intensely felt. Nothing would appear more alien to the American 1850s and 1860s than current debates about the waning of the nation-state and its fragile hold on our increasingly dislocated and global imaginations. And while critics reproach an earlier generation for its appreciative slant—few today would write, as F. O. Matthiessen does, that America was "coming to its first maturity and affirming its rightful heritage in the whole expanse of art and culture"—they still seem to agree on the singularly national character of everyday life in this period; they share with these classic accounts a sense, at least, of "America's" primacy over a larger field of cultural attachments.[2] But I argue in this chapter that a great many antebellum texts register a much different sensibility, an attitude toward America figured as an ongoing mystery of foreign affinities and international fixations, as a problem, first and foremost, in determining if cultural independence really mattered that much. I am suggesting, in other words, that a sense of national identity as inescapably relational and impossible to isolate within America's geography is a crucial aspect of these decades, though an aspect we have largely neglected, at least in part because it would seem an obvious distraction from the period's defining political dramas of race, slavery, and the threat of disunion. Canetti reminds us of how identity takes shape in the associations we imagine and the company we keep, and few associations were more possessing to antebellum America, yet more fanciful and perverse, than those with a culture of princes, lords, and liveries that was far less begrudged than we suppose. And while I admit that America's preoccupation with the grandest symbols and tiniest gestures of British culture may appear to constitute some sideshow, some space removed from the most pressing concerns of the national scene, I believe otherwise. Simply put, some of the period's urgent questions were addressed by confusing America with what it manifestly was not: the monarchy of Britain.

"*E Pluribus Unum*, or, in English, Welcome to the Prince"

In the late months of 1860, the heir to the British throne, eighteen-year-old Albert Edward, the Prince of Wales, became the first member of the English royal family to visit the United States. Accompanied by his donnish adviser, the Duke of Newcastle (who had a difficult charge indeed with the prince at such a tender age and all the American girls in fine feather), Albert Edward, who preferred ceremonial balls, was honored and feted first in Canada and then the United States from July to November when, to great cheer and adieus, he returned to his mother, Queen Victoria, aboard a man-of-war out of Maine. At each stop on his tour, the prince, otherwise known as the Baron Lord Renfrew, could expect crowds of thirty thousand and more, a grand ball and royal jubilee, rounds of addresses, state dinners and ovations, a torchlight march and cavalcade in full-dress and occasionally double-quick time down Broadway or State Street, with a chorus of hurrahs and a waving of handkerchiefs from sidewalks, the roofs of houses, porticoes and trees, all arranged in advance by municipal committees, ladies' voluntary societies, boards of governors, and public delegations. "We staunch republicans," says *Harper's Weekly*, "do 'love a lord' . . . so glad a day New York has never known," and so New York, like Philadelphia, Baltimore, and Chicago before it, met him accordingly with such "an overwhelming throng of human beings," so "densely packed as to be impenetrable," that *Frank Leslie's Illustrated* was left to admit, "we do not remember any turn out of the people in any way comparable with this."[3]

In the fall of 1860 the Civil War had all but begun and the Prince of Wales was simply everywhere. He was received at Harvard and the Astor Library, by academies of music and congressmen, by firemen, mechanics, and a Revolutionary War veteran: "Scores of policemen will never convince / The crowd, that it oughtn't to see the Prince."[4] Though the press would concede in unwonted moments, between its chronicles and daily sightings, that its subject was a little dull, that maybe the prince was not so quick as one had hoped, and for all that pretty short, too, and even inelegant as when, at the New York ball, he trips and "is nearly killed by a vase of flowers," still American society made such an exhibition of finery and dress, a glittering crowd surging, in the words of the

Herald, "backward and forward, shifting and changing like the figures in a kaleidoscope . . . a sea of heads," to greet him. The ladies especially, with something in the air about an American courtship—"Will the Prince of Wales," asks *Harper's,* "marry an American?"—adjusted their trinkets, smoothed their tresses and rushed him in a flouncy frenzy best described by the sonorous Edmund C. Stedman in the pages of *Vanity Fair:* "What were his thoughts I can never tell, / For sharply, as belle was jostling belle, / Each making a Flora Temple 'burst' / For the honor of dancing beside him first, / The staging before him fell in with a crash, / And fifty young ladies, as quick as a flash, / Sank down in a kind of ethereal hash— / As dainty a dish as a Prince could wish." [5]

Not so different from the 1986 visit of Charles, Prince of Wales, (himself only so bonny) to Chicago: the *Tribune* writes, "Most simply go ga-ga over the British, as when you saw so many squealing gala ladies stumbling out of their ball gowns trying to press the royal flesh." Yet the lure of Albert Edward is more astounding still, both for the plain fact of an American adoration for the great-grandson of George III and for its doggedness: months of matrimonial buzz—was it Miss Shelby Blackburn who "created a slight sensation underneath the Prince's ribs?"—of fashionables who "fought or bribed their way" to his apartments "to touch him curiously" as he passed, and all the parlor make-believe of fluttery beauties rehearsing, like the hopeful "Sophie" (who won't be taken by surprise), "Yes, dearest Albert Edward, if only I believed you were sincere." When the press at large could soberly thresh out the likelihood of an American princess, considering, for example, that, "if the Prince lives, he must marry," that "by law he is forbidden to marry a subject; nor can he wed any woman who is not a Protestant" and that, logically, "his choice is restricted to Northern Germany and the United States," it is no wonder *Vanity Fair* can take pleasure in imagining the ends to which an upstart teen could console herself on the near miss of a destiny in castles and courts if only she had been picked for a lancers and not the quadrille, eighteenth on his dance card: "Once, in the mazes of the giddy dance, *his hand touched mine!* A thrill of *fire* ran along my pulses—a pang of ecstasy *quivered* around my heart. I shuddered with delight. The—Be calm my *susceptible* heart, nor surge thus passionately in the *wild* tempest of thy thoughts! *The Prince is not for thee.*" Even after the prince is, in the words of George Templeton Strong, "at home again with his royal mamma" and, need I add, unbetrothed, something of his presence remains so vital that, according to *Harper's,* "thousands of young women, of otherwise robust constitution, now live exclusively upon the remembrance of having seen, spoken to, or danced with him," and yet so perfectly consuming that the very week of Abraham Lincoln's election to office, "in ninety-five out of a hundred drawing-rooms the Prince is the sole subject of conversation." [6]

Indeed, on November 3, 1860, South Carolina had committed to secede if Lincoln won, other states planned to follow, Lincoln's winning was assured, Wall Street was in a panic, and the Prince of Wales was on the cover of *Harper's* for the fifth time in six weeks (fig. 5). Never mind; the need to register his movements with extreme fidelity, the one-to-

FIGURE 5. "His Royal Highness Albert Edward, Prince of Wales," *Harper's Weekly* (October 6, 1860), front page.

one correspondence of happenstance to archive, meant that no item was too slight for the national record and that no one would even ask why, at the point of disunion, the American public would need to know that the prince departed from the Bay of Portland on "a fine day, but cold" and that the prince was fine but cold—"he is reported to have exclaimed, 'Hurry!—I'm cold!' "—before stepping on board the royal *Hero* with his woolly Newfoundland dog. Of course, such reporting produced an excess of occasions for lampoon and *Vanity Fair* rehearses a number of anecdotes in which the prince is noted for "witty morceaux" almost as apt as the one above:

> THE PRINCE OF WALES AND THE BOY.
> One day the Prince of Wales was passing along when he was met by a small boy in company with several other small boys.
> "My Gracious!" said the Prince.
> No more striking instance of royal sagacity has ever come to light.[7]

As Michael Kinsley says, "We Anglophiles don't care what the royal family do, so long as they do a lot of it."[8] There was nothing, it seems, more ordinary, or breathlessly gratifying, than the trivial facts of the prince's days in columns worth of "intelligence"—"It was 6½ P.M. when the Royal party landed at the foot of Twenty-second Street, North River"—and such dispatches of town talk as "The Prince Can't Bear Gas," "How He Plays at Nine-Pins," "He Picks Up an Appetite at Ten-Pins." Such talk, though resoundingly idle, is printed with all the technical solemnity of considerable news, forming, in *Harper's*, the greater portion of one continuous list of domestic and foreign items that includes "October Elections" on the one hand and "Rumored Victories of Garibaldi" on the other. In a paper where the "Progress of the Prince" in Baltimore is on par with the "Progress of the War" in Italy, shameless gossip about how "mosquitoes bit him dreadfully in Richmond" or how he "tore his trousers on the prairie" becomes so much the province of the man of affairs that even mockeries call attention to the seeming propriety of such reconnaissance for the movements of a royal minor:

> *Dear* Mr. Jenkins, we all want to know *one* thing. We feel *sure* you would have mentioned it had it *taken place*, because you are such a *perfect gentleman* that you do not fail to mention *every thing of the kind*. . . . Please

inform us in your *next dispatch*—for he is going to *Boston,* and you know how *icily cold* Boston is—whether the Prince has put on *his winter flannels.* And does he wear *Canton* flannel or *red* flannel? And have the shirts *long sleeves* or short? and if they are long, don't they *poke out* beyond his *wristbands,* and is he not obliged to *turn them up?* which must be so uncomfortable to his *arms.* And if they are short, *how* short are they? And *why* are they short?[9]

The eagerness about his nightie has an offhand civility because such intonated language with arcane emphases sounds obliging, like William F. Buckley. At least to notice his flannels is not to fail at being a gentleman, and somehow, at this moment of Civil War, public enthusiasm over Albert Edward, rude, trifling, and flagrant, is still the sign that some sort of civil society is functioning on—what starts to appear to be—a provocatively national scale.

Certainly by the time he was escorted to Portland by the quicker-witted duke, Albert Edward had become an American icon, and this is nowhere more evident than in a series of *Vanity Fair* cartoons where the matter of common life—a cigar's smoke, a hat, a household plant, the moultings of a pet—are metastasized into the prince's signature three-parted feather. The best of these imagines a pair of Prince of Wales spectacles that, enhancing and modifying, like the eighteenth-century Claude glass, would allow an artist to see the North American landscape as nothing but an assemblage of these recombined plumes. Trees become downy and trifurcated, as do clouds and distant hills (fig. 6). The fact that anything of the new British royalty could achieve such metonymic status, that some idea of the prince could be so normatively intimated, speaks not only to the scope of his tour but also to the generality of its impact. If the American system of representation was failing in 1860—if this, in fact, caused a war—we might say we have here one final and debased but purely representational moment; America had agreed on its symbols and its way of reading them, and all around an eighteen-year-old boy-prince who had come to visit. One need not have recourse to a "Renfrew glass" to see the prince's sprig erupting everywhere in the press, in Winslow Homer's illustrations, as dingbats on the page, so that locating it in America of 1860— what Strong calls "tuft-hunting"—suggests nothing so much as an antebellum precursor to "Where's Waldo" (we find it because we know it's there) played out on the national scene.[10] And in reference to this

A "LOVE OF AN EXOTIC!"
THE ICH DIEN FEATHER-FERN.

OUR SPECIAL ARTIST SKETCHING A CANADIAN TREE, AS SEEN THROUGH
HIS PRINCE OF WALES SPECTACLES.

A TAIL FOR THE TIMES.
MISS MOWERY'S MACAW, WHICH HAS BEEN VERY MUCH EXCITED LATTERLY, HAS JUST MOULTED
AWAY HIS TAIL IN THE FORM OF A PRINCE OF WALES' PLUME.

FIGURE 6. "A Love of an Exotic! The Ich Dien Feather-Fern," *Vanity Fair* (October 27, 1860), 209; "Our Special Artist Sketching a Canadian Tree, as Seen through His Prince of Wales Spectacles," *Vanity Fair* (September 8, 1860), 132; "A Tail for the Times," *Vanity Fair* (September 29, 1860), 161. The Library Company of Philadelphia.

single, promiscuous icon across the landscape of visual culture, there was, following Stanley Fish, a stubbornly functional "interpretive community," one that ensured not just recognition of the prince but also a coherence of affective response. Americans, in short, knew what was meant, and what to do, when shown the royal feathers, and if not fainting and genuflecting like the ladies of *Vanity Fair* (fig. 7), still we hear from Strong that "under all this folly and tuft-hunting there [was] a deep and almost universal feeling of respect and regard."[11]

We might well look again at anything that could be called a "universal feeling" in the fall of 1860; the prince inspired a rapture of consensus wherever he went, nothing short of the improbable, "national" acclaim President Buchanan had promised to Queen Victoria when requesting his visit: "You may be well assured that everywhere in this country he will be greeted by the American people in such a manner as cannot fail to prove gratifying to Your Majesty." [12] His tour, which took him through the cities of Detroit, Chicago, St. Louis, Cincinnati, Pittsburgh, Washington, DC, Baltimore, Richmond, and up again through Philadelphia, New York, Boston, and Portland, Maine, would semantically unify America at its point of dis-union; to speak of the prince's "United States tour" was to include Richmond and Boston in the same discursive landscape, and, as *Vanity Fair* reports, the visit was "a subject of thought among the high and low and the universal theme of conversation; even the newspapers which so seldom agree on anything agree on this topic and strive to outdo each other in chronicling the movements of His Royal Highness." A paper in New Jersey agrees that "his universal popularity, politically considered, is unaccountable." [13] It was a recovery, against the odds, of a common appeal, and if the occasion was a waltzing, bowling prince, it was nonetheless an emphatic moment of responsiveness on a federal scale. For the prince was pursued by the exact forms and rituals, the material practices, of nationalism itself:

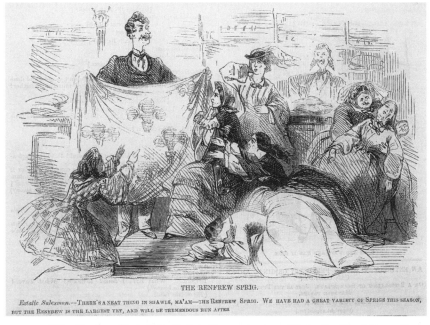

THE RENFREW SPRIG.

Ecstatic Salesman.—There's a neat thing in shawls, ma'am—the Renfrew Sprig. We have had a great variety of Sprigs this season, but the Renfrew is the largest yet, and will be tremendous run after

FIGURE 7. "The Renfrew Sprig," *Vanity Fair* (September 29, 1860), 164. The Library Company of Philadelphia.

all the processions and parades, the "gentlemen mobs" and takings to the streets, all the popular celebrations David Waldstreicher describes as the legitimating festivities of a nationalist culture are staged here around, in the words of the *New York Herald,* "that hearty love of merrie England which so many of us are proud to acknowledge." If, as Waldstreicher points out, "the assent of a unified populace" in the early republic had been secured by casting Britain's royalty as "a common enemy," to be demonstrated against, declaimed about, and burned in effigy, the ideological dramaturgy of national life is transformed and now a "general good feeling" toward the monarch-to-be affords this same communal fervor, the wide assemblies across party and class, the fireworks and flag-wavings that suggest nothing so much, to Strong, as "the unanimity and the depth of the popular feeling."[14] It is a unanimity announced and encouraged all over the press and not simply in Boston's accounts of a "solid mass of swaying humanity" surrounding the prince, or New York's accounts of "one continuous mass of human beings" awaiting as he passed, but in such reports printed and reproduced elsewhere: Richmond reports in New York, New York reports in Boston, so that each city registered both the spectacular corralling of its locals and the extralocality of their response. New York knew at least that its "five miles of human beings," from the Battery to Madison Square, had been preceded by a "standing mass of humanity" in Richmond, that the *Richmond Daily Dispatch* on Albert Edward sounded quite like the *Baltimore Advertiser* and the *New York Herald,* in which both were excerpted. It knew also, from Kinahan Cornwallis, a *Herald* correspondent who traveled with the prince, that in Detroit "there was a universal desire to pay him respect" and in Baltimore, too, "the thoroughfares . . . were lined with citizens, and thousands followed behind and alongside, cheering and waving hats." If regional difference defined the day, here is an offhand occasion where it cannot be found, where the sameness of ritual and report shows no conflict across states save the effort to honor him best, a competition without losers where, says the *Chicago Tribune,* "the press have vied with each other" to document the tour.[15]

I suppose that such claims of a patriotic alliance over the Prince of Wales may seem insecurely political, reflecting, if anything really, the need for a shared diversion—a last waltz, one's inclined to say, before America exerted itself in all the seriousness of war. The *Baltimore Sun* certainly wonders, and I am reminded of Poe's Prince Prospero with his thousand hale and light-hearted friends laughing, waltzing (senseless, magnificent pomp) in the midst of the "Red Death": "The external world could take care of itself. In the meantime it was folly to grieve, or to think. The prince had provided all the appliances of pleasure."[16] And so the *Sun* writes, "How long the United States will enjoy the advantages of domestic tranquillity is unfortunately a matter of serious doubt and uncertainty, and it is possible that when the Prince Albert Edward leaves these shores it may be . . . that the days of our peace and union are numbered, and that our institutions are a failure."[17] All the same, there is something about the prince that makes for a signally national moment, even as a holiday from national affairs, a moment, that is, for Americans to seem most exemplary as Americans, assembling together—over a hundred thousand in New York—filing out of businesses and homes in what the press describes as "voluntary" and "spontaneous" demonstrations of joy and assent, so freely performed across classes that the *New York Tribune* calls the prince's reception, most artlessly, "A Democratic Jubilee." I say "holiday" plainly; the royal visit was observed as a public holiday in, at least, St. Louis, Boston, and New York where ordinances from the mayors closed businesses, schools, banks, and even stock exchanges so that all could equally throng and hail, "many of whom," says Cornwallis, "would have sacrificed a month's wages rather than have missed a sight of the Prince," and with such Independence Day collusion that the *Herald* points out, "If there had been another Stamp Act to resent, more independence to gain, and a new Seventy-Six to be 'fought and bled and died' through, there could have been no more noise and confusion, no more drumming and fifing, no more training, marching and Yankee Doodling" than for the prince. The democratic character of mass public sentiment is revealed like never before, willing, unguarded, teeming, and jubilant across "the thew and sinew of the people," and we might wonder how the group psychology we take for granted as democratic—incorporating, identifying, of the people—is just as easily, is just as fairly called, monarchophilic.[18] Take, for example, the *New York Daily Tribune* on the prince and "the masses":

> While the suspension of business in the city was practically universal, and one great impulse directed the thoughts and the steps of all classes; and while all the conflicting elements that enter into the incongruous composite of the population were solidified in the enormous street assemblage, it was plain how a kindly feeling controlled all the exciting

affairs of the day. There could have been no fitter tribute to the honor and the worth, the traditional and the present grandeurs that are now so gracefully represented on the American soil by the fair youth Albert Edward, the Prince of Wales, than this immense democratic presence. Those huge collections of men, women, and children that met the eye in receding ocean stretches, swaying together as if with the irresistible tidal throb, compressed within often narrow limits, and compelled to chafe a good deal, but never sweeping over their bounds to do harm nor lost to the gentle but firm control of a sun of good humor: those spontane-ous, unstudied, inartistic, and chargefully picturesque symbolings of the wayside—the flags and flowers, the informal mottoes—and the stirring exclamations and delights that each first sight of the boyish form of the prince evoked; these, and with them the very confusions that were the natural fruit of such a preposterously fecund stock of enthusiasm, fitly typified the capacities of the people for a self-government founded on the immutable laws of human sympathy.[19]

Over and again, the press says "spontaneous"; it said it, too, in 1824 when the Marquis de LaFayette toured America as the "Nation's Guest." Then the people "chose to pour forth their feelings in acts of unrestrained hospitality," in "spontaneous bursts of admiration" that seemed to speak to the elective character of republican acclaim and were distinguished, so ardently, from the "mechanical" or, in Fred Somkin's words, "even unwilling homage" of Europe's subjects. Only, in 1824, the occasion was a figure in whom the virtues of the Revolu-tion were invested, "the embodiment," writes Somkin, "of the life lived for liberty"; and now, the same language of American exaltation, the same tropes of orderly, yet voluntary and ecstatic, enthrallment are rehearsed around an unreconstructed prince and his old-world cor-tege.[20] It is as if each public gathering for Albert Edward allows some-thing of American national life to be known and confirmed, and all in Britain's honor; an "incongruous composite of the population" is "solidified"—a union formed—by a wholly improvised symmetry of af-fections, and in a democracy, where everyone is free to feel what ev-eryone else feels, no formalities of class or rank can interfere with this American love of monarchy. It is finally the participatory suchness of these displays that renders the Anglophilia symptomatically American; thus the *Boston Evening Transcript* makes much of "the spontaneous ovation which the citizens of Boston have given Renfrew," and the *Her-*

ald, with improbable chauvinism, sets America's expressive devotions against Canada's obligatory "respects":

> The receptions here differed from those in Canada, also, not less in the part played by the prince than in that played by the people. There the government ordered out the troops and paid their expense; the canon boomed an official welcome; the people cheered the great peer of the realm; everything from the cars to the banners was bound, encircled and decorated with red tape. Here, on the contrary, the receptions were spontaneous. The people turned out of their own accord and cheered voluntarily and informally, doing honor to the boy, whom they loved, and not to the future ruler, whom they respected.[21]

A correspondent for the *London Times* also observes the elective character and mass aesthetic that distinguishes the love of democrats from the deference of subjects. Describing "the mingling of fervent, intense enthusiasm, of perfect good order, of warmth, and yet kind respect," the reporter notes a range of affect exceeding anything he had seen in Britain: "I am fairly at a loss," he says, "to convey in words to English readers any adequate idea of this most memorable event. I have had rather a considerable experience of Royal progresses both at home and abroad. . . . In the welcome to New York, however, I found that I had much to learn." While in Paris, a royal event would have been a "governmental affair of soldiers and *gendarmes*" and, in London, have required "an immense police force to control it," such measures were unnecessary on Broadway where "a gigantic meeting of the citizens" (he claims five hundred thousand) spontaneously converged for "one continued unanimous welcome that can neither be told nor forgotten" (the impression left by the surging crowd was "vague and undefinable, as that of the ocean in a storm"). He learned that "such an ovation as has seldom been offered to any monarch in ancient or modern times" was also an ovation that "only a free people could ever give . . . there was much, strange as it may seem, that made such a reception possible only in New York."[22]

For the author of an article in *Littell's Living Age,* "the honors which were paid to the English Prince could only have been offered by freemen, too confident of the greatness of their own country to fear any misconstruction of the applause which was voluntarily bestowed." After all, a Prince of Wales had visited America before: when Prince

William Henry came to the colonies in 1781, aside from deluded loyalists, there was no return to "ancient idolatry" and no evidence that the people of New York were "ready to worship the offsprings of the Royal Brute of Britain," at least according to the press. Of course we expect to hear this sort of language against the royal family in the midst of the Revolution. We expect less to hear a British reporter argue years later that the Revolution insured the fall into prince-love that only needed democratic forms to be indulged. Emotions are easy to produce for a purely emblematic prince because the pointlessness of the crowd's devotion guarantees that it expresses only what it feels: "The Prince of Wales," says the paper, "has been the object of enthusiastic applause from thousands who pride themselves on the knowledge that the establishment of royalty among themselves is impossible."[23] So we should see Americans reacting affectionately to the prince not as cynical but as enabled. Inasmuch as they pursued a psychic bond to him, they also enacted relations that were far more consequential among themselves. Albert Edward was the occasion for an event of politics that was not political to him.

It is not often, says one paper, "that a whole community is moved by one and the same sentiment. . . . Here it was otherwise." We are thus faced with more than a bit of transatlantic sport when the *Herald* says of the royal heir on the prairie that the Prince was thoroughly "denationalized," for a particular democratic process appears to have worked less on him than because of him, as he comes to embody the larger logic of association that Tocqueville describes as the gist of American civil life: "I have often admired," he says, "the extreme skill with which the inhabitants of the United States succeed in proposing a common object for the exertions of a great many men and in inducing them to voluntarily pursue it."[24] With each ad hoc marshaling of mass assent and spectacle of well-mannered frenzy, a version of the American ideology, a national measuring of the inner impulse to collective order, is staged and ratified: "The huge collections of men, women and children . . . swaying together with the irresistible tidal throb," the *Tribune* reminds us, are at the same time, "never sweeping over their bounds." Which is why the *Herald* also insists that the crowds assembling for the prince— boisterous, polyglot, and "popular"—are at the same time models of American self-governance, of a diversified citizenry that, just happening to pursue their own interests in public, cannot help but regulate themselves. The paper writes, "The most perfect order and good humor prevailed, too. Though the police were scattered singly and at intervals along the line of the march, no effort was necessary to preserve order; that was kept by the people themselves. . . . Nor was this peculiar to any one class of people." [25]

There is nothing, after all, like the love of a prince to inspire the best of democratic practice. What becomes increasingly clear to the press is not simply, as Harriet Beecher Stowe writes, that "the visit of the Prince to the States is a deeper and wider thing than it appears at first to be," but that some kind of unsought-for, needfully dramatic nation-building was taking place, "deeper and wider" because, like Benedict Anderson's "deep, horizontal comradeship," it was so unaccountably constitutive.[26] The reception of the prince does not speak to the ceremonious postures of a newly middle class, cultivating distinction and described, by John Kasson or Karen Halttunen, in all their relish for aristocratic forms.[27] Nor is it the sheer doings of an American elite who would solidify their own class status with claims of noble descent and British bloodlines, though this certainly plays a part. ("We cannot follow our ancestry more than a few generations back," says Governor Packer to Albert Edward of all his predecessors in the Pennsylvania Statehouse, "without tracing the line to a British red coat.")[28] Rather, the response to the prince is remarkable for just the efforts to prove that America is functionally classless, and why else, but that all classes are equal in their love of the prince? I refer not only to summons of the democratic process on his behalf, to debate, for example, over who should dance with him first—"shall it be by a majority vote of the Committee of four hundred, or shall the two-thirds rule prevail?"—or whether the reception committee itself "is strictly a representative list, and has no flavor of a clique." [29] What strikes me about the fascination of these months is finally the enfranchising work of Anglophilia, which allows for the vicarious endorsement of nation amid the self-effacing respect for a prince. It brings forth each particular constituency with nearly taxonomic effect, an *e pluribus unum* of tuft hunters, where royal devotion is so available, it is American nonetheless. "He came to visit us," says *Vanity Fair,* "one and all": the papers take pains to acknowledge the comprehending sameness of the nation's passion for the prince, how each last group—is it occupational, sectional, ethnic?—chose to take its day to celebrate with all the rest. "His visit," writes Strong, "has occasioned a week of excitement beyond that of any event in my time, and pervading all classes." So while *Harper's* admits the selectiveness of some events, it is careful not to claim privilege; certainly the rich would attend the New York ball, as the prince is accustomed to the richest affairs, but the ball isn't priggish (just pricey), and while "there is not a mechanic, or a farmer, or an operative on the list of names" that evening, "there was, of course," says *Harper's,* "no intention to slight any class." [30]

We are so used to imagining American flirtations with aristocracy as genteel behavior, a pursuit of refinement that seemed to promise some implied connection with a distant best society of noble births and high tastes, that such a presentist, realized monarchophilia of the masses seems at least a step removed from the emulating characters of Richard L. Bushman's *The Refinement of America.*[31] This is not, all told, the response of an Anglicized circle, the same aspirants, for example, who might paint crests on their dinnerware, but the totalizing affections of an American public who, more often and quite pointedly, had no historical claims to Britain. Here, again, is the *Herald:* "Every available spot from which there was a possibility of catching a sight of the face of the Prince was thronged, piled and crowded with people. . . . No class or nationality formed an exception to the general good feeling. Our adopted citizens of Irish, Scotch, German and other national origin were as numerously represented and as hearty and sincere in their testimony of respect and kindly feeling." Some sense of a subcutaneous allegiance, a fondness for British royalty oddly prevalent within all strata of the republic, and regardless of ethnicity or even race, a sense, too, of this allegiance as a kind of fortuitous common ground within a hugely diverse nation, informs accounts of the prince that stress how "a bond of kindred" with England among themselves "was felt in every bosom."[32] The visit becomes a street-level enactment of the melting pot, making "Americans," Crèvecoeur's promiscuous "mixture of English, Scotch, Irish, French, Dutch, Germans, and Swedes," out of this compounded affection and public outpouring for the prince; Old World identities are dissolved within the general Anglophilia of the day, which thus comes to function as a displaced patriotism, binding and transforming these urban masses around a symbolic pageant of nationhood that belongs, strictly speaking, to almost no one involved. At a time when the peaceable nature of such ethnic interminglings could not be assumed—take the Astor Place Riots or the nativist anxieties over Irish and German Catholics—there is a remarkable absence in these reports of anything we might call chauvinism, save that, of course, for England. It is a generosity not lost on a (fittingly ceremonious) *Richmond Examiner:* "People, to whom Episcopacy is an offense, flocked to gaze upon a beardless boy, who has, as yet, exhibited no talents whatever. The prospective head of English Episcopacy, receiving the homage of American Episcopalians, Presbyterians, Baptist, Methodist, Catholics, Jews, and that larger portion of the people who belong to no sect, was neither in proper keeping with our religious or political principle."[33]

It is the appeal of an Anglophilic pluralism that provokes the defensiveness, and as I will observe shortly, it is no coincidence that a paper that was soon to be published from the Confederate capital would find this "principle" most disturbing. That the symbols of Englishness may allow—indeed, may solicit—the allegiances and identifications of people otherwise defined by ethnic or religious differences is part of a culture of assimilation that remains central to models of U.S. national identity. Thus Peter Salins recent account of how Latino and Asian immigrants become acculturated to America seems to revisit the reports of 1860: "No immigrants, regardless of their original nationality, can escape [American culture's] pervasive 'Anglocentric' influence nor should want to. Americans, whatever their ethnic heritages, enjoy the best of all cultural worlds," one shaped equally by "America's English traditions" and "America's ethnic diversity." His vision of American society evokes a myth of British cultural formation that has long insisted on the availability of an imagined Englishness to a diverse cross section of the world's populations. As the signature of England's imperial ambitions, first in the British Isles and then almost everywhere else, the "anti-ethnic features of Royal-family nationalism," to borrow from Tom Nairn, reflect the fact that organic ways of figuring national identity—as the expression of a single, *volk* community—have never been the model for the Anglo-British state. British nationality, for Nairn, is "undoctrinaire"; and by this he means that Britain's fixation with monarchy in its most sentimental and cultish forms has managed to bestow a "sense of belonging" without the need for ethnic coherency. Anglophilia fulfills this logic of fungible attachment, and writers far less polemical than Salins still pay tribute to its assimilating effects. Adrian Peracchio writes that Anglophilia is "an obsession that seems to afflict each successive wave of American immigrants and citizens, not simply those whose ancestry legitimately belongs to England. All sorts of hyphenated Americans snap their cameras at the changing of the guard at Buckingham Palace and bask in the reflected glory of the troubled British royal family." Or as Geoffrey Wheatcroft says of the same "obsession": "Pretentious WASP, simple Midwesterner, New York Jew—all are vulnerable. I have seen them all suffer, and pitied them all alike." [34]

The more casual reflections chart one historical trajectory for the discourse of almost universal feeling that surrounds the prince's visit in 1860. They remind us that Anglophilia's emotional investments and representational strategies refer to a style of state that allows for "our" citizens to emulate "their" subjects in a way that tests the limits of nationalism's assimilative drive. It would seem wrong to describe the frankly multiethnic version of Anglophilia that sweeps indiscriminately across German and Scottish, Catholic and Jew as just a first shadow of the racial Anglo-Saxonism that has received (in the work of Reginald Horsman, Alexander Saxton, David R. Roediger, Dana D. Nelson, and others) the vast majority of critical attention. Anglophilia in 1860 operates with a force that is far more liberal in its embrace of difference and, thus, far more difficult on the question of ethnicity. I did, after all, say "almost universal," because, while the turnout for the prince is usually adoring, there are acknowledgments that at least some Irish and others depart from the sentiments that prevail among the masses. Kinahan Cornwallis tells of an "Irishman" who exclaims, on watching the prince depart from Washington, "I only wish I'd a ould shoe to fling afther yez, for its not the likes of yez as come here every day." The *Liberator* disapprovingly reports that "an enthusiastic Irishman slapped [the prince] in the face with his shocking bad hat." And Colonel Michael Corcoran received press attention for refusing to lead his predominantly Irish militia in New York's procession for the "Famine Prince"; papers as far away as Chicago reported on his protest, the court-martial that followed and at least one resolution in support of "his conduct in refusing to do honor" to Albert Edward. The same techniques of mass communication that show most Americans loving the prince also show that some did not; still, these read as exceptions to the fuller extent of Albert Edward's ecumenical appeal. [35] If the Irish use his visit to recall old partisan positions, this only sets them apart from the collectively American determination to forget "our sturdy republicanism, the turgid rhetoric about monarchies, [and] all matters of rivalry and prejudice." The displaced populism of the prince's visit unites Americans in a moment of good will—"whatever our social po-

FIGURE 8. "Broadway.—Respectfully Dedicated to the Prince of Wales," *Harper's Weekly* (October 6, 1860).

sition, whatever our party politics, whatever our theological creed"—that is heuristic for the kind of community that the nation is supposed to be. Anglophilia presents a relationship to Englishness that is open to anyone as social practice, civil behavior, or public expression; because it compensates for differences in "position" by the accessibility of its affect, Anglophilia brings most Americans together while leaving many in their place.[36]

Nowhere is this more evident than in *Harper's* illustration of the prince's parade down Broadway. Amid windows and galleries of onlookers, an affable assembly of preternaturally composed New Yorkers prince spotting in the late afternoon, a single black woman also peers out at the scene below (figs. 8 and 9). She occupies a space in the picture that is downright overdetermined: deep in a window, behind a curtain, in the shadows, and, even still, at the margin of the print itself; she is patently a figure of the "Mammy," with her wide, heavy face and hair beneath a kerchief, and also of the "Africanist other" that Toni Morrison has found both decorating and disrupting the fringes of the American representational world. But she is ostentatiously there, and her presence—all eyes and, with large lobular rings, all ears too—

FIGURE 9. "Broadway.—Respectfully Dedicated to the Prince of Wales" (detail).

signals an aspect of this day's event that is captured in astonishing detail by Cornwallis's narrative:

> To convey an idea of the crowd, which, next to the Prince, was the great curiosity of the day, is difficult. It was huge, immense, enormous, exaggerated, stupendous, infinite, and indefinite. It was a multitude as countless as the leaves of the forest—one of those crushes which are perfectly bewildering to the senses. Below a stratum of humanity was so wedged in and Macadamized together that to move one individual was to stir the whole mass; while above, every window-sill was a rough frame, within which the face of beautiful women and smiling children made up an attractive picture. Every opening, every story, every roof, was a parapet,

from which constantly played a battery of bright eyes. . . . Those who could not enjoy the privileges of a window were content to take to the street, and the quantity of well-dressed ladies and children, mixed in with the not over fragrant crowd of unscoured publicans and sinners, was painfully amazing to behold. Once in, it was almost impossible to get out, and the poor females were compelled to endure the pains of purgatory to gratify the curiosity they couldn't help.[37]

Harper's depicts a class that seems unmoved by every violation and travesty of bodily decorum that so interests Cornwallis; they are in close quarters but still above the jostling of the crowds at street level that are, even so, drawn as prim silhouettes of men and women, umbrellas and hats, "respectfully dedicating" Broadway to the prince. Yet, the spirit of the event remains inscribed in the "bright eyes" of the black, who alone registers the expectancy, the tense, gaping desire *to see* that ruffled all the tens of thousands, including, says Cornwallis, the well-dressed ladies. Her eyes are oddly paired with the binoculars' huge lenses; both "Mammy" and "miss" are linked in their exaggerated ocularity, and the prosthetics of the cool, white spectator betray a visual imperative whose intensity is displaced onto the anxious countenance of the black. She is not only the emotional cathexis of a scene that has been overcomposed but also a surrogate for us, the viewers, who observe not really the prince—he exists somewhere outside of the image—but the crowd observing the prince. Her response to the crowd, which she certainly sees, along with any of the troops and cavalry and prince en suite, is nothing less than Cornwallis's own. This scene, she seems to tell us, is "perfectly bewildering to the senses." *Harper's* may be invested in picturing a solemn audience, but the truth of the occasion is there in her face; this was not a homogenous, genteel gathering but a teeming, anxious, unscoured mass that was, for all who watched, "painfully amazing to behold," just as it remained, to those like Cornwallis, "harmonious, melodious, and good." The black woman, after all, turns out with the rest, and even a guarded print shows this vagrant proximity; from her own proper station, servant and swell find themselves amid a military pageant just the same, with a singular and mutual interest. In Richmond, where the matters of "station" are even more profound, this likeness of occupation—pursuing, rushing the carriage—becomes itself news in New York: "The sons and daughters of light and darkness (I speak of complexions) collected in front of the hotel in large

numbers this morning, in order to witness his Royal Highness' departure, and I again observed that the blacks and the whites manifested
an *equal* curiosity to catch a glimpse of our illustrious visitor; neither is
'God's image carved in ebony' behind the rest of mankind in opening
his mouth and throwing out an idea or two about what he sees."[38] The
prince bests racial insularity—everyone is curious—and when he is not
"flying from the eager crowd of negroes and boys" or attending church
with all "the darkies, who turned out strong," he's the sine qua non of a
reconstituted public sphere in which blacks, Catholics, and women can
also "throw out an idea or two" before the attentive press.[39]

That some feeling for the prince could provide for a casual moment of consensus, that Anglophilia, moreover, could have this general "look" of American assimilation, was not beyond the recognition
of papers that were everywhere else describing the failure of Union. In
the North, the extent of this "universal" fixation maintains a distinctly
national character. If that fixation is, for the *Tribune,* a "strange fever of
which Americans are, of all nations, the only true subjects," it becomes,
whatever else, a kind of "crowd symbol": one of the common, continuous symptoms of a population that Canetti says can enter a nation's
consciousness of itself.[40] When the *Herald* claims, from Richmond, that
the "mob" gathered for the prince "will afford the rest of the world
some evidence of their civil nation," it says not only that manners can
inhere in such a diversified assembly but also that manners, civil tolerance, and impartial enthusiasm, from New York to Richmond, will
effectually distinguish the nation as a whole. Look, says the *Herald,* the
South has some comity with the rest of us: this fawning, ingratiating,
prince-gawking behavior has brought all Americans to one place. On
the streets, that is, where the progress of the prince is the "absolute
topic," where all classes stand and yell, where cherished associations
with a nominative English homeland has claimed native and immi-
grant alike, no "polluted partisanship" can interfere, and most surely
from state to state: "The Prince and his suite regretted that they could
not go further South. . . . If her Majesty could have anticipated that the
Prince would have met with a tithe of the honors and friendliness that
have attended his tour in the United States, a much longer time would
have been prescribed."[41] Without any hope of fair share—the prince's
visit was short, the queen waited at home—we see the South demanding inclusion in a "Union" event; in a letter circulated in the Northern
papers, a committee of Southerners claims to feel left out of an itiner-

ary that was weighted to the North, federally arranged, and that made much of "Old England in the Embraces of New": "When the course of the royal party was first laid out, the route included no spot further south than Washington. . . . So there was no thought of Richmonds, or Savannahs or Montgomerys, or Charlestons, any more than of Salt Lakes, or pi-Utah settlements. But there came a wail. The voice of Virginia was heard in lamentation. Is this a sectional visit?"[42]

More often than not, the tour provides a "prospect view" of the nation, a panoramic fantasia of regions and landscapes—like the *Herald's* survey of his progress through "the prairies of the West, the Old Dominion in the South, the Federal City and along the route of intermediate places"—that assimilates an assorted geography into a transcendent, broadly allegorizing vision (a *discordia concors*) among the daily reports of secession and war. If not all papers agree with the *Baltimore Sun* that "the royal visit to this country, and the interest it creates, form a pleasing interlude in political excitements at this crisis"—if the "crisis" does indeed seep into accounts of the commotion and display—it remains partisan in a wishfully diminished way. Like the "internecine conflict" the *Herald* describes between the ladies of New York, triumphing over "provincial rivals" and one another in honoring the prince, the North's assaults on Richmond reduce political strife to social jockeying so petty—even the ladies hope "to outvie all others on this great occasion." When the Northern papers, in other words, claim that the prince was rushed in Richmond and "came near being crowded into a jelly" or that the groupie mob had made "the pillow-cases of his bed unfit for use by handling them," the sense of regional bigotry is less a national problem than the kind of civic one-upmanship made light of in a headline about the prince's reception in Boston: "The North against the South End."[43]

Indeed, in months when almost all stories of the traveling prince share pages with those of the "Revolution at the South," the "Arming in Virginia," and the "Plan in Georgia for Dissolving the Union," the royal tour provides not only for an image of the states "united" in spontaneous feeling on his behalf but also for an oddly convenient, and most deliberately noted, anti-revolutionary moment. The visit of the prince to America, "the friendly visit," that is, "of a member of the royal family of England to the revolted colonies," becomes a historic, elaborate spectacle of reconciliation, one where Albert Edward, planting a tree at the tomb of Washington, reviewing the cadets at West Point, or simply being on Boston Common, has "eradicated every vestige of the fraternal bitterness that once existed between us." [44] "Our sweet, young Prince," writes Strong, "Long May He Wave." A reconstructed star-spangled banner trades the nationalist fervor and separatist program of 1814 for renewed, familial affections; Strong's avuncular bonhomie toward the prince evokes the same, belated pooh-poohing of the revolutionary grudge as Harriet Beecher Stowe: "How much better such greetings between two noble kindred nations than the old family quarrel, all whose remembrances should now be grown over with the green harvests of advancing union." [45] In Detroit, *Vanity Fair* finds the "revolutionary spirit of seventy-six" in the way the least repressible of the crowd could hang onto a wheel of his carriage as it passed, "revolving" on the axis like a knife thrower's assistant, and so making for a hopelessly slapstick recantation of American partisanship; that is, a spinning of wheels for His Royal Highness that quite literally "rolls over" the small matter of independence. [46]

When Albert Edward meets with the Revolutionary War veteran Ralph Farnham, the last survivor of the Battle of Bunker Hill, they "chuckle," exchange autographs, and tell war stories. The Duke of Newcastle concedes of Burgoyne's surrender, "You rather had him there," and the old soldier (he's 104) remarks, "that hearing so much said in praise of the Prince, he began to fear that the people were turning royalists." The encounter is a lavish show of respect and mutual admiration for the prince, who is all "courtesies" toward the former rebel, and especially for Farnham himself, who "speaks of the interview with the greatest pleasure, and says that he wished to show the boy and his soldiers that he bore no anger for old times," a gesture made symbolic for the rest of us when the paper concludes, "The old man represents the general feeling." [47] Where, we might ask, has all the rebelliousness gone, when we see not only this apostate minuteman but also "the representatives of 'Young America' "—the nationalist movement otherwise "united by an antimonarchical" stance—leaping from car to car on the track opposite the prince's train, following his progress into Baltimore, where "the intensest clamor and curiosity was manifested by all to catch a glimpse of his royal highness"? [48]

Certainly all this conciliatory talk looks forward to a new internationalism, an Anglo-Saxon alliance that saw Britain and the United States as equal partners in a progressive drama of advancing civilization and influence. The Revolution could be figured as just an interlude—"dark days when fraternal war ended in political severance"—that isolated two nations in pursuit of "a common path of development," two nations that were now ready to join together again, "peers in all things." The worldly benefits of such a diplomatic relationship were reckoned without any hedging whatsoever from its imperialist overtones, and without much concern that this future *Pax Anglo-Americana* was here embodied in a teenager on vacation and the acclaim he received. "It was not a fiction of the over-excited brain," we read in the *Tribune*, that his "pleasant courtesies foretokened the closer blending of the interests of England and the States, and a fond union of their noble energies in the cause of truth, justice, and love for all people under heaven."[49] But while the prince's visit encouraged thinking along these prospective, fusionist lines, and thus "foretokened" a whole nineteenth and early twentieth-century discourse of imagined empires and joint enterprise—a "world mission," as Horsman writes, awaiting the Anglo-Saxon people—I would like to suggest that this rhetoric also served, on the strictly national scene, for the glorification of "Union" itself. For the language that was used to dream up a triumphantly Anglo-American future was not just resonant with, but often identical to, the language used to envision the thinly sublimated ideal of an undivided America. The two-way referentiality in the Northern press functions almost as a political innuendo, exploiting what might be called, following Roland Barthes, a "diagrammatic" relationship between entirely congruent frameworks of significance. Thus immediately after the *Herald* pictures "St. George" and "Old Glory" in coequal dominance, it adds that "such a union will reanimate the hopes of nations everywhere, and give an impulse to the cause of constitutional law and the reign of liberty and order throughout the earth."[50] No discursive arrow here points either to the South or from it; but the lexicon being celebrated—"union," "constitutional law," and "order"—is more than just portentous in regard to the crisis that is not, of course, the subject at hand.

And sometimes the domestic payoff is quite explicit. The urban exuberance, the peaceableness of the celebrations, the prosperity and goodwill of the crowds, the universal desire to please: these all seemed to prove that it takes a union to make one, that if the prince's visit signaled a new fraternity with Britain, it also made plain an existing one at home. "The historical societies of some of the Northern States," writes the *Baltimore Sun*, "have taken especial notice of the visit of the Prince of Wales to the United States, regarding it as an interesting il-

lustration of the progress of this country in prosperity and power under the present constitution and Union."[51] We need only see, beside
and above headlines of the "Irrepressible Conflict," how all Americans,
gathered for the occasion, "exhibited in some way the emblems of fraternal union"—how, likewise, "the bond of kindred was felt in every bosom, and its utterances welled forth from every lip"—to realize that the
prince's reception had at least as much to say about the congeniality
of Americans toward themselves and the possibility for these moments
of common, well-mannered affection. "The delightful ties of consanguinity have been renewed": a belated alliance between America and
Britain, a revolution diminished with time, or a hopeful answer to daily
reports of Southern secession? We check twice, because the language is
the same and a paper that describes "the reestablishment of fraternal
ties" with Britain will just after regret an impending civil conflict that
would "efface the last vestige of brotherly feeling." From descriptions of
the Fireman's Torchlight Parade in the prince's honor—"two nations
lovingly unite" / "We are one family"—we turn to descriptions of the
Union Torchlight Parade with its banners, "One and Inseparable. No
disunion," and understand that these two events are impertinently in
conversation, that the North is having this holiday of revolutionary
backsliding, of terrific rapprochement, while frankly addressing the
"revolution" to come.[52] The prince's visit encourages, with a sense of
what's at stake (this is, for many reasons, no "tea party"), a celebration
of patriotic conduct and sociable behavior, the reassertion of a common
culture, the sharing of symbologies and defining terms and, in short, a
referendum on whether "America" still represents a coherent national
identity, even as it is fastened on Britain and its dynasty of Georges and
queens: "And yesterday the drama—this wonderful and harmonious
drama of humanity—reached another climax, and the descendant of
the Georges entered the center of American independence, and met
no barriers but solid hosts of welcoming citizens, and the refrain of
chimes, and of all the instruments, was God Save the Queen! Not the
most dreary philosopher over the 'institutions' of his country could
come forth from the scenes of this occasion without a good hope for
the future of a people which is still so loyal to the domestic virtues."[53]

"Still so loyal": our resumed relations with Britain seem suddenly
pedagogical for our relations with each other. Our response to the
prince shows, whatever else, that these national virtues have remained
part of an American political character, latent within a culture out-

wardly devoted to revolution, independence, and the value of dissent, and "despite the sincere antagonism to princes as such which is felt by democrats." The prince allows Americans to discover these residual capacities for respect, restraint, and adherence to tradition and to bring them into focus around a single spectacular event that "has its origin in the love of fatherland, ancient memories, cherished associations." Once these qualities are discovered as having been there all along, and not affected from abroad, they can be staged and nurtured as alternative but still elementary national virtues and didactically used to revive the necessary, if forgotten, feelings of allegiance and "union." So when the prince attends the opera in Philadelphia, and the *Saturday Evening Post* exclaims that "the audience reverentially started to their feet upon hearing the first loyal strains of 'God Save the Queen,'" the emphasis is less on diplomatic cordiality and more on the American inclination toward reverence as such where Britain is concerned. What emerges during the prince's visit is a sense of some "other tradition," of a preexisting and Anglicized loyalism that has survived war and separation, equally American but imperfectly realized until this moment, just when our institutions are "dreary" and just when it happens to be needed most. Loyalism is brought forth as a parallel fiction of national experience and a different set of lessons to be learned from America's history. Here is the *Baltimore Sun* on witnessing the prince in Canada:

> The lady writes that Montreal was crowded with "States people," as we are there called; and that they (the Americans) had found that they had known nothing before of national enthusiasm—nothing of the principles of loyalty. Presidential inaugurations were tame affairs in their view in comparison with the receptions of a Prince among his loyal subjects. . . . I congratulate the Canadians upon the fact that they have some principle to which they can be loyal. If there is anything in these States to which our people, as a people, are loyal, I have not in my experience discovered it . . . our troubles arise from the want of loyalty to any national principle.[54]

Thus, in October and November of 1860, if allegiances were hard to gauge and patriotic commitments fraught, here at least, Americans were issuing forth, from all regions, with voluntary effusions of loyalism, apostrophes, anthems, and odes, like the following: "OH! Albert Edward, many-titled Guelph, / Lord Renfrew, otherwise the Prince of

Wales, / Or whatsoever else you call yourself— / Your glorious advent
each New Yorker hails; / All other things are laid upon the shelf, / For
you nor loyalty nor homage fails."[55] That the prince is so abundantly
named makes for an even stronger contrast with the vaguely signified
concerns being "shelved" on his behalf; but perhaps topical reference
was unnecessary and readers might easily have specified for themselves
the "other things" to which Albert Edward is opposed. After all, the
dialectic between an American crisis of and an Anglophilic return to
"loyalty" was rehearsed again and again; in a Boston paper, George
Henry Calvert pays "hearty homage" to the Prince of Wales and to the
love of England as "a flame nor quenched nor dimmed by changeful
Time's / Assault, but still old loyalty sublimes."[56]

On October 27, a page of poems to the prince, in the Herald, follows two folio pages on "the revolution at the South" and the "dissolution of the Union"; one poem promises, "Thousands of hearts resolved
and true / Hands ready and prepared, / Old England's bidding well to
do, / Her sacred throne to guard," and a past of bloodshed and fraternal conflict are reconciled into the consensual salutes and well-wishing
of loyal thousands.[57] The almost utopian project of the prince's visit, as
it is represented by many in the North, is to demonstrate a variety of
national devotions that certainly outlast, and perhaps may transcend,
both revolutionary ideology and nationalism's own sectarian impulses.
So Oliver Wendell Holmes, in an "international ode" set to the tune of
"God Save the Queen" and performed for the prince in Boston, allego-
rizes Albert Edward to Christ and the prospective king of England to
the almighty "King of Kings":

> God bless our Fathers' Land,
> Keep her in heart and hand
>   One with our own!
> From all her foes defend,
> Be her brave People's Friend,
> On all her Realms descend,
>   Protect her Throne!
>
> Father, with loving care
> Guard thou her kingdom's Heir,
>   Guide all his ways:
> Thine arm his shelter be,

From him by land and sea
Bid storm and danger flee,
   Prolong his days!

Lord, let War's tempest cease,
Fold the whole Earth in peace
   Under Thy wings!
Make all Thy nation's one,
All Hearts beneath the sun,
Till Thou shalt reign alone,
Great King of Kings.[58]

Love of one's "fatherland" is a piety, so while this poem is most directly about America's newfound attachments to Britain, it still makes patriotism itself, one's "fathers' land" in "heart and hand," akin to the kind of devotional respects colonies have toward the metropolis, subjects toward kings, and Christians toward God. A belief in this global alliance begins at home, but what interests me even more than Holmes's sense that "one nation, under God" is a world affair is a small detail of punctuation. "Nation's," with its curious apostrophe instead of the logical plural ("nations"), reduces all this holy peace work not to the act of making two nations, the United States and Britain, "one," or all nations, for that matter, "one" (within God's kingdom or the Anglo-American kingdom—it isn't clear), but of making a single nation, one nation, that is, *as* "one." Somehow celebration of the prince cannot help but turn in on ourselves, and if a divisive America is not addressed in the poem, it is not quite missed either, with so much totalizing, unifying atonement and so much emphasis on war.

Holmes's appropriation of the British anthem for this seemingly American moment only confirms *Vanity Fair* in its translation of a different sort of scripture: "*E Pluribus Unum,*" it writes, "or in English, Welcome to the Prince." I take this quite seriously in the end. The prince's visit, after all, was the closest Americans would come in the fall of 1860 to having this "one great impulse," a preposterous stock of royal curiosity that nonetheless brought Americans out in Richmond or Baltimore or New York "not as sectionalists"—I borrow from Rufus Choate here—"but as sons and daughters of our united and inherited America." Anglophilia, it seems, has an American payback. All that loyalty, reverence, respect, that affection for lost bonds, in the *Herald's* words, "never completely sundered by wars and revolutions": Anglophilia, it turns out, provides nothing less than a language for reimagining the Union itself.[59]

Anachronism and Style (More Twaddle about the Queen)

The Americans are Queen mad. We have Victoria bonnets, Victoria shawls, Victoria songs, Victoria marches, Victoria mint-juleps, and somebody has just opened a shop on Broadway called "Victoria hair-dressing emporium!" Victoria fiddlesticks.
—*New York Mirror* (July 14, 1838)

The prince's visit was not the first time the American obsession with royalty had become a national experience and ritual of consensus. With the coronation of Victoria in 1838, the fact that Americans were, in no uncertain terms, "queen mad," that the national demand for news of her daily costumes, equestrian exercises, afternoon levees, and the coronation, most of all, meant a constant stream of intelligence from London, was treated with knowing consternation in a press that still never failed to satisfy.[60] The *New York Mirror* writes, "All the newspapers from Maine to Texas are filled to overflowing with magniloquent descriptions of the ceremony. It is the universal topick in our republican circles. No particular is too minute to be interesting. One of our editors actually fretted himself into an apopleptick fit the other day, because none of his London correspondents had sent him word whether her majesty's slippers were of velvet or satin."[61] Indeed, the fetishism of the queen's person, the "Reginamania," as one corespondent calls it, for the meticulous knowledge of her toilette—"I understand she rises between eight and nine o'clock, breakfasts at ten"—often extends to her feet. At least her feet: for a queen who could otherwise be described (by cynics and Tories, say) as occasionally unbecoming, and fat, especially on the palace grounds where she never bothered not to appear in green riding dresses, her feet are always very "elegant." The newspapers in London and the United States alike, says the *Herald*, are "under the necessity of dwelling constantly on the beauty, not only of the queen's person and features, but of her *feet,* and even of her *slippers.*"[62]

The need for courtly information functions here no less than in monarchies where the excess of desire for the body of the queen, and all the ordinary facts that comprise her gestures of eating, grooming, loving, and generally behaving herself, turns each trivial thing into the far more compelling symbol of a transcendent thing. If her body charms and delights, it is because it points synedochically to an other, sublime body that is made manifest in the very fascination with the physical form of the queen and that grants the doubleness of the monarch's body—her "two bodies" (mortal and immortal, secular and scared)—that has become a commonplace of what we know about how sovereignty traditionally was conceived. The queen's feet, like her son's pajamas, are both the material things they are and the emblem of the "evasive" thing, in Slavoj Žižek's words, that marks the auratic function of a queen whose extraordinary properties come to inhere in the most ordinary properties of her everyday. Thus the paradox of sovereignty that projects perfectly abstract ideas onto prosaic details, so that the more insipid the amassing of these details is, the more absolute is the charisma of the queen, and the more her admirers can continue the practice of exalting by means of their "addiction to trivia," as Tom Nairn minces no words to call it.[63]

"I have driven in the Park several days," writes Nathaniel Parker Willis, "admiring the Queen on horse back." His investment in the person of the queen is rarely less concrete; such reliable pleasures are bound to the ways in which asserting what is there to see makes an idol of the queen but also makes the fact of her being there as reassuring as all the homely acts of smiling, waving, riding, and eating breakfast. In other words, the reporter abroad, faithfully recording his awareness of the queen palpably doing what she does, makes the very existence of a queen doing it seem just as incontestable. Needless to say, such journalism is short on critique (Willis just gossips), but in a way that allows our response to the monarchy to feed on such comfortable exemplifications of it, glad for the accidents and variety and most of all for the familial articulations of an institution that invites such immediate rapport. The small details, confirming a royal niceness in the meticulous attention to gestures and routines also confirms the traditionary, social order that has made such a royal culture part of the reality of common life. "Her Majesty seems to me to ride very securely": Willis's observations are tedious, but they are not experienced that way as he reproduces for the American public what Nairn describes as an "abstract cult *of* the concrete" that replaces the principle of the thing (whether, for example, anything like a royal family should be there to observe) with the irresistible images and intuitive commitment to its being there. Willis is both venerating the monarchy and doing so with a naive enchantment with "what it is"; his attention to the habits of the queen reproduces for his audience a characteristically British practice of empiricism (at least as it was understood) that likes particularity over principle and that shrinks from analysis more generally. The English, writes Emerson, "love reality in wealth, power, hospitality"; they "surrender to facts." Which is not to fall prey to the same folk mythologies of national character but to suggest in any case that Willis's weekly dispatches from the palace for *The Corsair* are a conservative affair of a kind with those that worked to legitimate the monarchy in Britain. Such involvement with the body of the queen rededicates American readers to, what Perry Anderson calls, a "simultaneous philistinism towards ideas and mystagogy towards institutions, for which England has won an international reputation." [64]

What does it mean for democrats to uncritically love a queen? If we believe Edward Shils's sociology of power, we could say that these displaced sentiments are psychic compensation for the ambivalence toward authority; such positive devotion arises out of the deepest compulsion to resist, and the democrat who finds these state symbols most sacred is the one who will dispense with them first.[65] If the monarchy is a vital object of attention, it is because it is mercifully of no importance for a people that have successfully relinquished it. The desire for symbolic authority, and all the splendid measures of its rites and show, corresponds exactly to the loss of real power for a queen who can only reign over the imaginations of a people who she no longer rules. The reverence of Americans for the queen is the function of their distance from her; their pure rituals of deference are completely insignificant except that they allow for a sincerity of devotion to the ceremonies of state that is most possible where the monarch is derealized as a figure of authority. Willis, for example, likes to contrast his own vigilance to the person of the queen to the indifference of her British subjects. At a concert in Kensington, he tells us that

> the Queen rode by, pulling up to listen to the music, and smile right and left to the crowd of cavaliers drawn up in the road. I pulled off my hat and stood uncovered instinctively, but looking around to see how the promenaders received her, I found to my surprise that with the exception of a bald-headed nobleman whom I chanced to know, the Yankee stood alone in his homage to her Majesty. . . . She is as completely isolated in England, as entirely above and out of reach of the sympathies and common thoughts of society as the gilt grasshopper on the steeple. At the opera and play, half the audience do not even know she is there;

in the Park, she rides among the throng with scarce a head turned to look after her.[66]

If she is just a queen in a crowd at Kensington, a tiny bauble ("gilt grasshopper") atop the class hierarchies of Britain, she is the sole occupation of this Yankee who "instinctively" and sympathetically knows to "look after her." If she is outside the "common thoughts" of Englishmen, she is the "universal topick" in the American circles that admire her freely and that express an homage based on spontaneous emotion and natural response, both of which far surpass, in Willis's national fantasy, the protocols of subjects. While the British are immune to her imperial nods, each royal gesture for Americans abroad is a blessing of pure communication from a monarch whose radiant acts testify to the affective power that ritual ideally ought to have but rarely can achieve, for it is only Willis's innocent remove from the real functions of the monarchy that lets him fully experience the dignity of its aesthetic. The tremendous lack of purpose that distinguishes his attentions is thus the highly improbable signature of what Shils might call, in terms derived from Émile Durkheim, the "sense of the 'serious'" that patterns any ritualized desire for "contact with the charismatic or sacred."[67] If "ritual is not technological," and thus finally calibrated on no mechanical exchange of means and ends, its force and pleasure is proved again by noting just how little consequence attends to what American observers of the queen actually observe. The accumulation of small details about her personality allows chroniclers like Willis to witness and reproduce the way that Victoria, as her reign extends across a liberalizing nineteenth century, provides a purely social medium for political belonging that increasingly makes community and consensus out of nothing much at all.

Walter Bagehot is most famous for articulating the separation in nineteenth-century Britain between the "dignified" elements of government that inspire reverence and the "efficient" elements that govern, between a numinous queen and the locus of power. His *English Constitution* (1868) insists that the business of the nation not only is increasingly beyond the role of the monarchy but should be as well. Monarchic ritual serves as a "disguise" for the reality of power that is, in turn, all the more efficient for concealing itself behind the pageantry of a sovereign who is "brilliant to the eye."[68] The problem for Bagehot is that such a glorious monarchy did not sufficiently exist in the Britain of midcentury. Bagehot's belief that "to be a symbol, and an effective symbol, you must be vividly and often seen" is also his lament for the paucity of royal spectacle at a time when, even before Prince Albert's death and Victoria's prolonged period of mourning, the ceremonial presence of the monarchy had been greatly reduced. For one, the first decades of Victoria's reign marked the height of her political power in affairs of state. She was responsible, most memorably, for the reinstatement of Whig leader Lord Melbourne, despite the Parliamentary victory of the Tories, and years later, she managed to remove Lord Palmerston as foreign secretary after disapproving of his imperial policy and, more so, his sexual conduct. Victoria's interference in government and political favoritism made her the target of the press, which called her "Mrs. Melbourne" and "the Queen of the Whigs" and which, in any case, was suspicious of the Germanic temperament of Prince Albert, who it also accused of too much authority. "If continuing royal power made grand royal ceremonial unacceptable," writes David Cannadine, "then renewed royal unpopularity made it impossible." This was, says Cannadine, a dowdy crown, the object of criticism in a press that was otherwise indifferent and that at best lacked the wide distribution and cheap illustrating technologies to make Victoria more vivid to her public. What pageants and rituals existed were managed locally and incompetently; they were not so much national events as provincial group rites, and the lack of what Eric Hobsbawm describes as "invented traditions" of anachronistic grandeur around the monarchy made such efforts at pageants visually dull.[69]

Certainly, Victoria was on her way to becoming the wholly symbolic monarch she would be by the end of the century, but the exchange of power for popularity, of executive function for ceremonial presence, was not yet complete enough for Willis's own sense of her public neglect not to have truth to it. The narrative that Cannadine tells, and that Margaret Homans and others allude to, finds the prestige of Victoria strengthened with her empire: her assumption of the title of empress of India in 1877 marks the rise of a radiant myth of royal influence that extends well past her diamond jubilee and relies on her new representative function as the head of state and not the head of government. When Joseph Chamberlain brings the colonial premiers and troops to Britain in 1897 for the jubilee procession, the crown they celebrate is the ornament of an imperial system that is putatively bound together through the forms and ceremonies that only a crown can inspire. If this crown has ceded the control of its empire to a network of far-flung bureaucracies and institutions, its impotence in this respect is also the means to its veneration as the vital center around which a feeling of collectivity can be ritualized. Because, in other words, the Britain to which the crown refers is imagined as an ideal community of tribute and devotion that need not—and perhaps cannot ever again—coincide with the everyday administration of society and government, it functions as a space where being a British subject at least in part demands an affirmation of belief. Of course, what is sacralized here is not so much Queen Victoria herself, but the occasion for belief she represents; the mystique that comes to surround her figure at the center of British Empire lives entirely within its own exertions and displays, and this is at once a sign of her diminished force in actual affairs of state and a concession to her increasing hold on the public imagination. That the most flamboyant expressions of this attitude toward monarchy largely originate in the colonies before returning to distinguish the culture of the metropolis thus makes perfect sense. The frontiers of empire, where the residual power of the sovereign is less real than the management of colonial rule, is also where the sovereign can overwhelmingly dictate the response of society to her distance as though it were a compelling form of transcendence.[70]

At least, this is the mythology of the monarch in the age of empire. When the Prince of Wales toured India in 1875–76, just as Victoria became empress, the amazing display of pageantry and homage projected a new idiom of empire that was shaped around the hierarchies and traditions that royalty manifests. The desperate anachronism of these gestures orchestrated a show of British rule as traditional, as rooted in the local character of even its most "exotic" habitations, and, despite all logic to the contrary, as participatory for how it invited colonial subjects to embrace the theatricality of their own domination. Thus for the various bureaucrats, administrators, viceroys, and other classes of imperial "impresario," to use Cannadine's term, the elaborate exportation of a social order modeled on a profound nostalgia for the whole culture of monarchy transformed the queen into a sacred relic of national community within an international context.[71] But the very public nature of the aesthetic forms that communicated this iconology of royalty also asked, and quite frequently demanded, that mixed audiences of both British and colonials shared in performances of their asymmetrical relations—through parades and pageants, coronations and processions—as if the spectacle of imperial power could guarantee not just obedience but also belief in the customary, time-honored status of the empire itself.

It is a version of this colonial vicariousness that Americans such as Willis seem already willing to indulge in their response to Victoria's coronation in 1838 and, of course, to their own reception of the prince years later. This is well before historians mark the emergence of an ambient culture of the British Empire predicated on the dramatic presence of its sovereigns. But then, the United States was not a part of the British Empire. The American investment in the queen is both a precursor and heuristic parallel to the later imperialization of the monarchy, but it is a parallel whose differences speak to something less historically fraught, which is, namely, a colonial structure of feeling without empire. For if historians argue that the potency of Queen Victoria as sovereign serves also as an index to her abdication of political authority over the course of the nineteenth century, it is very much the case that for Americans, adoring her at her coronation and later welcoming her son, she has no such authority in the first place. So the magical appeal of monarchy, for antebellum Americans, is certainly nostalgic but too far past the Revolution to suggest the psychic effects of British power in any convincing way, nor does it disguise, as it later will in India, the brutal practices of imperial rule. This is why Americans are uniquely able to celebrate an aesthetics of royal sovereignty that is much like Britain's own fantasy of its empire in which the costs are elsewhere. The garniture of the court and queen can stand in the same relation to Americans as the "reserve of features" that attract Roland Barthes to invest symbolically in foreign lands. If the empire, in both cases, becomes "an empire of signs" it is because the referent that lies behind this spectacular set of figures is, for better or worse, "a matter of indifference." [72]

How is a nation mystified by a queen who isn't theirs? "The American in England," writes Caroline M. Kirkland, "walks in a sort of mystification," criticizing the deluded "democrat" who, while paying homage to the queen in St. James Park, fails to grasp what is "absurd and degrading" about her liveries and hovering footmen. Horace Greeley, reporting from London, describes countrywomen desperate to see the court who had "not yet been long enough in Europe to forget what it cost our forefathers to be rid of all this"; others gaze at the queen "to catch the sunlight of Majesty." [73] The "new religion of monarchy" that

Perry Anderson and others describe as a specifically imperial formation around Queen Victoria later in her reign—a "traditionalism" that
both manifests and internalizes the "motifs of Empire"—promoted a
consecrated model of state style, if not more provocatively, a model of
the state *as* a style.[74] That this aesthetic of British power inspires converts among a citizenry at home, and among the functionaries and authorities abroad, should come as no surprise; this is a gospel preached
mainly to the choir. But the accounts of Americans abroad suggest that
it was also possible to make converts out of them, and not merely because a history of prior colonial relations provided a kind of psychic
preparation to regress.[75] The emphasis on the elective character of the
American response and on the contrast with Britons who remained
unmoved by their monarch in 1838 indicates an experience of royal
splendor that is predicated on what the Revolution has made possible:
a nation of republican individuals who can appreciate the baroque machinery of monarchy because they will never be its subjects.

A queen who no longer counts politically can be a beautiful queen,
but for Americans to acknowledge her appeal in stories of the coronation and in prints, accounts, and exchanges throughout these decades
of her reign is to participate in the formation of a culture that ineluctably returns to politics. Americans finally seem to adore the spectacle
of monarchy that reminds them of the nation they are not and, yet, offers them a style of state that, in the availability of the images through
which it is exerted, they can unite together to love. The desire to see
Victoria, and to have this desire realized in the elaborate theater of
public ritual, becomes the index to a more basic impulse to participate
in the common aspiration of all the other people who go to London
just to see her. "I know not whether this court gossip pleases your readers," writes one American reporter to another, "but I know that we are
exceedingly interested in all about the queen, and therefore I think
you may be also."[76] In a gesture that anticipates the forced identifications of Whitman's "what I assume you shall assume," the communication of common interest enacts the similarity from which it supposedly
proceeds; the attraction of the queen plays an indifferent part in the
grammar of the equation because readers are left with the unifying
vision of a public identical to themselves. The doubly comprehensive
nature of this devotion—"all about the queen" must be there for all to
read—requires that the capabilities of the press and correspondence
answer to the needs of a self-nominating audience whose collective de-

sire for contact with Victoria shades into the collective fantasy that the feeling is somehow mutual. If this is an experience of relationship that is ultimately illusory in respect to the queen (especially someone else's queen), it nonetheless makes for a sense of happy coincidence among atomized individuals, including those who *Herald* reporter James Gordon Bennett greets on his way to the coronation:

> I go . . . to describe, in a particular manner, the character, capacity, person, and history of the young Queen Victoria, who has set all the Aldermen of New York beside themselves, and inspired, with new-born veneration, every loafer in this great loafer community. It was but yesterday, as I walked along rascally Wall street and beautiful Broadway that I was accosted, oft and again, by some of the finest looking men—and richest too—and some of the dirtiest looking rascals of the day—"give my love to Victoria"—"remember me to the Queen"—"present my compliments to the royal maiden"—"don't forget to mention me to Victoria, and tell her to have nothing to say to Kinderhook." Such is the interest taken among us democrats in the maiden Queen of our fatherland. Thus we go.[77]

The accounts of leaving for England to see Victoria have a light agreeableness. They read as exceedingly unfraught moments and the friendly regards and courteous exchanges to each other on her behalf seem designed to show the unanimity of feeling on the streets where all Americans love the maiden queen. Bennett's opposition of "new-born veneration" to "loafing" makes the queen herself an American vocation, inspiring a revived sense of duty both vaguely devout and traditional—"born again"—but also implicitly aligned with a sort of energetic Jacksonianism that may be described as a vibrant, participatory investment in not loafing. Royalty here is not only removed from associations of decadence; an invigorating interest in Victoria gets even the rascal off his duff in a mobilization of the American public so complete that Bennett remembers we are "democrats." The sheer absorptive nature of everyone's "remember me," rich and poor, certainly anticipates the prince's visit with its complete sociality and personal wishes that become part of the cooperative action of sharing respects. Here the *Mirror* stages a royally inspired scene of instant fellowship: " 'Why, Singleton! good morning, Singleton. Where are you posting in such a plebian hurry?' . . . —'Don't detain me; farewell. I'm for the coronation.' —'Singleton!' —'Dawdle!' —'The races are over—the opera is over—the

gay season is over—and, egad, *I'll* be over—over the sea and far away!'
—'Bravo! come on then—the bell is ringing—no time to lose. No matter for clothes; I'll share my valise with you. Come, hurry, hurry!' " [78]

Two Americans meet on Broadway, one risking a faux pas in his "plebeian" rush to the coronation, the other joining him in the nick of
time, with no plans and no valise. Singleton, like a white rabbit with his
summons to the queen ("Oh dear! Oh dear! I'm late"), offers Dawdle a
breezy companionship, one swell escorting another to London with un-
characteristic haste, so that Singleton is no longer single and Dawdle is
no longer dawdling; they are similarly invested in the very literal sense
that they share the same clothes but also in their shared desire to behold a spectacle of state that seems both to transcend and to exemplify
the entertainments (operas, races, theater) they leave behind. To the
extent that Singleton makes a friend, and Dawdle achieves a purpose,
their sudden engagement to each other more than compensates for the
autonomy they defer.

Some years later, Sarah Orne Jewett's story "The Queen's Twin" returns to the surprising social effects of a vicarious investment in Victoria. The title character, Abby Martin, "born the same day as Victoria"
and "at exactly the same hour, after you allowed for all the difference
in time," dedicates her life to loving the queen because, with magical
thinking that makes meaning of coincidence, she believes that this is
her "birthright." Turning her best room into a shrine, covered with stories of the queen and portraits framed in hand-decorated frames, the
Twin leads her life in the inner life of her projections. Her psychic involvement with the queen is a reliable pleasure that fills the days of wid-
owhood on an island off Maine with intimations of a greater life that
is also unmistakably her own. The version of the queen that the Twin
assembles and indulges is not so much an antidote for her existence as
it is an allegory: in reading Victoria's book about the Highlands, Abby
Martin discerns the queen's preference for being "right out in the wild
country," which is just where Martin finds herself in Maine. "We do
think alike about so many things," Martin says to Jewett's narrator, emphasizing the degree to which the bond to Victoria depends on the
fiction of such correspondences between the queen and her Twin, so
that the idea of the sovereign's "two bodies" (local and transcendent) is
played out poignantly in the delusions of the widow who sees Victoria
as her second self. "I sometimes seem to have her all my own," says the
Twin, which is a way of insisting that such devotion incorporates the
queen who is loved into the secret life of her subject, which is as much

to insist, with only a little irony, that making the sovereign her own is the means to a kind of self-sovereignty for the Twin who lives alone in her thoughts on an island.[79]

"There's something between us": Abby Martin's statement of sympathy for Victoria is also an index of the great distance that such sympathy must bridge between Maine and Britain, between her own station and that of the queen who she make-believes will come see her. In the story, there is also something else between them on one particular night that the Twin revisits with the narrator and Mrs. Todd, the narrator's guide. The Twin fixes her house for the queen, "just as if she was really comin' ": she makes the bed and prepares a meal. She waits with disappointment, losing hope, when a poor cousin from nearby arrives instead. It is a guest who the Twin "was apt to be shy of" but who she is now ready to welcome, and Mrs. Todd, delighted to hear this, remarks that "it seems just as if the Queen might have known and couldn't come herself, so she sent that poor old creatur' that was always in need!" The phrase "as if" is Jewett's favorite device in *The Country of Pointed Firs* and in the other Dunnet Landing stories that, like "The Queen's Twin," appear later. It makes correspondences that link the attenuated lives of local characters to a worldly range of associations; every thing and act in Dunnet has a likeness beyond it and the similes that are invented bring so many atomized experiences into contact with the awareness of something else. The rage for resemblance that makes a queen of Abby Martin can also make a cousin of a queen, and, here, the fact of thinking there is "something between" herself and the queen has the fortuitous effect of letting something else happen, actually happen in Dunnet, between Martin and the poor cousin who needs her. The Twin could not have expected it, but loving the queen prepared her to receive her neighbor and to improvise the most familial connection at home.[80]

Is there an allegory in this, for us, about the love of Victoria in the accounts by Willis and others? How does identifying with a sovereign at a distance allow for rituals of reception at home? When the Twin sees the queen in person, on her one trip to England aboard a cargo ship, her response to the beauty of the queen, riding in a gold carriage through the palace gates, is both subjective, for its startling effect on her, and transcendent, since it also feels like a "moment o' heaven." But in Jewett's sketch, this aesthetic pleasure, which sustains the Twin through her life in Maine is also what makes provisions (literally, I suppose, in the food on the table) for her accidentally ethical encounter with her cousin and also for the good society—of Mrs. Todd, the narrator, and the Twin—brought together because it is fascinating to be fascinated by a queen. There is no society without the spectacle of the queen, so Jewett frames for us a story that in an unsuspecting way tests a Kantian logic that predicates the possibility of social bonds on the aftereffects of aesthetic experience. For Kant, because what is beautiful has nothing to do with us, no purpose can be ascribed to our interest in it, and from this disinterested response we forget ourselves enough to behave with a certain measure of nobility. Thus to have an aesthetic response, even to the apparatuses of state that, like the Twin's Queen, are so absolute, is to move some measure toward the humility it takes to be a citizen. Abby Martin's pleasure in the queen makes her at last treat her cousin *like a queen*. Our adorations make us hospitable to each other.[81]

Sovereigns, Substitutes, and Emptiness

It can be psycho-politically confusing to think that worshipping a queen is a democratic commitment. In an 1839 poem, "To Queen Victoria," the speaker claims "fellow" feeling with a sovereign who he has just placed powerfully out of reach, and it is hard to see where this gets him:

> I feel for thee such interest deep,
> As one who sees, on towering steep,
> That rises far above him, stand
> A fellow wanderer in the land—[82]

How disorienting: is the queen lording above our speaker or approaching him from the horizon? But the surreal absence of any logic to this landscape also offers the most objective of correlatives for the vertigo that patterns the relationship between them. Perhaps it is the undecidability of whether the queen is a supreme ruler or fellow traveler that speaks best to the strange contortions in perspective that are sometimes necessary for a republican emotional outpouring to carry a charge of courtly awe. The place where such an affect can be indulged appears entirely figurative, with any view of Victoria herself beholden to the metaphors that render her both near and far, familiar and remote. If the auratic object, in Benjamin's terms, retains a sense of distance no matter how close to it we come, the aesthetic contradiction that determines the speaker's response to Victoria seems especially apt for an American understanding of her sovereignty, which at once makes her recognizably what she is but also the symbol of a state we have cast away from us.[83]

American painter Thomas Sully's 1838 portrait of the queen represents a decidedly magnified Victoria, who climbing her throne in the

FIGURE 10. Thomas Sully, *Queen Victoria*, 1838.

House of Lords is seen, quite simply, as much larger than she was (fig. 10). Taken from Victoria herself, who agreed to the sitting, Sully, in an act of flattery and with all due respect to her stature, depicts the queen ascending rather than on the throne because, in his words, "she was too short . . . had she been seated, the draperies would have spoiled the whole effect."[84] With the throne as her stepstool, and the robes trailing down and even lengthening the figure, Sully's queen, like the queen on the "towering steep," rises above the eye level of the viewer, who looks up as she looks back. The result is a heightened, numinous queen who effectively ascends as she recedes, who gains in stature as she moves farther away from us toward the obscured rear of the painting. If the *North American Review* finds, in phrenological terms, "from the Revolutionary epoch . . . in the American cranium . . . the organ of reverence diminishing," Sully optically corrects this, as his young, solemn queen, on her brilliant feet, ingeniously grows before our eyes. The picture is a conservative proposition; indeed the figure that enlarges with distance seems somewhat akin to George Perkins Marsh's 1844 definition of "conservatism" itself, which he calls a "reverent regard" or exaltation of a past that is always regressing: "The mental eye," he says, "unlike the natural, magnifies objects as they recede, and every true man cherishes for his ancestry an affectionate partiality." This trick of sight—an illusion of memory and history—also recalls a moment in Wordsworth's *Prelude:* the narrator, rowing out from shore, looks behind to see a cliff suddenly and hugely appear. It looms above him with greater height, "growing still in stature," as he increases the distance between himself and it.[85] Sully's painting seems all about this form of "looking back" (the queen's own actions give us our cue), and the work was indeed a production of ancestor worship—a nostalgic portrait commissioned by a genealogical society in Philadelphia called the Anglo-American Sons of St. George. Yet the painting was also a broad success: a second version of it (Sully painted two) showed in New York, Boston, Washington, DC, and Charleston, while the St. George Society showed theirs in Philadelphia. The portrait also inspired a number of copies and engravings that sold and circulated nicely: "In every show shop," writes the *Corsair,* "in every bookseller's window, and in half the parlors in the city may be seen a 'decided likeness' of her Majesty. . . . Republicans as we are, we were half inclined to bow the knee in homage."[86]

If Sully's portrait turns on a manipulation of perspective that treats distance as something that, literally, elevates the queen for the viewer, it is only fitting that Victoria's celebrity in the United States would be heightened through these increasingly diminished images. The eccentric nature of republicanism in these accounts always involves the drama of a choice to defer; freely chosen, these acts of subjectification are, as Nairn describes them, an "enjoyable mode of psychic bondage" or, at least, the kind of renunciations that speak for our power to have them. A poet for *Godey's Lady's Book* writes, on seeing the portrait:

> *Victoria;* —she by Sully's skill
> Enshrin'd on canvass, for the usual fee
> Is view'd and worshipp'd—whosoever will
> Adores, *Domestic* deities for *me!*
> Each to his own taste, however;—all are free;—
> "Our glorious ancestors," *et cetera—fought*
> For liberty;—their proud descendents, we,
> Worship or not, as suits us;—so we ought;—
> That privilege we claim, being free in deed and thought![87]

The grammatically baroque defense of choice and "liberty" that unfolds within the poem's last lines seems wrought in part because it must make allowances for preferences that are not the speaker's own. We are more than free—we are historically entitled—to worship Queen Victoria if it "suits us," but we are reminded that there are other "deities" entirely ours and available for adoring without paying what is somewhat leeringly referred to as "the usual fee." There is perhaps too much to this business with the queen that turns our interest into idolatry and that renders both her ease before a gazing public, and her popularity with the masses, as too brazen for a speaker who likes women when they are more "domestic." But "each to his taste": if the memories of our "'glorious ancestors'" are better abbreviated *"et cetera"* than elaborated ad nauseum, we still function as their true "descendants" when we give ourselves over to perverse pursuits of happiness.

Sully observes a version of this same lesson in the journal he keeps during his visits to the queen:

> I found my way without help to my quarters in the Palace, set my Palette and all in apple-pie order long before the Queen entered with the Baroness and a pet dog—a Republican dog! so independent in his taste, that he turned a deaf ear to the Sovereign of England when she

called the audacious animal to her, in the most endearing terms—and when the whim took him would mount the throne and lay his head in her lap to be fondled![88]

Sully gives us a "republican" dog who is so "independent" and self-possessed, he only yields to the queen when he wants to mount the throne. It is a strange breed of servility; the idea alone of a "republican dog" yokes freedom to fidelity and makes it possible to believe that if none of his desires are denied, neither are the queen's. This game of disobedience between a sovereign and a dog resolves itself when the whim to comply affirms the proper order of his relationship to the queen but also grants him the autonomy of his tastes. So while there is something a bit salacious in the image of an "audacious" dog who jumps the queen for a good fondling, I would certainly not insist that this anecdote's appeal to Sully can be explained along these lines. The dog is not actually a republican, but Sully is: so I would more cautiously suggest that this scene from Sully's journal, which anticipates with great economy the contradictions that attend upon a "free" love for Victoria, provides a language to describe the displacements that seem crucial to represent the desirability of a sovereign to an American audience.

In the portrait, the royal robes that seem to lengthen her from behind also leave her pretty exposed, for a queen. The décolletage they create at once invites considerable attention to her naked back but just as certainly reminds us that her front remains chastely out of view. Her bare right arm is luminescent at the center of the image, and the single glove she has removed hints further at the way the painting gingerly approaches the temporality of a striptease. That is to say, I find it even more revealing that the other glove is still *on*, which suggests a show of her own decision to show herself not fully clothed or, just as curiously, the calculated ease with which she has let us catch her at this supremely liminal moment. With her left hand already on the throne, and the crown of George IV clearly visible but also cropped and shadowed at the painting's edge where it sits next to a scepter, she has not yet assumed the implements that will fully objectify her as a symbol of sovereignty, which leaves her here disarmed to greet us as a figure who is not quite a queen. The bit of undressing, to use a Burkean analogy, might leave her to that extent without the symbols or drapery, "furnished from the wardrobe of a moral imagination," with which to represent the dignity and the power of the state.[89] Which is just fine, since the queen represents, for an American audience, the significance of a sovereign who is already stripped of power.

The turning back to face us calls attention to Victoria's somewhat peculiar posture at the captured instant of action: the care that Sully takes to have Victoria raised across two stairs lets us imagine any number of impertinent physical details, be it the backward extension of her right leg or her instep arched across the stone edge that marks the culmination of her rise. But we need not start on such an exercise in embodied seeing to wonder more about Sully's emphasis on Victoria's feet, which, as we have seen, were a constant point of reference in American accounts of the coronation, and so here peek out, as if on cue, from beneath the golden tassels of her robes. They are bright and pointy—far shinier than her tiara—and the fact that there is a third foot visible on the pedestal she will use to climb the throne lends an excessive, and classically fetishistic, quality of both animation and detachment to their appearance.[90] If they are offered to the viewer as highly wrought replacements for the erogenous zones that Sully cannot picture for us in the shapeless mass of Victoria's lower torso, they are far more pathologically attended to in Sully's journal. There he describes his desire for "some trifle that [he] might bring away, as a relic" of the sittings—some *thing* of Queen Victoria. "Nothing presented itself," Sully confesses, "but her foot-muff; out of which I plucked a little of the wool."[91]

The graphically detailed and sexualized attention to Victoria— which is only possible because of what there is to see when she is not yet on the throne—also speaks to the painting's more deliberate and more formalized displacements of the queen's relationship to the sovereignty she embodies, which is as much to say, the sovereignty that the painting itself renders material. Since the longing for the fetish, in Freudian terms, "actually *takes the place* of the normal aim," it provides a compelling logic for the unusual uses and pleasures to which the artist puts a monarch who he adores as something other than a monarch.[92] In the portrait, the displacement of sovereignty is most plainly begged by the crown that is incorporated within one of the original frames. Strikingly large and sculptural in its relief, this crown not only makes the crown inside the painting look like the dimmest shadow of an object on the table to the left but also draws the viewer's eye across the blank space that occupies the canvas above Queen Victoria's head. This emptiness is necessary insofar as it allows for the perspectival illusion of Victoria's continuing ascendance, but it also seems to thematize this void as the absence that she can fill. The space in the painting where the Crown of England should be (on her head, that is) is left vacant; the crown and scepter are laid aside on the table, and into this evacuated locus of power, Sully raises up his figure of the queen. Her portrait more than represents her: what Sully pictures is a sovereign whose power inheres only in the manner she is framed as a work of art, which is why we find the symbol of her power so obviously in the frame. Sully's queen is exalted not by the apparatuses of the state (which are put down) but by the aesthetic act that frames her for a devoted audience.

Of course, the absence that a queen can fill in the United States is one that Claude Lefort famously argues is fundamental to democracy: if a monarch embodies the power of a state, in a democracy this "locus of power becomes an *empty place*." Democratic politics constitute the successive attempts to occupy this place, but it is only ever by proxy because the public remains aware that power does not essentially inhere in those who make claims to exert it. When the throne is empty, to return to Žižek, we are left with what was once the "anguish of the interregnum" as the normal state of affairs in which every (elected) pretender to the place of power is a temporary "usurper." Politics, then, are presented against the background of a radical loss; the emptying out of what Kant describes as "pathological" content leaves within rational government the most nonrational "kernels" of enjoyment in the contingent objects of affection. If all democracy may be figured as the Interregnum, then the surplus desire for the displaced monarchy finds expression in an attachment to its material remains, which then function for a democracy in ways that, if not useless, are certainly, in the Freudian sense, not *normal*.[93]

There are quite a few antebellum paintings of the Interregnum, some focusing on Oliver Cromwell and the Puritans, others on the Cavaliers, often wounded or returning from battle. Critics tend to read these in two ways: on the one hand, the Interregnum prefigures America's own revolution against monarchy and the triumph of a Protestant principle of liberty; on the other, the war of Puritans and Cavaliers looks forward to America's Civil War and the divided culture of Northern utilitarians and Southern planters who also evoke nostalgia for the lost ethos and order of aristocracy.[94] Emanuel Leutze's *Cromwell and Milton* (1854) certainly suggests the last point (fig. 11): his Cromwell, listening in a parlor to Milton playing the organ, is unaccountably

FIGURE 11. Emanuel Leutze, *Cromwell and Milton*, 1854. In the Collection of the Corcoran Gallery of Art.

severe; sitting with a staff, like a scepter and more, squarely between his legs, he seems to represent the austere authority of the Law that has replaced a king. He is easily compared to the king in Leutze's lost painting of *The Last Soirée of Charles II at Whitehall* (1856) shown alongside *Cromwell and Milton* at the 1858 Munich Exhibition. There, Charles II, at the center of the canvas, entertains a crowd of revelers in a rich hall, including the three women he woos. The chandeliers shimmer in mirrors and refract the sensuous pleasures of court—a rococo confusion that is very much a foil to the composed scene at Cromwell's.[95] But as a painting about the power of the Interregnum, Leutze's *Cromwell and Milton* also returns to the enjoyments left to us in a space constituted by such authority. If these enjoyments are not so seductive as the ones displayed in the picture of the Restoration that hung beside it, they nonetheless restore something of what is missing in Cromwell's society.

In the painting, Cromwell sits in a circle of spectators around the figure of John Milton playing at the organ, his face and body almost entirely void of detail within the shadow that envelops him and that fades as it extends almost to the tip of Cromwell's toe. The shadow at once contrasts with the bright illumination that is cast elsewhere on the largely empty floor but also conforms to, and indeed is contained within, the larger circle formed by the audience of listeners. Another sense of geometry operates in distinction to these circles: planks on the floor and ceiling beams draw the viewer into the domestic space, helping the image to sustain its depth of field but also indicating, perhaps explicitly and in regard to Cromwell, too, the strict rule that makes a rational space of this interior. Nobody looks at Cromwell, not even the small child in the foreground who raises his arms as though asking for care (but not from the Protector). Nobody looks at Cromwell because he is not central to the image. This is odd if we compare it to Leutze's painting of Charles II, in which the ruler commands the scene but not so odd as an expression of the different authority that Cromwell represents and that rests, as he does, with the assembly. If the power here sits out with the people, it is also true that the semicircular plan forces the viewer to reach that site of power across a negative space, one that is emptied of all things but the dainty silhouette of the poet making music while staring (we can just see it through the shadows of the organ) directly at us.

A Philadelphian, though German-born, Leutze moved to Dusseldorf to study art but soon left the academy there, objecting to its ties to the Prussian government, to open an independent studio. He was, writes Barbara Groseclose, "one of the first representatives abroad of the hustling, energetic American," which is one way of explaining his commitment during the revolutions of 1848 to organizing an artists' coalition for the liberation of German states from the rule of petty princes. Leutze was stridently committed to the idea of popular sovereignty, and, for this reason, the few critics who have read his *Cromwell and Milton* see it as a chastened vision of the type of leadership that corrects for the wrongs of monarchy.[96] I agree; but the vision of how this new order works is also mediated by its equally pronounced commitment to an aesthetic that reincorporates the symbolic character of the lost regime. Which is just to suggest that even though the image is unequivocal in its sense of Cromwell's authority—his severe countenance only confirms how tightly he grips his staff—the fact that he commands no one's attention speaks nonetheless to a regard he has lost or, just the same, has never enjoyed. Most eyes are on Milton, and those that are not belong to figures whose faces and postures show they are largely absorbed by his music; and the few who look distracted, such as the children in the left foreground and the girl looking back to Cromwell's side, seem also to be keeping quiet, so that Milton's playing does not so much compete with, as accompany their other engagements.

What do they see when they look at Milton? They see the production of art in the open space that Cromwell has left for it. It is not simply that Milton occupies the center of the scene that could belong to Cromwell; for in fact the most crucial feature of their relationship—which is, after all, what names this scene for Leutze and the viewer—is that Milton must sit where he cannot be seen precisely because the focal point of the society that Cromwell has made possible can only be imagined as a site of loss. But, then, this is the place where the artist must go to work, the place where the people turn for the elaborate performances of symbolic value that give, in Clifford Geertz's words, "a sign of being near the heart of things."[97] That the aura of religiosity suffuses Milton's playing—on the organ, with the women in the window seeing the light—is thus to be expected. Art itself is burdened and ennobled with all the seriousness of ritual and, in this form, conceived as the means by which the structures of belonging are animated. At the center of this society are the expressive and ritual acts that offer a purely formal space of identification while also offering, in transmuted forms, the sacred character of the sublime life that is lost in Cromwell's realm. So this is a scene of culture acting as a supplement to the state. Milton's music—but also, of course, his poetry (with the organ as the symbol of his voice)—unifies the people where the head of state does not. The aesthetic experience that Milton creates is the vital instrument through which Cromwell's citizens are brought together at Hampton Court with feelings of reverence and with deep reflection on both the image before them and on each other. His art is the organ of the state.

In the years of his protectorate, Oliver Cromwell removed organs from places of worship, so that by 1660 there were more organs in taverns than in churches. It was part of his polemic against rituals, which he both despised and feared as the sign of arbitrary power and popery. Still, Cromwell loved music, as long as it was not in church, and permitted private performances at secular festivities and at his residence at Hampton Court.[98] In Leutze's painting, the church organ has been brought home and incorporated into the secular entertainments of the drawing room. Cromwell may hope to eradicate the images and rites of worship he saw as corrupt, but in the act of suppression, they reemerge. The Puritan protector listens to music from the rationalized space of his home. A classical bust presides over the scene linking the arts that Milton makes to the historical arts that are also represented by the globe and the books—over time, as it were, since a clock marks the progress of things in the background. But Milton is so mysterious in shadows. The organ, which rises to the left of a woman boxed in by the walls that frame her, looks intriguingly like a confessional. Above the woman, a wreath reinforces the iconography of the scene and hangs on a print of Adam and Eve, which reflects back on Milton at the organ and seems to tempt us with the idea of a Paradise Lost. Flowers are strewn in front of Milton as if at the altar of his art, and behind him two beatified women look upward.

To what degree this image of the Interregnum is pure historicism in the service of Leutze's republican politics I cannot say. But it is safe to assume that these intimations of idolatrous worship and popish veneration are not placed there to contest the painting's ideological sensibility from within but, rather, to picture its most persuasive incarnation. This is the model of a civil religion, in which the relationship of the subject to the state, of the people to Cromwell, can only be imagined, if at all, through the intervention of these expressive acts that draw on art and religion to encourage attitudes of awe. Of course, Leutze's audience worships, too: as Milton looks out from the painting, he invites our response to the exalted scene before us, which serves to make us members of the society that is constituted around such works of art. In adoring the art, we join the circle of republicans.

"A world wholly demystified," writes Geertz, "is a world wholly depoliticized." If Leutze's *Cromwell and Milton* dramatizes this equation with particular insight, it is because the picture directs our attention to those "theatrical" elements that Bagehot believes can exist comfortably within the larger function of government. Such theater may be, strictly speaking, "irrelevant" to the everyday administration of civil authority but is both structurally and aesthetically necessary for sustaining the feeling of "common human nature" that makes politics not just effective but pleasing. The idea that art operates within an autonomous sphere does not presume a belief that it is divorced from the world of politics but, rather, describes just how it is most useful to the life of the state. For what art makes possible, in regard to the state, is the spontaneous experience of a resonant, general humanity—"the brilliant edition of a universal fact," says Bagehot, that "rivets mankind"—which renders the political as a mere aspect of the social but does so only to furnish the ground of shared feeling and abstract collectivity that is necessary for politics to flourish. To participate in the separate sphere of culture, according to the logic that Bagehot articulates, is not so much to be distracted from affairs of state but to be prepared emotionally to feel their significance and respond in kind—and more, to feel the significance of others feeling exactly the same as us.[99]

There was nothing more "irrelevant" to the administration of civil affairs in the United States than the theatricalized image of Victoria as it circulated in the press or in the prints of Sully's painting. Just so, the attention of the nation to a queen doing interesting things might be said, with Bagehot, to sweeten civil life "by the seasonable addition of nice and pretty events." Seeing Victoria in the magnificence of her reign provides what Friedrich Schiller might describe as an aesthetic education for communities of citizens; but seeing her at the same time more familiarly, as Sully urges us to do, is to reinforce the sense that the queen is just a "brilliant edition" of the common life that is shared by these citizens.[100] The popular image of Victoria in the United States as a young woman on the throne, and later as a new wife and mother, aligns her sovereignty with her ordinariness in a way that redoubles her effect as exemplary. But as an aesthetic attraction, and a feminized one, she also registers the transformation of both art and womanhood as they come to define differentiated spheres that exert their influence over civil life only by being irrelevant to it.

It is not inconsequential that the power of art in Leutze's picture takes place within the home. To feel its effects we must enter a domestic space, where the scene of aesthetic enjoyment makes its viewers part of the family circle, perhaps even holds them in its embrace like the children cradled at either end. Culture as such is gendered female, but to the extent to which it is contained within this private scene, it is also imagined as answering to a set of needs for which public politics as such has little vocabulary (Cromwell remains so stiff). Of course, the pleasure and seduction of these arts can be threatening too, like Eve with the apple in the print, which is why Cromwell tries so hard to domesticate them.

The American devotion to Victoria figures her cultural place in similar terms. The iconography of a feminized queen attends from a recognizable ideology of separate spheres that treats her cultural influence as a force that works from within an absence of power. There is more than a passing resemblance between this particular notion of what femininity can accomplish by means of its own circumscription and the kind of politicized sway Victoria is said to have achieved through her remove from the business of state; as Homans, for one, reminds us, monarchs and women were equally expected in nineteenth-century Britain to refrain from overt political action. In the United States, of course, there is neither the need nor the choice to refrain: the queen is already without power, which makes her status all the more able to articulate, almost allegorically, the marginal position of women as the key to their greatness. If Victoria's powerlessness is a matter of our national being, the model of influence she comes to embody can be all the more pure in its appeal.

It is acceptable for Americans to defer to the queen, insists a character in Francis Grund's *Aristocracy in America* (1849), because "a man cannot be too humble before a woman." Victoria becomes the idealization of the middle-class woman who has exchanged political power for moral influence; as a queen, she is extraordinary for just how representative she can be in this respect. Even before *Queen Victoria's Memoirs of the Prince Consort* was published in New York in 1867, the "domestic excellence" of the royal marriage set the "perfect example of true love and self-sacrificing devotion . . . before all the young people of America." Where else but in England, writes Sarah Josepha Hale in *Manners; or, Happy Homes and Good Society All the Year Round* (1868), "would the domestic virtues of a sovereign Queen and a Prince Consort have ennobled their high rank," making clear the way that "home happiness" and the well-being of the nation are one and same for a queen. It is Victoria's simultaneous role as "Queen of the mightiest kingdom (not country) on earth," and "a wife noted for her domestic qualities," that inspires a correspondent for the *Southern Literary Messenger* to imagine her as the supreme woman; in fact, should England ever wish "to attempt a real Republic" (a country, not a kingdom), her death would serve as the ideal occasion, since the influence of her feminine virtues are felt most when she is least present. In a morbid variation on a logic of separate spheres, the correspondent can only dream of what the "model wife in all points" could accomplish if she were "a sainted memory." His fantasy of political transformation is as weird to picture as it is finally conservative; the writer dreams that the "Phenix of Liberty" will arise from Victoria's ashes, producing a nation technically free of a monarch but only so monarchy itself can undergo "a sort of apotheosis" that will let Victoria be "revered forever." That this correspondent seems as much to describe a republic that already exists—indeed, the American revolution had made it—lends a curious note to this regicide fantasy, which needs the queen to pass away to love the queen even more. The apotheosis of monarchy is as the republic's object of reverence.[101]

The operational paradox of the structure of feeling around the queen is that it must not confess its social function if it is to achieve its desired effect. Victoria's power is radically indirect, which is, after all, the nineteenth century's primary mode for imagining the power of women. If Victoria is, as the *Ladies' Repository* describes her, "the exponent of female nature rightly cultivated," then it also follows that all women have the implicit power of a queen, whose power is, in turn, just that of a woman "exponentially" raised. During the first decades of Victoria's reign, figurative "queens" appear throughout American households in a widely available discourse of royal prerogative that treats any woman of worth as "a perfect queen," "a queen of society," "a reigning belle," or "a queen of the occasion" (fig. 12). The celebrated qualities

FIGURE 12. "The Queen of Beauty," Currier and Ives, 1860. Courtesy of American Antiquarian Society.

of the queen—her duty and devotion to family, her benevolence, her compassion—are redistributed throughout the classes, so that the effect of any beautiful woman on society may be likened to her "imperial authority" over the people who are drawn to her. "Some friends," writes Elizabeth Ellet in *The Queens of American Society* (1867), "have objected in advance to the title of this volume on the ground that the term 'queens' as applied to the subjects, seems out of place in the society of a republic. But if we call to mind how continually and universally the expression is used in ordinary conversation, it must be conceded that no other would do as well." [102]

For it is their functional equivalence that earns American women the right to be called queens: it is not just that their manners or refinement make society pleasing but, rather, that the virtues they embody and express make society possible by instilling principles of decorum, continuity, and obedience that are, to return to the *Ladies' Repository* on Victoria, "the superior moral endowments of the female" that she exemplifies. Victoria provides the model for female sovereignty as a "reign of feeling" that is at once distinguished from the world of politics but, then, altogether mediated by its terms. Within the language of domestic monarchy emerges an alternative epistemology of U.S. citizenship, one that attributes our attachments to each other to sentiments that exceed—because they have no place within—the realm of abstract, impersonal identities that the nation's ideology entails. The fantasy of a female sphere that is "essentially royal," in Ellet's terms, displaces the experience of national belonging by investing it with a rich aesthetic of personalized authority. "Every belle," writes Ellet, "every leader of the *ton* . . . is absolutely inseparable from her state." [103] At its limits, this discourse gives symbolic shape and form to values that are highly feminized—subservience, loyalty, reverence—in respect to both the subjects who are likely to indulge them and the icons who are likely to inspire them. Ellet would appear to capture best the character of a society that wants queens to keep us faithful to such virtues when she says, "there is nothing republican about it"—which is true, even when it is thoroughly republican.

Just after the start of the Civil War, Daniel Huntington painted a portrait of Martha Washington holding a levee in the early days of the republic (fig. 13). She is pictured as a queen: standing on a dais in a room with Corinthian columns, curtains, and statues that could line the halls

FIGURE 13. A. H. Ritchie, after Daniel Huntington, *Lady Washington's Reception,* 1867, engraving. Courtesy of the Mount Vernon Ladies' Association.

of palaces, Martha Washington oversees her reception by sixty-four brilliantly assembled guests including the Duke of Kent, Queen Victoria's father. The pamphlet accompanying A. H. Richie's popular engraving of the image admits that both its setting and its assemblage are imaginary. These people never gathered in Washington or Philadelphia where the levees were held, nor were there residences like this where they could be held, but we are told not to mind since the image only suggests the seriousness with which the Washingtons took the social demands of the presidency. In the engraving, Martha Washington so exactly resembles pictures of Victoria, in the white dress she had popularized as a bride, that a critic for the *New York Daily Tribune* attacks the portrait on the grounds that it fails to recreate an impression of the famously unassuming first lady who "no effort of the imagination can make look like a queen." But she is resplendent here in the midst of her "republican court," with George Washington conceding the floor to her. His image, copied from Gilbert Stuart's Lansdowne portrait, is in a context that makes the convention of his oratorical pose look like a gesture of deference to his queen.[104]

Painted in 1861, and circulated as a print throughout the war, *Lady Washington's Reception* reclaims a shared national heritage at a moment of sectional conflict. Hamilton and Jay, at the far left, join the Washingtons in a federal scene that commemorates the dignity and civility of the Union. "It was finished," writes Henry Tuckerman in 1867, "just at the outbreak of the Southern Rebellion. It is eminently a national picture, appealing so forcibly to the glorious past in our history." Huntington's picture offers a purely formal space of reconciliation in which the worship of idealized founders becomes the occasion for a common feeling of nostalgia. But it is through the image of a queen that the painting works: Huntington's adoring reconstruction of the past admits that the familiar symbols of the early republic are of little use when the bonds of republican loyalty have failed. If a nation declared by the will of the people is a nation the people can undo, Huntington's painting offers a vision of the republic as a traditional state that is more an expression of ritualized order than an invention of ideology and will. The picture asks us to revere the state as we would revere a queen: the "collective effervescence" of the scene before us asks for no commitment to the government it represents but an uncritical awe. The picture says, the state is magnificent. Lady Washington presides over a dazzling scene that depicts not the operations of government but the social functions that are ancillary to it, and they are affecting. This is not a rational public sphere but a court circle that cultivates, in a devotion to the beauty of its forms, a humble and obedient response to the state. It is not that Americans need a queen to stop the Civil War, but they need to learn how to love and honor their republic as if it were as constantly and universally true as the womanhood that a queen exemplifies.[105]

This is, for Huntington, a political proposition staked in part on religion. Critics made much of his Episcopalianism, which veered toward not only an ardent respect for the pomp associated with the Church of England but also a profound fascination with a Catholicized mode of worship that emphasized sensuous iconography. Tuckerman tries to defend this, despite what he calls "the recoil of the world's free spirits from the civic tyranny of Papacy." Huntington, he says, admires "the attempt to set forth what is most touching . . . in melody that wraps the soul in a holy trance, or in forms and colors that bring worthily before the eye examples that cheer and soften." Does not this aesthetic, asks Tuckerman in the face of secular views to the contrary, "commend itself to reason?" Tuckerman hopes to convince us that, in the case of the resplendent image of a queen, the symbol does not necessarily "shroud the fact" of the life it adorns; rather, "the pleasurable and soothing contrasts thus afforded between life and art, the holy efficiency of the latter in cooling the fevered pulse and awakening the heart to better aims and a nobler faith . . . yield some of the choicest joys."[106] Thus in the case of *Lady Washington's Reception*, its content is precisely in its form: Martha Washington's display of social grace and benevolence is also about the benevolence of social display; and the painting's depiction of her exemplary status is also about the pleasure and importance of having examples to learn from. Her appeal puts aesthetic cultivation at the service of civil society, for she teaches us how to admire the nation she represents by the pure force of her feminine grace, making our loyalty an almost instinctive response to the beautiful and the good. What Americans learn from Lady Washington is a political sensibility predicated on the transitive properties of female icons, who inspire an excess of feeling that is grounded in an individual devotion to personalized majesty but that remains always available for larger social ends—for conscription, that is, on behalf of the nation that assembles around its queen.

The Renewal and Uses of Filial Piety

These early decades of Victoria, from her accession to the throne, were not good years for Anglo-American relations. While the first transatlantic steamship crossings of the *Sirius* and the *Great Western*, just one week apart in 1838, seemed to diminish the distance between Britain and the United States and to promise a new period of collaborative enterprise and commercial alliance, violations of diplomacy and disputes over national boundaries were far more pronounced exchanges. In 1837, the capturing and burning of the *Caroline*, an American boat whose owner was accused of aiding Canadian insurgents, began a series of territorial conflicts with Britain over the eastern border with Canada. The United States demanded reparations, the British refused, and in 1840, the American government arrested a Canadian sheriff, Alexander McLeod, in New York for destroying the vessel under British orders. Until the British paid for damages on the condition of McLeod's release, both nations thought the incident could lead to war. Further contention over the boundary between Maine and New Brunswick became threatening when Canadian officials seized a U.S. land grant agent, sent to the region to expel Canadian lumberjacks. Maine and New Brunswick called out their militias, and both the United States and Canada passed appropriations for war funds and authorized conscriptions. In the meantime, British refusal to return slaves who had mutinied on board the American brig the *Creole* and sailed to refuge in the West Indies seemed to violate American sovereignty and international law. It was not until Lord Ashburton and Daniel Webster drafted their famous treaty of 1842 over a round of meals and conversations—Webster was said to have brought the duck, Ashbuton the wines—that hostilities ended. The borders of eastern Canada were defined and the United States agreed to station ships off of Africa to prohibit the slave trade, though Webster still rejected a request to allow the monitoring of U.S. ships by the British navy.[107]

So much for the east. Disputes over borders with Canada and the balance of power continued in the Pacific Northwest, and when the United States finally signed the Oregon Treaty of 1846, so that it could turn its attentions to Mexico, Britain became involved there too. During the years of war, the British government encouraged Mexico to abandon its claims to Texas, while encouraging Texas to maintain its independence, and to choose British favor over U.S. annexation. Such efforts to frustrate U.S. expansion into the Southwest, while also freeing Britain from dependence on American cotton, were finally abandoned in favor of amicability, but not without straining relations.

Of course the reliance of British mills on U.S. cotton was at issue again during the Civil War. When the Confederacy placed an embargo on exports, thinking that withholding the crop would compel the British to break the Union's blockade of Southern ports in order to obtain cotton, it may have miscalculated. But Britain's failure to rebuke the South caused suspicion in the North, as did its policy of "cold neutrality," and later, when the effect of the embargo felt real, the British discussed the possibility of mediating peace based on a diplomatic recognition of the Confederacy.[108] In 1861, Britain was nearly brought into the war when a Union vessel captured two Confederate envoys aboard a neutral British steamer, the *Trent,* on their way to Europe to pursue diplomacy. The British government considered it a violation of international law and demanded immediate redress, though finally dropped charges when the United States released the envoys. Later, relations between the United States and Britain were again at risk when Confederate agents contracted with private British shipyards to build warships; two of them, the *Alabama* and the *Florida,* were responsible for sinking or capturing nearly a hundred of the Union's merchant vessels. In 1863, a firm in Liverpool built two armored ships for the Confederate navy, designed with iron spikes at their prow for ramming vessels in the blockade; the British government eventually seized them to avoid a diplomatic breach.

Still, hostility to the British government did not considerably extend to the queen (who nonetheless signed its proclamation of neutrality during the war), perhaps confirming for posterity, in Daniel Greenleaf Thompson's words, that "the Great tends finally to become the good." [109] Certainly some envoys went to London with no intention of being moved by "the sound of an empty title." Senator Stephen Douglas, conferring with British radicals like Richard Cobden and John Bright, refused to appear before Victoria in court dress, much to the satisfaction of his friends. The royalism contested by radicals and Chartists would be echoed by American emissaries who were also suspicious of the queen's appeal to popular sentiment. Like Thomas Paine's attack on royalty as governance by "fraud, effigy and show," George Mifflin Dallas, minister to Britain in the 1850s, insisted that the theatricality of statecraft would soon vanish like "the hues of a rainbow" and give way to a politics of reason: "All this magnificence of ceremonial and pretension is being fast undermined, even among the proudest peers, by our republican principles." [110] But others describe the queen's character "without blemish." Edward Everett liked the dignity of her office, if not her government, which he found "selfish and grasping" in foreign affairs. James Buchanan thought the queen was "gracious and dignified" on his social visits to the palace, though his mission to London was troubled by unresolved disputes over the governance of Central America. When told that the queen might find it disagreeable if he appeared before her in "the simple dress of an American citizen," Buchanan reasoned that, inasmuch as the queen was "a lady," concessions could be made. The American minister wore a black coat and white cravat, according to common usage, but, as a democrat, swore off gold lace, and Victoria was so delighted with the outfit that at the first levee of the 1854 season she met him with "an arch but benevolent smile." [111]

Following the assassination of Lincoln, the queen wrote a letter of condolence to his widow. "They say," writes Bagehot in *The English Constitution,* "that the Americans were more pleased at the Queen's letter to Mrs Lincoln, than at any act of the English government. It was a spontaneous act of intelligible feeling in the midst of confused and tiresome business." [112] Such were the "irrelevant facts" that the monarchy introduced into the business of government that the matter of a letter from the queen might be a complicated thing to take if it were instrumental to the politics of nations that were sorting through disputes. But there is no idea in it—just arbitrary gestures of felt experience that preserve a naive emotionality within foreign affairs that are very confused. A queen sending wishes, as Bagehot might write, is "very small indeed," because the feeling of relations it articulates can seem like nothing more than what it is: a comprehensible moment of decency. Because her act is an exercise in simplification and because it is not diplomatic in any real sense, the rapport it manifests might be, like Paine's sense of monarchy itself, entirely without "substance." [113] The letter of condolence is fundamentally irrational, an empirical detail that takes the mind out of the history of Anglo-American relations. It is a reflexive show of bonds that are fictive within the crisis but too comforting to give up.

In "The Doctrine of Loyalty," George M. Fredrickson describes a conservative campaign of propaganda during the Civil War aimed at commanding dedication to the Union by redefining loyalty in America as a "respectable word." He traces the campaign to 1863 when, in response to an increase in Northern antiwar sentiments, intellectuals, including Francis Lieber, Henry W. Bellows, and Charles Eliot Norton, founded "Loyal Publication Societies" and "Union League Clubs" committed to strengthening respect for the Union and to denying that radical democracy was in principle above duty to the laws. For Fredrickson, transforming the nature of U.S. patriotism from belief in abstract ideas of freedom to "a kind of loyalty no different in its essential nature from the loyalty of an Englishman to his king" was brand new work and meant that the American Revolution was firmly over and its ideologies outdated. This sometimes involved a recovered notion of the "divine right" of government: Horace Bushnell, for example, sounds much like John Winthrop in his belief that the U.S. Constitution is providential and that one's loyalty to a federal authority is like one's loyalty to God. At other times, it derived from the historical premise that the Revolution had not been revolutionary at all but a conservative legal act in line with traditional British practice. Charles J. Stillé claimed in 1863 that the founders were loyal Englishmen applying and upholding the tested doctrines of British constitutional liberty and that U.S. patriotism was the natural product of the nation's veneration for British law and its fixed customs of state. In any case, the return to loyalty was made possible only by the exigencies of war, a situation so unique that conservative nationalists imagined that the "winds of history had changed direction" and the time had come when dissatisfied Americans could at last promote a position "which re-

quired no lip service to democratic idealism." Rufus Choate or Daniel
Webster may have argued earlier for a nationalism founded on loyalty to
institutions or a filial affection for the past, but Fredrickson insists they
were "out of phase with the currents of national feeling." [114]

National feeling, however, was never so plain, at least where Britain
was concerned. Fredrickson points to what may well have been a dramatic shift in American devotions but underestimates its provenance.
(Even pamphlets from 1862, he says, did not gain effect until they were
reprinted in 1863.) In the decades before the war, Americans had already improvised a whole discourse of loyalty that, in the free and unusual uses to which it was put, became answerable to conservatives at
the lecterns. The effusions of love for royalty as such were not partisan;
to the contrary, we have seen moments when their effects were "democ-
ratizing." The queen and her son inspired forms of veneration that did
not so much preclude democratic idealism as allow for consensual acts
of respect across parties. Still, the phenomenon of feeling they inspired
was widely advantageous for Whigs who were trying to bring back loyalty as a public good. Their rhetorics of Union parallel the unbidden
return to public sentiments of devotion that were already attentive to
the idea of a sacralized government. So while Choate or Webster may
have been "out of phase" with the general feeling of politics, where they
historically held minority views, they promoted a culture of traditionalism that was already a popular response to British symbols of the state.
The queen got there first, but the renewed ties to her person served as
the pedagogical ground for a Whig culture of citizenship in the United
States, one that also acknowledged—with amenable belief in the capacity of its forms—the ambivalent origin from which it came.

For a generation before the Civil War, loyalty was the performance
of a response to Britain, though not the way it used to be. Writing in
1838, George Putnam describes "seeing the *Queen* on a public occasion, when a full vocal company, and an immense audience joined in
the national anthem 'God Save the King.' The effect was quite inspiring—it made every body *loyal,* at least for the moment." This is not a
surrender of Putnam's identity but a kind of "participation mystique"
whose irony points to the eccentric nature of the range of rituals that
Americans enact as themselves. Some persons, writes Edward Shils, are
more "musical" in response to the past. At least while the anthem is
playing, the givenness of singing in company recommends the primacy
of attachments; thus culture bests politics in the claims of allegiance. [115]
But this happens in part because the British loyalty that enters the

American scene and to which Putnam momentarily avers is historically his to claim. If he can forget that he is American in Britain, he can be inspired to forget it at home. Consider this scene that the *Mirror* narrates on the arrival of the *Sirius* from London:

> The royal banner was waving from the attick windows of the "Carleton House," in Broadway, and that splendid thoroughfare was thronged with British subjects, among whom an extraordinary excitement seemed to prevail, indicating that something out of the usual course of things had occurred. We began to be apprehensive for the safety of the republick, and to imagine that our good citizens had renounced their patriotism, and were on the point of swearing allegiance to Her Britannick Majesty. . . . "Have you seen her?" asked one. "She's a noble specimen!" remarked another. "Hurrah for old England!" exclaimed a third; and "God bless John Bull and Queen Victoria!" shouted a fourth.[116]

What is the appeal of renunciation? What is the fun of the sport of jeopardizing the republic to behave as subjects of a crown? One form of belonging is exchanged for another in a way that denaturalizes the relationship between patriotism and the nation. But a sense of allegiance continues to operate, and its emotive texture and social purpose remain much the same, even though its source—which is also its object—is revealed as a matter of whimsy. These ritualized expressions of loyalty seem largely improvised, as if what is communicated between citizens is not just their sentiments toward Britain but also their ability to perform an identity that feels oddly contingent—as much a reaction to what is heard on the street as a reflection of deep-seated affections. The phenomenology of patriotism functions perfectly without the ontology of a nation behind it.

"National existence," says Rufus Choate in an 1858 Fourth of July oration, "is, to an extraordinary degree, not a growth, but a production." He means that the guarantor of the nation is not the inevitable outcome of its institutions and forms. By the nineteenth century, Whig rhetoric had largely dispensed with the idea that the principle of government, and the justice it delivers, was enough to ensure the civic order. If the framers of the Constitution thought they had devised a system in which the Union could cohere through the intelligence of its design, conservatives increasingly turned back to the belief that the security of a republic rests on the acquired devotion of its people. The Union, writes Choate elsewhere, is only preserved "by carefully cultivated and acquired habits and states of feeling . . . by a voluntary determination to love, honor, and cherish." The state may be a just proposition, but what perpetuates it are inchoate feelings of loyalty and reverence that shape a consciousness of national belonging. These must be learned: for Choate, citizenship relies on an ongoing education in filial piety toward the institutions of government that may be rationally good but are otherwise unloved. How, he asks, can the state and its laws, "gain a moment's hold on the reverential sentiments of the heart?"[117]

Whig sentimentalism stages an antithesis between the idea of the state and the habit of response to it, between a comprehension and an intuition of its virtue. In the context of a republican system of government, predicated on revolution and valorizing liberty, there is a foreignness to a psychology of political feeling that aspires to continuity, tradition, and deference. Obedience is not native to the ideology of the Union; it must be incorporated into it, in Jean V. Matthews words, through a "complex web of memory" and a supplementary aesthetic of social symbols. This is the age, writes Emerson, "of severance, of dissociation, of freedom, of analysis, of detachment. . . . The social sentiments are weak; the sentiment of patriotism is weak; veneration is low." Loyalty must be constructed out of behaviors and interests that, though not needed for a rational understanding of the state, provide a way for it to please on both formal and functional grounds. That is, to the degree that obedience is, as David Hume acknowledges, a "factitious" imperative and a "new duty" contrived to support the justice of the state, it is so because "such is the frailty or perverseness of our nature," that its justice is not enough.[118] Whig politics say that we require a culture that allows for an excess of attachment to authority, for a richly aestheticized and affective network of relations to power in the abstract, and to the state in particular, to stave off the waning of social desire. This is why Whig theories of government so often take shape as theories of culture, for it is in the domain of largely surrogate relations to power as they are lived in symbolic gestures, performances, and narratives, that Whigs enjoy their greatest success.

That loyalty, in the antebellum United States, was understood to be essentially British in character meant for Whigs that the future of the American nation depended on putting a little Britishness into it. If, as Daniel Greenleaf Thompson observes at the end of the century, "the progress from monarchy to democracy has been marked by a decline of this sentiment of loyalty," we see ample signs here of a similarly anxious view of the state as an attenuated presence for the vast majority of its people. Whether in respectful visits to Queen Victoria or in the energetic welcome to her son, the desire to pay homage to these emblems of Britain suggests the cure to democratic anomie that Thompson himself offers some decades later: "The general remedy lies in the education of men so as to restore, if possible, the sense of duty; to find some way to renew the spirit which existed in the sentiment of loyalty to the king."[119] Through their recourse to patterns of veneration, Americans invent a style of obedience that both is and is not their own. In borrowing from British idioms to express a nationalist sensibility, they recover the purportedly moral function of traditionary forms, while engendering a strongly presentist experience of community. This is a process that critics and historians of the British Empire, from C. L. R. James to Arjun Appadurai, have described as a crucial aspect of postcolonial politics; while there are limits on the applicability of such models for the U.S. context, there is also no mistaking the manifest intent of many antebellum figures to rehabilitate an iconography of loyalty as a way of accessing the emotional immediacy that they associate with a subject's relationship to the state.[120] Thus we find toasts to England like this, made at the St. George's Society of New York, but cheered on by the mayor and city dignitaries:

> If I may be permitted to allude to any one point of character, which beyond all others, distinguishes Englishmen . . . it is their loyalty,—their ardent attachment to their sovereign, and to the glorious constitution of Old England! [Great cheering.] Your cheers attest the truth of my remarks; what better can I do then, than give you as my sentiments,—
> Patriotism and Loyalty! Blended into one in every English heart.[121]

Such testimony asserts a deeply sentimentalized loyalty whose hold always precedes the events of the moment and whose sense of Anglo-American consanguinity cannot be upset because it derives from a past already fixed in the imagination. Suddenly Americans are touting loyalty and not, for example, the love of liberty, as the basis of patriotism itself. If this is an emergent political vernacular that speaks to the pressures of the antebellum moment, it does so in a "borrowed language," to recall Marx's famous passage from *The Eighteenth Brumaire of Louis Bonaparte*, that men use to summon "the spirits of the past to their service . . . in order to present the new scene of world history in this time-honored disguise." For Marx, the lesson of such influence, and thus the cause of his resignation, is the impossibility of making history new; any dream of "creating something that has never yet existed" is always haunted by "the ghost of the old revolution." [122] Which is not to say that this thick aura of pastness keeps the love of Britain alive only as a mode of nostalgia but, rather, it is to identify the historical formation that keeps it safe in the present and that patterns an American loyalism that can both retreat from, and rise above, national politics.

Look, writes the *American Whig Review* in 1849, at "the deep-rooted, world-renowned, inextinguishable loyalty of the English people ever since they tried the prescriptions of Cromwell with his regicide 'rump.'" [123] The deep loyalty here is the postrevolutionary return to loyalty; we might say that the desire for an old order comes back with a vengeance—it practically spanks Cromwell. The journal places the American Revolution within a typology of "restoration"; 1776, like 1688, reclaimed an "ancient and unquestionable inheritance" of English rights from "the innovating encroachments of the then Parliament." True revolution is the practice of loyalty, and loyalty is immanently English. It makes for the kind of devious logic in lines such as these: "Our ancestors were loyal to what has justly been called the first requisite of a gentleman,—independence." [124] The Whigs do more than replace a language of contractualism and natural rights with a historical model of the state. They choose their history so as to suppress the Puritan Revolution in favor of the Glorious Revolution and, in Perry Anderson's terms, the "official, radiant myth" of national identity. But we also hear, in the compensatory apologies for rebelliousness, a straining of self-definition that, following Freud, we might well attribute to "deferred obedience." This is a narrative of U.S. history that makes the revolution into an unlikely opportunity for expiation; the practice of independence becomes a guilty working-through of displaced English virtues and their symbolic forms. Such professions want to organize a national mythology around a "substitutive formation" that finds, in the expressions of a revolutionary will, a collective wish to bow down before power that was ancestrally overthrown.[125] These conservative Anglicizations of the American Revolution treat insurrection as a roundabout means of tribute, a gentleman's duty to both England and loyalty; such images of elective and belated acquiescence mark the place where a politics of Whig loyalism shades into Anglophilia's more cultural domain.

If by 1863, as Fredrickson suggests, Unionists could salvage for the United States the most un-American of virtues, it comes via a rehabilitation of Englishness that finally exceeds its usefulness. In *The Republican Court* (1854), an homage to the Federalist era, Rufus Griswold praises both the "regality" of Washington's government and the "nobility" of those who opposed it:

> The loyalists were in a large degree people of good condition, accomplished in manners as well as in learning, and by their defection the country lost many persons who at the end of the contest would have been among her most useful citizens, and the brightest ornaments of her domestic life. The Fairfaxes, Galloways, Dulaneys, Delanceys, Robinsons, Penns, Phillipses, Whites, and others, if of the Whig party would probably have been even more distinguished in society than in affairs, though the military and civil abilities that some of them displayed against us, or in foreign countries, showed that they might have nobly served their fatherland in these capacities, and participated with the most successful and most honored of her faithful sons, in her affections and her grateful rewards.[126]

This has an astonishing effect. It is not just that Griswold is technically seditious. He also concocts a tortuous logic in which America loses its best men to loyalism, who should have stayed to serve the cause of . . . loyalism. Griswold gives us a puzzler of terms, where allegiance to Britain sounds no different than allegiance to America, where "Independence" is the work of "faithful sons" on behalf of "their fatherland," and where rebels "nobly serve." There is even a transvestism of the "fatherland" itself with "her" affections and "her" grateful rewards. And just what "Whig party" is in play here—would the Fairfaxes and Galloways have been the "brightest ornaments" of the English Whigs, had they chosen lives of politics, or of American Whigs, had they stayed? Indeed, Griswold's mourning for a lost generation of Whigs seems undeniably in response to the dissolution of the American Whig Party in that same year, 1854—could these "good" people, in other words, have saved it?—and yet this passage is so wistful, so firmly historical, it imagines Americans as players in English politics. But this is not, in the end, even about politics. It is about the need to register the loss of a courtly style in which even elected authority operates through aesthetic forms. Making the Revolution English may partake of a conservative doctrine, but it finally offers such a bewildering range of response—from melancholia to abjection to outright imitation—that its partisanship seems only incidental to its awe. Our "most useful citizens" were loyalists—that much is clear, if nothing else, in Griswold's revisions.

Griswold's valorization of "faithful sons" points to a language of filial piety that is deliberately antiquated, that uses a colonial nostalgia of ties to Britain to reimagine American citizens as children, and patriotism as a set of sacred obligations to the "fatherland." It speaks to a longing for dependence that is purely indulgent: a vogue of the past in which American "unions" were involuntary and affectual—more Burkean than Lockean—and maintained by a child's love and reverence for the state. It reinvests in patriarchal authority by understanding national ties through anterevolutionary metaphors of familial connections and ancestral duties. "The American visits England," says Edward Everett, "with something of the feelings with which a dutiful son, after wandering long in foreign climes, returns to the roof which sheltered his infancy, and makes his pilgrimage to the churchyard where his parents are laid to rest." [127] The prodigal son returns but the father is dead: it becomes the essence of such devotion that its object is unattainable, the idolatrous tie to what is unambiguously gone. "It is well," Rufus Choate writes, "thus filially, thus piously, to wipe away the dust, if you may, which two hundred years have gathered upon the tombs" of the pilgrims who themselves cherished a "deep filial love of England and the English, which neither persecution, nor exile, nor distance, nor the choice of another and dearer home, nor the contemplation of the rapidly revealing and proud destinies of the New World, ever entirely plucked from the hearts of all the Colonists." [128]

Of course, I would not go so far as to say that some standing dream of Britain is recalled in Lincoln's "mystic chords of memory," nor that all *these* "bonds of affection" could change anything back home. I only suggest that the interests of Union seem implicitly at hand in these narratives of nostalgia and return and that the vague ties to Britain—"the silver cords, which bound distant, but affectionate colonies to their parent country"—could sound surprisingly similar, for example, to Edward Everett's pleas for the Union: may we join together, he says, "so that all the cherished traditions of every part of the country may be woven and twisted into a bright cord of mutual goodwill, to which every honored name, and every sacred spot, and every memorable deed shall add its golden and silver thread." [129] "Behold," says Daniel Webster in his second reply to Hayne, "the gorgeous ensign of the republic."[130] The stars and stripes are figured in his speech as "arms and trophies," and the emblem of liberty as the lustrous insignia of an inseparable Union. Webster gives us a grand symbol of America in which consanguinity seems like a set of old-world attachments and the banner of patriotism like family heraldry.

Indeed nowhere are the resonances of Union so great as in the antebellum mania for genealogies, in which even the most avid Americans sought the distinction of British ancestry by adjusting their names or appropriating coats-of-arms. The "extraordinary passion" for British genealogies, which "has raged during the last twenty years in the United States," writes the *North American Review* in 1863, has "the tendency to draw closer the sacred ties of blood." In offering an elaborate symbology of relatedness that necessarily precedes the Revolution, the genealogies not only enoble filial piety as a matter of course; they also invoke a language of belonging central to the Whig investment in national identity as an expression of loyalty and heritage.[131] "The most consistent democrat among us," we read, "will find nothing inharmonious with his principles" in resuming such dynastic practices. For while the rage of American pretenders gave rise to what Hawthorne calls the "diseased American appetite for English soil"—to Americans arriving in Liverpool with blood claims to the queen or dreams of dukedoms—it also recalled the rhetoric of patriotism itself: "By the considerations of a common ancestry," writes Jonathan Prescott Hall, "the emotions of a natural sympathy might be excited, and the bonds of union strengthened."[132]

Americans ransacked Sir Bernard Burke's *Peerage and Baronetage* (1863), James Savage's *A Genealogical Dictionary of the First Settlers of New England* (1860–62), William Whitmore's *A Handbook of American Genealogy* (1862), and Charles Boutell's *A Manual of Heraldry, Historical and Popular* (1863), with its seven hundred illustrations of insignia. They published their family histories and paid special attention to Britain— John C. Warren's *Genealogy of Warren* (1854) and Isaac Appleton Jewett's *Memorial of Samuel Appleton* (1850) are two of many.[133] Burke writes, "For ten or twelve years before the civil conflict broke out, the most intelligent and zealous of my genealogical clients were from the other side of the Atlantic, all yearning to carry back their ancestry to the fatherland, and to connect themselves in some way with its historic associations."[134] Indeed, with the first publication of the *New England Historical and Genealogical Register* in 1847, Americans managed to sustain what, in Burke's words, "Britain never did": a magazine devoted solely to genealogy. Before and during the war, Americans, with their genealogical tables and taste for the science of heraldry, were "extending the bounds of recognized kindred, because their hearts and sympathies were large enough."[135] And while the American pastime may seem more like bourgeois affectation—"It's the genuine thing," says one literary "Yank" of his coat-of-arms, "I paid a deal of money for it"—there remains an excess language about the "community of ancestry" in the pieces that are claimed and restored.[136] As Stephen Spender tells us more recently, "There is an implicit idea in the books written a century ago by American visitors to Europe that in reentering the traditional sources of their own country, they were piecing together their divided selves."[137] This evokes a Puritan sense of loss as separation and of totality achieved through the reintegration with one's past. The ennobling of old relations suggests a "family Romance" with Britain at its center but, also, a rhetoric of identity that makes these magnifications ("surely there can be nothing offensive to the purest democracy") fundamental to the American self. No actual Britain inspires them but its idealized and totemic replacement: what the revolution cast down is restored in Anglophilia's genealogical romance of a historic homeland and source of self-fashioning to which all Americans—as members of a widely extended "kinship"—could subscribe. "At any rate," says an article on the practice of heraldry, "it seems to be almost an instinct . . . in our country."[138]

Anglophilia, to paraphrase Michel de Certeau on history, does not resuscitate anything. But it evokes a whole system of figures and mythologies that are productive in the present and exchanged for the present, while being cautiously rehearsed as the past.[139] Revisiting Britain is a way of revisiting childhood; if, says Van Wyck Brooks, "America has no childhood—in America. We left our childhood in the Old World," then Britain involves a memory of dependency that is phylogenetically unfraught and a resumption of filial piety that is, in no case, un-American. "I love Old England!" writes Thomas Brainerd in *Sartain's*, and continues,

> During the war of words on "Oregon boundary," I saw stuck up in the windows of London, a caricature of *John Bull and Jonathan* . . . [John] stood bolt upright, with a stout cane in hand, before Jonathan, and gave him a look in which irritation, jealousy, impatience, and pride struggled,—with a little of the relenting and respectful air of relationship and good-will,

while he said—"*Boy,—will you strike your own daddy?*" . . . It did my heart good to see even in this caricature, that the parental and filial relation was still recognized. . . . As an American, my eyes often moistened while crowds before me acknowledged their paternal relation to my country-men, and their desire for perpetuated good-fellowship.[140]

How, asks Rufus Choate, can the state "impress a filial awe; how can it conciliate a filial love; how can it sustain a sentiment of veneration?" If the point of Whig rhetoric was to esteem the past and preserve the nation by encouraging a "filial love" for its laws, then the attachments to "Old England" could be pedagogically recovered for the "bonds of Union" themselves. "The American in Britain," writes George Calvert "is filled with filial reverence. . . . He runs about refreshing, verifying, and rectifying his vague memories."[141] Where else could you find the individual recollections of a childhood that is by no means one's own? Calvert neither has personal memories of Britain nor requires them for the experience of national heritage he is determined to retrieve; because the remembered space of childhood is always indeterminately possessed, it provides an ideal domain in which to find—which is as much to say, imagine—signs of an originary sensibility that exists only at a fugitive distance from the nation's present. Calvert's nostalgia maps a romantic temporality of childhood onto Anglo-American rela-tions. More important, it treats Britain as an anthropological reserve where a vanished world of meaningful attachments and social impulses still manages to survive. Following on Jacqueline Rose's provocative un-derstanding of childhood as something which exists outside the cul-ture in which it is produced, it seems only fitting that Calvert appears enthusiatically confused about the way a fantasy of national childhood makes it possible to reclaim a privileged set of values from which Amer-icans have been estranged.[142] Childhood, in short, provides a natural-izing metaphorics for the profound and, ultimately, presentist allure of Britain.

Americans become children again in Britain not so much to revisit the political nativity of the nation but to recapture an immediacy of relations that redeems the lost world as a physical place. Here are Fred-erick Law Olmsted's remarks on an American's first trip to England:

We cannot keep still, but run about with boyish excitement. We feel in-deed like children that have come back to visit the paternal house, and who are rummaging about in the garret among their father's playthings,

ever and anon shouting, "See what I've found! see what I've found!" If we
had been brought here blindfolded from America, and were now after
two days' visit, sent back again, we should feel well re-paid for the long sea
passage. If we were to stay here a month, we should scarcely enjoy less than
we do now, rambling about among these relics of our old England.[143]

Olmsted gives us an emotional response to Britain that is, above all,
innocent. That he would sail "blindfolded" is certainly suggestive: it is
an Anglophilic equivalent to "blind faith." We arrive at this point of
devotion, but only because we uncritically believe in it. England provides Olmsted with a phantasmic experience of "reunion" and an elusive way back to filial feeling. His "vague memories" of England are
figured as latent aspects of the American consciousness, an inheritance he rediscovers while "rummaging about" a shared past. Still, as
second-hand recollections or "relics" they are appealing. Olmstead's
enthusiasm for his discoveries—an unmediated thrill at the presence
of the "playthings" he has found—suggests an experience of the past
that lies, as William James might say, "altogether in the sphere of sensation." England reimmerses him in a world of embodied meaning that is
intuitively felt and navigated with a child's totality of engagement; the
mythical past is lived in material ways. Feeling like a child in England
evokes a time of sentient pleasures but also identifies England itself as
a place where an intuitive sense of things offers tacit compensation for
growing up American. The empiricism that both Locke and Rousseau
ascribe to the concrete psychology of childhood becomes the character of Englishness, too, and what Olmsted's pilgrimage makes possible
is nostalgia for both childhood and England as worlds where he can
adoringly accept what he feels.[144]

The cultural fantasy that Olmsted articulates is finally concerned
with an extraordinary sort of homecoming: a return to a place he has
never really left having never been there in the first place. His unem-
barrassed veneration of England thus gratifies American wishes in two
emphatically different ways: it produces a sense of auratic wonder that
also promises the most familiar comforts of home. "Dear old mother
England!" Olmsted writes, "It would be strange if I were not affected
at meeting thee at last face to face."[145] The American "rectifies" and
"verifies" his innate bonds to England and thus undergoes what we
might call a remedial education in Whig virtues, through all the fond
accounts of dotage and filiation, and the narratives of childhood (with

its intense feelings of attachment) regained. This is what it feels like to pay respects and, also, to recall childhood as a category of dependence. But the Whig logic that remembers the relationships of duty and deference it entails also promises that such an infantilizing nostalgia can sustain an American mythology of nation. The "affectionate colonies" may have been "severed" from their "parent country," writes Jonathan Prescott Hall. "But all the fruits of that vine which God had planted in the wilderness were to remain to the descendents of those who had nurtured and cherished it. . . . They established institutions, which we are bound by all the sacred obligations of filial affection, or parental reverence, and common gratitude to preserve and maintain." [146] If antebellum Americans, in Michael Rogin's words, "turned political inheritance into family descent" in which "their union was a house, held together by loyalty to the fathers," then stories of Britain provided for a romantic nationalism based not, as Rogin says, in hero worship of the revolutionary patriarchs but in an older mythic heritage that absorbs even them and that has their forefathers in debt to their forefathers. [147]

While Americans traveling in England recall a set of historical relations in a forgotten national childhood, England also reminds them of their own childhoods, which were everywhere filled with English nursery rhymes, fairy tales, and legends of the court. For the American abroad, Britain remains a predisposition that is infixed in the lessons of a more personal past. Here is the *North American Review* on the "home feeling" of an American in London:

> In the part within the old city limits, with the familiar names of streets, the well-known haunts of old worthies, and the frequent memorials of the representatives of England's true glory in the past, the American feels more at home than in any unfamiliar city of his own country. St. Paul's dome and cross seem to be a part of his own youth, and at every step there is some old and familiar sight that seems to have belonged always to the life-experience. One feels that he knows many who have lived and died here better than he knows his next-door neighbor at home. He cannot believe that he has never before lived in those scenes. [148]

London is a never-experienced "life experience." It is a part of our prehistory, and we return to it, says Van Wyck Brooks, with "a kind of half-dreaming instinct," an incomprehensible longing that seems to forget "this really wasn't our childhood at all." [149] In Jacob Abbott's children's book, *Rollo in London*, even a direct experience of seeing the queen registers as a figment of the boy's imagination: as Rollo watches the cortege leave Buckingham for St. James, "It passed before his eyes like a gorgeous vision, leaving on his mind only confused images of nodding plumes, beautiful horses, gay footmen and coachmen clothed in the gayest colors." For the young American in London, the queen is more than a vision of herself; Rollo's wonder and delight at seeing the queen makes her actual appearance feel like déjà vu, which is exactly Brooks's sense of touring England: "It's not sight-seeing really. We feel as if we had lived there in a dream sometime." [150]

Indeed, Britain was an integral part of antebellum youth culture: it furnished its heroes and myths, its folklore and its tales of other children. We feel "at home" in London, writes George Putnam in 1838, because "even the associations of childhood connect us with it. We remember it as far back as the happy days, when we loved nursery songs and 'rode a horseback on best father's knee.' Whittington and his cat lived there. All our picture-books and our sister's dolls came from there; and we thought, poor children! that every body in London sold dolls and picture-books." [151] It was not just, as Ruth Elson reminds us, that the continued publication of British schoolbooks in America and the pirating of these books and spellers meant that early lessons were infused with a sense of the virtues of Britain. Even consciously American primers by mid-nineteenth century taught an ancestral respect; more often than not Americans are seen as acknowledging a familial love for Britain, whose common language and kindred laws bind the nations together, in the words of the *Hillard Reader* (1856), "with cords which neither cold-blooded policy, nor grasping selfishness, nor fratricidal war shall be able to snap." The Whiggish orientation of both new schoolbooks and educational curricula more generally meant countless reprints of orations that taught children obedience through invocations of history. Edward Everett, for example, appears in readers to say, "Who does not know that every pulse of civil liberty in the hearts of our ancestors, the sobriety, the firmness and dignity with which the cause of free principles which came into existence here, constantly found encouragement from the friends of liberty there [in Britain]? For myself, I can truly say that, after my native land, I feel strong reverence for that of my fathers." Washington Allston's poem, "America and Britain" is reprinted with frequency ("yet still from either beach, / The Voice of blood shall reach, / More audibly than speech, / WE ARE ONE"), as are John Kirke Paulding's allegories of the American Revolution as a family quarrel between John Bull and "John's own boy, a true chip off the old block." [152]

But, even more than in lessons, the Englishness of childhood in America resides in the character of play. The Mother Goose melodies that filled antebellum nurseries with songs of sixpence, Cock Robin and Henny-Penny, and other rhymes of Charing Cross and St. Ives, let the aimless noises of youth bear, as one songbooks writes, "all the marks of their English origins." Picture books, printed in Philadelphia, made few alterations from their English sources to tell the tales of *Dame Trot and Her Comical Cat* or *The History of Mother Twaddle* and *Tom the Piper's Son*. Even before the end of the century when Sidney Lanier popularized Arthurian tales and Frances Hodgson Burnett's Little Lord Fauntleroy becomes heir to an earldom (well before Peter Pan, Pooh, and Paddington), the diverting, poetical enchantments of youth were made of English subjects, royals, and knights but, especially, of English words and sounds: Humpty Dumpty and all the king's men, goosey gander, and Georgie Porgie. [153]

Hey diddle diddle: the detractors from nursery rhymes who insisted that children should learn sensible language also objected that rhymes in which cows jump and dogs laugh "[are] suited only to the old countries." Samuel G. Goodrich, whose Peter Parley's tales offered more useful knowledge for the modern world, said that imaginative verse that aimed to cultivate the affections and fancy was also an effort, by the English, to "woo back the erring generation of children to the good old orthodox rhymes and jingles of England." In a dialogue written for his magazine, *Merry's Museum*, in 1846, Goodrich laments that it is such foolish rhymes that stick, so while a mother recommends hymns to her son instead, the boy keeps reciting the rhymes back to her—"higglety, pigglety, pop" and "doodledy, doodledy, dan"—until he doesn't "care so much" when the book is taken from him because he knows "all the best of it by heart." Rhyming without purpose may not be educational, but its formal effects on children so attached to their own enjoyments and pursuits does suggest an aesthetic desire for expressions with no semantics to them. "The human being," writes Elizabeth Peabody a bit later in the century, "comes into the world with an aesthetic nature." [154] In the dialogue that Goodrich creates, the boy admits that he sees no meaning in Mother Goose's rhymes, "but I really do love them," he says, which amounts to a rejection of language as a process of telling in favor of language as play. But if play is the prerogative of childhood, it is also the Englishness of it that allows for an aesthetic release from the utilitarian lessons of Goodrich and others; the nonsense he sees in English forms also defines a period of youth in which love itself is a pre-rational response to pleasing and immediate effects. The reiteration of nonsense says that the empirical experience of words may appeal more than their import, but to suggest that such nonsense is English in character is also to suggest that Englishness is where the susceptability of childhood to such pure sensations is most effectively relived.

Hawthorne's Mystic Threads

The American's return to Britain is nowhere more symbolically in-volved than in the two manuscripts Hawthorne wrote from Concord in 1860–61, now published in the Centenary Edition as the *American Claimant Manuscripts*. These aborted attempts at a romance —later "fished" out of his papers and sold by his son Julian as *Dr. Grimshawe's Secret*—are most famous for their candor in recording the mistaken launches of the author's late career. In older age, Hawthorne's origi-nating ideas no longer seem to work: they are increasingly arcane and his whole symbolic getup is finally unimaginable, especially to himself. It is not just that the project is so vast and that it remains, while as ambiguous as other works, not even slightly schematic. The *American Claimant Manuscripts* are the most awkward read: they are strewn with false starts and dangling elements; mysteries that are never lifted but, unlike the "minister's black veil," have no "desirable effect" for being there; characters that disappear and reappear as other characters— Mr. Hammond is a secret agent, but an unrelated Mr. Hammond runs an old men's home; no final moral or, in Hawthorne's words, no "cen-tral effect"; and yet central actions that effect nothing. The problem is that these manuscripts have always failed to deliver a sense of refer-ence, not just within their own sketchy contents but also as a text of their time. For, critics have always asked, what more spectacular recoil from national concerns in 1861 than a story about (1) an American fascination for English noblemen; (2) the unspeakable history of an occult English quack; and (3) a thicket of ancestries that may make its hero heir to an immense English estate or may—like Hawthorne's at-tempts at this novel—lead to nothing at all?[155]

What we can now make out of the narrative proceeds something like this: Dr. Grimshawe and his two wards, Ned, a foundling, and Elsie, a probable niece, live with their aboriginal housekeeper Hannah in a cobwebby home on the brink of a Salem graveyard. The cobwebs—no sign of domestic neglect on the part of "crusty" Hannah—are spun by one enormous South American spider ("The pride of the grim Doctor's heart, the pearl of his soul") and saved for a certain extract of cobwebs the Doctor claims can cure diseases of the "inflammatory class." As Ned grows, the Doctor, who may or may not possess a secret that bears on a hereditary title, impresses his ward with tales of Old English nobility and estates with towers, turrets, and painted windows. When Ned then asks, "where do I come from," the grim Doctor replies, "out of dust, clay, and mud" but tells him that if he must dream about his race to dream of an ancient county seat, a thousand years old, with a secret chamber where a renegade Puritan (who may have killed Charles I) was confined by his brothers until he escaped—leaving behind a bloody footprint on the threshold—and headed for New England where his descendants were born. One day, a schoolmaster arrives to Salem with his own legend, and the papers to prove it, about an old English family with a renegade and Quaker son who was confined by his brothers in a secret chamber for loving the wrong lady, until he escaped, leaving behind (no less) a bloody footprint on the threshold, and headed to New England; once there, the schoolmaster continues, the Quaker's ladylove sent him a fancy silver key to a coffin, where something important was hidden, and their newborn child, who, to be sure, had more children in time. The schoolmaster tells his story to Doctor Grimshawe and then mysteriously disappears, as do his papers; but soon after Ned finds a new grave in the graveyard with the impress of a foot on it and a fancy silver key nearby, and later when the Doctor dies, he also finds some papers in the wall. Years pass, and Ned Etheredge, after losing his bid for a second term in Congress, goes to England with the key and the papers and some claim in his head to an English estate; it is an estate with towers and turrets that he dreamily roams about but is mistaken for a poacher and shot and hospitalized in an almshouse for old men, where he is cared for by an old pensioner, before finally meeting the current owner of the estate, the villainous Brathwaite; Ned attends a banquet at Brathwaite's house, wanders off, finds a bloody footprint on the threshold as well as a big, tropical spider in a cobwebby room; he makes his claim to Brathwaite who, in turn, drugs, kidnaps, and confines him in a secret chamber. At the novel's end, Ned is rescued by the old pensioner and Elsie, who is back from who knows where. They find a fancy coffin and use the fancy silver key and somehow, what they find inside, bundles of ringlets of golden hair, reveals, after all, that not Ned but the old pensioner is true heir to the estate.

That this romance did not work—that the transatlantic spider never does do its office—was a cause of lament for Hawthorne, who racks its margins with notes and rationales, but still can not make hay of its antiquated forms, golden locks, silver keys, or even Dr. Grimshawe who, to be honest, has no "secret." And though Hawthorne spends pages hatching explanations for the bloody footprint—is it the mark of a tortured Quaker or of a regicidal Puritan?—and for the coffin of hair, he is left with such impossible lemons that the manuscripts keep stalling to ask, in stupendously weary ways, just "how to get on," before devolving into potty lists of gothic glossolalia. Of the Lord of Brathwaite Hall, says Hawthorne,

> Something monstrous he must be, yet within nature and Romantic probability—hard conditions. A murderer—'twon't do at all. A Mahometan?—pish. If I could only hit right here, he would be the centre of interest. . . . A Resurrection Man? What? What? What? A worshipper of the Sun? A cannibal? A ghoul? A vampire? A man who lives by sucking the blood of the young and beautiful? He has something to do with the old Doctor's spider-theory; the great spider has got him into his web. The Doctor, before he left England, has contrived a plot of which this man is the victim. How? He has been poisoned by a Bologna sausage, and is being gnawed away by an atom at a time. . . . Ye Heavens! A man with a mortal disease?—a leprosy?—a eunuch?—a cork leg?—a golden touch?—a dead hand?—a false nose?—a glass eye? . . . What habit can he have? Perhaps that of having a young child, fricasseed, served up to him for breakfast, every morning? . . . All this amounts to just nothing. I don't advance a step. . . . A propensity for drink? A tendency to feed on horse-flesh? A love of toads?[156]

The collapse of his English romance into so much literary backfire meant that Hawthorne would turn his *English Notebooks*, the garnered record of his residence abroad, into *Our Old Home* instead, a series of broad and expository essays on England. All the everyday particularities of English life—the ladies and lords, fox hunts, toasts, tea tables, Americans slobbering over toasts and tea tables—all, says Hawthorne, "intended for the side-scenes, and back-grounds, and exterior ornament" of his English romance would become the book itself. For, critics tend to point out, this was the middle of the Civil War, and what other authors found "inspiring," feeling the impact of the crisis in some fiery and imagined way, Hawthorne found a hindrance to his romance. He says so in the first paragraph of "Chiefly about War-Matters," and again in his dedication to *Our Old Home:* "Of course, I should not mention this abortive project, only that it has been utterly thrown aside, and will never now be accomplished. The Present, the Immediate, the Actual, has proved too potent for me. It takes away not only my scanty faculty, but even my desire for imaginative composition, and leaves me sadly content to scatter a thousand peaceful fantasies upon the hurricane that is sweeping us all along with it, possibly, into a Limbo where our nation and its polity may be as literally the fragments of a shattered dream as my unwritten Romance." [157]

But what strikes me about Hawthorne's opposition between his "Romance" and "the Actual," is that we see the same fantasy of England paramount on both sides, and not just in stories of American claimants or dreams of family nobility (Hawthorne, too, sought advice from the genealogist James Savage), but in a superb fascination for England itself. We see it in the warm language of "instinctive" longing everywhere in the ruins of the manuscripts—in Ned's "old, very deepest, inherent nature" (168), so haunting it has to be gothic—but also in the only geography of "the Present, the Immediate" about which Hawthorne can write. Because, despite charges of jingoism in *Our Old Home* by English readers (Hawthorne *could* be confrontational at times, calling the English an "unfragrant crowd," unacquainted with the washbowl, and English women "all homely alike" [235, 239]), still it is hard to see. Somewhere between apostrophes to the Earl of Warwick and his love for beef, we realize that Hawthorne, like Ned, is "enthralled"— certainly he croons at a singing of "God Save the Queen"—and that this account of the Actual is just a Romance by other means, one more confused American's claim to England. Indeed, critics saw in *Our Old Home* an escapist charm, the malingering of an "isolated genius" when "civilization itself" was at stake. George William Curtis rued such aloofness; in 1863, after all, the North was nearly at war with Great Britain for its sympathies with (and financial interests in) the South, and no one should have been more attuned to this fact than such an unremitting New Englander. [158] And yet I would like to suggest that Hawthorne's reflections on England are not "isolated" at all. Rather, his seeming retreat into genealogical legends and ancestral attachments—even the amusement at these attachments—suggests not simply a method of coping but a mechanism of solution and accommodation located firmly within "the Present."

It is not that Hawthorne liked England; as with most of his convictions, he never quite decides. Nor does *Our Old Home* deflect from our sense of his nationalist bent or from Melville's claim, for example, that Hawthorne was a "Shiloh" of "Young America in Literature" who could lead away from "flunkyism towards England." [159] Rather, Hawthorne's turn to England feels surprisingly tactical. His likings, even regret for his likings, are rehearsed in the same historically specific language of affinities—"roots which were never snapped asunder by the tug of lengthening distance, nor torn by the violence of subsequent struggles"—which read, all over this period, like a deliberate and suggestive response to the problems of Union. Take Hawthorne on seeing Old Boston in England: "It is singular," he says, "what a home-feeling, and sense of kindred, I derived from this hereditary connection and fancied physiognomic resemblance between the old town and its well-grown daughter" (165). The invocation of old ties and filial respects—what Hawthorne calls the "blind" (19) American tendency to wander back again—is also this one American's feeling and deep capacity ("a sort of innate idea, the print of a recollection in some ancestral mind" [63]) for the practices of an affective loyalty that have been deplorably disused. "It was the first time in my life," Hawthorne says after watching a company of Englishmen sing "God Save the Queen," "that I had ever seen a body of men, or even a single man, under the active influence of the sentiment of Loyalty; for though we call ourselves loyal to our country and institutions . . . still the principle is as cold and hard, in the American bosom, as the steel spring that puts in motion a powerful machinery" (324–25).

So while Hawthorne may find England a little ludicrous and too quaint and fossilized in its forms, the sentiments that it seems to elicit in him, and in Americans more generally, are spontaneous and quickening—something he seems to take seriously if not for England itself, with its outmoded earldoms (a particular peeve), then for the way in which "her vagrant children may be impressed and affected" (253). Hawthorne is aware, at least, that he is addressing a "home-feeling" wide enough to bring thousands to the American consulate to trace supposititious pedigrees (wide enough to sell his book, too). So Hawthorne's late, failed romance and the book he salvages from its wreckage are indeed more about the nation than they appear and not just because history can return when repressed. Hawthorne's subject in 1861 and 1863, respectively, had so much to do with what he saw as "American" at the time—and with a roundabout, but nonetheless enduring, symptom of national life. Hawthorne, like the young American Rollo, experiences England with an "innate" sense of déjà vu: "Almost always in visiting such scenes as I have been attempting to describe, I had a singular sense of having been there before" (63).

So what does it mean for Hawthorne to write a romance just then of how a Congressman, with no apparent blood ties, defeated by party politics, goes to England to reconcile two branches of a family and reclaim a "consanguinity" that has been lost? Hawthorne, after all, is the most fabulous of reconcilers—"in politics," says his contemporary Edward Dicey, "he was always halting between two opinions; or rather holding one opinion he never summoned up his courage to adhere to it and it only." "Ideologically fixated," says Sacvan Bercovitch, "like some Ahab of compromise."[160] It is almost remarkable, then, how much Hawthorne can sound like Hawthorne when insisting that loyalty toward England is no apostasy for the devotedly American: "I hope I do not compromise my American patriotism by acknowledging that I was often conscious of a fervent hereditary attachment to the native soil of our forefathers, and felt it to be our own Our Old Home" (40). Because, Hawthorne seems to confirm, there is something about Anglophilia that accommodates, that allows for these confessions of loyalism (for even a prince fetish) while taking no toll. It reintroduces such past sentiments as hereditary reverence, while keeping one's democratic principles in tact. ("No community worships hereditary rank and station," says George Templeton Strong in 1860, "like a democracy.")[161] And my point is that, for such a consensus broker as Hawthorne, nostalgia for England could provide a rare moment of community and tap into something so "inherent" in all Americans that, like Hester Prynne's return to New England, so the New Englander's return to his "old home," it need not be explained. Ned Etheredge, finally freed from his legislative cares, seizes the opportunity to visit England,

> whither he was drawn by feelings which every educated and impressible American feels, in a degree scarcely conceivable by the English themselves. And being here (but he had already too much experience of English self-sufficiency to confess so much) he began to feel the deep

yearning which a sensitive American—his mind full of English thoughts, his imagination of English poetry, his heart of English character and feeling—cannot fail to be influenced by, the yearning of the blood within his veins for that from which it has been estranged; the half-fanciful regret that he should ever have been separated . . . from these men who are still so like himself, from these habits of life and thought which (though he may not have known them for two centuries) he still perceives to have remained, in some mysterious way, latent in the depths of his character, and now to be reassumed, not as a foreigner would do it, but like habits native to him and only suspended for a season . . . it seemed as if he were gradually awakening to a former reality. (148)

This language, of course, is not Hawthorne's alone but an already-available phantasmagoria of the blood ties and kinships, the "half-fanciful" reunions, that antebellum Americans had been inventing for years and in just those terms: a symbology that was as overplayed—to cite Hawthorne on haunted houses—"as the familiar tune of a barrel-organ."[162] Like Twain's "American claimant" of the 1890s, who misapprehends a true Englishman for "a Thing, a Materialization" of his own hokey conjuring—an ancestral earl he has brought back from the past—Ned's English connections are nothing but an "insubstantial resurrection" and a mistaken identity.[163] Yet his very expressions of consanguinity, of filial yearnings "awoke all afresh," might reclaim something in their own right. "Ah;" says Lord Brathwaite, "it is very curious to see what turnings up there are in this world of old circumstances that seemed buried forever; how things come back, like echoes that have rolled away among the hills and been seemingly hushed forever. We cannot tell when a thing is really dead; it comes to life, perhaps in its old shape, perhaps in a new and unexpected one; so that nothing really vanishes out of the world" (284).[164]

In Louisa May Alcott's first novel, *The Inheritance* (1849), Edith Adelon, a poor orphan from Italy, has been brought to the English manor home of the deceased Lord Hamilton to serve as playmate for his daughter. Honorable and true, Edith enjoys a "wealth of warm affections" from the family, who treat her generously as their own, until a haughty cousin, Ida, envious of Edith's beauty and her pursuit by a rich nobleman, frames Edith for stealing funds from a cashbox and disaffects her from the Hamiltons who feel betrayed by her "ingratitude" and "disobedience." Later, when fortuitous circumstances reveal that

Edith is actually heir to the English manor, that everything of Lady Hamilton's is rightfully hers, and furthermore that Edith has known this for "a while" and kept the secret in her "grateful heart," Edith asks, not for the restitution of her title and estate but for Lady Hamilton's parental love: "Take," says Edith, "all that I can give, and in return for this act, let me call you mother and be a faithful, loving child." As for Ida, an always "self-denying" Edith is quick to say, "The past is all forgotten and forgiven. We are cousins. Now let us be friends." [165]

The story of the American claimant, for Hawthorne, as for Alcott, is not about status or sudden riches or even a fantasy of independent wealth but about the recovery of an inheritance that can tighten one's bonds and provide a world of faithful attachments. Edith's first "independent" act is to choose dependence, to seek the exact loyalties she had as a child. In fact, it is the otherwise relentless desire to exist on one's own—the way the highborn but poor Ida "longed for freedom from dependence"—that is at the core of the treachery that follows. Ned Etheredge, with some of Edith's "deep, longing wish for tenderness and true affection," looks for his ties by nature—it is a surrender of autonomy that seems to Ned like a "happy notion," all his democratic "sovereignty" aside (240).[166] So we discover that grim Grimshawe's hostility toward England is "something that, in the natural course of things, would have been loyalty, inherited affection" (368), and elsewhere Ned concedes that as long as "the path seemed to lead onward to a certainty of establishing me in connection with my race, I would yet take it. I have tried to keep down this yearning, to stifle it, to annihilate it, with making a position for myself, with being my own past, but I cannot overcome . . . this feeling that there is no reality in the life and fortunes, good or bad, of a being so unconnected" (258).

I would suggest, then, that Hawthorne's romance, like Ned's, is not only an escape from the "uneasy, agitating Conflict" of the present but also the return to an older order—to the original, loyal feelings that at least aim to be a reparative and "natural" response and in some circuitous way an assurance of "reality." Indeed, Ned's final, unexpected, reunion with Elsie, who appears unaccountably in England, is the happy and very real outgrowth of his visionary claims. All these fantastic, genealogical relations, inspired by the relics of a distant past, end in a much less fantastic (in a renewed) fraternity that had been lost for twenty years. Ned's rapturous return to England—"Oh home, my home, my forefathers' home! I have come back to thee! The wanderer has come back!"—is answered by a slight stir nearby him, and the true sight of Elsie sitting on her mossy seat, taking a sketch of the landscape. "Elsie," Ned cries and continues, "What has brought us together again? Away with this strangeness that lurks between us. Let us meet as those who began life together, whose life-strings, being so early twisted in unison, cannot now be torn apart" (260). This kind of allusive cause and effect—one renewed relation sitting so paratactically next to another—gives Hawthorne's treatment of such reunions in 1861 the feel of innuendo. Take this line from the third preliminary study for his romance, which, given his narrative and its situation of production, I cannot quite read straight: "It must be shown, I think, throughout, that there is an essential difference between English and American character, and that the former must assimilate itself to the latter, if there is to be any union" (477).

I think to see this is to see all over the *American Claimant Manuscripts* some sense of the American crisis, perhaps remote and stealthy, like the papers in Grimshawe's wall, but close enough to Hawthorne's more conservative moments, in letters and notebooks, when politics do play a part and when he regrets, at least, his country's deep "irreverence" for how it is. In one of Hawthorne's *Biographical Stories for Children,* two quarreling brothers, Edward and George, listen to a tale of Samuel Johnson doing penance for an old act of filial disobedience. Johnson returns to the market in Uttoxeter where he had been too proud to accompany his father, a bookseller, fifty years before and, with deep "humiliation of heart," asks forgiveness from his now deceased parent and from God. The boys hear the story, and hardly is it concluded, "when George hastily arose, and Edward likewise, stretching forth his hands into the darkness that surrounded him, to find his brother." [167] The story, then, is not really about filial piety; it is about a renewed sense of filial piety that becomes, in turn, the means of (and the impetus for) a renewed fraternity expressed in the reconciliation of the two brothers at hand.

I would suggest that a similar dynamic is at work in Hawthorne's romance: the filial devotions, the return to the "father-land," and the posited amends for old rebellions all seem at times to address—to want to effect—unions of other sorts. Certainly, this novel about a New Englander's desired reunion with his "estranged brethren" evokes a prerevolutionary loyalism that Ned Etheredge feels again, despite himself, on English grounds, in the hall where James II feasted or while seeing a company rise to its feet for "God Save the Queen": it was a spectacle, he says, "being so apart from an American's sympathies—so unlike anything that he has in his life or possibilities—this active and warm sentiment of loyalty, in which love of country centres and assimilates and transforms itself into a passionate affection for a person, in whom they love all their institutions" (240). Such sentiments echo later with Hawthorne's dedication of *Our Old Home* to Franklin Pierce—a dedication that manages to find its place in a frothy English travelogue for the celebration of an unredeemed Unionist. Pierce was a president, says Hawthorne, who remained at any cost, "faithful forever to that grand idea of an irrevocable Union, which, as you once told me, was the earliest that your brave father taught you. For other men there may be a choice of paths—for you, but one; and it rests among my certainties that no man's loyalty is more stedfast" (5).

And then there is the big spider dangling over the narrative—a spider that spins "flimsy" ligaments that Hawthorne audaciously calls "mystic threads," not to be confused, of course, with Lincoln's "mystic chords" though they, too, make "millions and millions" of "vibrations." They are threads that are spun at great length and exertion, carefully "encouraged and preserved" to cure, no less, eruptions of the "inflammatory class" (347). "Let me alone, Ned," says Doctor Grimshawe, "and I shall spin out the web that shall link you" to other men (359). Indeed, the entire fantasy of this novel, in Hawthorne's words, is one of "making plain the links, the filaments, which connected this feeble childish life" (359), with delicate ties to old relations in unlikely places. And the point, I think, is that, for such a reclusive book, the crisis of Union keeps stealing in, phrased as a problem, that is, of preserving these ubiquitous links or tying together a romance of belonging. One need only return to Hawthorne's potty lists of blabber to see how the unraveling of his English romance freely associates its own symbolic breakdown with breakdowns of a grander kind, as Hawthorne looks into that fussy coffin for some kind of sense and seems to find, of all gothic things, America itself:

> The object of the book, to find the treasure-chest, which the silver key, found in the grave-yard by Etheredge, will suit. This at last turns out to be the coffin of a young lady, which being opened, it proves to be filled with golden locks of hair. But this quest must be merely incidental. Under the hair, or upon it, is a roll of obliterated writing. This nonsense must

be kept subordinate, however. 'Twon't do. Crambo. Mary Mumpson. Cunkey. Miss Blagden. Miss Ingersoll. Mr Roberts.—Marshall Rynders. President Buchanan of dis United States. (220)

This United States, dis United States: a tremendous pun, the romantic and "the Actual" at once, the state of affairs as it might be, the state of affairs as it is—there is even an echo of minstrelsy that hints at questions of race, "dis United States." Of course Hawthorne was not an unredeemed Unionist, and we are finally left with very little here, a symbolism that makes nothing happen, claims of kinship that are false and, in the end, no inheritance for the young American. If we are thrown back on the Actual, we are thrown back on a lack of consanguinity, on a set of relations that, like the creaky machinery of this novel, seem far too contrived—the "mystic threads" are more and more just cobwebs in some funereal plot. This is not, after all, "Our Old Home," but something closer to an antiquated, disintegrated House of Seven Gables that, Hawthorne decides, must finally be abandoned.

CHAPTER TWO

Imperial Nostalgia

American Elegies for British Empire

Oh, dullness! dullness! I do wish Harry was at home, or Sir William would march some of his troops this way! What's the use of an army in the country, if one can't have a dance once in a while?
—OLIVER BUNCE, *Love in '76* (1859)

The Dullness of Patriotism

"The age for declamation upon the American Revolution has passed away," and George Ticknor Curtis is really so glad. Each successive Fourth of July, growing millions of Americans had turned out to commemorate the declaration and been "wont to listen to its great truths . . . its doctrines and the doings of its afterday of strife and sacrifice and blood and triumph and final peace." What a bore! Look, says Curtis, in his own Fourth of July address, this is 1841: for more than half a century the American mind has rehearsed the associated recollections of this day in the most emphatic orations, and it is always the same story of liberty and progress. The public is exhausted of independence—its topics "pall upon the wearied ear"—so perhaps it would be more patriotic to say, "we have done all that we can well do, with this mode of treating our history." [1]

But there are other ways of celebrating the Revolution: Curtis, a lawyer famous for his Constitutional histories, does not want us to forget the past—just stop talking about it. Maybe, he suggests, history is better written and read; then, in the place of these tired forensics, we can enjoy such a degree of exactness of knowledge, such familiarity with the doings of our national heroes (and others besides) in all the antinomic mess of thousands of pages of history derived from remote and irregular archives—maybe then we can free ourselves from

Independence Day preaching. For it is the laborious historian, "grop-
ing among archives"—"where the worm feedeth swetely on treasuses
[sic] covered by the dust of time"—who inspires a sense of nationalist
exhilaration far beyond any of the jubilating orators. Fourth of July
celebrations have become both annoyingly ahistorical and dull; though
how surprised would Emerson be to find here, amid what he would no
doubt call the dry bones of the past, the very things to invest our American holiday with new interest, making it, for Curtis, "like nature's day,
which dawns successively just like the preceding, but yet is ever novel
and fresh to the craving sense of novelty." Patriotic homilies leave us
cold, but the public has recourse to grittier knowledge and tales of the
Revolution, and it is these that Curtis puts faith in: a patently transcen-
dental experience of arcane historical refuse.

So far so good. There were a number of historians in this period who
found the Fourth of July trite and hoped to fill in its abstract subject
of nationalism with the particular impressions, anecdotes, and modest
amusements of intimate, physical facts. Which was to say, with Richard Hildreth in his *History of the United States,* "Of centennial sermons
and Fourth-of-July orations, whether professedly such or in the guise
of history, there are more than enough." Better to eulogize the Revolution "exactly as it was" and "unbedaubed with patriotic rouge," which
meant, for Hildreth and others, the free use of original documents,
laws, official records (printed and manuscript), letters, and memoirs to
tell a story of the Revolution somewhat more "life-like" for being pictur-
esquely inside the "sometimes defective, and sometimes contradictory"
material record.[2] The fact that such records were increasingly available during the first half of the nineteenth century—through public
archives, historical societies, and congressional preservation acts—and
the fact that such "documania," as David Van Tassel calls it, could em-
barrass the more syncretic, moralizing histories of the Revolution so
deadly suffered in oratorical commemoration, I will return to later.[3] But
I will note for now that more than 110 historical societies were founded
in the early nineteenth century and that many of them published magazines that put such newly acquired revolutionary pamphlets, diaries,
correspondence, and government papers into print. Between 1815 and
1861, Congress also funded sixteen extensive documentary projects
chiefly about the Revolution, including the *American State Papers* (38
vols; 1832–61), Peter Force's *American Archives* (9 vols.; 1837–53), Jared
Sparks's *Diplomatic Correspondence of the American Revolution* (12 vols.;

1829–30) and *The Writings of George Washington* (12 vols.; 1834–37), Charles Francis Adams's *The Works of John Adams* (10 vols.; 1850–56), H. A. Washington's *Writings of Thomas Jefferson* (9 vols.; 1853–54), and Henry D. Gilpin's *Papers of James Madison* (3 vols.; 1840)—all-told, 184 government-sponsored volumes of uneconomically bound particulars satisfying an antebellum impulse to conserve. In these same years, other revolutionary sourcebooks were increasingly popular; alongside the documentary histories of Sparks and Hildreth were Benson Lossing's *Pictorial Field-Book of the Revolution* (1850), Frank Moore's *Diary of the American Revolution* (1860), Abiel Holmes's *The Annals of America* (1820), Timothy Pitkin's *A Political and Civil History of the United States* (1828), the slighter, anecdotal accounts of John Warner Barber, and countless local, regional, and personal histories of the war.[4]

Antebellum historiography of the Revolution is moved by the "objective" recovery of these minute particulars, and such objectivity seems to say that the prevailing histories, including oratory and including progressive accounts by George Bancroft and other "romantic historians," overrate the will of the historical event. What we find, in other words, in the "collection of small things" that make up such documentary commitments, is a mass of little realisms—the truth of a child lost to war, a love affair across enemy lines, how it feels to have the British quartered in your home (and what to feed them)—that are a nuisance to histories that see the past as only instrumental to ideas of autonomy, democracy, and liberty as they reside in the present.[5] There are antebellum Americans, then, who turn to the Revolutionary War not for patriotic continuities but for occasions to worry over wreckage and loss; and quite a few melancholy materialists who, like two-bit "angels of history" (following Walter Benjamin), perceive not an unbroken "chain of events" from past to present but a desultory riot of colonial debris accumulating at their feet. For Benjamin, history is what we salvage from a past that always devolves onto its particulars; and progress is the "storm" that leaves the past so catastrophically strewn to pieces.[6] For antebellum historians—even for casual enthusiasts among the proliferating archives—the "storm" is independence.

John Fanning Watson evokes this graphically in his *Annals of Philadelphia,* first published in 1830. As he chronicles incidents of the Revolutionary War in that city, from the testimony of survivors, he says that it seemed as if the stillness and repose after the great storm had passed by. I felt eager to look upon some of the remains of the desolating epoch; but little or none remained to the eye; and what I could contemplate and consider, came home to the feelings through the ear—by hearing the recitals of those who had been familiar with the incidents. What I failed thus to get at closely, concerning the war and its people, I came at last, in subsequent years, to see and feel on other objects, seen gliding down the stream of time, like floating drift-wood, and which it has been my pleasing business, and useful occupation, to snatch from the ebbing tide, and to ware-house (or chronicle) as the relics and remains of olden time—gathering up for my own contemplation, and for the wonderment of another gen-eration, the passing and dissolving characteristics of men and things of a passing and a dissolving age. "Oh, sweet is a tale of the olden time!"[7]

I am not sure which is more surprising to hear from a "professed his-torian" of this period: that the age of independence was a "desolating epoch" with an arbitrary legacy or that the "stream of time" carrying independence to us is not the course of progress but a slipstream back into "a dissolving age" through the accidental truths of its flotsam.[8] If, as David Levin claims, the "basic assumption" for the romantic histo-rian was human progress—if indeed John Lothrop Motley, "went so far as to say [in the 1860s] that were it not for progress, history would be the most 'contemptible' subject to study"—then Watson's *Annals* are a mean business.[9] Rummaging through the shards of independence, Watson sees and feels not the origin of democracy in America or a per-vading principle of freedom advancing irresistibly to the present but such a sense of the "passing" of the past, of its quaint singularity, that any lessons of the war seem lost to these piles of colonial "olden"-ness. Watson's wondering "Oh" severs the eighteenth-century past from the nineteenth-century present just enough to look at independence not as a set of "vague traditions" that inform us now but as an eccentric as-sortment of men and things from a residual, warring age that at least one historian keeps finding "sweet."[10] There is no scheme to Watson's story of independence; in fact, there is no story at all, just a "chronicle" he compares to a "warehouse" of matter from a distant, unaccountable period—a revolutionary time "pleasing" to consider because it never exactly anticipates our own.

It is not that the so-called romantic historians liked the individual fact any less; both Bancroft and Motley lavishly indulged in original

documents, visits to state and foreign libraries, the purchase of manuscripts, and the employment of copyists in the archives. They pursued
their sources scrupulously and left the footnotes and bibliographies to
show it.[11] At issue between Bancroft and Hildreth or Watson is not the
industry of scholarship or the pains of discovery but the willingness to
stop at the facts—to see the multiplying details as essentially attractive
and too empirically involved to serve the historical design that Bancroft finds intuitively beyond them. The facts in Watson are signally un-
invested; they add up not to a justification of history as it happened but
to an unreconstituted mix of revolutionary moments made visible on
the page and then defined there as "dispassionate inquiry." The plea
of objectivity is what matters most, for what could not be published in
its name, if only to prove that every last unassimilated anecdote was
merely the effort of the "honest historian," in Watson's words, "to record the truth without partiality?"[12] For even as Bancroft was identifying the laws of an "absolute" American history derived from Hegelian
romanticism, these compilers were finding that the laws were contradictory and that fitting the facts into an illuminating pattern had
caused them "to be twisted and distorted in a thousand ways."[13] Some
still shared the Enlightenment's encyclopedic approach to knowledge:
it is behind Force's claim that such efforts to acquire and know everything originate in "the liberal and inquisitive character of the age." But
others were discovering their own version of Leopold von Ranke's idealist belief that empiricism, if exhaustively practiced, might produce
a definitive understanding of the past. Rejecting history based on a
priori laws, Ranke believed that the divine order of the world (assuming that there was one) would not be manifest until all of its historical
truths were assembled like the pieces of a puzzle. In the meantime,
historians acquire and collect, and this sense of archival purpose—of
one day perhaps harmonizing the small facts of the past into a know-
able history—motivates Lossing and Watson. Lossing claims that "each
apparently insignificant event in the wondrous history of our continent
is a link as important in the great chain of human deeds, directed by
divine intelligence, as those which arrest the attention and command
the admiration of the world."[14] So we indiscriminately return to the
scenes of war, both the great events and the variety of contingencies.
There is, in the grand scheme of things, nothing irrelevant and nothing inadmissible; the historian's task is not to judge or interpret the
past but to respect its vastness essentially.

What, then, are the consequences of such objectivity for antebellum accounts of the Revolution? What happens when suddenly everything that is found becomes historically admissible? If Bancroft sees a providential plan and national destiny in the drift of past events, compilers such as Watson entertain more options for the archive in the acknowledgment that much of what the past means might be apropros only to the past. So the true use of American revolutionary history, to invoke Curtis's address, is perhaps to admit that the past is rather more useless or that the revolutionary world we restore is not so material to the iconic project of America now.

Indeed, Watson wants an objectivity that brings with it a receptivity to the aspects of the revolutionary past that do not foretell Jacksonian democracy or reveal the "tendency toward independence" that Bancroft found latent in the very texture of colonial life.[15] Watson's "truth without partiality" rejects the ardor of romantic nationalism, but—to be clear—it does not aspire to academic detachment. Making way for a more exhaustive reckoning of a great many attitudes toward the past, it allows for a history fashioned as "impartial" precisely because it has a sympathetic place for every irreducible partisanship. Or to quote Thomas L. Haskell, "Objectivity is not neutrality": it would be a mistake to think that such historiography requires an ascetic, scientific absence of emotional investments, or that detachment marks the affective end of deep engagement with the scores of contending prejudices that the archive puts on display (remember it is not objectivity but patriotic sermons that leave us cold).[16] Watson seems to say that if we leave the revolutionary period well enough alone—if we do not construe it to explain or predict the present but let it reside, anachronistically, in its sweet "olden time"—then there may be a lot for us to feel besides the spirit of liberty that led to independence.

If Hegel is the figure most powerfully associated with purposive history, abandoning what it cannot use, it is worth remembering that the nineteenth century also witnessed a renewed interest in the writings of Vico, whose seventeenth-century *New Science* helped to legitimate the modernity that Hegel enshrined by describing the anachronisms that did not belong. Anachronisms are "the poetic origins of history," to follow Srinivas Aravamudan following Vico, that no longer function within stories of progress, though, like Barthes's "obtuse meaning"—holding our attention for no reason at all—they may be poetic still. It took the nineteenth century to notice that, in Shakespeare, clocks chime for Julius Caesar; such anachronistic and mistaken details may communicate meaning within history (Caesar is doomed) but only symbolically and according to the rules of art. For nineteenth-century Americans, the poetic origins of their national history operate as "epistemological aporia" between the lived immediacy of the historical event and the structure of meaning that explains its "longer-term conditions." [17] They are fascinated by the contingency that patterns the relationship between our democracy and its constative moment, because it suggests that the histories we abandon speak to a complexity of emotion and experience that survive the histories we inherit. The Revolution becomes a drama in which independence is rightly gained but at the expense of prior ways of being colonial in America that were "multiply and deeply constituted" by more traditionary social orders. Nineteenth-century Americans did not debate the politics of the Revolution but displaced them for the "encumbrance" of society and identifications that marked a vanished world of "situated subjects" who, in Bonnie Honig's sense, "have no occasions for politics." [18]

The examples are always specific. For Watson, they are the pains of a Tory widow as confided to her diary or the ecstatic reception of the British in Philadelphia as remembered to him by loyalists. "Detachment," writes Haskell, "both socializes and deparochializes the intellect": the historiograpically sensitive writer brings such a collision of rival perspectives—so many peculiar, spontaneous responses to anomalous moments—that to look back fairly is to become more aware of the nation's seductive illusion, which is that the United States took shape inevitably.[19] All these diaries and letters, detailing the conversations and affections of still-colonial characters in their parlors or war camps, locate the Revolution in such distinction to the nationalist nineteenth century that to historicize at all is to be almost ethnographically estranged from the progressive narratives that claim these British Americans begot us. At least, our encounters with the past remind us that quite a few Americans loved the king, while others loved Americans who loved the king (that there were feelings of loss in independence); and in showing "how very much has been omitted" by the authors of history, Watson restores the homely, particularized pictures of war's "vicissitudes and emotions, more touching than many [tales] of far more consequence." [20] The heterodox appeal to objectivity and sentiment implies that we should not think about emulating these early Americans, nor advancing admonishingly beyond them; we should just take pleasure in the exceptionality of their early Americanness. That is, whatever analogies may suggest themselves between now and then, the historiography teaches us, to borrow from James Chandler, that "individual character could be differentially derived from the peculiarities of different epochs" and that the revolutionary epoch was peculiar indeed.[21] That it played by its own rules may not be obvious, though our impartiality toward the past allows us to understand finally, in light of the archive, the emotional sway of assorted chauvinisms shaped by remote, half-intelligible circumstances in equivocal relation to our own.

This is why Curtis, in his Fourth of July address, hopes at last to impress us with a range of allegiances left out of nationalist paradigms and concludes that colonists of all classes held "a deep affection for the mother country, which made them reluctant to sever ancient ties."[22] So, all in all, while patriotism as we know it is stupefying, we are left believing that the true story of America's respectful attachments to Britain inspires all the cathexis one needs in a proper holiday celebration. Just what are the fireworks for?

A Case of Surrender

"I don't embrace trouble," says Oliver Wendell Holmes, Jr., "that's as bad as treating it as an enemy. But I do say meet it as a friend, for you'll see a lot of it and had better be on speaking terms with it."[23] The Battle of Saratoga was a sanguinary affair, but it is not long before the student of the conflict comes across—in the documentary histories, but also in the fictional accounts to which they give shape and inclination—an anecdote that puts familiar faces on Holmes's precept. For the historiography that recovers this anecdote in the nineteenth century suggests we should not embrace our trouble as trouble (so morbid!) but welcome the experience we may gain in addressing it. And if trouble looks like an amiable, accomplished officer, a gallant gentleman and distinguished man of letters? All the better.

In October 1777 British general John Burgoyne signed the articles of capitulation at Saratoga and watched his troops march sorrowfully from their encampment on the hills to the banks of the Hudson River, where the companies were drawn up in parallel lines and ordered to ground their arms. Many wept, but General Horatio Gates did not see it: it was a decisive victory for his branch of the American army, but the least he could do was distance himself from the spot and not suffer his men "to be witness to the sad spectacle."[24] Benson Lossing, taking his version of the surrender from Burgoyne's own letter to the Earl of Derby, writes that the British "were not subject to the mortification of submitting under the gaze of an exalting foe, for General Gates, with a delicacy and magnanimity of feeling . . . had ordered all his army within his camp out of the sight of the vanquished Britons." It was an exercise in civility, but the wartime decorum of gentlemen too full of feeling to shame the enemy says something exquisite about the enemy, too. Certainly Gates was encouraged in his conduct by the desire "to draw forth the expressed admiration of Burgoyne and his officers," nor did it hinder the principle of politeness that Burgoyne was so divinely "arrayed in splendid military trappings" or was such an elegant speaker and excellent versifier, the general knowledge of which is plain in the revolutionary letters and diaries that Lossing found years later. "Among his literary productions," Lossing notes, "are *The Maid of the Oaks, Bon Ton,* and *The Heiress,* dramas which at one time were highly popular. Benevolence and humanity were strong features in Burgoyne's character, and I think the fierce anathema of Philip Freneau, a poet of the Revolution, was altogether too severe." [25]

When the British grenadiers laid down their arms, Burgoyne asked to be introduced to Gates and met him at the head of his camp; he reined in his horse, tipped his hat, and said, "The fortune of war, General Gates, has made me your prisoner." Gates quickly replied, "I shall always be ready to bear testimony that it has not been through any fault of your excellency," and then the parties, writes Lossing's source, General James Wilkinson, who includes the account in his memoirs (published in 1816), "repaired to Gates's headquarters" for a "sumptuous dinner." A becoming ceremony followed in which Burgoyne, in front of Gates's marquee and "according to previous understanding," presented his sword to his victor, who received it with a "courteous" inclination of the head and then delicately (because he couldn't possibly take it) presented it back to Burgoyne, thus ending the "drama upon the heights of Saratoga." The two men then retired to the tent to resume their banquet.[26] Burgoyne soon after removed to Albany to stay as a guest at the residence of the American general Philip Schuyler, whose family met the British general with warmth and cheer, though (all accounts remind us) "he had without necessity ordered their splendid country-seat near Saratoga to be burnt." Never mind: atrocities are to be expected, but they're so tiresome at dinner. "Such is the fate of war," Schuyler said to Burgoyne; "let us not dwell on the subject." [27]

I have just quoted from E. F. Ellet's *Domestic History of the American Revolution* (1850) but I could have turned to almost any documentary history of the period for this anecdote of Schuyler and Burgoyne trading esteem and good humor in Albany, which was first published in the wartime journal of Friederike von Riedesel, the wife of a German general in Burgoyne's camp.[28] The anecdote is pert enough: the felicitous number of occasions on which it appears teases us with Maurice Blanchot's sense that feelings of community come not of, say, common work or common causes (revolution included) but of just such baffling contingencies. There are moments, that is, when the immediate distractions of war—for example, the fact that Burgoyne just happens to be good company, and witty besides, and in any case has to eat— suggest an appeal to ad hoc social ties that operate at the very limits of partisan attachments. Indeed, this tale seems less an account of fraternizing with the enemy than a drama of sociability in which fraternity itself is fully realized *only* in such hesitations within the logic of conflict. The histories I am describing, of course, do not neglect the right of independence and the bonds of those united in its cause, nor do they treat all enemies with General Schuyler's easy grace. Still, they pause at many instances when hostilities are spectacularly suspended to expose such impromptu moments of human communication across the social divide. Burgoyne provides for just the sort of "interruption" that, to enlist Jean-Luc Nancy, "turns community toward the outside instead of gathering it in," and the fascination that this bit of historiographical static seems to have held for nineteenth-century readers reminds us that the American Revolution was, in fact, terrifically "radical" for the way that it made new forms of society possible.[29]

So the fun with Burgoyne began: nineteenth-century chronicles of independence tell how "Gentleman Johnny" and his troops became ornaments of American society in captivity, discussing over tea, in the china brought with on their detail, just "how Pope is preferred in England to Prior" or getting up parties and balls in honor of the king's birthday, among other events. The patriots attended such parties, if reluctantly for the occasion, then most willingly for the company: the captive army, for example, displayed such fellowship in their renditions of "God Save the King," drinking the monarch's health, "with feelings of the liveliest attachment to his person," that Schuyler's own daughter and son-in-law, says Riedesel, "could not forbear participating" in the enthusiasm. Notwithstanding the presence of the enemy, such anecdotes insist on showing that the war necessitated a certain measure of indulgence: even the English must expect the usual courtesies; it would be impolite to exclude them from sleighing parties, for instance, when the winters are dull, and *could* the ladies of Burgoyne's army visit Cambridge, asks Ellet, *without* an invitation from Mrs. Hancock?[30] It is exactly this collateral sociability—all the engagements made possible by such an influx of the English (and Germans, too)—that these stories turn to account not merely to argue that war has its protocols but to remember the Revolution as well for its immanent globalism even as it inspires our national politics. The calculus of hostility and hospitality is, not surprisingly, tortured: with the redcoats in marvelous abundance, and America thoroughly occupied, antebellum stories of the Revolution can seem coy on how patriots and Tories come to close quarters. Thus Alexander Graydon, captain of a Pennsylvania regiment whose memoirs were published in 1811 and reprinted in 1846, tells of a German prisoner's introduction to the "dancing parties" of his custodians: "Overhearing a dance called for, one evening, which we had named *burgoyne's surrender,* he observed to his partner, that it was a very pretty dance . . . and that general Burgoyne himself would be happy to dance it in such good company."[31]

Antebellum tales of the Revolution tend to turn on such niceties, with the assurance that even colonial defiance could be somehow finessed. We see just this kind of maneuvering in Benjamin Franklin's laconic letter of 1775 to a Tory friend, William Strahan, reprinted often in nineteenth-century biographies of Franklin and in accounts of the Revolution itself. "You are a Member of Parliament, and one of that Majority which has doomed my Country to Destruction," Franklin starts, before appending a short list of bloody incriminations. The letter's signature then closes the hostile communication with a gesture of radically indeterminate affection:

> You and I were long Friends: You are now my Enemy, and
>   I am,
>   Yours,
>   B. Franklin.[32]

The artful play that makes the language of war recall the language of affection—enemy or friend, Franklin is truly "yours"—is ironic, of course. But it is also sincere, inasmuch as the flash of wit suggests at least a liberal intercourse and humor that remains between friends. That violence can be waggish pays tribute to this common ground; Franklin defers to the enemy even as he names him and insists on saying that, while he takes the offensive against this Tory, he will never be offensive *to* him. That many recounted instances along these lines sublimate resistance and compliance in a language that avails itself of either motive force suggests the appeal, for antebellum Americans, of commemorating the Revolution as a period of aggression that is also distinguished by its formal concessions.

Deference, in other words, is not dependence; indeed, we might say that voluntary submission to the British at such moments is the mark of a new *independence,* which can be affably and conversationally conceded precisely because it is at last secured. "Deference," J. G. A. Pocock writes, "could not corrupt men or reduce them to servility, because in the last analysis it was concerned with what [James] Harrington called the 'goods of the mind.'"[33] For Pocock, deference acknowledges the value and self-esteem of both parties; it is not servility, but a stylistic exchange of respect and consideration between equals. Only "great" men could defer. Franklin's formal surrender—that epistolary moment of saying "I am Yours"—is also the revolutionary's assertion of autonomy: I am so self-possessed that I can play this gorgeous game of giving it up to you. Because I declare independence, I can love you as well.

The need to preserve good form in the midst of violence is not simply pretense. Where it occurs in revolutionary narratives, it has little calculative effect and no bearing at all on the outcome of the battle or campaign it interrupts. Such affability is a legitimate end in itself, relieving the pressures of war by changing the subject or abstracting it into an aesthetic play of forms that guarantees, above all, no real business but conversation. Still, far from reality, to quote Georg Simmel, this affability "nourishes itself from a deep and true relation to reality."[34] And the reality it seems to want to affirm is that Americans, at this revolutionary moment *are* great—great enough to follow these rules of civil behavior and, even more, great enough to inspire goodwill. It takes, in short, a rather elevated amount of *ton* to give joy and relief to one's enemy, especially to want to give them, and these Americans show respect irresistibly. In the thick of the seriousness of war they find pleasure in the mixed company, and in the free and exhilarating conversation, that comes of this war's accidental encounters between gentlemen.[35]

"The worst thing about war," writes Ellen Glasgow, "is that so many people enjoy it," but this is not what she means.[36] For the accumulation of "trifling details," in Graydon's words, that "mark the temper of the times and shew, that they were not all fire and fury," says also that revolutionary America was a theater of innumerable odd and personal exchanges that could be, in fact, simply pleasurable, insofar as dances, courtships, birthdays, and sleighing parties go on amid the dark ex-hilarations of violence that are war's worst thing. That war sees better things is only half the point; Graydon's argument is finally historio-graphic and aimed at "modern pretenders to the spirit of *seventy-six*" who would have "patriotism in the nation" remembered as the archive's only lesson for the nineteenth century.[37] For Graydon and others look-ing back, these moments of civil conduct and play come to represent the "typical anomaly," which not only punctuates the totalizing wholes of historical narration but becomes the irreducibly particular event that most powerfully estranges us from the assumption that the past is like the present, only earlier.[38] This historicizing warns against an anachronistic sense that the spirit of 1776 is like the spirit of 1846; the frame of reference that might have allowed Burgoyne's men to dance through "burgoyne's surrender" with, say, a glass of grog in hand is just weird enough to suggest that any exercise in history might hold some of the benefits of ethnographic discovery. At least such untrou-bled attention to a world of ritual, gesture, and individual response in which nineteenth-century Americans might not feel at home implies that history does more than chart a course of progress and that revo-lutionary history, in particular, can involve a thorough reckoning of loss, not gain. These historiographical interruptions, in other words, add up, and a feeling for the "temper of the times," which compounds nostalgia and desire for the cultural terrain of the Revolution, depends on an understanding of how these delicate performances of niceness are small, though no less treasured, incarnations of a once coherent period whose moment has passed. It takes no historical imagination, Graydon might say, to claim that Gates's victory over Burgoyne leads to further victories down the line; it asks considerably more of us to stake our interest in this battle on the finer equivocations that figure largely as its social aftermath.

By the end of the nineteenth century, such historiography has re-stored to popular imagery a distinct regard for the receptive, frater-nizing culture that the Revolution brought to an end. Edward Percy Moran's painting of Burgoyne's capitulation (ca. 1911) seems so in-clined toward these agreeable tales of the event it effectively reverses the choreography of defeat: Gates extends so much courtesy to Burgoyne

FIGURE 14. Edward Percy Moran, *Burgoyne's Surrender at Saratoga,* ca. 1911. Prints and Photographs Division, Library of Congress.

that he practically surrenders to *him* (fig. 14).[39] How an image titled *Burgoyne's Surrender to Gates* could have Gates bowing to Burgoyne, hat in hand, would elude me except to suggest that the moment it commemorates is just the one that Lossing and others describe in which Gates returns Burgoyne's sword in front of the American flag (in the painting, Gates has the hilt). It is shrewd the way Moran figures it—that one might go with the scene after the scene of defeat in which the enemy is more honored then subdued and insist that *this* is the patriotic victory. From this moment everything in the painting admits to nostalgia: the manneristic exchange at its center plays at an "intimate distance" from the viewer, who is left well outside the circle of costumed observers who solemnize the scene.[40] This military triumph seems a little quaint, framed in the left middle-ground by a *repoussoir* of feathered Indians and washed in a filmy iridescence, as though we were seeing it through the smoke of the warrior's peace pipe. Can Revolution be picturesque? Moran brings before us no sublime clash of forces but the harmonizing arrangement of a small, gracious act that takes on meaning only when we understand how truly marginal it is to the battles of independence. The painting, much like Gates himself, seems so hesitant to let the British go, stopping them in their march off the American scene—they nearly exit the canvas—to insist on paying respects. What feels nostalgic is the niceness of the gesture, which assumes that the Battle of Saratoga is not over until the American bows; he could not have done it, after all, without Burgoyne (good man!), and the tribute that marks the surrender as a stylized exchange between gentlemen makes us linger wistfully on that exchange. If the victory at Saratoga makes way for America's future, this kind of gallantry amid the pressures of war seems as antiquated as the stoic, spear-handling Indian to the left. The Indian's red cloak not only reminds us of his collaboration with the redcoats but asks us to extend the analogy as if to say that once there were both noble savages and noblemen and now there are not.[41] But the Indians are also likened to us, Moran's viewers, who see such civility from their perspective: above and to the left, from behind the pointing spear and thicket, our entry on the scene (reading from left to right) is decidedly through them. As surrogates for our own spectatorship, they perhaps suggest that we too stand in relation to such acts of English civility (for even Gates was English then) as "native" Americans, a bit more rustic and uncultivated; their racial difference articulates our own cultural estrangement.

Were we not party to the title of Moran's painting, it would seem more foreign still. The forward march of the British, the drumming guardsmen in busbies, and the slow movement down a makeshift avenue, with Americans standing by, together look perilously close to scenes of British victory. Henry Alexander Ogden's image of Lord Cornwallis's entry into Philadelphia, based on anecdotes of the British occupation in September 1777, tells a different story than Moran's, but the well-appointed troops nodding agreeably to the crowd—"the younger ones were more dashing," recalls a witness in Watson's *Annals,* but the "officers of middle-age were in general polite"—give purchase to the same confusion of attachments that the archive puts amply on view (fig. 15).[42] In E. L. Cushing's 1824 account of the event, for instance, "the British and hessian grenadiers, with a detachment of royal artillery and a party of light dragoons, accompanied by Lord Cornwallis and many other officers of distinction, entered [Philadelphia] in triumph, and took formal possession, with great pomp; while the music played 'God save the king,' and the ladies showered flowers, and waved white handkerchiefs from the windows, to welcome the approach of the conquerors."[43] How, by the nineteenth century, the revolutionary moment is fungible enough to remember America's *admiration* of the

FIGURE 15. Henry Alexander Ogden, *The British Entry into Philadelphia, September 26, 1777,* 1905. The Library Company of Philadelphia.

British as they captured its finest city—how the clean fun and general huzzahs seem to have turned this invasion into a family event—is most striking in how Ogden preserves the idiom of patriotic celebrations. For some colonials, after all, it *was* a nationalist parade, and for others, left with everyday life of the city while American troops were encamped at Valley Forge, the British takeover was at least (say these characters on the right) worth taking the children.[44] For those who were less well affected, we hardly see resistance here: the scowling figure at the lower right, whose distemper has raised the eyebrows of Cornwallis, and the fifer, too, seems less patriotic than rude, as though whatever politics he may harbor are commensurate with the ill manners he shows the woman to his right by staring from behind.

"A superficial thinker," writes Watson, "may, possibly, deem it unimportant to attempt thus to preserve the facts transpiring in Philadelphia, concerning the war of independence; and especially that portion of them relative to the *entry* and *possession* of the city by the *British army*. But to minds of more reflection, many sufficient reasons will appear for preserving the memorial for posterity."[45] The superficial thinker likes bottom lines (*we* won), but the deeper thinker understands that how things happen to have turned out is a poor criterion for what historically matters, a way of looking back on the war that promises the loss of moments (like that memorable day when the British came to Philadelphia) that have no obvious place on a chronology of independence. For Watson, this loss counts against our own investments in the past, because the expectation of inapplicability—the fact "that Philadelphia will *never* again be invaded or possessed by any conquering foe"— allows for a recovery of feelings for the British that may be appreciative and fond, or as melancholy as Watson, but all less easy to appreciate if more were finally at stake.[46] It is not simply that history appeals in inverse proportion to its relevance; these antebellum writers are saying that history is always irrelevant, insofar as the past is made up of personalities and passions so unique to the past that they little speak to us now. The nineteenth century seems determined to show just how little, its literature reflecting the difference we feel on encountering those dispositions that made the revolutionary world into a place far from our own.

This stance makes for an uncanny sense that America is alienated from its own history, even to the degree that the British may recognize the revolutionary landscape better than Watson's antebellum readers. In John H. Mancur's *Tales of the Revolution* (1844), Henry Montresor, a young English officer in occupied Philadelphia, finds the city so accommodating that "he could not realize the fact that he was in a hostile land—in a city but two hours ride from an enemy's camp—and that the environs were the scene of almost daily skirmish."[47] Mancur has found the cultural moment of the Revolution in an "old" Philadelphia whose music and conversation—whose metropolitan companies, gracing the boxes of the Southwark Theatre in the winter of 1777—seem strikingly displaced from where we map the birth of independence. His *Tales* are only one example of the extent to which the war could be revived for its anachronism, for the distant and curious ways that these early Americans ate, drank, danced, talked, and generally conducted themselves, and the fact that the Revolution decisively determined what Americans would be by the time these tales were written makes almost perverse just how uninterested the historical literature seems in such connections. David Lowenthal and James Chandler both find in the early nineteenth century an emerging perception of the past "as a different realm": if the eighteenth century assumed a basic similarity among all people from all times, so that every epoch or event disclosed the same universal principles, the historicism that followed strived to preserve the past by promoting the textures of its difference. Lowenthal turns to a line of L. P. Hartley to capture the new historical sensibility that proceeds from an experience of dislocation in looking back: "The past is a foreign country: they do things differently there."[48] For antebellum Americans, remembering the Revolution could feel as exotic as sworn enemies sharing toast and tea on a battlefield, for the obscurity of such acts in the period that hoped to revive them only distanced them further. Even the recent past was a foreign country: in America, the past was Britain.

Delicacies of War

In William Gilmore Simms's Revolutionary War novel *The Partisan*, Lieutenant Humphreys lets the chef, Porgy, know that General Francis Marion will not be dining that night on his generous mess of eggs and turtle meat. "Terrapin, indeed, Porgy! how you talk! Why, man, he don't care for all the terrapin in the swamp." "Then no good can come of him," replies Porgy, "he's an infidel. I would not march with him for the world. Don't believe in terrapin! A man ought to believe in all that is good; and there's nothing so good as terrapin." Lieutenant Porgy lets no war burden his "cultivated" tastes. He gads about South Carolina sentimentalizing about hash, stews, and ragout, finding "dainties to human appetite" in the banks of reedy sludge and making epicures of officers. Our fat friend is a declined gentleman in the swamp who "might *play* the buffoon" but whose culinary arts—stretches of beef on the turf, fried eel in turtle-shell tureens—do nothing less than exercise the "humanities" of the militia; good taste, Porgy tells us, makes good officers, and certainly where decent people could enjoy a proper dinner, a war might be won. A man ought to believe in all that is good: sorry Doctor Oakenburg, "a fellow of the most perverted tastes," and with little relish of marsh hen, is a "wretch" indeed, with "no more soul than a . . . lizard" and no respect for the dignities of the war. For even love—love of one's country, love of one's cause—may be, for Simms's laughing philosopher, "considered as a delicacy."[49]

But what about poor Marion? He, too, is not swayed by the terrapin and, while outfoxing the regulars with his guerrilla menace, cares so little for taste in his torn and dirty habit—not even carrying a long sword, says Simms, which was positively "then in fashion!"—he offends the "nice taste" of General Gage who, in turn, needs the most "well-regulated sense of politeness, formed closely on the models of foreign service" just to keep from laughing.[50] Coming to terms with Marion, the ragtag patriot-hero of the Southern campaign, better at killing the British than eating a meal, is certainly a pastime of this novel. He cannot cut a figure: small of person, lame of leg, with hesitating manners, it takes all the deep stores of civility and edict from the annals of diplomacy just to speak to him. And why a folk figure, freeing the borders of Charleston from British encroachers in a nationalist novel about a national victory, should seem, because of his tastes, so decidedly "foreign" is worth another look. By the time *The Partisan* appeared, in 1853, Marion's Lenten diet was popularly rehearsed: an example of American deprivation to English overelegance, Marion rather grazes his way to independence on potatoes and roots, sharing his messes with horses. With opposing officers at "two hundred pounds" and up, on nightly spreads of beef, and Cornwallis especially "portly," even the British admit in these accounts that, under such miserable conditions, Marion really *should* win. But what, asks James Kirke Paulding, in his own tale of the Revolution, is "the Price of Liberty?"[51] For while Simms does honors to martyrs in an earlier biography of Marion, his most lovable, honorable characters here, in *The Partisan,* do, most ceremoniously, eat. And eat, I will add, with all the gastronomy and pleasure seeking that are otherwise reserved in revolutionary lore for the more felicitous, more gratifying British. "I am," says Lieutenant Porgy (sotto voce) of his love for food, "a true Englishman in that, though they do call me a rebel. I feel my origin only when eating; and am never so well disposed towards the enemy as when I'm engaging, tooth and nail . . . with roast-beef."[52]

In 1840 the Apollo Association, forerunner to the American Art-Union, sent its subscribers a mezzotint by John Sartain of a decidedly different Marion. The print, *General Marion in His Swamp Encampment Inviting a British Officer to Dinner* (fig. 16), after a painting by John Blake White, has Marion in full, clean dress extending a mound of sweet

FIGURE 16. John Sartain, after John Blake White, *General Marion in His Swamp Encampment Inviting a British Officer to Dinner*, 1840, mezzotint. Courtesy of American Antiquarian Society.

potatoes to an Englishman.[53] The gesture is grand and sincere. With the practiced formality of Lady Hamilton's attitudes and some footlights to match (he is improbably luminous beneath the shade of a tree), Marion urges the enemy to stay awhile. And why not? The enemy is handsome. He and Marion stand in contrast to the ragged assortment of darkling figures around; the blacks who tend the fire and horse are not half so peculiar as the ambiguously turbaned brigands who stand armed or half-clad and glowering in shadows to the right. There is certainly something between Marion and the officer, like two-sies, with their breeches, sashes and aprons of buttons, all mirror images, or their arms, which rhyme instead in a funny duet of niceties—oh you mustn't / I insist. It is an exquisite moment of truce, and if the hatchet is not exactly buried—it lies in the open foreground of the image—it is certainly a pleasing détente with officer and officer deeply engaged in small potatoes. The image marks a historical event—a young soldier is dispatched from his British post at Georgetown to effect an exchange of prisoners—but this is not a history painting. It is a "conversation picture" with all the warmth and intimacy of eighteenth-century scenes by Arthur Devis, for example, depicting gentlemen sharing a meal or music, netting partridges or just plain "conversing," gentlemen most often of the prospering middle classes being gentlemen outdoors. Which is not to say that it is not a nationalist image: the Apollo Association chose the print, for its first issue, precisely because it rehearsed and popularized a bit of revolutionary lore. Still I would ask, in describing this lore, why an American picture of a famously homespun, semiliterate hero, known for intuitive guerrilla tactics and audacious victories, would hang its patriotism on a moment of such cozy hospitality toward the British and such supreme rapport.

The picture is based on an anecdote that first appears in Mason Locke Weems and Peter Horry's 1809 biography of Marion: a British officer, invited to stay for dinner after a diplomatic visit, is aghast to find that "dinner" is a pile of sweet potatoes. Surely, he says, "this is one of your accidental lent dinners. . . . In general, no doubt, you live a great deal better." Marion informs him that, no, he mainly eats potatoes and launches into a bit of, what Simms later calls, the "exuberance" of Weems's account: "I am in love; and my sweetheart is liberty. Be that heavenly nymph my companion, and these wilds and woods shall have charms beyond London and Paris in slavery . . . to be my own master, my own prince and sovereign, gloriously preserving my national dignity, and pursuing my true happiness; planting my vineyards, and eating their luscious fruits; and sowing my fields, and reaping the golden grain: . . . This, sir, is what I long for." The Englishman hangs his "honest head"—is Marion the upbraiding ghost of "his illustrious countrymen, Sidney and Hampton?"—and returns to Georgetown defeated. How can the British ever hope to best a collection of loobies who can live, "almost without clothes," on roots and water, and are not adverse to being so Puritan? He resigns his commission to the heap.[54]

I will put aside for a moment the implications of this as a turning point of battle: it is not a partisan offensive that shows the British our resolve but the American willingness to eat dirt. To surrender one's commission may be the fair shakes of war, but an evening's supper? (Doubtless, says the Englishman, what you lose in meat, you must make up in beer?) And while Marion and his scraggly, naked militia had dared to dash up to Nelson's Ferry and recover their prisoners, to pull off, incognito, two other exploits including a full plunder of

English weapons and goods, this officer is finally duly impressed—you can imagine, says Parson Weems, "his great mortification"—when, at mention of "dinner," he looks around and sees no sign of a Dutch oven! "Ah!" he cries to British Colonel Walton, "what can be worse?" We may wonder just how the opposition can be so correct—a meal is a meal comme il faut—even a pile of potatoes sets off his scrupulous decencies; quite a lot of work is done, for example, to carry the food to the mouth: "The officer, who was a well-bred man, took up one of the potatoes and affected to feed, as if he had found a great dainty; but it was very plain, and he ate more from good manners than good appetite." The outstanding delicacy that sets the Englishman apart from, what Simms describes as a "motley multitude" with sabers and from Marion himself, equally "strange or savage in costume," is nearly a commonplace of these accounts: the enemy, perhaps, but these Englishmen are enthusiastic admirers of the table. Who wouldn't withdraw for a draft of fine Madeira, or "a tête-à-tête" around a "petit-souper"?[55]

In the mezzotint, Marion's theater of operations makes the dirty camp into a consular cook-off: the demurring that ensues has all the good warmth of Melville's paradise for bachelors where *any* meal, among gentlemen, can look "like Blucher's army coming in at the death on the field of Waterloo."[56] The popular engraving of the Revolution chooses to depict the reconnaissance of war as a grammar of table manners; Marion's civilities make his camp the perfect host to English forces, even amid the "shady" characters. An entirely manufactured moment of treaty with the English is offered as an American nationalist event, and even then we are left to work out where Marion stands. Marion is so akin to the British officer (grouped with him as it were), and with so many "savages" around, this looks more like *Penn's Treaty with the Indians*.[57]

Then there is John Blake White's judiciously cooked up slave: he appears nowhere in Weems (though an aide-de-camp, Tom, makes potatoes). If Weems and Horry describe Marion as "a swarthy, smoke-dried little man, with scarce enough of threadbare homespun to cover his nakedness!"—if Marion surprises the British officer, most of all, because he is not "gaily dressed"—is it not fair to say that this black servant, in his rumpled shirtsleeves and in his "swarthy" disarrangement, reaching toward potatoes and, in fact, very "smoky" (the fire fans toward him), sits in for our hero himself?[58] The slave is dark so that Marion does not have to be; Marion's been verily polished and, like his image in the mezzotint that, unlike a copper engraving on flat plate, has restored various degrees of smoothness to a roughened plate (up to actual burnishing where white was desired), he and the officer are the most "finished" figures we see. Indeed, in a much cruder rendition of the image in Simms's own *Life of Marion,* Marion and the Englishman are the only whites around. The militia that stands beside with powder horns and firelocks, as Marion tiptoes through civilities, are as dusky and leaden as the slave who, again, echoing Marion's gesture of "here, potatoes," reaches toward a pile. What strikes me, though, is the way this new figure at the corner of the assembly seems not just some embodiment of Marion's "slavery" to the cause but a bold incarnation of the work being done in this scene. This is a picture about doing service to the English: Marion's surprising attentions are projected onto the black who, kneeling before the opposition, with his potatoes in hand, is quite literally ready to serve. He is only surpassed in readiness by a small black dog who lies faithfully at the end of White's compositional diagonal of open, catering arms. Marion, the slave, the dog: this is a nationalist picture engraved for a nationalist organization, that finds its revolutionary ideals in escalating models of obeisance.

In her novel *The Linwoods* (1835), Catharine Maria Sedgwick rewrites the episode of the sweet potatoes. This time, an abstinent patriot is invited to the table of Sir Henry Clinton and asked, over a sumptuous menu, by the splendid St. Clair, about the pleasures of the American camp: "Pray, Captain Lee, have you a good fish-market at West Point?"[59] The patriot Eliot Lee, who "felt an honest pride in being one among those who contracted for a glorious future, by the sacrifice of animal and present indulgence," and having frustrated St. Clair's line of inquiries about any trout, goose, turkey, or woodcock on the American watch, is finally asked what officers *do* do ("We have none of these delicacies, sir." "God bless me!—how do you live?"). Eliot retaliates with a show of "pardonable pride" that recalls the mezzotint's scene quite expressly, right down to its nibbling horses: " 'I'll tell you how we live, sir'—the earnest tone of his voice attracted attention—'we live on salt beef, brown bread, and beans, when we can get them; and when we cannot, some of us fast, and some share their horses' messes.' " His speech, which swells with all manner of declamatory dash—Revolution is the manna that comes down from Heaven; our faith is our nutriment, et cetera—excites patriotism in the hall; every breast vibrates to the "burst of true feeling"; women open the door of their hearts and cry; the guests drink virtuous bumpers of plain water in honor of their "native land." But this is not finally a tale of Marion. Eliot sits down and his speech feels funny, overdone: "After the momentary excitement had passed, Eliot felt that he had perhaps been a little too heroic for the occasion. Awkward as the descent is from an assumed elevation, he effected it with grace, by falling into conversation with the major on sporting and fishing; in which he showed a science that commanded more respect from that gentleman, than if he had manifested all the virtues of all the patriots that ever lived, fasted, starved, and died for their respective countries."[60]

Something has happened: Eliot, awkward with his pieties, effects a smooth return to "conversation." His revolutionary fervor has been embarrassed and resolved into the fireside backchat of (satiated) bench fellows. War is less affable than unmotivated sport, and Eliot has been rude. His revolutionary principles *do* inspire a sympathetic response—his own to St. Clair. The British simply cannot stomach these histrionics and Eliot needs to rely on his store of genteel pastimes as a hedge against the brazen affect of "too heroic" a display. It is not the gigantic meal that is plethoric, but patriotism itself. The hubristic heights from which the hero "descends" are too showy for gentlemen. Lake fishing, for instance, is more felicitous. And as Eliot becomes convivial—as he manages his fortunate "fall" into grace—all the living and fasting and starving and dying for one's country seem pretentious (don't you think?), kind of stiff or "assumed."

So Eliot Lee puts down his proud patriotism and decides "to play citizen of the world." The Revolution, it turns out, is lucky for this, for each hawkish scene can be rehearsed in an America that is now, with all the Englishmen and Europeans on shore, newly global, that requires, for its nationalist project, an emphatically cosmopolitan look. By this I mean the sheer worldliness of such events—the kind of circumstances that had the American, General Schuyler, inviting an Englishman, General Burgoyne (and a German, Baron Riedesel) to share smoked tongue and wine after Burgoyne's defeat at Albany. The literature is clear: political fervor is hard to sustain, and when the quotidian affairs of dining, drinking, shopping, and generally conducting oneself became occasions for metropolitan intercourse (where the colonies could aspire to civilities) a certain amount of pleasure had ensued.[61]

In Diana Treat Kilbourn's revolutionary novel *The Lone Dove* (1850), Doctor Brown tells Mrs. Maitland of his intentions to attend a grand ball and "be merry" in the midst of the war. "The human mind," he says, "seems not only to possess the power of assimilating itself to any situation, no matter how repulsive, at first, but, in time, to experience a species of enjoyment in that situation."[62] At least resistance could be avoided at those moments when the freighted consequences of war were lifted for the blessing effects of society. For the very design of society was its stylized elevation over the sordid details of revolution, so that William Dunlap, for example, could reminisce about the "beaux and belles" during wartime evenings in New York or about walking by the ruins of Trinity Church "with thoughtless gayety or with measured steps to the music of military bands placed by the officers amid the graves of the church-yard."[63] The Revolution brought with it these rites of the elite, which now involved loyalists and patriots in the inconsequential amusements that came with forgetting the war in mixed company— with marking off society from the business of conflict enough to decide, as Alexander Graydon does, who of the enemy could dance and who dabbled best in theatricals. Of the British officer who occupied his family home in Philadelphia, Graydon writes, "But what imports the reader to know that Sir William Draper was a racket player? Nothing, certainly, unless we reflect that he was a conspicuous character, the conqueror of Manila, and still more the literary opponent of Junius. Without granting something of celebrity to this latter sort, what possible interest could we take in learning that doctor Johnson liked a leg of pork, or that he could swallow twelve or more cups of tea at a sitting?"[64]

Graydon became a Federalist who saw in the drives of the Continental army the seeds of present-day American opportunism and ruthless self-interest; he became so disaffected with the military because of its system of favors and spoils that he resigned his commission.[65] So it might be tempting to read Graydon's mythologizing of Draper for his sports and letters (and colonial conquest?) as an idiosyncrasy all his own if not for the affinities it shares with so many nineteenth-century accounts of the Revolution. What Graydon fastens onto are the attributes of Draper's social character as an English gentleman, which is why his previous military exploits in the Philippines during the Seven Years' War give pride of place to his defense of monarchy against Whig rhetoric (by "Junius") in the London press. His relation to the celebrity of Draper, like that of Doctor Johnson, is structurally and essentially irrational, but it is precisely this that makes the extremity of his attachment more than mere show. Recent historians, including Aaron S. Fogelman and Michael Zuckerman, have challenged the idea of a "deferential society" in colonial America by claiming that theatrical effusions of appreciation toward the British were coerced and empty displays.[66] The rebel who has chosen to respect the occupying power nonetheless must either strategically dissemble or bear the psychic brunt of domination. But Graydon's *Memoirs* (1811) are not the "pose of the powerless"; they are the anecdotes of a revolutionary officer who has effectively isolated his public politics from his personal attachments to a socializing British elite in which deference—among gentlemen—can be given freely.[67]

Zuckerman is particularly suspicious of efforts to locate deference as a central aspect of eighteenth-century America and has little patience for historians, from Jack P. Greene to Pocock to Bushman, who have argued about the various origins and ends of deference without paying sufficient attention to the evidence of its existence in the first place.[68] For Zuckerman, there is instead a rich archive of unruliness that has not been reckoned with; indeed, as Robert A. Gross writes of Zuckerman's work, this devotion to the actual records of contempt for social betters and traditional authority "exposes the flimsy foundations on which the construct of a deferential order has been built."[69] Rather, Zuckerman finds hundreds of cases of contempt for distinction and rank, moments of rioting or rudeness in which colonists mock their pastors and politicians in bumptious displays of egalitarianism that help explain why so much of the populace rallied to rebellion. If deference lives anywhere at all, according to Zuckerman, it is as a "convenient fiction" that provides "a *frisson* of nostalgia for an imagined past that is not merely of the colonial era." He continues: "Assertions of olden days of deference are not just mistaken interpretations of the colonial character but also invincibly dreary and uninteresting ones."[70] I question this last claim, less because the narratives and iconographies of the Revolution offer proof of real deference, after all, than because they show how thoroughly spirited and energetic nineteenth-century Americans could be in their imaginings of a past where the fine points of social hierarchy seemed almost constantly diverting. Whether the spirit of the revolutionary times is, at any given time, most defined by its disorder, disrespect, and reduction of ritual or whether it remains a last moment in which Americans were deferential as now they are manifestly not is, at least, worth pursuing *as* a historical perception. This is not to overlook, as Judith V. Van Buskirk reminds us, that civility is often beyond reach in these accounts, which tell of cruelty and sadistic acts against prisoners on both sides and of generally inhumane conditions for privates and noncommissioned officers especially.[71] But even all the violence, when it appears, occurs as a departure from a deeper sense that some civilities did flourish in the midst of war. Whether or not the war truly was civil, in other words, the nineteenth century clearly found it interesting to search out archives that suggested that it was. The fact of this search, in response to Zuckerman, is more challenging than "dreary."

So when Americans finally do face the British, and then defer to their enemies with idealized aplomb, we see ritualized displays of decorum that refashion the history of hostilities into the occasions for politeness. These scenes reveal a whole network of respects and affections that not only survive but improve under conditions of war. That is, antebellum narratives of the Revolution seem doubly motivated: on the one hand, determined to commemorate how Americans bested the British and won a new nation; on the other, how Americans bested the war and won a new proximity to British society. It is an odd tactic for nationalist fictions—using the Revolution to emphasize how very British America was.

The Elegiac Return to Dependence

It is something of a commonplace in the recent popular press that the Revolution makes bad culture. Representations seem ponderous and stiff and, in film especially, like scholastic reenactments. Insipid, really: Sons of Liberty singing "Yankee Doodle" fight songs, George Washington riding tall in slow-motion silhouettes (gliding actually, as if perpetually on the Delaware), John Adams calling for "order, order" in quick, rhyming recitative (in the musical *1776*). Hollywood versions seem to have trouble keeping up with the orotund discourse in which the Revolution always lives. Al Pacino is traitorously bad as the hero of *Revolution* (1985), playing a sort of glottalized Sam Adams, and in *The Howards of Virginia* (1940) Cary Grant brings the itchy, manic energy of *His Girl Friday* to the role of a minuteman torn by family ties, though no one else talks half so fast or seems about to take a pratfall. Writing of Mel Gibson's would-be summer blockbuster *The Patriot* (2000), the latest screen version of the fight for independence—and perhaps the last for some time—David Denby puts it squarely: "The Revolutionary War has never been much of a movie subject."[72]

Denby and others attribute this failing in part to the age or distance of the event. There is no *drama* in the national drama because it is, finally, so foreign: Americans have wigs with "ribands" and all those *clothes.* The Revolutionary War does not look like war, either: war is speed and chaos, frenzied violence, and the cold, lonely carnage of *The Red Badge of Courage.* Or war has the monumental, mechanistic scale of films about World War II, or else the stark, photographic vérité of Gettysburg. But because we have no graphic archives of the Revolution, our representations take their cues from the manneristic iconographies of Trumbull paintings or jingoistic pamphleteering: all dying soldiers finish their sentences, all children have Patrick Henry on the brain. There *are* ferocious Indians, corny rustics, and wildly articulating patriots. There are genteel women who get dirty with the cause. But it is all so awkward and schematic: the Revolution, critics seem to say, cannot stand on its principles. Of course, the absence of a photographic record does not lessen the popularity of other wars: Napoleon and Josephine do well in sales (*Napoléon, Master and Commander*), as do Elizabeth and the Spanish Armada (*Fire over England*), the French Revolution (*The Scarlet Pimpernel, A Tale of Two Cities*), and Scottish independence from the tyranny of Longshanks (*Braveheart*). Even the French and Indian War makes a fine period piece: *Northwest Passage,* starring Spenser Tracy, and *The Last of the Mohicans* are considered the best, and purest, hokum. The problem with the American Revolution, it seems, is that there is no genuine menace: who really thinks that the English are evil? They are so droll and polite or fat, or outrageously flouncy, with bad buckteeth. And they have been an ally for so long; Christopher Hitchens describes best how the American cult of Winston Churchill, for example, became the sine qua non of a "special relationship" politics with Britain that, since the mid-twentieth century, has lent a "blue-chip" status to any Anglo-American front (the English aren't evil; the English fight evil).[73] Why, then, would any film go out of its way to "dredge up some long-reconciled misunderstandings when there was a globe full of German, Japanese and Russian enemies to conquer before the credits roll?"[74]

In antebellum America, the sense that the Revolution is natural, legitimate, and over—that while the truth of its eloquence remains, need we really carry on so?—informs these narratives that seem as intent on sounding the depths of our relations with Britain, as any (wearisome) obligation to throw them off. "The corner rock of our offense," writes C. M. Kirkland in *Sartain's Magazine* (1849), "is, of course, that old rebellion, so vexatiously successful, and, moreover, so particularly galling because brought on" by the "blundering arrogance of the mother country, which, by a little polite kindness could have held her sprightly children in leading strings for half a century more at least."[75] Kirkland's version is, of course, quite different from the eighteenth-century accounts that insist on less affective ties in which America had outgrown its familial bonds to Britain. In 1789 David Ramsay, for example, claimed that America's "affection for the Mother Country, as far as it was a natural passion, wore away in successive generations, till at last it had scarcely any existence." But Kirkland's is hardly a tale of broken contracts and violated promises either—of Britain, say, from 1763 on, conspiring to subvert a voluntary and constitutional affiliation with colonies that might have agreed to *remain* colonies had these violations not occurred.[76] Kirkland's Americans wanted to be dutiful—it is "galling" they wouldn't let us be—and Britain's blunder lay in stubbornly refusing to accept how loyal we were.

George Washington Greene continues in the same vein in *Historical View of the American Revolution* (1862). The American's "success," he says,

> awakened no pride; his filial reverence called in vain for maternal affection. The hand that had been held out in cordial welcome to the English stranger in America, found no respondent grasp when the American stranger returned to visit the home of his fathers in England. With a heart overflowing with love, with a memory stored with traditions, with an imagination warmed by tales and descriptions that began in the nursery ballad, and led by easy transitions to Shakespeare and Milton, with a mind elevated by the examples of English history and the precepts of English philosophy, he was received with the repulsive coldness of En-glish reserve, and the haughty condescension of English pride.

Greene is making an argument about the slow evolution of liberty—how Britain transformed loyalty into aversion, and "submission and love into defiance" by inches over time—but we are left not so much with a progressive theory of American history as with an elegiac return to dependence.[77] America had a "heart overflowing with love" and nostalgia but was spurned at home, and this cold, loveless repulse is otherwise known as liberty. Britain was less tyrannical than indifferent, and what the conservative Greene seems to condemn is not its overtaxations and demanding measures but its impossible excessive *laissez-faire*. The

Revolution was caused not by too much government but by neglect: the British were so reserved, so hands-off—choosing, says Greene, not to hold us in their "grasp"—that America had finally no choice but to assert itself.

There is, alas, little romance to independence: what these antebellum literatures seem to admit is that, while its ideals are everywhere and defining and its justice is entirely granted, the Revolution is not, in the end, so sentimental. "Ah!" says Isabella Linwood in Sedgwick's novel, "I am not skilled in metaphysics, but I *know* that we have no power whatever over our affections": the Revolution survives in principle and reason, but, when confronted with all these British admiring beauty and eating well, talking, loving, taking sketches of the landscape, or bringing *en scène* all the candidates for wives who can recite "like Fanny Kemble," "we may smile at their weakness but cannot deny them our sympathy."[78] Perhaps our literature of the Revolution is so prosaic, Greene suggests, because while great revolutions usually favor the cause of literature—the French mind was never so vigorous as during *its* contest with an "arrogant" rule, and a Protestant zeal gave us *Paradise Lost*—they are derived from both politics *and* "passion." But

> the American Revolution, with all its earnestness of purpose, with all its strength of conviction, belongs, in its intellectual relations, to the domain of reason rather than to the domain of feeling. It was the expression of a belief founded, indeed, upon those instinctive suggestions in which the heart and mind act together, but a belief that appealed for confirmation to the deductions of rigorous logic and the facts of positive history. . . . Hence, while it brought out in full light principles overlaid till then by old forms and customs, it started no new theories, opened no new fountains of feeling, left the floodgates of passion untouched.[79]

How do we monumentalize independence from a society so lovable and amusing? It is easy to lose track of the ideologies of war when the British soliloquize their way out of forests, dreaming of Windsor Forest, risking their lives, captivity, nay death, for single sniffs of roses or copies of Oliver Goldsmith—or, like Major John André, in Delia Bacon's *Bride of Fort Edward* (1839), stopping and dropping in war zones to draw miniatures of pretty ladies:

"These woods yield fairies,—come this way."

"For God's sake, André! Are you mad? . . . have you forgotten we are on the enemy's ground?"[80]

The British cannot help themselves: they are unremitting aesthetes looking for pleasingness wherever they go—Madeira, French wines, West Indian turtles, set pieces to stage and perform, cocks to fight, women to woo—or forming convivial associations with just about anyone at the Bunch of Grapes Pub or a ball. If only they could forget themselves long enough to ensure victory in the cruel desert of war, but that would require forgetting their amusements and conversation, their midday suppers of costly fruit and wine served by well-dressed servants, their devotion, as one account describes it, to their "own ease."[81] In these stories the British are sincerely uncommitted to the object of war—a sunset will divert them—and it is to the amusing distractibility of the British living beautifully that America owes its independence. "It is impossible to divine what might not have been the consequences to the liberties of America," declares Peter Van Schaack, a Tory refugee whose writings were published in New York in 1842, if, say, General William Howe had *not* allowed his army to preoccupy itself with putting on an ornate, medievalist pageant and masquerade in his honor during the spring of 1778 in Philadelphia (more on this later).[82] Neither high resolve nor moral purpose on their own part but the endless bumbling inflexibility of the British, traveling between campaigns with trunks of silks and calicoes, with tea, with furniture from London, with volumes to read, enabled the Americans to steal their liberty while the British astonished themselves with their own equipage. "Indeed," writes John McClung in his historical novel, *Camden* (1830), "it has been suggested by many writers that the quantity of baggage allowed to the British officers was extremely injurious to their efficiency in America; and perhaps formed one thread of that complication of causes which led to their failure." The Englishman, writes Emerson, "who visits Mount Etna, will carry his teakettle to the top."[83]

The British are not evil; the British are incompetent. The Manichean dramas of oppression and emancipation on which the lexicon of revolution relies leave little room for imperial legacies left by British who are "too fine!—too fine by half!"[84] The fact that the British are so uninvolved and untroubled by their empire that even in America the anachronism of their pageantry comes at the expense of their battles, and of their colonies ultimately, is what makes the Revolution appear tauntingly marginal, at least to some. The tales can be blunt: "As most of those on whom his majesty principally relied for chastising his refractory subjects, thought more of a dinner of sirloin than the conquest of a rebel province, the welfare of their country was in a measure forgotten amid the repeated scenes of pleasure with which they were surrounded; as hardly a day was suffered to pass without a splendid ball route, or levee at the house of some one of the royalist gentry."[85] This author means the *political* welfare of Great Britain, which seems worth casting aside if only it ensures the continued rituals of imperial pleasure and ostentation, including the "pomp and magnificence" of war. That "attention to one's appearance is the weakness of the British army" is perhaps not as derisory as it sounds, particularly when so many historical and fictional accounts describe the dazzling effect on American spectators of the splendid scarlet arrays, as if the colonies were not worth keeping if it meant soiling oneself in the process.[86] On this front the empire may be at risk, but the picture of empire is accordingly preserved in the uninterrupted amenities and celebrations of His Majesty's representatives, in the amalgam of costumes, fetes, processions, and loyal toasts that perpetuate the luster of the empire even as its own intractability disables it:

> "If you are thinking how your soldiers will look on parade, you will be very apt to spare their clothes, and to avoid putting them to dirty work."
> "Some truth in that. General Howe loses half his opportunities on that very account. Still, this pomp and circumstance are imposing. I do like a little of it."[87]

What strikes Americans looking back from beyond independence is the essential, unrivaled character of an Englishness that seems most concerned with reproducing the life of the metropolis overseas. In fact, the habits of a resplendent society become the very sign of imperial dominion, made immanent to Americans with each preening display of conviviality, warmth, and wit. Colonial power looks like so many glittering redcoats toasting royalty with burgundy, so that while the power is objectionable as such, the prevailing spectacle of it can seem pleasing, even to refractory colonists. These accounts are remarkable for how much they trust the British to have remained, in the face of the contingencies of war, so unequivocally themselves: their strong love of order and proper form, their layered, traditional chain of command, their sociable tolerance and ease based in personal feelings of respect, all fatefully unadaptable to the fact of revolution.

Patriots could rely on it, and this is nowhere more playfully remembered than in the anecdote of Mary Lindley Murray, a Quaker woman with Whig sympathies, who skillfully distracted the British in her home while Washington's embattled troops (under General Israel Putnam) escaped northward to Harlem. The story, first reported by James Thacher, a Continental Army surgeon whose journal was published in 1823, has Howe's regiments resting at the Murray mansion in New York at the behest of loyalist Robert Murray, while his pro-patriot wife and daughters, Beulah and Susannah, induce them to stay two hours too long by plying the officers with "cake and wine." "By this happy incident," writes Thacher, "general Putnam, by continuing his march, escaped" and "it has since become almost a common saying among our officers, that Mrs. Murray saved this part of the American army."[88] A nineteenth-century illustration of the anecdote has the officers jovially entertained by their drinks and themselves; using her feminine wiles, the Quaker lady contrives to divert them with their own conversation—to leave them, that is, to the joys of their own good cheer as they remove their gloves to fraternize and raise a glass around the table (fig. 17). *Dearest Enemy,* Rodgers and Hart called it when adapting this story as a musical comedy a century later.[89] The joke, of course, is that the American lady can detain the officers by being as invisible to them as her black servant, and coconspirator, to the right. She lets the British do what they do, dear enemies, when presented with morsels of cake and a footstool on a languorous afternoon: maintain a fine and regal sense of their pastimes. Though this image makes plain that such socializing here at the outposts of an empire can be gravely consequential, it is also very much the case that such socializing is what the outposts of an empire are for. If there is a lesson here about what Ian Baucom calls "the cultural imperatives of empire," it shares little with the cautionary tales the British tell themselves about the need to guard against the loss of their identity abroad. The British are never *more* exemplary as British than in American accounts of the Revolution that recall how the colonies could serve as wider homes to their acutely British forms.[90]

Historical recoveries of independence are fortuitous for remembering such impulses to empire insofar as they also aim to document the settled, hierarchized social order against which the colonies rebelled.

QUAKER LADY DETAINING THE ENGLISH GENERAL.

FIGURE 17. *Quaker Lady Detaining the English General,* ca. 1840. Prints and Photographs Division, Library of Congress.

It is precisely the vision of decorated lords exercising their prerogatives to stay and eat cake that could motivate an entire liberalizing rhetoric of popular authority and equality. But from the perspective of the nineteenth century, these vestiges of imperial privilege are so permanently eradicated by the Revolution itself that the British Empire, though only just about to achieve unparalleled breadth and amplitude, could seem serenely antiquated. Thus, while the British may still seek to control continents, what inspires them appears more about rank, titles, honor, courtliness, processions, and ceremony, about the far-flung extensions of an ancient system, than any modern threat to America now. Even in the eighteenth century, David Cannadine gorgeously argues, the furthest British colonies probably preserved more of the character of "old England" than the metropolis itself did: there, the royal images and icons of a once feudal society, the elaborate, "ornamental" presence of the British in their dominions, could be more traditionally maintained than in the increasingly industrialized and democratic center of London. "The empire," says Cannadine, "was not *just* as hierarchical a construction as British society in the metropolis: it was significantly *more* so, a kind of enlarged and heightened version of the metropolitan model, blooming with brighter colours, greater radiance and stronger perfume."[91] The culture of British imperialism was already so old-fashioned—so different also from the travails of mass democracy and capitalism in the nineteenth-century United States—that it was perhaps not too compromising to revisit these colonial scenes with a historical appreciation of their antimodernism, so proudly played out in the preferences of a resident gentry. Because the Revolution had brought a new social order, its effect on the old one was valedictory; the British system, with its baroque, overlabored machinery (with its inappropriate baggage), was simply obsolete.

"Remembrance, especially nostalgic remembrance," writes Baucom about the postcolonial experience of history, "is regularly intimate with forgetting." For Baucom, this structure of memory lets Britons at home lovingly avow their empire while disavowing its consequences. At the same time, and more productively, it makes a thickly symbolized sense of the English past available to colonial "act[s] of reinvention." For each scene of the colonial project attempts to animate a sense of England that exists in some timeless remove from history itself, and so it is not surprising that Englishness as such can also live on creatively, and even thrive, long after the empire fades away. Colonial improvisations on these abstracted English forms involve, says Baucom, a "disobedient labor of remembrance"; and nineteenth-century accounts of independence enact a striking version of this impertinence.[92] These accounts celebrate America's triumph of liberty from the abuses of England while seeming greatly reluctant to be liberated from the particular Englishness of that moment. Yet in describing the choice soirees of this "olden time," or the shops still trading in London fashions, the literature seizes on an Englishness that has become boldly aestheticized into an anthropology of empire without a politics behind it—an imperialism of considerable attraction because it is *only* cultural at last. For instance, in the novel *Ambrose and Eleanor* (1834), the day of George III's forty-sixth birthday celebration in revolutionary New York was ushered in by the sound of cannon from different fortresses on the Island, and [from] the shipping in the harbor, as the first rays of sun darted from the eastern horizon, and these were followed by strains of martial music, mingled with the shout of ten thousand voices proclaiming at the same moment, "*God save the king*," while the banner of *Old England,* was proudly waving from every steeple, tower and cupola, and the narrow and winding streets of the city, being thronged with a motley gang of different nations, colors, languages, showed that the day was one of general festivity and joy. But while such were the general scene [*sic*] of confused merriment within the walls of the city, Belmont Hall, the residence of Sir Arthur Percival seemed the centre of attraction, to the more fashionable class of the citizens, as well as officers of the royal army. From an early hour in the morning the hall and garden presented a scene of confused preparation for the approaching festival, servants and retainers crowding and dodging each other, some preparing booths and seats in the garden, others bearing to and from the refractory dishes of choicest viands, while through the open windows were seen barbers, tailors, hair dressers and mantua makers, flitting from one apartment to another, till past the hour of twelve, when at the summons of the old major domo each was posted in his proper station. . . .

   First came Governor Trion and his suite, in all the splendor of feudal magnificence.

"We shall not attempt to go the round of the ceremonies that followed," continues the narrative, "and which, thanks to our republican institutions have now become obsolete"—though this may be simple exhaustion from having just gone the round of "feudal" arrangements and stylized ranks, in which each retainer knows "his proper station," as all the fussing and accoutering resolve into ravishing tributes to the king.[93] Our republican institutions do not here prevent a reincorporation of such dazzlingness into our national myth at the moment of excluding it. This is "a tale of the Revolution"; still, with the colonial gentry's exaggerated display and a "gang" of ethnicities out for the pageant, the scene is enamored with the ancien régime it seems compelled to reproduce on the streets of wartime Manhattan. The fantasy that the republican ethos of the United States has eradicated such conspicuous models of hierarchy—and more so the fawning delight of multicolored colonials reinforcing them—seems merely enough to justify the inapposite detailing of these spectacles in the midst of revolution. The literary expenditure on such magnificence, and the English orthography ("centre") that indulges the task of describing it, while each reminiscence of the spangled troops returns New York to its exotic, elaborate prehistory, make England symbolically central just as it becomes politically peripheral to the new United States.

The number of sources to which the historical novelists could turn in the nineteenth century for documentary evidence of this imperial culture is staggering, and Moore's *Diary of the American Revolution* (1860) is one example of its intimate rediscovery. Transcribing excerpts from Whig and Tory newspapers published during the war, as well as diaries and other contemporaneous writings, Moore's history follows the anxious push and pull of revolutionary resentments and colonial affections. We see, for instance, in the scattered assortment of original sources handed up on each page, that while the nationalist *Pennsylvania Packet* is outraged at the visit of George III's son, Prince William Henry, to the colonies in 1781—"the governor of the garrison of New York thinks that [like the golden calf] we will be prepared to return to our ancient idolatry, and are ready to worship the offsprings of the royal Brute of Britain"—the loyalist *Rivington's Gazette* is worshipfully glad for the "condescension shown by this most pleasing manly youth when he appears abroad amongst the happy loyal subjects of the good gracious king." Though there is ample evidence of revolutionary dissent, just as much attention is paid to the everyday maintenance of colonial society, with its fashion, sports, banquets, theatricals, royal visits, and state events. We have the *New Jersey Gazette* on the queen's birthday at the King's Head Tavern: two hundred candles illuminated giant statues of the king and queen propped on a coat of royal arms. Elsewhere a ball was held: a Doric pediment was erected to frame paintings of their majesties at full length, under which the "general, field and staff officers of the army to the garrison and the principal ladies and gentlemen of the city" could dance among arbors and parterres.[94] All these festivities suggest, perhaps, in this utter confusion of context, that the discourse of independence is most accurately understood when it is immersed in the sometimes overwhelming background noise produced by British subjects in America. The implicit argument of such an archive is that these unexamined reproductions of imperial culture are a necessary aspect of our own national history, not simply as the other side of a more faithful record of the past but as an object lesson in the otherness of eighteenth-century America—a catalog of everything that

can contribute to a more coherent sense of national identity, which is
as much to say, the very material that proves its difficulty in the first
place.

"How gay the arrival of the army under Burgoyne will make the city,
Miss Wharton," says Colonel Wellmere in James Fenimore Cooper's *The
Spy* (1821). "Oh!" agrees the American girl, "How pleasant it must be."
Cooper's narrator looks back from an era in which Queen Street, "one
of the most fashionable quarters of the town," has become Pearl Street,
the home to auction dealers, warehouses, and counting rooms, and
perhaps it is no wonder that such a transition from gentility to utility
and commercialism yielded a wistful nostalgia for a paternalistic system
based on traditional, social obligations.[95] The patterns of respect and
civil behavior that Cooper associates with colonial culture have been
so abandoned by a liberalizing society that now the writers of historical
romance can indulge in such alluring institutions as the British army.
If Burgoyne's officers made the city gay, there is now a lingering fear
that the self-interested activities of nascent individuals will leave less
time for gaiety. But there is also a fear that the commercial spirit of the
present will overwhelm a productive reverence for the state that is here
made available by the colonial example. Lossing has his own melancholy response when, on returning to Carpenter's Hall, where the first
Continental Congress met, he finds nothing in the window but trade
cards for "Wolbert and Co. Auctioneers for the sale of real estate and
stocks" and, on the inside, walls echoing with the auctioneer's hammer
and every make of merchandise: "What a desecration! Covering the
façade of the very Temple of Freedom with the placards of groveling
Mammon!"[96]

What has been lost is not simply respect for the icons of the Revolution but enchantment with the past; love for the state has been for-
feited to crassly secular opportunities, and the sacro-political language
that Lossing employs is also firmly Burkean. As he tours the country to
record and sketch vestiges of the Revolution for his *Field-Book* before
they give way to "the plow of agriculture, and the behests of Mammon,
unrestrained in their operations by the prevailing spirit of our people,"
he feels "emotions of shame, such as every American ought to feel" in
remembering that such impiety is characteristically our own. Because
"while England erects a monument in honor of the amputated leg of a
hero who fought for personal renown, we allow these relics, sanctified
by the deeds of soldiers who were more than heroes as the world re-

gards heroism, to pass away and be forgotten. Acquisitiveness is pulling down walled fortresses." The historian, traveling the nation to preserve what he can from oblivion, has discovered that the historical impulse is itself English and that even the desire to memorialize the last remains of the American revolutionary tradition requires a foreign experience of attachment to the past. "I knew the genius of our people was the reverse of antiquarian reverence for things past," writes Lossing, and that "the glowing future, all sunlight and eminence, absorbed their thoughts and energies, and few looked back."[97]

If only we can learn from the British how to sanctify our national business, Lossing seems to say, we might inoculate ourselves against the nakedness of our ambitions. When he encounters on his tour of revolutionary battle sites in 1848 a group of volunteers returning from "the battle-fields of Mexico," they are weary and "spirit-broken" and their recollections of havoc on the fields bring none of the joy "which the soldier feels who has battled in defense of country and home." These are the representatives of the new American empire, but the forward-thinking militarism of their enterprise has no ready stock of historical capital on which to draw for consecrating imperial expansion with honor and "glory." Lossing's nostalgic historiography is framed as a retreat from the materialism of post-Jacksonian society—"I left behind me," he says at the start, "the cares of business life within the confines of our commercial metropolis"—but his "pilgrimage" to the hallowed sites of the Revolution is also a return to a model of empire in America that is less alienating for him (though no less troubling for us) than what these soldiers straggling home from the Mexican border exemplify.[98]

John Richter Jones draws a similar contrast of empires in his revolutionary novel, *The Quaker Soldier* (1858). Worrying over our predatory ambitions in the west—"the tiger had one lap of blood in the mexican [*sic*] war, and has been restless ever since"—he hopes to carry readers back to "that humbler national period when your grandfather—mine certainly—was a rebel against the British crown." The term "rebel" is important for Jones because the historical milieu he evokes around the British occupation pays tribute to the " 'rebellion,' viewed as it appeared before success had sanctified it into a revolution." It recalls a time when Americans were sufficiently immersed in this other, earlier empire not to think past its fall. The history of how empire looked this last time that it was operative in America becomes a way of working through the starkest aspects of its reemergence, and these writers are inviting

Americans to inhabit the colonial space once again. This is in part a fantasy of escape into a simplifying dependency, when the historical burdens of a continental destiny seemed less America's to bear. But such invitations also have a pedagogical commitment to Britain's imperial example, especially as it reflects on the nation's own "restless" expansionism. In *The Quaker Soldier* our empire is breeding nostalgia for *their* empire, and Jones claims that if that empire has declined, it is only because the British are "too fine by half." Detailing high society in Philadelphia in 1777, and the romances and intrigues that come of noble Englishmen taking up quarters in the house of loyal Quakers, Jones offers countless illustrations of what manner of imperial society—hierarchized, ritualistic, and intricately responsive to the discourses of tradition—best flatters its dominions. While the British are not above reproach (the villain in the novel is an English libertine), the world they import is so prepossessing—they apologize "so handsomely for their intrusion," for example, and are "besides so genteel and good-looking"—that even the rebelling subjects feel "fortunate in [their] guests." Such reminiscences of this still colonial society remain the "sweetest of our sweet fancies." "Your tastes," Jones tells his readers, "are the same—we hope." [99]

Of course, central to the ideology of the Revolution was a belief in the need to replace paternalistic social ties with contractual relations. If America had revolted against a tyrannical sovereign, it could now stand on its own as a consensual union of autonomous individuals. The idea that obedience to an arbitrary monarchy is coerced and ritualized—and that such a system relies on the power of influence, patronage, and personal obligations—provided the logic for a new society based on abstract principles and more rational interactions. But the revolutionary accounts considered in this chapter hesitate to leave behind the all-enveloping social worlds that were both ordered by and modeled on imperial rule itself. Can we occasionally recover, they seem to ask from the other side of independence, what it feels like to be a subject? It is not so surprising that a postrevolutionary culture, facing a breakdown of traditional authority and a certain social anomie, would offer up compensatory images of more codified communities. What remains striking are the affective identifications with Britain—imagined always as the reliquary of caste, stability, and anticapitalism—that these images specifically bring back. Elizabeth Fox-Genovese writes that the demise of "embedded paternalism, whether social, governmental, or religious, engendered regressive longings for paternal or organic authority."[100] Accounts of the war for independence can feel regressive indeed, and they often turn on what it means to see the British Empire—just as its moment in America is passing—as never more deserving of regard.

Empire of Beauty

There is perhaps nothing more arresting in nineteenth-century accounts of the Revolution than the enthusiasm for Major André's "Mischianza." An extravagant public festival honoring Sir William Howe in Philadelphia in May 1778, the Mischianza would be remembered as the most flagrant, obtrusively garish spectacle of imperial occupation. And fondly: the labor spent reconstructing the character of the pageant that John André, adjutant major to the British army, in part designed (before, that is, he was hanged by Americans as a spy), from its opening regatta to its medievalist tilt and tournament, speaks to the exalted, vivid notion of its place in wartime culture. But just how such an aristocratic splurge of feudal falderal, including banners, streamers, state barges, trumpeters, heralds, and men-at-arms in breastplates, exactly belongs to the American Revolution is one of the historiographical "specialties of interest" that Watson concedes should be left to "*individual* contemplation."[101] Remote, impractical, and dreamlike, the entertainments are remembered for the conundrum that they were: a token of history that shows a willingness to turn its back on history by retreating into a simulacrum of the past. For the Mischianza transformed the actual occupation of Philadelphia into a hypnotic stage show of "old English" grandeur, a nostalgic recasting of the modern army as a quintessentially English artifact. That the army contrived, in the midst of war, an elaborate fakery of war with all the glitter and show of knights in combat testifies to how great the imperial manufacture of iconic Englishness could be around their real English presence. That Americans in the nineteenth century incorporated this feudal ersatz into the histories, novels, dramas, paintings, and general national memory of their Revolution speaks to the haunting way the British could live on as such unlikely projections of themselves.

The Mischianza, from the Italian meaning "medley," took place on May 18 at Walnut Grove, the Philadelphia estate of loyalist Joseph Wharton, to commemorate Howe's command before his recall to England for military indolence. Howe was personally popular, and his theatrical send-off by admiring officers was calculated to show esteem for a general who, despite his gambling and dissipation—which "may have indeed tainted the army" and led to defeat—was nonetheless happy to share his indulgences with his men.[102] The fete began with a grand regatta on the Delaware and continued with a tilting contest in which two groups, "Knights of the Burning Mountain" and "Knights of the Blended Rose," mounted on caparisoned horses and attended by squires, jousted in honor of appointed American "ladies" left behind in the war. The women, wearing medievalist Turkish habits designed by Major André, watched from festooned pavilions. But why not give André's own account of it, from a letter to a friend, since Benson Lossing, John Fanning Watson, and others all quote it at length (the following is from Lossing)?

> After they had rode round the lists, and made their obeisance to the ladies, they drew up fronting the White Knights; and the chief of these having thrown down his gauntlet, the chief of the Black Knights directed his esquire to take it up. The knights then received their lances from their esquires, fixing their shields on their left arms, and, making a general salute to each other by a very graceful movement of their lances, turned round to take their career, and, encountering in full gallop, shivered their spears. . . . At length the two chiefs, spurring forward into the center, engaged furiously in single combat, till the marshal of the field (Major Gwyne) rushed in between the chiefs, and declared that the fair damsels of the Blended Rose and Burning Mountain were perfectly satisfied with the proofs of love and the signal feats of valor given by their respective knights, and commanded them, as they prized the future favors of their mistresses, that they would instantly desist from future combat.[103]

After which, the knights and ladies joined a full processional through two triumphal arches into the grand ballroom for dancing; then a rocket and fireworks display, in which Chinese fountains chimerically danced to military music; then a grand banquet attended by twenty-four black slaves in "Oriental" dresses with silver collars, and the ceremonial entrance of the Herald of the Blended Rose, who toasted the king's health, and so on.

"And thus closed the greatest and last exhibition of romantic grandeur, and extravagant folly, which the fair CITY OF INDEPENDENCE was ever to witness under foreign rule; for in one short month afterward, the gay soldiers of Britain departed, and, with them, every vestige of foreign authority, to return no more." Folly perhaps, but for James M'Henry who thus closes his 1831 novel on the Mischianza, the investment in the vaudeville of English gaiety is also a belief that this gaiety is the signature of a romantic aesthetic that is elegiacally linked to British sovereignty in the colonies. To win independence is to lose the British, but to historicize independence is to revive such auratic, imperial Britishness as a fetish, and M'Henry is very good at it. His own revolutionary romance preserves all sides of the war but plots them onto the Mischianza's ludic legend, so that Tories and patriots—finding themselves likewise enlisted in the feudal games—fight out the battles of independence by parrying in mantles. They confront each other on the field in expostulations of Tudor English: "Shame to thee, uncourteous and ruffian knight!"[104] M'Henry rehearses the Revolution through an iconography of chivalry, but he also admits that the British make this figurative transposition of American independence possible—it is *their* presence that imparts the "grandeur" to the moment that allows for its stylistic excess to be reckoned as historically representative.

The degree to which antebellum reconstructions of the Mischianza plainly revel in the atavistic world of medieval pleasures should not have us overlook the deeper play with tropes of war and empire that patterned the event itself. In making available to Americans once again a deliriously outmoded style of Englishness, writers such as M'Henry and Lossing are memorializing the culture of British Empire as it appears already cannibalized and motivated for colonial display; thinking back to Cannadine's account of the empire's historicizing fantasies, this may be just the sort of inauthentic show of tradition that could best confirm the place of Englishness abroad. "Let modern Britons act the ancient part": Major André's poetical address to the pageant's closing banquet, which biographer Winthrop Sargent reprints in full, is a sentiment that at once acknowledges the escapist theatricality of the affair but also resonates with the strenuous anachronism that the imperial enterprise makes work for itself. What might seem like an instruction for sheer diversion, an invitation to forget about the maintenance of a colonial presence in America—"the soldier," says André citing Plutarch, "tir'd of war's alarms, / Exalts to feast on beauty's charms"—is in fact deeply implicated in the power and hold of that presence.[105] "Modern Britons" acting "ancient parts" involves a reproduction of archeological Englishness that not only traditionalizes the sense of a British presence in America but becomes part and parcel of a nineteenth-century aesthetic that can now look back on the "romantic grandeur" of empire.

What is the nature of the experience of seeing a picture like "The Mc-schianza at Philadelphia," while reading a history of the Revolution (fig. 18)? Between stories and sketches of the war in Watson's *Annals*, following an account of the Battle of Brandywine, is another picture of battle: two sides front each other on the field, as one soldier hoists his weapon in a decisive call to arms. But this is not war; this is a war game in the midst of war, and the extreme imposture leaves us with all of the truths of pomp, circumstance, and martial display, but none of the consequence—a Simmelian play of forms in which there is no real friction because make-believe soldiers in a mock-up contest cannot really harm one another. The Mischianza is a pure symbol of war whose structural excess—the phalanxes stepping in time, the throwing down of the gauntlet, the general salutes and shivering of spears—unburdens war of its contents, so that all we see are these free extrapolations of its architecture and movement. There is nothing at stake in the Mischianza but the effectiveness of these forms and the quality of play, which is still a lot to involve the spectator watching its battle as a

THE MESCHIANZA AT PHILADELPHIA.—Page 290.

FIGURE 18. John F. Watson, "The Meschianza at Philadelphia," in *Annals of Philadelphia, and Pennsylvania, in the Olden Time* (Philadelphia, E. Thomas, 1857), 2:259. The Library Company of Philadelphia.

sport, like the ladies in the picture's pavilions or like any reader of Watson who stops to look at this picture amid the larger narrative of the war. Without violence or force, war is an occasion for the exercise of order and rank, chivalry and humanity, for noble encounters between noble men. Most of all it is pleasurable to see, as its rules and protocols transform the theater of operations into a dynamic ballet of passion and restraint. John H. Mancur describes the visual drama of André's tournament in his tale "La Meschianza" (1844): "The glorious pomp and Circumstance of war were emblazoned on every side, its grim terrors were hushed. Every balcony, window and housetop were occupied with spectators. . . . Mistress Pemberton who for many months had never ceased bewailing the presence of the spoilers, and the desecration of her dwelling, felt for once pleasure in gazing at the rich array." [106]

The aestheticizing of the Mischianza allows for an audience at war to be pleasurably entertained by war. The amusement produced by a trained military prancing around the occupied territory in knights' costumes with plumes—and tunics emblazoned with sunflowers and cupids—is neither cathartic nor jingoistically mobilizing but an offer of escape into the sublimated, ordered culture of war as if war were only culture. On their own, the profession of arms, the skill, tact, and naturally the notions of honor and duty that ennoble them—in short, the sum and substance of what is seen as the art of war—become an exemplary domain for thinking about order, civility, even beauty, despite the war itself. As Mancur makes clear, there is no denying the formal appeal of war's color and motion, its organic sequence of attractions, and affecting symmetries: "The next encounter," he writes, "was a general *melee* with swords, which to the spectators had every appearance of real combat, the blows flying thick and fast. . . . This diversity of action, and occasional fright and disorder of the steeds, gave a life, spirit and picturesque display highly pleasing and gratifying to the eye—while the ear was constantly assailed with the ring and clatter of conflicting steel." [107]

Mancur's dramatic climax occurs during the Mischianza's tournament when two rival suitors of an American girl—a profligate Englishman and Montresor, an honorable American loyalist (both fighting for the crown)—confront each other in the arena. Among the "amicable interchange of blows" between the other knights, their own duel becomes deadly (their hostility is real), and Montresor wounds his rival and wins the girl. But Mancur's romance does not like Pyrrhic victories: Montresor finds a surgeon who heals the Englishman who in turn feels so ashamed for "interrupt[ing] the social festivities" with his "breach of decorum" and "improper play," he courteously grants a last dance to the girl (according to his scripted role in the pageant) and takes his leave. As for Montresor, "he felt equal repugnance that the festivities of the evening should be disturbed by his 'unmannerly brawl.' "[108] The Englishman is passionate about the girl but even more so about the civilizing behaviors he relies on to regain his place in polite society after an awkward moment of emotional attack. Not merely his show of sublimation is instructive, but the consciousness with which all involved translate the commotion of deep unrest into a formal resolution that is, in the end, most engaging for its superficiality. The romance of the Mischianza is that "war" might be celebrated not for its victories but for its own sake—for the involved, self-regulating rituals that let its participants be so brave and decent, daring and deferential, exquisite and subdued.

While stories of the Revolutionary War certainly intend to confirm *its* victory, they also want to reengage with chivalric discourses in which the contest is not meant to be won or lost but rightly performed. The Mischianza points to a turn away from the history of the historical drama to concentrate on the spectacle of mutual interaction that war makes possible. But tales of the Mischianza are only symptomatic of how the Revolution becomes an occasion to glorify the high formality of military culture as a means of recalling a lost genteel world of symbolic, social relations. Just look at the frontispiece to Lossing's *Pictorial Field-Book of the Revolution* (fig. 19): what is a Revolution, it asks, but the chance to experience a decorated array of generals, lords, and marquises arranged by insignia on a medieval triptych? This is not, after all, an allegorizing image, nor emblematic of independence and its principles, but the kind of sampling of "historic costumes of the world" one might otherwise associate with atlases. George Washington's central place may be a nod to America's victory, but standing under the bunting of warring parties, surrounded by an equal distribution of stars and strips, union jacks, and fleurs-de-lis, it is hard to make out the contest behind the unifying arrangement of well-apportioned forms. Our national flag, in this context, is just one aspect of the ornamental garniture of war that also has Britain's banner and the French coat-of-arms harmonized into an ornate assemblage of war's trimmings. The image may be evoking the heraldic formalism of state flags, seals, and currency, but its feudalizing excess—the knight's helmet at Washing-

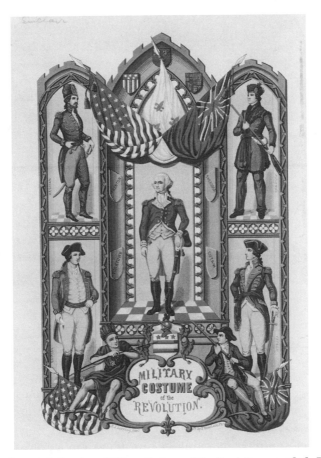

FIGURE 19. Benson J. Lossing, *Military Costume of the Revolution,* ca. 1876. Prints and Photographs Division, Library of Congress.

ton's feet, the battlements on top of the picture—feels semantically thin save to reconfigure a vision of chivalric types. Revolutionary history is about its dressings, and Lossing sacrilizes, on this altarpiece of war, the impulse to good form as such. We return to the Revolution not for narrative coherence or political inspiration, but for a pleasing iconography of idealized combatants within ordered and aestheticized schemes.[109]

Mancur's tale of chivalric conduct also speaks to matters at the heart of John Trumbull's masterpiece, *The Death of General Warren at the Battle of Bunker's Hill* (fig. 20). Painted in 1786 and again in 1834, circu-

FIGURE 20. John Trumbull, *The Death of General Warren at the Battle of Bunker's Hill,* 1786. Photograph © 2008 Museum of Fine Arts, Boston.

lated widely as an engraving, the picture represents the death of the patriot Joseph Warren by a musket ball through the head just as the British press beyond American fortifications. The central moment turns not on the fact of his death but on the noble gesture of British Major John Small who is shown on the left cradling Warren, the enemy's general, while attempting to save him from a grenadier's bayonet. Trumbull claims in his *Catalogue of Paintings* that, in focusing on Major Small, he hoped to honor an officer "equally distinguished by acts of humanity and kindness to his enemies, as by bravery and fidelity to the cause he served." The artist was criticized, by William Dunlap among others, for choosing to paint such a refined moment of British humanity—one derived from a possibly apocryphal anecdote about an internecine battle in which no one finally wins.[110] But Trumbull's subject of gentlemen acting beautifully in the midst of battle takes advantage of war's ability to produce dramas of chivalric sensibility that are both dependent on and aesthetically poised against the treachery of combat.

The circulation of Trumbull's painting is coincident with renewed historiographical interest in two particular facts about the Battle of Bunker Hill. The first is that the battle did not take place on Bunker Hill at all, but the adjacent Breed's Hill, and that Breed's Hill was not commanded by the iconic Israel Putnam as history had taught (*he* was at Bunker Hill), but by Colonel William Prescott who was lesser known. Israel Putnam, in other words, the epic hero of the Revolution, was really peripheral to the battle for which he was acclaimed, and the reestablishment of Prescott at the scene by archivists, braving the recalcitrance of Putnam's defenders in the press (including his son and Daniel Webster), was seen as a controversial move beyond filial piety and ancestor worship in histories of the Revolution. As Lossing writes, "This battle should properly be called the battle of Breed's Hill, for there the great events of the day occurred. There was much slaughter and fighting upon Bunker Hill, where Putnam chiefly commanded, but it was not the main theater of action."[111] Trumbull does include Putnam in the painting, as a tiny figure with an upraised sword at the left (presumably ordering Americans to retreat), but his own gestures toward meticulous historicism—privileging the anecdote over the national myth—resonate with this other, ecumenical act of remembering. Here, amid the carnage, Trumbull isolates an ennobling interlude of gallantry so eccentric to the American legend that it encourages an Anglo-American burst of consanguinity.

The other claim to critical attention was the much-adored fact that the Battle of Bunker Hill could be watched: from the windows, roofs, steeples and cupolas of Boston, across the bay, the battle on the hill could be advantageously seen—it "raged," says Lossing, "in full view of thousands of spectators." Women especially from "every elevation gazed with streaming eyes" on the bloodshed as their husbands, sons and brothers clashed on both sides of the conflict. Fought on high ground in the neighborhood of a populous city, "the operations and movements," writes Daniel Webster, "were of course all visible and all distinct" and the spectators, "far outnumbering both armies, thronged and crowded on every height and every point which afforded a view of the scene, themselves constituted a very important part of it." The presence of witnesses, continues Webster, following "every gallant effort," with all the force and sentiment of "their own throbbing breasts," had the effect of making "the troops of the two armies [seem] like so many combatants in an amphitheatre."[112]

Nineteenth-century accounts of the battle like to dwell on this exceptional theatricality, even as late as Oliver Wendell Holmes, Sr.'s "Grandmother's Story of Bunker Hill Battle as She Saw It from the Belfry" (1875), Edwin Blashfield's painting, *Suspense, the Boston People Watch from the Housetops the Firing at Bunker Hill* (ca. 1880), and Howard Pyle's

FIGURE 21. Howard Pyle, *Watching the Fight at Bunker Hill,* ca. 1899.

illustration, *Watching the Fight at Bunker Hill* (fig. 21), in which clusters of composed viewers see the engagement from a series of rooftops and gables across Boston Bay. In Pyle, the spectators are indeed crucial to the scene: it is about them. But the lack of any characterized response (their faces are hidden, and where is the fear?) makes this also about an aestheticizing remove from the battle, which can be watched like a sport from the bleachers or like a tournament from the Mischianza's pavilions. The image is conventionally picturesque, with the darkened foreground of shingles and the line of figures ascending to the left, and all serving to frame the battle in the distance: it is serenely far-off, luminously lit by its own fire and smoke and kept, one could insist without too much cleverness, visually "at bay." The audience, who we sit behind, helps sustain the illusion of a stage set.

Trumbull had famously witnessed the Battle of Bunker Hill just like this, through field glasses while stationed across the Bay at Roxbury. When it came time for him to paint it, he maintained the picturesque quality of experiencing it from afar, not only in its miniaturized size (only 25" × 34") and the shading and framing of the chosen moment in a safe middle distance but also in its universal orange tint that mellows sharp light and gives the composition the feel of being viewed through a Claude glass. But Trumbull has preserved the sense of spectatorship, too, in the figures at the right of the image: Lieutenant Thomas Grosvenor of Connecticut and his black servant, about to retreat, stop awestruck at the scene before them. Not simply Warren's death but the handsome gesture of the Englishman, brushing aside the bayonet, turns the figures in their flight as they spin around to see Small and Warren so affectively coupled as themselves. The black servant rests a sentimental head on the shoulder of the wounded lieutenant (who holds his bleeding chest), while pressed intimately behind as if to say, I've got your back. He looks much like Small, who leans over Warren in a feminized posture of devotion and care and has his back, too.

The black servant, who Trumbull describes as a "faithful Negro," is often misidentified as Peter Salem, a free black minuteman who allegedly killed British Major John Pitcairn, pictured here in the middle of the canvas falling into the arms of his son. But this is not Salem, who, if he appears at all, is more likely the black soldier just discernible under the aggregate of flags flying over the scene; this is mainly because Salem, as a soldier from Massachusetts, would not have served under a slave-holding lieutenant from Connecticut (nor be considered his servant).[113] Salem is a famous actor in the battle, but Trumbull foregrounds instead a black slave who is safe not only from imputations of violence but from any partisan affiliations save his personal responsibility to Grosvenor himself. He is, in the strict sense, kept outside the politics of the conflict—still serving within a system in which, as a slave, he can have no stake—but also curiously linked to Small whose own duty and deference to Warren have him acting against his own interests. Hence, the disinterestedness of the slave is sentimentalized as part of a larger social order that puts a premium on personal loyalties and bonds and that sees such connections as increasingly rare within a political culture so responsive to cold, abstract ideals it has Englishmen fighting Englishmen to begin with. Trumbull enlists the figure of the slave to function as a perfectly (and suspiciously) innocent observer, whose rapt attention to a death scene that has, for him at least, no consequences, makes us appreciate this scene in ways less conditioned by our own partisanships. What the slave sees is not a turning point in war but the aesthetic sublime of Small's humanity as it transcends politics and context. Insofar as the slave is a surrogate for our own viewership, he helps us to recognize the categorical imperative of that response. How can we think about the implications of Warren's death on the American campaign, when it forces us to pause in wonder instead at the breathtaking extent of human sympathy? "My dear friend," says Small to Warren in one novel's version of the anecdote, "I hope you are not badly hurt?"[114]

Like Trumbull's painting, representations of the Mischianza render warring sides as largely formal oppositions and discover in the anecdotes of the archive a polite culture of war that operates above the incitements of ideology or cause. The Revolution becomes a theater of heightened engagements where the aggressions of war serve as an expressive backdrop to an inapposite drama of manners. In the Mischianza's repertory of contests, scenes of victory are not so grand as to represent, say, the triumph of individual rights, just the exercise of personal incentives within bounds that have been exactly and admirably drawn. In the nineteenth century, such scenes are often set against contemporary fears that self-interest knows no bounds in a society that has come to favor ends to means and commercial transactions to stylized engagements. The histories and romances look back ruefully from a nation too caught up in progress to bother with inexpedient embellishments of grace. Lossing, for example, lets us know that the site of the Mischianza still stands in 1854 but is "devoted to mechanical purposes."[115] In Hawthorne's tale of the Mischianza, "Howe's Masquerade" (1842), the pageant of the past haunts the mercantile boardinghouse and bar that have come to occupy its historic space.

I am not the first to want to situate the Battle of Bunker Hill beside the Mischianza's spectacular arrangements. Hawthorne's tale of the fete relocates the Mischianza from Wharton's house in Philadelphia to the Province-House in Boston, in part to imagine what it might have been like to witness the pageant and the battle from the same place. So we keep the legends of Bunker Hill in mind as Hawthorne guides us through the revelries of the Mischianza as if the two events—both the battle and the entertainments conceived by Howe's men—are equally evocative of a vanished moment in America full of figures "who have flitted forth from the magic pages of romance" or, just as fantastically, "flown hither from one of the London theatres, without a change of garments."[116] Hawthorne's tale is explicit in portraying the masked pageant as the dramatic end of Britain's legacy: Howe's theatrical of steeled knights is interrupted by a spectral parade of colonial governors wending down the stairs and out the door—Winthrop, Bellingham, Phips, Andros, Hutchinson—and finally the proleptically shrouded ghost of Howe himself. The rulers of the "old, original Democracy in Massachusetts" are followed by tyrannical or careless royal authorities though now the movement of the march, like the march of history, seems fixed on their descent and expulsion. The Mischianza shows the British Empire "at its last gasp"—the imperial power playing out its anachronism in a hopeless procession that makes every officer of rank look like a mourner at his own funeral. But the narrator of Hawthorne's story, himself listening to the tale of "Howe's Masquerade" from the bar of the Province-House, is still gladdened "to be conscious of a thrill of awe" by the romantic forms that preceded him. As he looks around the old mansion, now subdivided into small rooms for city boarders and greatly decayed, surrounded by the traffic of a commercial street, he tries to "throw a tinge of romance and historic grandeur over the realities of the scene." The spectral figures of the pageant may speak to the passing of British rule, but inasmuch as they are invoked here "to throw the spell of hoar antiquity" over the living world, the narrator does not admit *their* passing. Such colonial spirits are raised from the "dead corpse" of Britain: they help to mitigate against the commercial transactions, the businesses, penny presses, cigar smoke, tumblers of whiskey, and customers that otherwise "woefully disturb" the narrator's "gorgeous fantasies" of the Revolution as belonging much more to the old world than new.[117]

If narratives of the Mischianza mark a sentimental recovery of prenational attachments, it is to the figure and person of Major André, its inspired author, that nineteenth-century devotions most turn. Caught and hanged as a spy while negotiating with Benedict Arnold for the surrender of West Point, André's untimely death elicited the most exceptional effusions of American sympathy. How pronounced was the impulse to weep for one's enemy to be so commemorated in ballads, broadsides, testimonials, newspapers, and, by the nineteenth century, innumerable historical accounts of the grieving and regretting by "all that were worthy . . . in the ranks alike of friends and foes." Critics have long remarked on the phenomenon of affection that attended memories of André for a century after his execution: pilgrimages to the Westchester tulip tree under which André was discovered and captured; reproductions of his self-portrait, sketched in haste from the prison cell; melancholic returns to the moment of his death through the reprinted tales of eyewitnesses. All the elaborate elevations of feeling over principle in which Americans loved their enemy traitor seem to suggest another, contending revolution of sentiments in the midst of the Revolution itself. Around the pretty martyr, the bonds of brotherhood would transcend the discordant claims of nations to share in obsessive, communal acts of mourning; "never," writes Lossing, "was sympathy more real or feeling more genuine than that exhibited by the American officers on this occasion." Americans went so far as to fault George Washington for the absolutism of his sentence and his blind adherence to martial law, not letting André be shot as a soldier rather than hanged as a spy. By the 1860s, the notion that Washington lacked the finer sensibility to bend the rules of justice this once had historians even claiming that his own death was "not universally regretted by the American people." [118] Was this, at last—to return to James Kirke Paulding—the price of independence? A lovely man sacrificed to the unforgiving measures of principle, reason, and law?

But not any lovely man: not, for example, Nathan Hale, the blue-eyed, Yale-educated patriot who went behind enemy lines in New York at George Washington's request and was hanged as a spy by the British. While the fate of André was cause for universal sorrow in decades of commemorative response on both sides of the Atlantic, the decent Hale has few artifacts from the period to recommend him. Certainly some noticed the slight, and by the 1830s petitions began to circulate for the erection of a Hale monument in Connecticut. A single anonymous "Ballad of Nathan Hale" appeared and occasionally one comes across a nod to the patriot in an antebellum novel or history: "Where," writes Jared Sparks in 1835, "is the memento of the virtues, the patriotic sacrifice, the early fate of Hale? It is not inscribed in marble; it is hardly recorded in books. Let it be more deeply cherished in the heart of his countrymen." Mostly, Hale became the pet project of ladies' societies in Connecticut, while André was the lost love of nations who could agree on nothing but him. As Oliver Bunce puts it in his *Romance of the Revolution,* "Any impartial reader will question the justice of history, which has done so much for the memory of André, and left that of Hale in comparative oblivion . . . we can discover but little difference in their cases."[119]

But what is different in the case of André? What is the shock of the loss in the battle for independence of something that wasn't our own? Of course, the handsome soldier and man of letters would benefit from comparison to the crippled, villainous Arnold whose double-dealing had jeopardized his country *and* the life of his young accomplice who was only guilty of serving his cause. In this sense, fidelity to one's county—whichever country—is set against the self-serving ambitions of Arnold. Nineteenth-century American schoolbooks rehearse the story of André more than any other anecdote of the Revolution to teach the lesson of his honor, fortitude, and loyalty (never mind his loyalty to the king): "Oh!" one children's book character exclaims, "had it only been Arnold instead of André!"[120] Historical accounts also tell the story of Sergeant Major John Champe and Major Henry Lee infiltrating the British camp in the guise of deserters with the hopes of delivering up Arnold to Washington in exchange for André's life. Their lack of success is the subject of at least one melodrama that sees the restoration of "the amiable and unfortunate André to his friends" on the British side as a "glorious project!": remember, says Champe's betrothed on his departure, you go in honor of "patriotism and fidelity" (no, replies Champe, "patriotism, *love,* and fidelity").[121]

Still, the contrast of André with Arnold does not account for the historical neglect of Hale, who was also true to his country and whose country was *ours.* And the same decades that came to revere André as exquisitely lost to Arnold's treachery were also beginning to soften on Arnold. New accounts of his heroism in American campaigns near Albany describe his turn from patriotism as a response to a series of insults by General Gates, who "was evidently jealous of Arnold's well-earned reputation and growing popularity with the army," and by the devious, careerist General Wilkinson who panders to Gates and cheats Arnold of his promotions. With resentment and shame, Arnold finds comfort in the fashionable high society of loyalist Philadelphia, where the biases of his new wife, Peggy Shippen, brought him "into perpetual contact with persons, who had no sympathy with the friends of liberty, the advocates of independence." But could the antebellum reader fault Arnold too severely when André himself was enthralled by the attractions of Peggy Shippen, the *belle* of the Mischianza, writing sonnets in her honor and sketching portraits from memory, even conducting an intimate correspondence with her when the British removed to New York? That Arnold may have deserted a company of corrupt mercenaries to find refuge in loyalist love was the cause of some speculation and a certain leniency toward the traitor who can sometimes appear as a pitiable turkey but is nonetheless not unsuggestive of the profound affective ambivalence of colonial relations themselves. At the end of Delia Bacon's play, *The Bride of Fort Edward,* Arnold has left the American campaign for the indulgent comforts of Britain's feminine grasp: "Ay, ay, come hither," he urges the rebels. "Look you there! Lay down your arms. Seek the royal mercy;—here it is. Your wives, your sisters and your innocent children;—let them seek the royal shelter;—it is a safe one."[122]

For even Arnold can be forgiven his psychic response to the ruthless aggressions of the American campaign. Rebel soldiers in Bacon's drama chase him and shout "to the death!" with all the purposeful drive of a maniacal mob. Meanwhile André speaks in Shakespearean verse and falls in love with a lady he thinks ("methinks," he says) "the heavenly revelation itself doth that." He wanders the war-torn fields of New York picking forget-me-nots and playing the flute, so inspired is he by his inamorata. Here is André with friend Mortimer overlooking a waterfall and glen:

ANDRÉ: I would have bartered all the glory of this campaign for leave to stretch myself on its mossy bank, for a soft hour or so.

MORTIMER: Ay, with Chaucer or the "faery Queen." If one could people these lovely shades with the fresh creations of the olden time, knight and lady, and dark enchantress and Paynim fierce, instead of Yankee rebel—

ANDRÉ: Twere well your faery-work were of no lasting mould, or these same rebels would scarce thank you for your pains,—they hold that race in little reverence. Alas—

No grot divine, or wood-nymph haunted glen,
or stream, or fount, shall these young shades e'er know.
No beautiful divinity, stealing afar
Through darkling nooks, to poet's eye thence gleam;
With mocking mystery the dim ways wind,
They reach not to the blessed fairy-land

That once all lovely in heaven's stolen light,
To yearning thoughts, in the deep greenwood grew.[123]

In the "daylight broad" of reasoning history, America wins its freedom, but André reminds us that in the shady glens and the sleepy hollows of romance, there is no liberty from the past. Nor should we want there to be: in these narratives of independence, Britain is, to borrow from Arjun Appadurai, "not now a land to return to in a simple politics of memory." The imperial presence may be gone, but it left a historic repository of knights, ladies and fairy queens, and of gentle cavaliers like André to which "recourse can be taken as appropriate."[124] All these cultic English forms, and especially the bygone excesses of chivalric address through which André summons them to the American scene, feel like recourse indeed since Delia Bacon offers them as compensation for the Revolution that would do away with Englishness to begin with. Most of all, these scenes in which André is at his most beautiful—lost in his impromptu—are symbolic restitution for the Revolution that has so rationally sacrificed him.

Because what finally distinguishes André from the respectable and pleasing Hale is the sheer compass of his beauty: "he was," writes one observer, "the handsomest man I ever laid eyes on." Major Benjamin Tallmadge, as custodian of André in the days leading up to his execution, was chief witness to the elusive, transporting experience of beholding the spy: not just André's gorgeous physique, he says, but his genteel deportment, his enlarged understanding, his affability of manners even while walking toward death combined to produce in Americans a longing response uninhibited by the extremities of war. Here is Tallmadge's testimony as it was cited throughout the century: "I became so deeply attached to Major André, that I could remember no instance where my affections were so fully absorbed by any man. When I saw him swing under the gibbet, it seemed for a time utterly unsupportable: all were overwhelmed with the affecting spectacle, and the eyes of many were suffused with tears." But wait: there was also the exciting and charming role André played in the Mischianza, the poems he wrote for *Rivington's Gazette,* his passionate love of society, his good ear and eye for writing songs and taking sketches throughout the American campaign—"not Goldsmith's flute was more useful to its master beside 'the murmuring Loire' than the brush and pencil to André's familiar hand." Tales even describe how André interrupted his military duties to teach the children of Pennsylvania how to draw. Most of all, there was André's indomitable capacity for love: having volunteered for active service to seek solace from the pain of a broken engagement, André tours the colonies in these accounts lovelorn for his Honora Sneyd—whose parents forbid the marriage—and then for almost anything at all that strikes him as worthy and good. He loves other women, and other soldiers, and even an American soldier who becomes his bedfellow when taken as a prisoner of war. He loves the landscape and the sudden intimations of truth he gains from its assertive shapes and forms: "Delectable mountains," writes one novel about André just before he is captured, "gazing at them he forgot for a time his disguise, the perils of his position, the great war which convulsed the land, and thought only of the glory of this wonderful earth." He loves his enemy, too, which is why, accounts say, he fought in a war that sought to preserve America's familiar and intimate connections with Britain: it was, says Sargent, "in the fulfillment of an enterprise that he believed would, if successful, crown him with the honors due to the man who had restored harmony to a divided empire, extinguished the flames of civil war." [125]

Now, whether or not André really was this pretty has little bearing on the remarkable investment that Americans had in proving that he was, over and above any action he took against their national interests. Hence, while an appreciation for Hale or other revolutionary figures could always drift into—or synecdochically become—a patriotic memorializing of independence, the love of André offered the appeal of a simply aesthetic sensation. "The heart of sensibility mourns when a life of so much worth is sacrificed on a gibbet," writes James Thacher in his military journal of the Revolution, published in 1823. How to understand that André is worth more alive than Hale—who history had insisted on valuing for his death—except to say that our pursuit of happiness is better served by having him to behold? If only Hale could die once again for our cause seems the point of immortalizing his last words, "I only regret that I have but one life to lose for my country"— but as the object of longing and desire, André becomes a fascinating keepsake of the Revolution who resists such use-value within the wages of war. [126]

This is at least Benjamin Tallmadge's feeling when in 1817, John Paulding, one of André's three captors, resurfaced to apply for an increased military pension. Tallmadge opposed the bid, claiming that André's captors were crass marauders who could have been bribed if

André had been carrying the funds, but the language he employed insists that the final good of their act—detecting the spy and saving West Point—itself deserves no recompense. Congress, moved by Tallmadge's testimony, denied Paulding's petition, and though this sparked a public debate, in which Paulding's vindicators spoke to his patriotic motives or, in any case, the national benefits of his act whatever his motives, the fact remains: the "rightful" work of detaining a spy on the neutral ground of Westchester forced the nation to choose between the rational transactions of war and "everything that is amiable in virtue, in fortitude, in delicate sentiment, and accomplished manners."[127] A Revolution, in other words, predicated on life, liberty, and individual pursuits had not counted on producing a man whose amiability and beauty gave rise to such an irresistible response that, in the Kantian logic of aesthetic judgment, one could not *not* be moved by his virtues. Even Washington Irving's gangly opportunist, Ichabod Crane, is haunted by the place of André's capture on the lonely roads of Sleepy Hollow: "To pass the bridge was the severest trial. It was at this identical spot that the unfortunate André was captured, and under the covert of those chestnuts and vines were the sturdy yeomen concealed who surprised him."[128] This spot is where the puny connivers of personal gain are reckoned against the romance of André's nobility. Ichabod, fresh from schemes to win Katrina Van Tassel (and the abundant food off her father's farm), approaches the tulip tree with trepidation. As he should, because his own dreams of self-sufficiency are soon lost to the tormenting specters of the revolutionary past in the guise of a Hessian ghost—his head blown away in the violence that finally satisfied the nation's craving for independence. The Headless Horseman may be just another opportunist in disguise (driving Ichabod away from Katrina) but he borrows enough awe from André's consecrated ground to rack the petty individualist with the phantasmagoria of bodies sacrificed to make a country where there is liberty enough to calculate one's returns.

"Independence," says André to an American friend in a novel of the Revolution, "what a delusive word that is. I wonder, Pemberton, that a man of your fine sense can be so deluded by it." Certainly, such uses of André allow nineteenth-century writers to take exception with the legacy of independence along lines made familiar by the work of Richard L. Bushman and others; anxieties about the potential for civil society to degenerate into a "democratic" mode of vulgarity come to the surface almost simultaneously with nationhood. They shape a network of postrevolutionary concerns about the cultural resources America has for rescuing forms and patterns of aristocratic refinement from its recent colonial past, for the allure of civility would always speak to the enduring hold of the forbidden ancient regime within a capitalist society that seemed increasingly less capable of rewarding character and culture. As this fictionalized André argues, "There is at least something noble, refined and glorious in Aristocracies."[129] The historical André offered a much grimmer challenge to American manners in 1821, when the British Consul, James Buchanan, arrived to convey André's remains to Westminister Abbey. Opening the coffin, and finding no indication in the dust and moldering bones that the corpse had been buried in regimentals, Buchanan complained that André's executed body had been rudely stripped of his uniform. His accusation was only one of several that surfaced in the British press claiming American indelicacy in the handling of André's death: others charged George Washington with erecting the gallows insultingly in view of André's prison window, as though to mock the officer with his disgrace; and still others alleged that André had been denied his proper rank and title by being executed as "John Anderson," the nom de guerre under which he was caught. James Thacher published an appeal to Buchanan and the rest, based on both his own observations and on corroborating testimony: the regimentals had not been plundered but respectfully returned to André's servant; the gallows were erected more than a half-mile from the house in which André was confined ("and there was a clump of wood standing between which entirely intercepted the view"). The nervous strain of establishing that Americans, far from violating the honor of André, showed every decency toward the man who they nonetheless dishonorably hanged also registers as an emotional proposition: might there be room to acknowledge the traumatic difficulty of sacrificing the English gentleman to the discipline of our cause, when human instincts inclined us to respect and preserve? Saying how he witnessed the death of André "with emotions of sympathy which will never be obliterated from my mind"—or how Washington's hand trembled as he signed the death warrant—Thacher wants to prove that our protocols were only in compliance with a feeling that we were not yet *at liberty* to violate something so "noble, refined, and glorious."[130]

Our fictional André's words of advice to Pemberton—why would a man of sense be deluded by the idea of independence?—speaks to a language of social attachment that might redress the affective failings of a culture that democratically denied the appeal of traditionary rituals and past structures of belonging. There is something so mischievously ambivalent about the fascination with André and his Mischianza in these stories of the Revolution, for the rediscovered attractions of colonial life come to offer momentary interludes where an always individualized American will to sovereignty may be pleasurably abandoned. Accommodating André in these narratives means making room for fantasies of more ennobling ties, for ideal communities of conduct and sensibility, and for an aestheticized reestablishment of dependence as a defining aspect of the historical enterprise itself. In his essay, "The Epochs and Events of American History, as Suited to the Purposes of Art and Fiction," William Gilmore Simms argues that the best subject in all of American history for a romance is the story of Arnold and André ("the future Shakespeare of our land will seize on the event"). From the obscure "period of twilight" for the British Empire in America, this one insufficiently excavated anecdote of crossed and mysterious allegiances is, for Simms, where America's romance begins. Because the facts of their cases are equivocal, and the archive of their history suggests untold probabilities, we are free to narrativize at will: it may, Simms ventures, not be difficult a hundred years hence, "to make it appear that Arnold was the victim of some great injustice" or that the Revolution is "merely a civil contest between rival parties of the same nation—a dispute involving only the success of contending factions, not principle." (We could even "endow" Arnold with a fetching sister who finally wins the love of André.) In the contradictory record of disputed facts, we have a range of interpretive movement that Simms likens to being on the "neutral ground" of revolutionary Westchester County across which Arnold and André slyly traverse between positions. If, as Cooper writes in *The Spy* (1821), "the neutral ground implies a right to move at pleasure over its territory," then Simms is also navigating pleasurably across the shifting, elusive geography of the colonial divide.[131] What he finds there is what he was looking for—not a settled history of independence but enough curious uncertainty and deficiency of purpose for the pages of any romance. These ambiguous intervals in the recovered matter of the Revolution are where we, Simms's imagined readers, find ourselves insufficiently nationalized; caught in the middle terrain between being the colonists we were and the citizens we are, the self-evidence of independence seems "delusive" indeed.

But as Simms sees it, this desire to be lost within the indeterminate world of colonial loyalties is itself a consequence of the uneven temporality of national experience. We are never thoroughly released from our colonial past, but the idea of our attachment to these anterior moments of history might be assimilated into the national romance. American independence simply feels like the vertiginous capacity to be both nationalistic and nostalgic for our antenational relations—American sympathies for the British, as they are gleaned from the archive, become some of the integral, honest truths of revolutionary separation. For Simms, our generous return to the memory of being subjects is the sign of nothing less than our unfettered liberty to do so: "We have our rights to it," he says in the essay on Arnold. "Their past is ours . . . their Chaucers—their Miltons—their Shakespeares are ours." And later, "The province of the romancer leaves him large liberties of conquest. It is difficult to say what seas shall limit his empire—what mountains arrest his progress—the liberties of conjecture are the liberties of creation." As the romancer in the archive travels the vectors of time and space into the past and over to Britain, his imperious imagination absorbs these antecedent forms into unequivocally national expressions of admiration. Such an emperor of the archive does not bring André to American histories, schoolbooks, or novels as English so much as an Anglicized model of exemplary traits and wished-for demeanors, transposing a foreign icon of the colonial past into a vernacular figure of the national present. These powerfully American incarnations of André suggest, following from Homi Bhabha, that Englishness itself is a belated effect, for only "*after* the traumatic scenario of colonial difference," is such a sense of Englishness codified in the minds of those other cultures that give it imaginative function and force.[132]

The nineteenth-century ardor of attachment to André suggests nothing so much as the way a homogenized assortment of English forms, left over from the imperial rule, enters the reserves of America's own national mythology. I say "homogenized," drawing again on Appadurai, because in these texts the figure of André always manages to call forth for us a miscellany of old English things as if to suggest the fungibility of eighteenth-century British soldiers of the Revolution with the worlds of Chaucer, Milton, and Shakespeare—at least for our purposes here.[133] Our relations to England have been lost, but all the Englishness remains as a stockpile of cultural memories that Americans can improvise on at will. André himself becomes one of these memories—both a figure of the English past and the most useful embodiment of the English past, to be reserved for articulations of ourselves.

In Sarah Orne Jewett's novel, *The Tory Lover,* one character looks to the aftermath of independence from Britain and presumes that "it may be a century before the old sense of dependence and affection can return."[134] It did not take half so long; but it would be a mistake to imagine that the sentiment is consigned in democracy, as it is in the novel, to the reactionary apprehension of elites, because the culture of Major André suggests that these feelings are the legacy of independence itself. Simms tells his readers to put Arnold or André "to use," which is precisely what he proceeds to do with all the liberatory language of free and conquering love. Derek Walcott believes that culture always begins with models there for us to emulate and that these acts of inscription from the center of somewhere else create forms of new consciousness at home. Ned Thomas puts it perfectly: the "colonial neurosis is always to look for approval to some distant centre, and even the protest against this dependent condition is still controlled by that which it reacts against: no reagent is a free agent. But whatever creates a new centre of consciousness is truly liberating, and this is what love does: it endears places to us, surrounds them with an air of glory, creates a centre from which we can look outward, in Donne's phrase 'makes one little roome, an everywhere.' "[135] These nineteenth-century stories of André may give credence to colonial anxieties and the bonds of dependence, but, as Walcott reminds us, when our attachments give rise to the possibilities of expression, love is liberating. Love, in these stories of the fated Major André, is, more precisely, revolutionary.

Loyal Archives and the Reluctance to Rebel

Lydia Maria Child's Revolutionary War novel *The Rebels,* written in 1825 and reprinted in 1850, has one of the more curious scenes of colonial recovery, centered though it is around resistance to the Stamp Act. Lieutenant-Governor Thomas Hutchinson, who appears as "Uncle Hutchinson" (this is ultimately the story of his nephew and adoptive American niece) is the most affable statesman of colonial "loyal town" (Boston), and, while he has been proven to show a certain amount of greed, it manifests itself nicely: his library contains the finest collection of books in the colonies, and bears "the obvious marks of the scholar, the antiquarian, and the man of taste."[136] He has, in fact, such a capacity for "refined pleasure," combining "intellectual vigor with the best affections of the heart"—not to mention a personal correspondence with Oliver Goldsmith—that Henry Osbourne, the most agitating patriot, keeps "forgetting how much he despised" Hutchinson and, as a fan of Goldsmith himself, admiring the "uncommon beauty" of the governor's library, house, and niece. In the novel, Hutchinson's English kinsman, Somerville, comes to Boston and is a dissolute rake, exercising his pleasing tongue to seduce the niece, Lucretia, and Grace, another American girl. But we should not see the novel as a tale of English corruption and American virtue and for the principle reason that, being a colonial story of 1765 that includes the repeal of the Stamp Act as a "national jubilee," all of its characters are and remain English, including Child's fictionalized, and voluble, Samuel Adams.

In fact, if the English fare poorly in the Revolution, it is precisely because, though they may have acquitted themselves well "in the gay reviews, exhibited for royal amusement, in Hyde Park, or on Wimbledon Common," they have actually "never fought with Englishmen." There are only good English and bad English, and Somerville is a particularly good example of the bad: he is fickle, unfaithful, shifting his affections at every turn, from Grace to Lucretia and back, in a thwarted effort to secure his financial "independence." He is, in other words, characteristically *disloyal,* and, like the villainous Colonel Wellmere in Cooper's *The Spy*—a flat-out bigamist with a wife back home—these recreant English can prey well, says Child, on the "unconscious deference" of American girls. Colonel Kit Dillon in Cooper's *The Pilot* (1824), a similar opportunist and foe, is chastised by Americans for his false loyalism: British Colonel Howard, says Katherine Plowden, "is a good and loyal subject, and no rebel. When I asked why [Kit] was not in arms in these stirring times, contending for the prince he loves so much, the colonel answers, that it was not his profession." How dare, these novels seem to ask, the loyalist not be loyal? Like Sedgwick's shifty, seducing Meredith in *The Linwoods,* the problem is never "affectionate" Thomas Hutchinson, or "benevolent" Henry Clinton, or "gay" Lord Howe, or "gallant" Burgoyne, or Cornwallis with his "quiet dignity," but this crooked assortment of trothless libertines who lack the faith to be significantly English.[137]

The fact that, to repeat, there are not bad English, but characters who are badly English informs the sense of Child's Somerville who, in his lack of discipline and self-possession—"Give me," he says, "nature, bold, impetuous, and unrestrained"—sounds more like the intoxicated American mob that storms and desolates Thomas Hutchinson's house in 1765 ("Liberty or death! . . . Hurra! hurra! hurra!") than like any of

Hutchinson's kin. Which brings me to Child's recovery. In describing the mob violence that tears with a "torrent of liberty" and brutal enthusiasm through every furnishing, curtain, plate, and royal portrait, so that all that remained was the decapitated bust of Mary Stuart, she decides to have Lucretia salvage two things: the manuscript of William Hubbard's 1680 *History of New England* and the second volume to Thomas Hutchinson's *History of Massachusetts-Bay*. Hutchinson's *History* had been famously scattered in the violence: Bernard Bailyn tells poignantly how the original manuscript of volume 1 was "savagely" lost in the flames and wreckage along with most of the historical papers Hutchinson had been gathering for years as the basis of a public archive. In Child, the return to the ruined library is a scene of the most melancholy regret for the patriot, Osborne, who keeps passing it that night, and, of course, for Hutchinson himself, who despite his deep "constraint," cries when he looks on the "wreck of that splendid library, which he had been collecting for thirty years."[138] Child is historically accurate in having Lucretia save what there was of Hubbard's work and of the second volume to Hutchinson's *History*: Hutchinson himself had helped pick them out of the wet debris and his manuscript, now in the collections of the Massachusetts Historical Society, still bears the mud stains of Boston's rioting streets. "With an involuntary wish to save something, she caught two rolls of manuscripts, lying on the table": for a novel about "rebels" to concern itself so plainly with the recovery of a loyalist archive would seem, as Child admits herself about this book, "quite too tranquil" for its cause.[139] But the American girl's unwitting compulsion "to save" speaks to its own gesture of defiance amid the mob's destructive fulminations. These are the endangered histories of the Revolution, and Lucretia, like Watson's capricious collector, snatches them at random out of the waste. Both shore up these fragments against the ruins of a Revolution that makes the emergence of national identity into an experience of cultural loss.

Lucretia's act is in keeping with antebellum works of historical preservation that were also attendant on suspicions of loss—on fears, for example, that the remaining curatorial treasures of America's past must now stand in for those manuscripts that had been axed and scattered by the mob or for the dispatches that (collectors would paranoically insist) had been dumped from captured vessels of privateers.[140] "We regret to say," writes Peter Force, "that we have found [colonial records], in some instances, in a lamentable state of deterioration, confusion, and decay;

many important documents and public proceedings appear to be irretrievably lost."[141] From the founding of the first historical society in Massachusetts in 1791, preservationists established at least 110 more by 1860, ninety of which published their proceedings. Historical magazines, often sponsored by these societies, also put newly acquired colonial and revolutionary pamphlets, diaries, correspondence, government papers, and other original documents into print for the first time. (Reading source materials, says the *North American Review,* is the "most delightful of intellectual recreations.")[142] In the 1820s, state governments, at the urging of the historical societies, began the work of compiling their own official records, often appointing a particular state agency or clerk to do so. The decade before, Congress had passed the first Archives Act for protecting government papers, after investigations found them scattered "in attics all over Washington," and in 1859 Congress founded the Public Documents Bureau for housing all past and present government publications. By the 1850s, the Library of Congress had initiated its own systematic collection of American papers, becoming at last an important depository of historical sources, though for decades Jared Sparks had been urging that "a copy of every book and manuscript relating to America" be secured there.[143]

Central to the archival project was the recovery and preservation of loyalist histories. The impulse that brought such accounts into print did not feel the teleological urge to find the origins of the United States in the revolutionary moment. The collectors anticipated the perception of the so-called imperial scholars of the early twentieth century, including Herbert Osgood and Charles McLean, who recognized the parochialism of not fully recognizing the scope of "the British standpoint."[144] In history, says Herder, "all, or nothing, is fortuitous": the loyalists in the archives are variously and vitally American.[145] Their rescue for the nineteenth-century public is premised on the fundamentally sociable idea that, in the distinct community of the colonial past, they count. Here is Charles Kendell Adams in an essay for the *Atlantic Monthly* late in the century:

> One of the erroneous impressions lodged in the popular imagination is the supposed unanimity, or approach to unanimity, with which the Revolution was undertaken; and there is also a popular impression, equally erroneous, that the logical and the constitutional objections to the revolutionary policy were weak and insignificant . . . there has never been

lodged in the popular imagination any adequate impression of the tremendous significance of those who always insisted on calling themselves "Loyalists," but who were early stigmatized by their opponents with the opprobrious epithet of "Tories." . . . It is now fair, however, to presume that we are far enough away from that exciting period to admit, without danger of bodily harm, that there were really two sides to the question as to whether fighting for independence was the more promising of the two policies open to the colonists.[146]

What might not be lodged in the popular mind was at least out there as fact about the Revolution, exposing the belief in the universal march of history to be, as Nietzsche described it, an "all consuming fever." [147] The war had left Americans with these fragments of loyalism; their Revolution was not inevitable but negotiated and contrived in an internal struggle with other Americans. Historians well before Adams betrayed the desire to incorporate them within a more imperial sense of the American self.

In July 1813, John Adams wrote to Thomas Jefferson:

> The Letters of Bernard and Hutchinson, and Oliver and Paxton, etc. were detected and exposed before The Revolution. There are I doubt not, thousands of Letters, now in being, but still concealed, (from their Party to their Friends,) which will, one day see the light. I have wondered for more than thirty Years that so few have appeared: and have constantly expected that a Tory History of the Rise and progress of the Revolution would appear. And wished it. I would give more for it than for Marshall, Gordon, Ramsay and all the rest." [148]

The first sustained and sympathetic account of a loyalist to be published after the Revolution was the biography, journal, and correspondence of Peter Van Schaack, compiled by his son in 1842. An ardent Whig who turned loyalist at the outset of the Revolution, Van Schaack suffered, in the war's few years, the death of his wife, father, and six children, the loss of his business, almost total blindness, persecution by the government (including a court martial) for opposing the war, and finally exile as a refugee to London. "Torn from the nearest and dearest of all human connections," writes Van Schaack in his journal, "by the visitation of Almighty God, and by means of the public troubles of my country, I am now going into the wide world, without friends, without fortune, with the sad remembrance of past happiness, and the gloomy prospect of future adversity." [149]

"It was," says his son Henry, "the arbitrary distinctions of a civil war" that interrupted the relations between Van Schaack and his friends, but their attachments to each other "were based on principles too pure and immutable to be permanently disturbed; and it was evident that on a fit occasion these kindred spirits would reunite the relaxed bonds of personal regard and friendship." The most poignant moments of this book attend on just such reunions as if the Revolution were an artificial barrier to the natural impulse of affections between men. Thus to move past the Revolution against British authority feels much like Jules Michelet's sense of society in the wake of the French Revolution, where the peremptory, social divisions of the ancien regime are exchanged for the expiating effusions of love and fraternity. Loyalist Van Schaack, hoping that partisan politics had not ruined his personal connections, writes to "old friend" John Jay in Paris after the war: "Whether what has passed has altered your opinion of me as *a man,* I own, is a question I could wish to have resolved. The artificial relations introduced by a state of society, may vary, or be dissolved by events and external circumstances; but there are others which nothing but deviation from moral rectitude can, I think, annihilate." John Jay replies: "In the course of the present troubles I have adhered to certain fixed principles, and faithfully obeyed their dictates, without regarding the consequences of such conduct on my friends, my family, or myself; all of whom, however dreadful the thought, I have ever been ready to sacrifice, if necessary, to the public objects in contest. . . . My regard for you, as a good old friend, continued notwithstanding. God knows, that inclination never had a share in any proceedings of mine against you."

Their letters begin as a cautious reacquaintance—such solemn gestures of détente that they mirror Jay's ongoing negotiations for the Treaty of Paris—but they soon fill with unguarded eruptions of intimacy and ease: "You see," writes Jay, "how naturally I slide into the habit of writing as freely as I *used* to speak to you. Ah! my friend, if ever I see New-York again, I expect to meet with 'the shade of many a departed joy.' My heart bleeds to think of it. . . . How is your health?" [150] The relief Van Schaack feels on receiving Jay's letter is just more than our own; because the Revolution has already been demythologized into a sequence of private, emotional trade-offs, we are prepared to be lenient with its principles, particularly when they interfere with the prevailing pathos of Van Schaack's need—and Jay's happy willingness—to resume the tangible pleasures of communication. These are war's interior spaces where the "moral rectitude" of honoring the oath of friendship prevails over public allegiances to moral precepts. "It melted my heart," says Van Schaack of Jay's letter, and "every idea of party distinction or political competition vanished in an instant!" If the ideology of the Revolution claimed that the British government, by its tyrannical enforcement of colonial bonds, had prevented Americans from forming an affectual union among themselves, then here are Americans declaring their perfect friendships. These are the most voluntaristic unions; they have not reconstituted themselves around new ties but sought, as soon as they were free, to pursue again the old ones. Now, says Jay, we can "indulge the effusions of friendship, without reserve and without disguise." [151]

"It is one thing," writes Watson in the *Annals,* "to show the evolution of battles, and it is another thing to show how the casualties and excitements of war affect families and individuals." The microhistorical drive to resurrect the loyalists for allegories of the Revolution as a civil war also seem intent on discovering forms of belonging to America that are not about nationalism per se. The argument pulled from these assembled fragments of journals and letters is that the loyalists are Americans nonetheless for being monarchists because their natural inclinations and familial attachments remain locally bound as such. "Could it be for the sake of Great Britain," writes Van Schaack to Jay, "that I could wish to sacrifice the welfare of my native country? My attachment to her (great indeed as it was) was founded in the relation she stood to America, and the happiness which I conceived America derived from it." Van Schaack is not British, even as a citizen in London; he is a colonially American subject whose longings for British dominance shape a distinctly native act of possession. When Lorenzo Sabine writes, in his 1847 biography of loyalists, that "*mere loyalty should have been forgiven*" at the conclusion of the war, he is thinking of Van Schaack and others whose incalculable desire to preserve their country's oldest traditions and character may have excited their loyalty to begin with. "My heart," Van Schaack continues, "warms whenever our country (I must call it my country) is the subject, and in my separation from it, 'I have dragged at each remove a lengthening chain.'" [152] These refugee sentiments, as they are recovered in the nineteenth century, suggest that American identity is a feeling rooted in historical culture and in the acute nostalgia that attaches itself—like Van Schaack's elastic chain—to a sense of place. For antebellum Americans looking back, such expressions of attachment provide evidence of a decidedly romantic nationalism at the moment of the Revolution, which in turn implies the degree to which these loyalist affections could resonate with nineteenth-century efforts to idealize the experience of one's nation as a higher form of emotionality. This is an unfamiliar aspect of early U.S. identity as we have come to know it and marks a departure from the work of recent historians who argue that a sense of being American takes hold around more abstractly motivated investments in the nation, its political institutions, and its practices of affiliation. Readers in the 1840s were fascinated by the ways in which the patriotism of figures such as Van Schaack obscured, and indeed often contradicted, the very language of U.S. nationalism and political commitment. Thus "Americans" disaffiliated by measure of their political principles—where is *their* rational love of liberty?—are welcomed back on the strength of their devotion to America as their "native" land. The editor of the journal and correspondence of Samuel Curwen, a loyalist refugee and admiralty judge during the war, hopes that by publishing his papers in 1842, he might "exhibit to [Curwen's] countrymen . . . the ardent affection he bore towards his native land." [153]

Sabine's popular *The American Loyalists; or, Biographical Sketches of Adherents to the British Crown in the War of the Revolution* (1847) and *Biographical Sketches of Loyalists* (1864) see the Revolutionary War as part of, what Hayden White might call, a comic plot of American history, in which conflict among Americans is explained away by the appeal to presumed reconciliation in the long run. In Sabine, the evident discord of the Revolution exists to be resolved in redemptive family dramas where the natural affections between loyalists and patriots overcome the arbitrary resentments between them. So the revolutionary "winners" in these sketches are most often identified as the children of "expatriated losers," or else the fathers of unremitting monarchists, and, in any case, Sabine seeks to do *"something for the cause of human brotherhood"* by memorializing their reunions. Sabine takes pains, for example, to tell how John Hancock becomes the beneficiary of the fortune and estate of his Tory uncle Thomas, who was "always on the side of Government." He also makes much of the dramatic reconciliation, after an estrangement of ten years, between Benjamin Franklin and his disaffected son William, last royal governor of New Jersey: "I ought not to blame you," says Franklin to his son, "for differing in sentiment with me in public affairs. . . . Our opinions are not in our power; they are formed and governed much by circumstances, that are often as inexplicable as they are irresistible." [154]

If, as recent historians suggest, the "belittling or ignoring of Loyalists," in the eighteenth century, "left no doubt that the Anglo-American conflict was one of nation against nation"—if the British here trespassed and "usurped"—then Sabine is rather insisting that the Revolution was not a revolt against foreign power but an American civil war. Or an English civil war: "It is difficult to decide," says the *North American Review* of the sketches, "whether the theme of this volume is more peculiarly English or American," and indeed its loyalties are profligate, to Tories, Whigs, even loyalists who are Whigs. We have such a confused prodigality of attachments, such a deep desire to honor, and to revive, in the words of Benjamin Franklin, "the affectionate intercourse that formerly existed," it is difficult, in the end, even to define "American" at all. Except to suggest, as Franklin himself seems to here, that whatever sentiment it names reflects, in any case, a mystery of pure response to dimly perceived circumstances, as thoroughly "inexplicable as they are irresistible." If our political opinions are "not in our power" but, rather, conspiracies of influence and circumstance we can only retrospectively name as matters of volition or belief, it is obviously difficult to hold anyone accountable for one's own—a convenient enough theory of ideology to enable the reconciliation of Franklin and his son. This all comes quite close to Bernard Bailyn's sense that political belief, at the moment of the Revolution, was something of a syndrome to which Americans "indeliberately, half-knowingly" succumbed, despite the rhetoric of the elective use of reason to defend their various positions. Indeed Sabine's interest in the case of Franklin and his son seems finally to attend from a perspective that Bailyn would approve: their renewed relations become exemplary for showing how patriots and loyalists can appear as perfect versions of each other. Their respective differences are essentially dissolved into a larger story of Americans, so swept up in the phenomenality of events that partisan specifics fade away in mutual recognition of the shared experience of belief as such.[155]

What is more, Sabine premises this urge to reclaim loyalist history as part of American history on the forgotten fact that all Americans were once loyalists, including founding fathers, firebrands, and military patriot heroes. In the "historical essay" that opens the *Sketches,* Sabine quotes Washington, Franklin, Adams, Madison, and Jay all professing

their early devotions to both the Crown specifically and the whole ideological megillah of monarchy itself: "the Tories," he boasts, "may be
relieved from the imputation of being the only 'monarchy-men' of the
time." For unless, Sabine suggests, "the sincerity and truthfulness of
some of the most eminent men in our history are directly impeached,"
we must promptly admit that, had American grievances been redressed,
not one of our Continentals would not "have been willing to rescind the
Declaration of Independence, and to forget the past" or to restore, in
the words of James Madison here, "*the Colonial relations to the parent country, as they were previous to the controversy.*" This, Madison continues, "was
the *real* object of *every* class of the people." Indeed, to acquit the bold
claim of these biographical sketches—namely, that all "Loyalists are to
be excused"—Sabine offers many such isolated outtakes of Congressional regret from the recovered letters and journals of its delegates.
Drawing, too, on certain whispered anecdotes (was Hancock obsessed
by coronations?), Sabine offers up a set of Anglicized colonials, midwar,
who we only now know were our first statesmen. "What, eastward of
New York, might have been the dispositions towards England before
the commencement of hostilities, I know not," says Thomas Jefferson in
Sabine, "but *before that* I never heard a whisper of a disposition to separate from Great Britain; *and after that, its possibility was contemplated with
affliction by all.*" "*I never did hear,*" says John Jay, "*an American of any class,
or of any description, express a wish for the independence of the colonies.*" [156]

While this sort of voiced regret for a lost dependence on Britain derives, in part, from an eighteenth-century politics of representation—
one that says that America was good and faithful until the violent imperious offices of the king forced the colonies to rebel—there remains
a shift of affect, if not inference, in antebellum accounts that have
nonetheless retained a prenationalist investment in the Crown. This is
more than to suggest that nineteenth-century historiography sees the
Revolution as an unusually conservative affair, involving no social up-
heaval, no leveling tendencies, and a reticent set of rebels qualmish at
the war they must endure to protect the principles they had inherited
to begin with. The founding fathers in Sabine have a palpable aversion to independence that preserves for their nineteenth-century readers a naive emotionality and imaginable sense of belonging with the
familial embrace of empire. The reluctance to rebel in these histories
is nontheoretical as such, binding Americans together within a traditional or organic community animated by a communal attachment to

the Crown. Such "familial" patriotism, in Tom Nairn's words, is quite different from the nationalism we have come to associate with the late-eighteenth and nineteenth centuries and their populist assertions "from below." [157] Rather, these loyalist histories tend to suppress such democratic aspects of national awakening in a prior language of instinctive, historical feelings for Britain that still evokes a *sense* of equality in the psychic structure that respectfully levels subjects before their king. As loyalist George Chalmers argues in *Introduction to the History of the Revolt of the American Colonies* (1782), which Jared Sparks "discovered" and published for the first time in 1845, the colonists were not inferior to Englishmen because all were equally beholden to Britain's sovereign law. Without any awkward populism, Chalmers recalls for the nineteenth century a consensual and elective national identity articulated by all colonists, like all Englishmen, around the quasi-parental authority of the Crown.[158]

But Chalmers, a Maryland lawyer who escaped to England during the war, also maintained that a rebellious irreverence for the traditions, laws, and institutions of Britain was characteristic of Americans themselves, and Jared Sparks takes issue with the *History* not for its allegiances to Britain but for doubting the colonies' own. So, while Chalmers puts forth his belief that Americans before the Revolution left loyalty to chance—though they everywhere enjoyed the privileges of Englishmen—and that Americans are always inclined to "disobey the edicts of prerogative," his nineteenth-century editor's view of Anglo-American relations is (to use a word of John A. Schutz) considerably more "sunny." Certainly, says Sparks, Chalmers had no real proof of American disloyalty, and to examine the preponderance of newly collected archives on the subject is to see that the colonies had at no time "acted with a direct view to independence, or even meditated schemes for such action, till very near the first conflict of arms which opened the war of the Revolution." The *North American Review* gives this abstract of his argument: "Mr. Sparks has examined the subject with his usual care and ability, and has arrived at the conclusion, that separation from the mother country was not desired by any of the Colonies while hope of redress remained. Such is the opinion of American authorities very generally." [159]

For the lesson of the archive in the nineteenth century was that a measurable colonial affection, which was the bond of union with Britain, could withstand claims by professed nationalists such as Bancroft or scolding loyalists such as Chalmers that the colonies were designed for disobedience. The colonists, in fact, saw few contradictions between their allegiance to Britain and their desire to reform the imperial relationship. As Benson Lossing tells his readers, the delegates to the First Continental Congress looked forward to reconciliation between Great Britain and the colonies, "*so ardently desired by the latter*," and insisted on their loyalty as Englishmen even while petitioning Parliament for a redress of grievances. "To the king," says Lossing, "they expressed their continued devotion to his person." To the people of Great Britain, "they truthfully declared that their acts were wholly defensive; that the charge which had been made against them, of seeking absolute independence, was a malicious slander."

I do not mean to step into debates over whether the Revolution was radical or not as a case in fact and will leave to Gordon Wood, Jon Butler, T. H. Breen, Richard L. Bushman, J. R. Pole, and the others whether prerevolutionary America had been sufficiently "Europeanized" as to retain its deferential character toward the institutions of Britain right up to the moment of war. Butler, for one, would say no, but, even if we believe him, the historiographical insistence in the nineteenth century on the Revolution as a doctrinaire and unpopular war suggests an old-style desire to hold onto the myth of colonial acceptance as long as possible.[160] That is, the indisputable success of independence seems to animate the consciousness of a totemic, sentimental longing for the authority of Britain that is socially conceded only after maturation from a colony to a nation has made such filial piety seem quaint. As Henry Van Schaack writes, "The great body of those who afterwards became the pillars of the Revolution, were slow in coming to that unwelcome conclusion. . . . Indeed, the attachment of the colonies to the mother country, and their solicitude for a continued political connection, notwithstanding all that had taken place, is claimed to have been one of the brightest features in the Revolution which established the independence of these United States."[161]

The archive of empire in America seems to diffuse the weary plots of ministerial aggressions and stolen rights with the familial guarantee that loyalism itself was a revolutionary experience and that the dependence of the colonies on the metropolis could be esteemed—against the counterassertion of nationalism—as "essential" to their happiness. The empire's constrictions can appear rather more sensible, in fact, than the popular, liberatory ferment whose chaotic and unforgiving measures made Britain's lack of egalitarianism seem like the best safeguard of personal freedoms. The nineteenth century could now look back to a Revolution that relied for its success not on the consensus of a deliberating public but on the coercive acts of an insecure Congress and martial law, on the "military dictatorship" of Washington, and on the suspension of personal liberties. Better to be, as Lossing calls it, "*free men* and *loyal subjects*," under the protection of the Crown, than vulnerable to the arbitrary measures of incensed democrats who, denying the love of that state to which they belong, were compelling the colonies into nationhood. Not only, said these loyalists papers, did Congress disarm Americans adverse to independence; it also confiscated their property, dismantled their businesses, and instituted a draft, for which failure to comply meant imprisonment. By the spring of 1778, most states had also enacted loyalty oath statutes requiring voters, officeholders, and all suspect persons to swear allegiance to their state while abjuring loyalty to the king. Thus patriots were made of the threat of poverty, persecution, and banishment, swearing allegiance to America with as much hesitation as the "pausing American loyalist" in Frank Moore's *Diary* who is caught Hamlet-like between the path of least resistance (taking his state oath) and avenging the wrongs to his king:

> To sign, or not to sign? That is the question.
> Whether 'twere better for the honest man
> To sign and so be safe; or to resolve,
> Betide what will, against associations,
> And by retreating shun them.
> To fly—I reck not where: And by that flight, t'escape
> Feathers and tar, and thousand other ills that loyalty is heir to.
> . . . .
> Thus, dread of want makes rebels of us all.[162]

Papers of loyalist refugee Joseph Galloway, published in the mid-nineteenth century, make a similar case: colonists were coerced into rebellion not by the decisive acts of Parliament but by the extreme and arbitrary power of a Congress willing to make use "of every means that art and force could suggest." The transcript of Galloway's examination before the House of Commons in 1779 (during its inquiries into the efficacy of the British campaign) and reprinted for the Seventy-Six Society of Philadelphia (1855), describes at length the unwillingness of Americans to rebel until drafted. Some, he claims, "were even pushed into the field by bayonet." For Galloway, the revolutionary Congress did not signal a more perfect union of virtuous citizens but a fictional consensus arrived at through contrivance and misrepresentation. He tells Parliament, for example, that one of the rebel delegates from New York "was chosen by himself and his clerk only, and that clerk certified to the Congress that he was unanimously appointed!" Indeed, while Galloway's own 1774 *Plan of Union* for a legislative compromise with Britain was defeated in Congress by a vote of five to four, Galloway insists that "many more than four-fifths of the people would prefer Union with Great Britain, on constitutional principles, to that of Independence." [163] Conscious, in fact, that his *Plan* would be agreeable to the people at large if published, Galloway reports that the independent faction of Congress, with much alarm, erased it from the minutes.

It is hard to imagine a more plausible expression of the nineteenth century's investment in such colonial attachments than the reappearance of Benjamin West's *The Cricketeers* (fig. 22). Painted in 1763 but exhibited

FIGURE 22. Benjamin West, *The Cricketeers*, ca. 1763.

at the Pennsylvania Academy of Fine Arts in 1819 and again in 1831, *The Cricketeers* is a group portrait of five young Americans gathered after a game of cricket during their years of studying abroad in England. West depicts the collegians in a moment of repose and reconnection after the contest: whatever the teams had been, the men are now intimately in league. Such corporate connection: hands rest on arms, and arms on legs. At the center of the painting, two dovetailing cricket bats preserve the visual link between the cricketeers where their legs cannot. The figures appear spent, leaning on bats and each other with all the postgame fraternity of a locker room, the one player, second-to-left, holding a sweaty rag and the player he leans on as particularly peaked as the dog that mirrors him at the right. They are all dog-tired, but—insofar as the general legginess of the image suggests, with so many drooping limbs and dropping bats—it is with a playfully homosocial spirit of detumescence. These are colonial boys who have come to the metropolis for their education, entering into forms of sociability that here seem as much an English institution as the cricket game that elicits them or the imagined Cambridge that West paints as a background of columns and the Thames from his studio in London. What makes this painting's popularity compelling in the postrevolutionary United States is neither simply the association of England with knowledge and authority nor its pedagogical inscriptions that seem to mark the passage of these colonial youth into members of a mature Anglo-American fraternity. By the time West's picture was exhibited in 1819, its subjects had lived and died with more famously complex histories: some were patriots and some were loyalists in the Revolutionary War.

There is disagreement over the position of West's sitters, but they are usually identified as, from left to right, Ralph Wormeley, the brothers James Allen and Andrew Allen, Ralph Izard, and Arthur Middleton—five wealthy colonials pursuing their education abroad, the Allen brothers at Middle Temple in London, the rest at Cambridge. Twenty years from the painting of the picture, these players would come to represent the full spectrum of colonial response to the Revolution. Wormeley of Virginia returned to America after Eton and Cambridge to hold British government posts and remained a Tory throughout the war. Andrew Allen of Philadelphia fought in the British army and later fled to London after his property was confiscated; his younger brother, James, retired to the country during the war and died, in 1778, opposing it and "very obnoxious to the independents." Izard settled in

London after his years of schooling but left in protest for Paris in 1776 and finally returned to South Carolina, where he was elected to the Continental Congress. Middleton became a revolutionary in South Carolina, a signer of the declaration, and a member of the Continental Congress; he spent 1780–81, as a British prisoner of war.[164] To look back on this painting from the nineteenth century is to return these loyalists and revolutionaries to a prior scene of fellowship before the politics of war split allegiances and before the demands of a national culture estranged them all from the specifically colonial play of identity we witness here among the pillars, swans and cricket bats of a fabricated Cambridge. Real adversaries had met once on these old English match grounds, where sides as such meant less than the stylistic rituals of sport itself. In focusing not on a game of cricket but its denouement, the painting emphasizes the kind of fellowship that is the more profound accomplishment of a match played well and with a pure investment in the rules of the game. That the painting fails to offer any sign of teams is entirely the point: five Americans have participated in a contest that has been carefully structured and authorized to produce this close community of "cricketeers."

The nineteenth-century viewer stares back on a world that is inscrutable to the politics that overwhelm it: there are no loyalists or rebels yet, only Americans; there is even a future rebel in a red coat (Izard). We see cricket here providing for an early version of a now familiar drama of colonial self-making that, as perhaps best described by C. L. R. James, rehearses English models of acculturation for all the ways in which they finally can express and shape the imaginable rituals of shared experience that are more particular to somewhere else.[165] For James, colonial engagements with such English institutions could animate—even in their most sincere rehearsals—a singularly mobile and adaptable structure of communal feeling among colonials though organized around a mutual deference toward imperial forms. West's painting is no exception: as it travels past the Revolution, the nostalgic return this picture invites to a time of belonging within Britain feels much more nostalgic for a lost community among ourselves. For what else would this fraternity of eventual enemies offer but the chance to indulge in an elegiac fondness for how unified Americans had been, as colonials?

A funny thing happens when reading Benson Lossing's *Pictorial Field-Book of the Revolution*. Designed to follow the progress of Lossing's own itinerary over more than eight thousand miles to record and sketch every last site made memorable by the war, the history unfolds not as a chronology toward independence but as a wayward travelogue through the war's events according to the narrative of his tour. Here, the *fabula* behind the story of the war insists on the superior appeal of Lossing's own journey from one locale to the next, taking in the scenery and last ruins and remnants of the Revolution as they appear to view in graves, forts, or battlegrounds. Traveling from New England to South Carolina then back up to New York, Lossing chronicles the Revolution through the connective record of his journey in a way that, in his words, "necessarily break[s] up the chronological unity of the history, and, at times, produce[s] some confusion."[166] We read of Burgoyne's defeat and return to England before we read of his march up Lake Champlain; Cornwallis surrenders at Yorktown 300 pages before he happens to take over New York. Thus following Lossing's history of the Revolution through the particularity of places that animate the war as a series of individual anecdotes, impressions, ties, and conversations has the disorienting effect of securing independence and then retreating from it, abetting the course of history, then backtracking. The progress of the Revolution matters less than the pleasures pursued by such personal reconstructions of it; in Lossing's hands the events of war are dealt out as whimsically as they are in the contemporary *Game of '76* that leaves the fate of independence to every contingency of a card game (fig. 23). The moments of war are so shuffled as to make us look again at whether we must always end up with independence.

Women Folks Are Natural Tories: Love in the Age of Revolution

"I think I may safely say that more than half the men will refuse to take a part against the King."
   "And all the women."
   "True, and their influence is something."
—J. B. Jones, *The Monarchist: An Historical Novel* (1853)[167]

What if Burgoyne arrives safely in Albany, asks a soldier in Bacon's *The Bride of Fort Edward*, "And what becomes of us all then? We shall go back to the old times again, I suppose; weren't so very bad though, Sam, were they?" Oh no, says Sam, "we have seen worse, I'll own." In Bacon's play, a fictionalized story of Jane McCrea in Shakespearean verse, the Revolution is the end of love and romance. The war has separated Helen Grey from her Tory lover, an officer in Burgoyne's army, and on her way to meet him, she is killed by Indians in the woods; her lover,

FIGURE 23. Cards from the *Game of '76*, ca. 1840. Courtesy of American Antiquarian Society.

Edward Maitland, finding her dead, with her long golden hair "dreaming heavily on her mantle," goes mad. The actual death of Jane McCrea was a celebrated atrocity of the Revolution: it helped to articulate anti-British sentiment by publicizing the reported brutality of collaborating Indians employed by British in the war. But Bacon's work need not be craven. It is an elegiac closet play about an American woman and her dashing, versifying loyalist lover who are prevented from marrying. The Revolution has interfered with ties "which the war cannot undo," and, as an absurdly present Major André (he was nowhere near McCrea) narrates from the side (when not busy sketching), "This was Love." For as André sings out in part awe and part lament, the America that the Revolution would ineluctably bring forth "shall make Romance a forgotten world."[168]

In the eighteenth century, the story of Jane McCrea was circulated as evidence of the depraved character of Burgoyne, whose alliance with the Indians seemed to sanction the brutal scalping of the young bride on the way to her nuptials. The facts were these: on July 27, 1777, as the armies of Burgoyne and his Indian mercenaries were pressing south through New York, Jane McCrea was killed on her passage from Fort Edward to the British camp to meet her intended, David Jones. There were some doubts as to whether Jones had sent the Indians to escort her, but whether it was due to an altercation among Indian parties over a reward for her deliverance or to an act of premeditated barbarity, McCrea's scalp was returned to Jones who flew to the scene of the crime and recovered the bleeding body. General Gates, in a widely publicized letter to Burgoyne, puts McCrea apocryphally in her wedding dress as she met "her murderers employed by you": this is not simply the tale of a reckless British alliance with savages, who are paid for scalps in gold, but of Burgoyne's tyrannical intervention in the betrothal of two people who would love across enemy lines. For, as Jay Fliegelman points out, the death of Jane McCrea could be rehearsed as an assault on romantic love by the abuses of paternal authority, a theme familiar enough to American audiences from sentimental fiction and a theme symbolically linked to the predations suffered by the colonies at the hands of their parent country. Burgoyne's savage emissaries could stand in for the British threat to all voluntaristic unions, including that of thirteen colonies with the most affectual hopes of uniting themselves.[169]

But the nineteenth century has its way of forgiving Burgoyne. Corrective accounts describe the betrayal of Burgoyne by the Indians, who were unable "to regulate their passions," despite Burgoyne's refusal to pay for scalps and despite his effort to forbid bloodshed outside of open warfare. Burgoyne's fatal error, writes one historian, "sprung from an overweening confidence in his own influence—an influence he vainly flattered himself was sufficiently powerful to restrain the ferocious spirit of the savage, within the limit of civilized humanity." After all, Burgoyne had explained to his Indian allies the difference between a war waged against a hostile nation and the present conflict in which "the faithful were intermixed with the rebels, and traitors with friends."

Burgoyne had warned the Indians, in a speech that historians like to cite, that in a civil war between gentlemen indiscriminate violence was not only inhumane warfare but risked sacrificing friends and loyal subjects. Burgoyne was only guilty of trusting in the honor of the Iroquois who had pledged their compliance with the rules of war and moreover their affections for the paternal embrace of the empire: "I stand up," said one Indian chief, "in the name of all the nations present, to assure our father that we have attentively listened to his discourse. We receive you as our father, because when you speak we hear the voice of our great father beyond the great lake . . . our hatchets have been sharpened upon our affections."[170] The death of Jane McCrea, then, was not the story of a cruel father denying his loyal (Tory) child her nuptial rites but the story of a virtuous father cruelly forsaken by his rebellious charges. The Iroquois's promises to the British, writes Benson Lossing, "were all very fine, and Burgoyne, to his sorrow, had the credulity to rely on them. At first the Indians were docile, but . . . their faithfulness disappeared; and in the hour of his greatest need they deserted him."[171]

Or not: still other accounts vindicate Burgoyne by attributing the death of Jane McCrea not to the brutality of his Indian allies but to the errant bullets of American rebels who attacked the Indians on their way to the British camp. While the popular legend of McCrea's death, as told by George Bancroft, for example, has her killed by quarreling Indians with a tomahawk, "the actual circumstances of the case," writes William Stone, "stripped of its romance" and corroborated by "veracious and industrious" historians, are considerably different.[172] They suggest that McCrea and her loyalist chaperone, a Mrs. McNeil, were forcibly taken from their house by the Wyandot Indians who sought payment from the British for their delivery. Nearly overtaken by a detachment of American soldiers, McCrea was fatally hit by crossfire from the pursuing party and only later scalped by her guide, the Wyandot Panther, in revenge for the lost reward given by Burgoyne for any white prisoner. So while McCrea's body was found slain, scalped, and tied to a pine tree, that tree remained (until it was chopped down in 1853 and converted into McCrea souvenirs—canes, boxes, etc.) thickly scarred by bullets in evidence of a skirmish whose witnesses included Mrs. McNeil after she was ransomed and taken to the British camp.[173] That McCrea was likely killed by American gunfire and not a tomahawk or scalping knife was also confirmed by members of her burial party, who testified to three bullet wounds on her corpse, and by a surgeon years later who, during the disinterment and removal of her remains to the cemetery at Fort Edward, saw no sign of gashes to her skull.[174]

From the story of a brutal scalping that justifies independence, the legend of Jane McCrea becomes about the melancholic fact of independence in which the pursuit of the Indians by the rebels prevented the consummation of loyal affections. The woman-at-risk in these versions of the tale does not want to be freed, but with the compulsive longing to be, like the Jane-figure in Bacon's drama, "his wife, his wife, *his*," renounces the cause of liberty: "Let the big cause of right and freedom, whose sad banner, now, on yonder hill, floats in this summer air . . . let it prevail—though *I*, with all this sensitive, warm, shrinking life; with all this new-found wealth of love and hope, lie on its iron way."[175] No longer an allegory of the Revolution, McCrea's death becomes a folkloric reminder of a colonial loss. The surfeit of sentiment that surrounds her murder attaches itself to the social practices of souvenir hunting or the visits to her grave, but the tragic point of such remembering is more intimate than civic. The loss of love in the tale is functionally ambivalent except to say that youth and innocence were sacrificed to the object of war, while this object is so remote we have trouble recalling it. The death in these accounts no more justifies the act of warring than the deaths of Romeo and Juliet; what had been symbolic of nations becomes the diminished partisanship of two families that the lesson of love transcends. Jane's fiancé, says D. Wilson in 1852, "depicted the peaceful times that would ensue—a return of the happy days when husbandmen were singing in the fields, and before the voices of love were drowned by the bitter clamor of contention. The feud that had sprung up between members of their families would then cease. Then—ran the current of their hopes—old friends would unite over the graves of forgotten animosities, and the spirit of good fellowship would return with their allegiance to a lawful king."[176]

In Wilson's biography of McCrea, it is not Burgoyne who interferes but Jane's zealous brother, John, a colonel in the American army, who objects to the marriage and who hopes to separate the lovers by taking Jane south with him on the American campaign. John's "laborious toil" for independence is set against Love itself, which gets characteristically allegorized as this account proceeds, as in Wilson's remark that "it was Love's reinforcement" that sends Jane to Jones. While John McCrea "would rather that the bones of the young lieutenant [Jones]

should bleach within the dank recesses" of the wilderness that separated the British from the colonials, Jane "would have smoothed a
pathway through it with her own hands, if it would have led him safely
to her side." For his part, and in response to the "violent animosity"
of Jane's brother, which threatened to "tear asunder all those endearing ties which so long had bound [the lovers] fondly and affectionately
together," Jones suggests they marry at once, the logic of which makes
John's "rebellious obstinacy" responsible for Jane's fateful trip through
the woods. "In the heart of the maiden," continues Wilson, "there was
a contest between duty and affection. . . . Should she fly to the protection of her lover, she would forfeit the affection of one who, for years,
had treated her with more than fraternal kindness; should she depart
southward with her kindred, the sweet dream of her youth would never
be realized."[177] That Jane yields "to the voice that was pleading in her
heart" is in keeping with the volunteerism of the eighteenth-century
legend, only now her choice speaks to the romantic appeal of British
love over the responsibilities of American allegiance. Jane's "duty" and
"affection" effectively reverse the moral of the tale: on the one side
are the pressures of the cause of independence and, on the other, the
courtship of "a faithful subject" in the "ranks of his lawful king." On
one side is the tyrannical fraternity that is the signature affect of revolutionary nationalism. On the other is a great chain of belonging that
would place Jane under the protection of her loyal lover whose own
ties to the king suggest more personal sources of feeling. From the insistence on fraternal bonds, Jane dreams of refuge in the British camp
where Jones's promise of romance emerges as a politics of return to the
absorptive dependencies of the empire.

Jane's remains were moved twice in the early nineteenth century:
first, in 1822, for a proper burial in the town cemetery and, again, in
1851, to a less disclosed location after the pilfering of her bones and
the chipping of her headstone by souvenir seekers. Of the first occasion, Jared Sparks recalls, "The ceremony was solemn and impressive.
A procession of young men and maidens followed the relics, and wept
in silence when the earth was again closed over them."[178] Even after her
remains are secured, the pine tree that marks the site of her death provides the materials for the manufacture of still more keepsakes; to the
degree that all such souvenirs, as Susan Stewart reminds us, replace the
meaning of the original occurrence with the ritual of "perpetual con-
sumption," the specific historical content of McCrea's death becomes

a grandly generic occasion for sentiment and melancholy. Thus each cane and box made from what Lossing calls "the patriarchal pine" rehearses a repression of colonial trauma through a language of longing. What had served as a call for revolutionary action becomes a token of lost relations. The "patriarchal" tree has fallen but only to make possible the ownership of such lost icons as the private gratifications of kitsch. A political allegory of rights denied by tyranny is remembered as a romance of love denied by politics, and what gets increasingly displaced in the transition is an argument for the Revolution itself. This is perhaps why the anecdote of the events comes to focus finally on the derangement of David Jones, whose madness on recovering Jane's decaying body ("[bending] over her mangled remains") demands a carefully maintained oblivion to the war that caused it. Wilson tells us that Jones's mind "seemed to be wandering and lost; he was not himself," and from that time forward, "his friends were careful to avoid any allusion . . . to the incidents of the Revolution." [179]

The historical investment in Jane McCrea does not so much renounce the Revolution as suggest that its legacy is most powerfully felt at a distance from its politics. The claims of this investment are smaller than the grand-style applications of her death by the colonial propagandists, which is only to say that they prophesize little on the Revolution itself. If this does not entirely constitute what Ann Douglas would call an "apostasy from history," it at least releases the moment of Jane's death from the inscriptions of more romantic histories in order to operate with a degree of abandon. [180] The antiquarianism that gives us, for example, John McCrea's ultimatum to Jane is wholly gratuitous. It is also an instance of the kind of historicizing in this period that Douglas describes as a temporary turn from national events to more local moments of social interest. The death that had once changed the course of history is now a melancholy tale of lost attachments that made little happen but lets us indulge in the therapeutic return to the breadth of emotions it puts impertinently on display. Such, for Douglas, is the "feminization of American history," though I quibble with her claim that the rise of domestic or private histories over national ones is the work of women and the clergy (as she insists) since the demographic of guilty antiquarians is as wide as their range in this chapter. Well beyond the legend of Jane McCrea, we might take enough from Douglas to suggest that all the acts of historicizing we have looked at thus far, including the reconstruction of battles and military victories, redeem just the smallest, most intimate contingencies of the past that allow for feminized rituals of compassion. The dialectics of progress, all the collisions of achievement and force that change the past into the present, are suspended in the pious attention to private moments of love and loss. Only Douglas does not say "suspended," she says, "fossilized, weakened." While the romantic historians chart the rise and speed of liberty through the ambitions of great men, the mementos of the past that the antiquarians bring forth are not interested in change. So we go down the slippery slope of feminization, where the excitements of progress give way to the ceremonial revisiting of relics, and where history itself gets stuck in the local feelings that it comes to elicit on the page.

But to measure the meaning of this affective historiography, we might look again at what the antiquarian investment in Jane McCrea—and, by extension, the larger realm of sundered bonds and ruined feelings she embodies—makes possible for the nineteenth century, and for the men and women who recounted her story and those of women like her, in such particular detail. In this regard, Douglas's emphasis on historical evasiveness may well obscure the more tortured dialectic between national imperatives and emotive universals that these sometimes maudlin recoveries of revolutionary women entail. These are stories in which appeal to the private and domestic as a register of higher feelings is not so much a timid backsliding from the demands of history as an overt and entirely self-conscious argument against the demands of American history as such. And if this seems only like a disagreement with Douglas over nuance, I would suggest that it is precisely the importance of the nuanced and trivial gesture that this dimension of revolutionary historiography salvages. We see not just a "separate sphere" of feminized experience as constructed and maintained by domestic ideology; we see an attempt to use this structure of experience to reckon with a profound sense of separation between antebellum America and its colonial and revolutionary past. The attraction to an archive of individual trauma and personalized response speaks to the way that women's isolation from, and resistance to, the inevitability of historical progress provides something of an allegory for the historian's own immersion in a world of social textures, minor details, and past forms that are far more abandoned by the course of history than they are implicated within it. But this is the true measure of their resonance: they suggest that there is a felt devotion to the historical that may never be relevant to the logic of national destiny.

That women make this devotion possible is, to be sure, a reflection of their assumed remove from the politics of the nation's founding. Yet it is just as much the case that the partisan politics of the moment are figured as troubling enough to make us respect this remove. "You must not begin to talk politics," says Lucretia in *The Rebels* to the patriot Osborne, warning him to behave on an outing with Thomas Hutchinson. "Give to the winds your political differences," says Isabella Linwood to her Tory father of her rebel brother, "and leave the war to camp and field." [181] Outside the principles of the conflict, the women of these narratives are at liberty to obey the allegiances of their hearts, which is to say, they put on display an enabling incapacity to resist. "Thank God," says Aunt Archer to Isabella Linwood, "we womankind are exempts— not called upon to take sides." So it is not surprising that women in accounts of the war are given a great license to love the enemy and are then celebrated, like Jane McCrea, for their reflexive impulse to love. This is made considerably easier by the terrific fact of mobility that women enjoyed during the war and that rarely goes unnoticed in the stories about them. Freedom from the weight and content of war meant freedom to travel with impunity, between camps and men, to shop, trade, give care, and mostly bestow their affections. As Lossing writes, "While every [British] man who went to the river for water became a target for the sure marksmen of Americans, a soldier's wife went back and forth as often as she pleased." [182]

Such liberty of movement, the freedom to engage multiply on both sides of the conflict, can seem a very literal way of rendering the character of sociability itself in Simmel's terms. The capacity to move between positions with no consequence, to accommodate all parties and commit to none, while prioritizing the functional play of relations that such indifference permits is what women do and what sociability is. Simmel analogizes such sociability to the female practice of coquetry which perhaps helps us to explain why coquetry is so often rewarded in these revolutionary tales. It is not simply that the stories put no probation on anticipated pleasures: the women who fill the pavilions of the Mischianza and let the British fight in their honor dally with all amnesty across enemy lines. (It was natural, writes Winthrop Sargent, for "many, particularly of the softer sex, to look back with real regrets to the pleasant days, the festive nights that prevailed during the British occupation.") It is also quite usual for the most free and wanton pursuits of desire to end happily. Take one story from Frank Moore's

Diary of the American Revolution: "A young lady, having forsaken her father's house in Wales, in the beginning of the American war, leaving
only a letter behind her to bid them be assured her honor and her
life should be secure in her own care, followed her lover (a cornet of
horse) to whom she engaged herself privately, during his recruiting in
the town in which she lived. She married him the hour she arrived at
New York, where his regiment was at the time."[183] How different from
the most exemplary stories of women-at-risk just after the Revolution.
Susanna Rowson's *Charlotte Temple* forsakes her father's house in England to follow her lover (an officer in the army) on his tour of duty
to America; when she arrives in New York she is abandoned and dies,
while giving birth to a child out of wedlock. Thus these later stories,
including Moore's, turn a cautionary tale about a dangerous latitude of
affections into a celebration of love's most wayward tendencies. If the
British officer had been a rake, he is now an ideal husband who honors
the heroine's risk by ratifying it as proper form. And these undoings of
Rowson's tale mark not only a thematic rewiring of the revolutionary
romance but also a historiographical intervention in the nineteenth
century's understanding of its colonial affairs, as the preface to one
novel makes clear:

> In strolling about what is at present the most fashionable part of our city
> . . . one sees but little to recall the scene of former days, when the fash-
> ionable of both sexes resorted hither to enjoy the freshness of the sum-
> mer breeze, and to tell or listen to tales of love. It was however during
> the scene of our revolutionary struggle, when the enemy was quartered
> within this then infant city, that this part of the lovely island of Manhat-
> tan, became the scene of many a love adventure, that have long since
> passed into oblivion, while others like the mournful tale of Charlotte
> Temple still survive the reak [*sic*] of time."[184]

In James Heath's novel of independence, *Edge-Hill* (1828), a staunch
royalist tells his rebellious son that he should "attach himself more to
female society, and less to revolutionary doctrines."[185] While his strategy is one of diversion—why not transfer your passions from the cause
to a woman?—it indicates the degree to which these texts treat radical politics and romantic entanglements at cross purposes. It is neither
simply that courtship plots require departures from the male sphere
where partisan positions are held nor that they involve attractions more
tangible than the talk of rights and liberty. Women come to represent

the deeper pleasures of fidelity as both an abstract principle and a social practice; they are at once the agents by which the work of loyalty goes on amid the Revolution and the model for a network of attachments that, though ostensibly apolitical, are quite readily described as conservative to a fault. Loyalty is troped through images of domestic love with a logic suggesting that women retain the predilection for dependence that the Revolution otherwise tests. So while the most ardent rebel in Revolutionary War novels almost never marries—the mad Ralph and Job Prey in Cooper's *Lionel Lincoln* (1825) or Harvey Birch in Cooper's *The Spy*—the woman not only pursues romance but makes a "very obedient wife." She marries, into whichever side of the conflict, and "yielding allegiance," like Cooper's Katharine Plowden in *The Pilot*, "adheres with instinctive dependence to the side of her lover." Thus William Gilmore Simms's calls a running header in his novel, *The Partisan*, "The Loyalty of Women."[186]

"Women folks is natural Tories [*sic*]," says old Mr. Philpot in Sarah Orne Jewett's *The Tory Lover*.[187] He means to suggest that women are predisposed to do those very things—respond adoringly to hierarchy, defer to power, subordinate their wills to the larger social order—that would map a very explicit politics, if not the doings of women. But because such inclinations reflect a "natural" psychology of gender and not an ideology, the Tory leanings that women characters indulge are met (even in narratives aligned with the cause of independence) with responses that range from gentle, temporizing irony to impassioned approval. The character of loyalty in revolutionary America is not explained away by projecting it onto women and their sphere but relished as something apart from the appeal of independence. Cooper's Katherine Plowden or Jane McCrea become surrogates for a fugitive structure of political feeling that allows postrevolutionary Americans to cherish a Tory aesthetic without claiming it.

The same can be said for Lady Harriet Ackland, whose melodramatic journey to the American camp to care for her imprisoned and wounded husband, Major Ackland—at night in an open boat in the rain—becomes iconographically central to such reinvestments in loyalty. That a lady of delicate form, and rank and fortune, would "brave the darkness of night and the drenching rain for many hours, and to deliver herself to the enemy," was an act of connubial devotion that, Elizabeth Ellet writes, "touched the feelings of the Americans, and won the admiration of all who heard her story." A popular print of Lady Ackland shows her en route to the camp of General Gates accompanied

FIGURE 24. Martin Johnson, after Alonzo Chappel, *Lady Ackland's Visit to the Camp of General Gates,* 1857, engraving.

by a British chaplain, her waiting maid, and Major Ackland's valet, who had been wounded in the search for his master when he disappeared from the battlefield (fig. 24). To this foursome, the image adds a small dog, likely the invention of painter Alonzo Chappel, but altogether appropriate for the thematics surrounding Lady Ackland's passage: it makes clear, as only a bit of symbolic redundancy can, that the emphasis is squarely on fidelity, with all the figures defined by their subservience, whether wife or pet, a servant of the Lord or a servant of the major. The composure of Lady Ackland and her maid on the choppy waters of the Hudson—for which the dog's calm demeanor is both rhyme and proof—is one more index of the beatifying steadfastness that the anecdote enshrines as a counterpoint to revolutionary turbulence.

In the anecdote of Lady Ackland, an idealized language of marital relations and a disavowed language of political identity not only meet but become decidedly confused. It is not the possibility of such confusion, but its certainty that patterns the way that women are commemorated for "the shining virtues of connubial constancy, heroic devotion, and unbending fortitude."[188] If these are taken only as the defining attributes of the bond between a British wife and her British husband during the Revolution, then the explanation of their attraction for nineteenth-century Americans must at least reckon with the oddity of going so far afield to celebrate what is entirely conventional. But to the degree that such historicizing rediscovers figures capable of moving freely between the conflicting sides—and to treat these figures as "newly" emblematic of a revolutionary moment that has been insufficiently remembered—no one makes more sense than Lady Ackland. Her fateful crossing from the British to the American side of the Hudson takes place on the very "no man's land" it metaphorically suggests.

The women at the center of this project remain devoted with a "constancy" that is hard to incorporate within the governing ideology of Revolution. It is Jefferson, after all, who insists, in his draft of the declaration, that "manly spirit bids us to renounce forever these unfeeling brethren." But in offering a language of domestic affections as a language of loyalism, women speak for a love of Britain that dare not speak its name. The connection between love and loyalty, in these tales, is so involved that even love between confirmed patriots (patriots who marry patriots) is often mediated through an understanding of the way we submit to our devotions. One cannot help feeling, for example, the pull of loyalism in Aunt Archer's concept of being "in love" (as she reflects on Isabella Linwood):

> Belle thinks and feels independently. No woman in the unimpaired perfection and intensity of love does this. Milton understood our nature best when he put those words of dependence and tenderness into Eve's mouth:
> God is thy law, thou mine: to know no more,
> Is woman's happiest knowledge, and her praise.

All in all, a fitting psychology of feminine devotion for a novel of independence that concludes by making a case—to our great surprise—against the "unscriptural doctrine of divorce."[189]

CHAPTER THREE

Freedom and Deference

Society, Antislavery, and Black Intellectualism

In the summer of 1848, English patrons offered Alexander Crummell, then pastor of New York's Church of the Messiah, the opportunity to pursue a university education abroad, in a grand though by no means isolated gesture of British support for black abolitionists. Crummell's choice seems to have inspired some excruciating deliberation, especially in a long letter he writes to white antislavery partisan John Jay, a letter structured as a numbered dialectical exercise, four points in favor of the offer and two against. Would years in England make Crummell more useful to the abolitionist cause in America? It is an elaborately choreographed show of argument and disputation, before Crummell decides that, since "there is not a learned black minister in the whole U.S.," the potential benefits—"to myself, my people, & my race"—practically demand an extended stay abroad. I find one of Crummell's arguments to Jay particularly compelling, not just because it reminds us of abolition's transatlantic scope but because it reveals an anxious and adoring language of national wanting that suggests a much wider phenomenon of response to Great Britain. "You know," Crummell explains: "the *English English* universities are superior to our colleges. An English degree is of great value in America. Shd. I prove a faithful student and pass honorably through an English University . . . would not the learning of an English University in my own person and an English University degree, place me in a position among American Clergymen, wh. wd. shame contempt, neutralize caste—yea even command respect & consideration?"[1]

In so making his case for an "English English" education, Crummell suggests that Britain's place in American antislavery was not just as a provider of sanctuary and capital but also as a repository of less tangible, more imaginary contributions—contributions that are political only by way of a peculiar and involving fascination with "Englishness" itself. "English English," as opposed to what? Wouldn't just "English"—since "our colleges" are not—do? Crummell appears to be after some quality of English national identity that is best stated in the form of a national *identity*, strictly speaking; the education he receives will be somehow more English than English and, at the same time, grant him a transitive status back home, a new "position" derived from whatever comes to be most closely associated with England as Americans imagine it. This is not England but some pure essence of England, and the echoic moment of sheer, elicitory English—of Englishy English—indulges with the same considerable relish as Julian Barnes's *England, England,* an eponymous theme park in which Big Ben is next to Stonehenge in a moat full of sheep.[2] Crummell, that is, evokes a curiously augmented England—an England with all the attributes of England (dons and gowns, sociability and conversation, tradition and status)—and it is perhaps difficult to understand how just such a class-ridden mix is supposed to "neutralize caste" back home. We ought not be surprised that Crummell's editors gloss this reduplication with an apologetic "*sic,*" as if what we have here is only an instance of semantic prattle, to recall Roland Barthes, and not a canny play to the strictly national insecurity Crummell assumes on his correspondent's behalf. That Jay, just two generations removed from the founding fathers, must implicitly know the social and political "value" of a wholly "English University degree," shows the measure to which nineteenth-century Americans could devote themselves to fantasies of an idealized England that retained an unlikely sense of national priority in the years after independence, despite skirmishes over geopolitical turf, and despite the more usual claims of American nationalism. That Crummell's Cambridge education might possess the power to "shame"—"yea even command respect & consideration"—in America at least begins to uncover what the black abolitionist abroad had to gain from the "English English."

I want to look closely at the "England" that figures prominently in abolitionist discourse, an England shaped as much by the material conditions of antislavery politics—by the fact, for example, that British abolitionists helped organized and finance the movement—as by the compulsive patternings and devotional respects of what I can only call American Anglophilia. Thus I examine how an extreme regard for England made some of the material conditions—the singing of anthems for West Indian emancipation, the soliciting of nobles for moral leverage and funds, the London Antislavery Convention, antislavery fairs and bazaars—into eminently pleasurable activities for a great many abolitionists, both black and white. My concern is with the ways such an Anglophilia underwrote the American antislavery movement as both an ideological mission and a cultural project and, at the same time, supplied abolitionists with an available symbology of a country worth emulating, far beyond the mere adoption of emancipationist politics.

The Importance of Being English

Of all the transatlantic attachments in *Frederick Douglass' Paper* only some seem unlikely, but it is these I am concerned with here. That Britain figures prominently in the black abolitionist press makes a great deal of sense: the primary historical example of emancipation in practice, Britain was essential to the antislavery cause in America and at once a political refuge, financial resource, and ready audience for slave narratives on stage and in print. What surprises about the black disposition toward England is the extravagant fixation on aspects of British culture far removed from, and far surpassing, the political imperatives of abolition itself. To pay Wilberforce homage, to give lectures in Leeds—these were customary, if not requisite features of abolitionism; to acknowledge the fine points of petticoats at Queen Victoria's Birthday Drawing Room—"the Duchess of Kent wore white satin trimmed with gold and white blonde and tulle"—to seek out the very spot in Holyrood House "where Mary, Queen of Scots, stood when *she was married to Bothwell*" is altogether something else.[3] And to profess a collective nostalgia for an old English homeland on behalf of African-American ex-slaves, as the following does in 1852, is, historically speaking, just short of absurd:

> So numerous have become the descriptions of England, that the peculiar features of its scenery, its cottage-homes, its parks and hedge-rows, its palaces and mouldering abbeys are familiar as daily sights to many of us who have never left our hearth-stones. We should know St. Paul's at a glance, and could find our way at once in Westminster Abbey to the spot where the 'sweet swan of Avon,' and 'rare Ben Johnson' sleep their last dreamless sleep. Yet we cherish in our hearts so warm a love for our beautiful mother country that we do not weary of the 'oft told tale'; and

we like to hear about her palaces and monuments, her wealth and her poverty, her Queen and her great men nonetheless, because the white cliffs of old Albion have never greeted our eyes.[4]

What is perhaps most striking about this passage in *Frederick Douglass' Paper* is its impossible location of African American national origins in the land of Shakespeare and Victoria. We might call the dissonant history and fantastic geography this passage imagines, following Paul Gilroy, something of a "black Atlantic" in Wonderland, for it carries a sense of identity-in-transit between Africa, England, and the Americas forward to the radical conclusion that the diaspora of slavery has tragically removed blacks from the world of England that is, after all, their maternal inheritance and birthright.[5] This fantasy of virtually English African Americans is both phantasmagoric yet strangely concrete, a travesty of historical logic phrased in a language of precise detail, particular observation, and carefully sounded dialect—"oft told tale." What is more, this fantasy indexes a much larger body of texts and practices in antebellum America that discovered the central meanings of black intellectual experience in "old Albion," a land of cricket, liveries, and lords, with aristocrats vying with abolitionists as the main population of interest. In a paper produced largely by African Americans, an attempt to engender sentiment for Dover's "white cliffs," an image not without a certain racialized coloring, appears at first glance so bizarre as to be almost certainly an aberration. Yet we find similar sentiments expressed by such figures as Frederick Douglass, William Wells Brown, Samuel Ringgold Ward, and Crummell, of which only Crummell's extreme attachment to England may be explained away as the product of his Cambridge education. Even in Crummell we get a sense that England's supreme fascination outstrips whatever material advantages it offered to American blacks seeking higher education and social mobility in the nineteenth century. So I suggest below that the imagined "England" of the abolitionist press and the travel narratives of ex-slaves is only partially defined as a place "cherished" for those reasons we might expect and often more cogently as a wider field within which African Americans could operate in ways *not* circumscribed by the project of abolition. My hope is to understand better the networks of national ideology and cultural style that tightly linked a preoccupation with England to the emerging category of the "black intellectual"; and to point out, in the meantime, just how this fixation was part of a larger national devotion that patterned an astonishing degree of cultural life in the antebellum United States, including the cultural life of a great many "Americans" whose "beautiful mother country" was quite pointedly not Great Britain.[6]

Let me begin, then, by saying that Anglophilia was alive and well in black abolitionist culture; sex and ancestry made little difference, nor did it matter if one was a Garrisonian or an anti-Garrisonian at a time when "English society" would be described, by at least one ex-slave, as "perfectly captivating."[7] Anglophilia lurks in the interstices of black journals and black speeches; between fears of Anglo-Saxon racialism and British "neutrality," it is uncannily transmitted, like the spirit of Byron in William Wells Brown, even (and this is the heart of it) when British economic interests meant closer sympathy with the South. Indeed, while abolitionists protested not just Britain's traffic in slave-grown cotton, but its own labor practices as a form of "wage slavery" (with poverty and dispossession for the Irish especially), there remains, throughout the black press, an unflappably Anglophilic conceit. This amounts not only to swoonings over Kenilworth Castle and Windsor Palace, to articles in *The Colored American* about "our" Lady Jane Grey, or lavish apostrophes to Charlotte Bronte's dead father.[8] Nor is it limited to lengthy extracts in Frederick Douglass's *North Star* from the apocryphal diary of John Milton's wife, extracts written, no less, in false archaisms that give modern English a Tudor spin (never mind when Milton lived), much like the fakes of Thomas Chatterton, whom Brown adores—"But ah! unhaillie pilgrim, lerne of me"—or our standing fad for "ye olde" as an impertinent honorific, for anything ("ye olde coffee shoppe," "ye olde cyber-shoppe"). Here is Milton's wife:

> Yesterday morn, for very wearinesse, I looked alle over my linen and Milton's to see could I finde anie thing to mende; but there was not a stitche amiss. I would have played on ye spinnette, but was afrayd he should hear my indifferent musick. Then, as a last resource, I tooke a booke—Paul Perrin's Historie of ye Waldenses; and was, I believe, dozing a little, when I was aware of a continual whimpering and crying. I thought 't was some child in ye street; and, having some confits in my pocket, I stept softly out to ye house door and lookt forth, but no child could I see.[9]

Given the orthographic contortions to which black speech in America was subject, we might well wonder if the *North Star*'s interest in the

"Journal of Mary Powell" discloses a deeper play of linguistic politics, a deliberate show of just how unfamiliar the most patently legitimate English could be made to look. But I do not sell short the possibility that such language, "whether authentic or not" (as the paper concedes), speaks just as forcibly to a certain pleasure in experiencing one's native tongue as antique, and though a pleasure of no apparent use to antislavery, there remains the fact that such a readerly investment in a strenuously outmoded England just appears, here, in 1848. Somehow Milton's wife is more effectively *like* Milton's wife when her language is behind the times—*her* own times almost as much as ours; a sense of the past is produced only by these forms of poetic license, which make Restoration English sound more real to whatever extent it sounds like Tudor English, and far from an astute philology of that. Because this is not Tudor English, but a more operatively concocted "English" English—the anachronistic inflection, after all, does not extend much past the substitution of "ye" for "the," the phonetically irrelevant misspelling ("lookt"), and, of course, the additional "e" wherever it fits, but the result is still estranging in a way that reminds us that "our" language is never assuredly ours alone.

The *North Star* does not explain how all this might work as abolitionist allegory, and while we might discern a phantom pedagogy in Mary Powell's kindness toward servants or distaste for corporal punishment, the connection is not just obscure—as the invocation, perhaps, of a typically Puritan revolt on tyranny?—but rather at the mercy of its form, which is so excessively labored it becomes the main event. A testament to freethinkers, maybe, but need we hear about this Puritan's practice on "ye spinnette" and the getting up of a masque in Ludlow Castle? A celebration of England's radicalism seems to make room for a cult of England's past, and all at once the "hoar tower" of a country church or "mailed knights" and geese and gables seem as appropriate to the abolitionist press as those politics that, says *Frederick Douglass' Paper,* "made the spirit of liberty inseparable from British soil." [10] " 'Old England' is a wonderful country," writes William G. Allen to William Lloyd Garrison. "There is grandeur in the looks of it. There is poetry, too." [11] Brown's return to the site where Milton wrote *Comus* ("the exquisite effusion of the youthful genius") finds him overcome, not by a lingering spirit of the English revolution but by the "baronial fortifications" of the same Ludlow Castle where the remnant recesses of passages and towers, engrafted in ruins on the headland, need their "divine poets" as much as their dynastic histories. Brown tells us, after all, that he is rehearsing the "picturesque," and the heap of overgrowth and old gray stone, hallowed by Milton, is as to-order as the verse he adoringly recites from the "visitor's book" at the gatehouse: "Here Milton sung; what needs a greater spell / To lure thee, stranger, to these far-famed walls."[12] If Brown somewhere hopes to establish critical distance from such a redolent discourse of aestheticized travel, to inflect this tall prose with abolitionism itself, it is not at Tintern Abbey, where an "unusually perfect" ruin gives rise to an odd sauce of British Choctaw—feathered songsters and artless lays, bleating flocks, lowing herds, Gothic pillars, Christian martyrs, and a weakness for Martin the Regicide.

There are, of course, times when African Americans in England recall the language of abolition quite explicitly and also times when accounts of enjoying the freedoms of Great Britain turn sharply on matters of political consequence: "England," says Frederick Douglass, "is responsible for our civil war. The abolition of slavery in the West Indies gave life and vigor to the abolition movement in America. Clarkson of England gave us Garrison of America; Granville Sharp of England gave us our Wendell Phillips; and Wilberforce of England gave us our peerless Charles Sumner."[13] But there are too many moments when the rhetoric of antislavery mixes haphazardly with a profound engrossment in "old England" and results in an Anglophilia that seems less a way of flattering contemporary Britain for having rid itself of slavery and more a way of savoring its extravagantly historicized past of royal intrigue and feudal legend. It is not simply that black abolitionists like Ward fondly rehearse narratives drawn from periods when most British peasants were little more than slaves themselves but rather that British history can be so casually, so needlessly interpolated into their own stories of daring and exploit. In taking his surname from the rebel hero of Sir Walter Scott, Frederick "Douglass" makes retrospective claim to a standing mode of Romantic radicalism, perhaps even a whole typology of nationalist endeavor.[14] Many transactions, however, between British lore and emancipatory longing appear decidedly more arcane. Ward relates the following tale of his "escape" from a historic chamber at Holyrood House:

> We took our *tour* . . . and were first shown into the room in which King James is *said* to have been born. [Our guide] made some stupid blunder about the lock of the door, so that he could not unfasten it to let us out.

There we were . . . locked in the room in which, he said, James the Sixth of Scotland and First of England was born! After the far less sober guide had exercised his skill upon the door, the lock, and the key, sufficiently to convince us that he could never release us, I took an old battle-axe, affirmed to be 600 years old (everything is ancient in such places, according to the chronology of guides and servants), and broke the door open, effecting deliverance from durance for myself and party. (235)

New meaning indeed for the autobiography of a "fugitive Negro," though it is hard to tell exactly what is at stake here, halfway through a castle tour, and so unlike the first "deliverance" he and his parents pray for, at the beginning of the narrative, while still slaves in Maryland.[15] The echo is as inappropriate as it is elaborate, for just as his mother's "undaunted courage" carried him through the "dangers of *exodus*," here Ward's own ready action also brings to an end the "durance" of his party. He is certainly having fun with this diminished moment of captivity and flight, and the language of slavery and antislavery seems only to inspire a language for enjoying Britain more—they are "released" so that they may be, as he says elsewhere, "wended on their way" (across "the bedsteads of the princes"). Even so, there is a visceral quality to the scene that is less easily explained: a violent delivery from close confines rhymes most awkwardly with the birth of King James. Having already made himself "familiar with the history of Mary, Queen of Scots," Ward's fascination with this particular royal family takes on a strategically self-aggrandizing cast as he is "born again" a hero in this place of kings. Yet there is truth in it, too: these tours through Great Britain *are* a renascence of sorts of the kind Douglass describes when he finds himself in England newly living as "a man" ("I seem to have undergone a transformation. . . . Instead of the bright, blue sky of America, I am covered with the soft grey fog of the Emerald Isle. I breathe, and lo! the chattel becomes a man").[16]

Ward's engagement with the trumperies of grand tourism is not untouched by a certain irony, but only to the extent that it complicates— much more than mitigates—the ecstatic identification that marks his gestures of knowing remove. Such irony seems never to detract from the enthusiasm for what Ward sees, in "the fabulous blood of Rizzio" and the "thousand and one curiosities" of the queen's indelicate bed.[17] Ward's *Autobiography* suffers an inscrutable detailism, of each person, custom, thing, and form, and while long rosters of sympathetic abolitionists and supportive politicians seem only fitting in a text conceived, at least in part, as tribute to Ward's British backers, there is still a sense of privilege for the padding and too fine an investment in the British drill. This suggests an attitude toward empirical detail in the black abolitionists that is more than a bit mystifying and yet "absolutely anatomical and enumerative," to borrow from Edward Said, in its dedication to ethnically specific facts.[18] Under the sway of Anglophilia's psychology, it seems impossible to find anything English that is not worth registering, so that even what is unnegotiably political seems over and above politics: I think of Brown's neatly dioramic reconstruction of the House of Commons with its illustionistic depth, real-time narration, and full ascription of hairdo, eyewear, and dentition ("Look at that tall man, apparently near seventy, with front teeth gone") or Ward's own fatiguing accounts of Parliamentary ado (just *how* Lord Lyndhurst asked a question of Lord Clarendon and *how* the noble secretary answered to the satisfaction of the great ex-lord chancellor, and suchlike, and so forth, before the orders of the day).[19]

The ceremoniousness and ritualized coherence that lends character to the array reproduces on the abolitionist's page the same kind of prolixity that is itself seen as "peculiarly English." The casual expatiation on any thing or fact aims, too, at the conversational epicurism that is so often admired by Americans in London. Here is Charles Sumner on Lord Brougham: "My wonder at Brougham rises anew. To-night he has displayed the knowledge of the artist and the gastronomer. He criticized the ornaments of the drawing-room and the dining-room like a *connoisseur,* and discussed subtle points of cookery with the same earnestness with which he emancipated the West India slaves and abolished rotten boroughs."[20] We can see a similar surplus in the black press, mixing antislavery reform with dainty *virtú*—political memory with British desire—where Julia Griffiths may write, in 1861, on the pleasure parks and hedges of Loxley Hills or her lucky encounter with Victoria's jewels: "The new crown made for the coronation of Queen Victoria is a purple velvet cap, enclosed by hoops of silver, and studded by a great quantity of diamonds. The upper part is composed of an orb, adorned with precious stones, and surmounted by a cross. Amongst those diamonds is a magnificent ruby, worn by the Black Prince, and a sapphire of matchless beauty. The value of this crown is calculated at £111,900."[21]

There is in all this an anthropologist's method, an "Anglomaniacal imagination" capable of divining talismanic importance in the trivialities of someone else, codifying the everyday nonesuch of British life as if it possessed a degree of meaning unmatched by our own. But then there is also something beyond the anthropological in all this, because no larger laws are finally deduced, no sense of structure is fashioned from these vast accumulations of the particular, the endless lists of lords and ladies, the carefully reconstructed itineraries from one summerhouse to the next, the compulsory observation of "English" dialects and habits of speech; we are left to wallow in these details as if the interest they possessed was utterly intrinsic, as if only a lunatic would even ask why Americans, black or white, needed to know on what day Prince Albert will be arriving in Liverpool, and whether he will be received there by the Earl of Seftan at Croxteth Hall. Take this report from *Frederick Douglass' Paper* in 1851:

> In all probability, the *Manchester Guardian* announces, the Queen and His Royal Highness Prince Albert will reach Liverpool from the north, on the evening of Wednesday, October 8. . . . On Thursday the 9th October, the Queen and the Prince will visit the town and port of Liverpool, and his Highness will probably inaugurate St. George's Hall. Her Majesty and Prince Albert will leave Liverpool in the course of the afternoon, and arrive in the evening at Worsley New Hall, the recently erected mansion of the Earl of Ellesmere, on a short visit to the noble Earl and his Countess. On Friday the 10th October, both Her Majesty and his Royal Highness Prince Albert will visit Manchester, and, we believe, also the sister borough of Salford.[22]

In other words, the black fascination for England, while usually acknowledging the London Antislavery Conventions and the British and Foreign Antislavery Society, was still only about abolition to a point and, at the same time, so plainly implicated in the flattering attentions of other Americans abroad, of Charles Sumner, for example, who is so powerfully drawn to "famous London town" he declares it socially "bewitching."[23] Compare, for example, Ward's apostrophic swoon, "I had never before seen a Lord Mayor," to Sumner's own unguarded taste for royal show: "I could hardly believe that I was not on the stage, partaking in some of the shallow banquets there served, when the herald, decked with ribbons, standing on an elevated place behind the Lord Mayor, proclaimed that 'the Right Honorable the Lord Mayor to his guests,—lords, ladies, and gentlemen, and all,—drank a cup of loving kindness.' The effect of the scene was much enhanced by the presence of women decked in the richest style; among them was the Princess of Capua."[24] Or *Frederick Douglass' Paper*'s first-hand report that "the Queen wore a train of white silk, richly brocaded with a running pattern of flowers" to Nathaniel Parker Willis's Victoria-spotting for *The Corsair*—"there's no word yet whether her slippers were velvet or satin."[25] What I am suggesting is that we read the black response to Britain as at least somewhat informed by a rather causeless enthusiasm, a psychological *fixe* that was also white, rampantly American, and most liberally shared. For while Horace Greeley notes the extent to which Great Britain is "glorified" by blacks as "the land of *true* freedom and equality," there are as many occasions when such moral responsibility is, quite simply, "allied," to quote Crummell some years later, with "its palatial residences and fine equipages, its grand Cathedrals and noble churches, its marvelous sanitation" in a way that treats the structures of aristocracy as the signs of moral largesse and also resonates, quite directly, with white Americans on tour.[26]

Britain may well *be* better accommodating of antislavery, but we also begin to realize, in the tributes to its morals and manners (there is no separating them after awhile), that the regard, alas, depends on an American faith in Britain as just plain *better*—cleaner, smarter, more smartly dressed. Anglophilia plays to a whole complex of American inferiorities that often seem most stubbornly rooted where there is apparently less at stake, which is perhaps why radical politics and cultural enrichment appear so evenly matched as abolitionist concerns. Anglophilia, that is, provides a discourse that ties these minor affects of British culture to improbably larger questions of American identity and offers a fantasy of self-fashioning that seems to work more vigorously on the image of one's "Americanness" than on the image of one's race. What if Brown's statement, "I had come to fancy myself an Englishman by habit," is, along with a celebration of black rights in Britain, also akin to a *Life* cartoon some years later in which high-hatted Americans who would "pass" for British become unrecognizable to themselves?— "Aren't you an Englishman?" "No, aren't you?" (fig. 25).[27]

Or might we see in fugitive slave Samuel Ringgold Ward's apology for "using an Americanism" (110) to describe the British landscape, the same sense of shame that appears with epidemic frequency in the writings of Americans on Britain, in Edward Everett and George Putnam,

FIGURE 25. "Two of a Kind." *Life* (April 17, 1884), front page.

in Hawthorne's *Our Old Home,* and in Stowe's *Sunny Memories of Foreign Lands* and, a generation later, provides Henry James with the material for thousands of pages where Anglophilia is, as he might put it, the very consciousness in which other relations are involved. I speak more to "Americanisms" later but note for now that Ward's skittishness at using such an ambiguously "Yankeefied" term for a bit of scenery as (the dreaded) "none better lies out of doors" is exactly like Sumner's distress at being corrected for his own idioms by Walter Savage Landor: "Why will you, Sumner, who speak with such force and correctness, employ a word which, in the present connection, is not English? Washington's body was never *burnt;* there are no ashes,—say, rather, *remains.*"[28] I note too that Americans were long in the habit of appearing British "by habit," with a reluctance to own their Americanness—and a joy in being mis-taken—that George Putnam for one admits in his recollections of Britain: "I seldom confessed that I was any other than 'a native born and bred,' but whenever I did plead guilty of being an American, I always observed an expression of wonder, if not of absolute incredulity."[29] And it shows no sign of fading: we might see Ward's self-abasing sense of nation as proleptic of an old *Ellen* episode in which the character "Emma Thompson," played by Emma Thompson, will broadcast her lesbianism but is horrified of being "outed" as the American that she is—from Dayton, Ohio, no less—the fiction of her heterosexuality finally less dear than the fiction of her Britishness. ("They're going to find out eventually anyway," says Ellen Degeneres, "that British accent you have is not very good.") Ward suggests that in the context of American Anglophilia no category of identity is more disgraceful than that of "American" itself, a proposition that *Ellen* seconds, for while clearly intending Emma Thompson's embarrassing nationality as the allegorical double of her homosexuality, the allegory works only too well when we are left, in the end, much more comfortable with the notion that the *real* Thompson might be a lesbian than we ever could be with the scandalous possibility that she might *not* be English.[30]

Simply put, black Anglophilia was part and parcel of a much larger cultural formation in American life, a devotion to Great Britain that seems to outperform, in the words of Rufus Choate, any "overrated diversities of interest" and an affinity Charles Sumner insists on, when he writes to Lord Morpeth, "We love England; and I hope you will believe it, notwithstanding the vulgar cries to the contrary."[31] I think we might look differently at Brown's "I felt my identity with the English" when we realize that just a few years later the white and Whiggish *North American Review* would similarly declare that "an American gentleman or lady is constantly mistaken for an Englishman even by the English. . . . If we are to be afflicted with any national manner, we prefer the English."[32] So while the claim of antebellum black writers to be, according to Ward, "the most loyal of Her Majesty's subjects" is undeniably a tribute to the fact that in Britain blacks *could be* her subjects, or full-fledged citizens, it also resonates with the Anglophilia found simply everywhere in the texts of admiring white Americans, of Joseph Story, for example, who writes to Sumner: "You are now exactly where I wish you to be, among the educated, the literary, the noble, and, though last not least, the learned of England, of good old England, our motherland,—God bless her! . . . Oh, for the coronation! the coronation! and you in your Court-dress! We all shouted hurrah!"[33]

Seeing black loyalty to England as the mere function of abolitionist sentiment is only part of what is going on. There are occasions when another kind of expression takes over, an almost compulsive iteration of Englishness that falls just short of political, that is just too baroque. There is a difference between Ward's canny accounts of English cordiality toward blacks—"the Reverend Thomas Binney received me most kindly" (170), or "the Earl of Shaftesbury bade me call upon him" (206)—and such moments of sheer and ecstatic fanfare, of touristic gawking, as "I had seen a nobleman, a lord, the Marquis of Cholmondeley—for the first time!" (33). And although these narratives are designed to show, most of all, how blacks might live in a land without "Negro-hate," as Ward puts it, somewhere among all these tours of Tintern Abbey, and dinners with Tennyson, and teas with the son-in-law of Sir Walter Scott, the antislavery cause gives way to something else more distracting and diffuse, and to the pleasures of Britain as such. Thus Brown writes to Wendell Phillips about the latest antislavery bazaar, and the choosing of delegates for the Peace Congress, but seems always to run out of time: "But I must stop," he says, "The Queen prorogues her Parliament to day, at 2 o'clock, and my girls want to see her." In a column for *Frederick Douglass' Paper,* "Letters From the Old World," Julia Griffiths, after reporting on the house where the poet Moore was born and the church where the Duke of Wellington was baptized, Loch Lomond and the Scottish Alps, after three folio columns and nearly three thousand words, needs finally to end by confessing, "Something I had intended to say of Antislavery, but must defer it."[34]

Caste and Conduct

What makes these spectacular exhibitions of Englishness important for the emergence of Douglass, Crummell, Ward, or Brown not just as reformers but also as the public intellectuals they were considered to be? I am interested in these moments of Anglophilia run wild because they reveal the peculiar qualities of American intellectualism at work, an intellectualism that always seems to define itself as a cosmopolitan susceptibility to other nations, and to Britain most of all. This is not just because Americans have always imagined the work of the mind as something that happens elsewhere, though this too plays a part. The 1840s and 1850s are filled with rhapsodies on just how clever Britain is—it is Britain that has spread an "intellectual Empire" across the globe and that has, says Ralph Waldo Emerson, "inoculated all nations with her civilization, intelligence and tastes." From Emerson's concession—that "the culture of the day, the thoughts and aims of men are English"—to ex-slave Ward's advice that any "man wishing to improve his head" (175) must visit England, the belief that everything British spells Culture, that the British accent itself is intellectually and morally superior, is so pervasive—perhaps Ellen says it best in that same episode: "English people are smarter than regular people. Everyone knows that." [35] Here is Sumner on the theme: "In England, what is called society is better educated, more refined, and more civilized than what is called society in our country. You understand me to speak of society,—as society,— and not of individuals. I know *persons* in America who would be an ornament of any circle anywhere; but there is no *class* with us that will in the least degree compare with that vast circle which constitutes English society. The difference of education is very much against us." [36] It is not just the offhand way he summons England's (axiomatic) excellence; for Sumner writing home, it is as if "English" needs to be translated— "you understand me," he says to his friend—because American society is, quite simply, not *society* (like our public schools are not their *public schools*). Society takes distinction; so this is far from Tocqueville, where "society in the United States" means "all men are alike," but a more guarded sense of society as, finally, a proper class. [37] And finally English, too; Sumner makes a deeper likeness to England the very sign of American accomplishment, and so Anglophilia is the expression of a better education that—in an argument that runs in these "circles"—is defined in terms of Anglophilia to begin with. This is why Sumner writes that a "deep love to England" in America "is borne by all the educated classes." [38]

Antebellum blacks put to work a similar mythology, at times rehearsing the language of grand tours—a sense of learnedness that only Europe makes available—but, at others, a logic of acculturation that effectively distinguishes identity. African Americans will be refined in England *as* African Americans and, for all their Anglicizing, much more perfectly themselves. In his introduction to *My Bondage and My Freedom*, James McCune Smith writes that England "awakened" in Douglass "the consciousness of new powers that lay within him." [39] Becoming English is not foppish appropriation but something closer to the developmental model of Emerson's "American Scholar" who evolves from a degenerate "victim of society," and the "parrot of other men's thinking," into *Man Thinking*," at just the moment when the world and its attractions are wide around. If, in America, Douglass's public self was an "irresistible mimicry" of Wendell Phillips or William Lloyd Garrison, and a continual replaying of the "pathetic narrative of his own experiences of slavery," in England Douglass is inspired "to carve out for himself a path" of more "intellectual manifestations," a path that carries the life battle of abolition onto a genteel terrain where he is not bound by political needs:

> A visit to England, in 1854, threw Mr. Douglass among men and women of earnest souls and high culture, and who, moreover, had never drank of the bitter waters of American caste. For the first time in his life, he breathed an atmosphere congenial to the longing of his spirit, and felt his manhood free and unrestricted. The cordial and manly greetings of the British and Irish audiences in public, and the refinement and elegance of the social circles in which he mingled, not only as an equal, but as a recognized man of genius, were, doubtless genial and resting places in his hitherto thorny and troubled journey through life. There are joys on the earth, and, to the wayfaring fugitive from American slavery or American caste, this is one of them.[40]

The associations here are rather "thorny" themselves, between the exhilaration of Douglass's "spirit" and the loosing of his "manhood," between British "elegance" and black "genius," between "the bitter waters of American caste"—from which he escapes—and the refinement of English class—through which he comes into his own. The passage gestures toward a calculus of intellect and identity that cannot be resolved in America, perhaps because it is so difficult to imagine back home how white "women of earnest souls" might be the "cordial" audience of a black manhood "free and unrestricted," or how Douglass might be recognized as just slightly more than "equal" (not *only* an equal) to the abolitionists whose patronage he sloughs off. England is not offering heroic inspiration—we're in drawing rooms far removed from where Ward wields King James's ax—so much as a flurry of adulation that makes Douglass's socializing into a ritual of discernment along patently Anglophilic lines and thus confirms, as Douglass himself writes later in *Life and Times of Frederick Douglass* that the British "measure and esteem men according to their moral and intellectual worth."[41] The "genius" of both ex-slave and English culture are reciprocally esteemed, with the argument that (racial) caste proves no hindrance to blacks abroad who may then enjoy distinctions only (social) class provides.

It is an argument, too, that celebrates, within black abolitionism, a rather curious form of individual liberty—the right to stylize one's self as reformed by British manners, and enriched by British ways, while insisting that these privileges are American. Douglass may have been forced "to seek a refuge in monarchical England from the dangers of republican slavery," but he frames his exile nonetheless as the occasion for a *republican* national experience: "A rude, uncultivated fugitive slave, I was driven to that country to which American young gentleman go to increase their stock of knowledge, to seek pleasure, and to have their rough democratic manners softened by contact with English aristocratic refinement."[42] He advances his position here from "slave" to "gentleman" almost immediately, on the strength of little more than an analogy and a common destination, but the effect is striking: the American, whether slave or free, now stands exposed as desperately seeking a cultivated "Englishness." There is no middle ground between "slave" and "English," because there is no appreciable means of discriminating, from the vantage of "aristocratic refinement," between Americans of either race, all of whom are rude and rough, and go to England. Douglass's evolutionary pattern aspires to be a "type" of national life itself, and this universalizing reach is more than simply signaled in Smith's introduction but made the key to understanding Douglass as a thinker. "He is a Representative American man," writes Smith, "a type of his countrymen. Naturalists tell us that a full grown man is resultant or representative of all animated nature on this globe; beginning with the early embryo state . . . and passing through every subordinate grade or type, until he reaches the last and highest—manhood. In like manner, and to the fullest extent, has Frederick Douglass passed through every gradation of rank comprised in our national make-up, and bears upon his person and upon his soul every thing that is American."[43] Douglass is Emerson's "Representative Man"—the man who in the "fluxions and mobility" of his mind can assimilate the ranges of human existence—but Smith is slyer than this too and builds in a liberal polemic of upward mobility that moves from slave to the highest rank of "manhood," just as the exemplary Douglass moves from America to England. In Smith's dizzying phylogenic vision of the narrative to come, the womb of slavery is the first stage in a "strictly national" American progress toward maturity and, follies of sociobiology aside, it is a language we have heard before, both in Smith's sense of Douglass's "manhood" in the drawing rooms of Britain and in Douglass's own sense of becoming a "man" on British soil. The path of the American Man is the path to Britain; Douglass moves through every gradation of our national makeup to reach this highest rank of being an American, in England, where with new "refinement" and a "stock of knowledge" he is, so to speak, "finished."

Black antislavery preserves class; it calls for a liberal ideology of open-mindedness that links freedom to status and impartiality to good discernment. It makes the abolition of slavery into another social improvement that we Americans acquire abroad: "There's so much to be learned here," says Ward of England, "civilization being at its very summit—society, in consequence, presenting every attraction, and every form of social improvement and instruction" (175). Seeing England as a place of self-education allows black abolitionists to use and extend one of the central tropes of the slave narrative, literacy—and literacy's symbolic affirmation of "status within the human community"—with a turn of the screw.[44] For such moments evoke the same desire for cultural elevation, the same dream of "civilizing" a degraded race, only now this insufficiency of learning and refinement becomes a broadly *American* phenomenon—a condition answerable not so much to slavery but to the shoddy education anyone gets if it is not finally English. In Ward's assent "with those who hold the opinion that the best specimens of the Colonial or the American gentleman need European travel for their finishing"—with "English travel," of course, being "the best, choicest portion of European travel"—we hear a mediated play of cultural performance that aims less at destabilizing English authority, than at appropriating it on behalf of all mistaught Americans and their laggard "civilization." It is not just that Americans, when it comes to Britain, are all lumped in with colonials. These black writers *are* making a hash of America as the dominant culture but only by way of ratifying this other more dominant culture—more central center—that is still not their own. Ward's language suggests a thorough affectation of regard, which is not to say black abolitionists are altogether endorsing this culture but to venture that they are cannily aware that even Americans so highly polished as Sumner are liable to be shamed by the failings of their own "English." At least, Brown's descriptions of language acquisition in *The Black Man, His Antecedents, His Genius and His Achievements*—of Phillis Wheatley, for example, having "mastered the English language"—or Abigail Mott's descriptions of "Uncle Jack," a Virginia slave who interpreted obscure passages of Scripture and "spoke pure English," read slightly differently when we hear Landor accuse Sumner, in these same years, of using words that are "not English."[45] Literacy narratives remain about literacy pure and simple, and yet many of the arguments for black intellectual refinement sound like so many narratives of American refinement more generally, where the terminus of every self-education is the cultivation of English talk.

Abolition trades on a discourse of intellectualism and cultural advancement that is teleologically Anglophilic, that says that Great Britain is simply further along in ways America has yet to manage for itself. When Ward finds "the anti-slavery feeling" in Great Britain "prevalent, deep, earnest, and intelligent," he is suggesting that abolition travels in smarter circles abroad but also that the British engage a higher, more enlightened faculty and "are abolitionists from intelligent conviction" (230). The British, it would seem, are of a better mind toward antislavery because their minds themselves are better used.

For Ward, among others, Britain represents, much more than intellectual insecurity, a whole fantasized realm within which a cosmopolitan universalism gets realized. Here Anglophilia shapes a style of intellectualism that lets black abolitionists operate on an open terrain of cultural concern, one where investments in British customs do not always circle back to slavery, and where race counts among a variety of interests that are as undiscriminating as the British themselves—as the British, says Sumner, who may pour forth on "law, literature, and society" in a morning's tea, or pass, like Macaulay, "from the minutest dates of English history or biography to a discussion of the comparative merits of different ancient orators" while giving you "whole strophes from the dramatists at will."[46] It is as if in observing everything that was beside the point, the ostentatious marginalia of abolitionist England, the ex-slave fetishized into being the very world of an unfettered mind, free to skip wantonly from detail to detail, to treasure each oddity of dialect and euphony of proper name ("Cholmondeley"), a mind released from the single-mindedness of "the cause" and its rhetorics, to take pleasure in the frippery of royal salons. For black abolitionists are never so much public intellectuals as when, finally dis-affiliated from anything in particular, like Russell Jacoby's New York intellectuals, they are *not* talking about abolition. What do we make, for example, of Brown in Oxford when, after lamenting the lack of op-portunities for black education in the United States and the lack of reform in educational laws, he apologizes for his polemic—"But I am straying too far from the purpose of this letter"—and proceeds instead with maundering sketches of a stroll through Christ Church meadows and the university's founding by "good King Alfred"?[47] As Ward writes in his autobiography, "It will be seen that I have freely made remarks upon other things than slavery. I did the former as a man, the latter as a Negro. As a Negro, I live and therefore write for my people; as a Man, I freely speak my mind upon what concerns me and my fellow men" (xiv). Yet what most concerns Ward, the "Man," as opposed to Ward, the "Negro," are not the theological and humanitarian implications of the antislavery movement but rather the protocols of English manners and the matrimonial bed of James the First, matters almost ludicrously mismatched to the universalist language of his preface. Or put another way, that England might not be an entirely cosmopolitan matter seems never to cross Ward's mind.

The association of intellectualism with cosmopolitanism has been long observed, certainly since the Dreyfus affair when, as Ross Posnock points out, Émile Zola rejected national "chauvinism" for universal val-ues and especially now when such self-conscious intellectuals as Martha Nussbaum and K. Anthony Appiah have revived a rhetoric of cosmo-politanism intent on replacing nationalist projects with, in the words of Stanley Crouch, "the commonality of human concern."[48] But even as early as 1845 the *North American Review* would say, "Mere nationality is no more nor less than so much provincialism. The demand for na-tionality bounded historically and geographically by the independent existence and territory of a particular race or fraction of a race . . . is a sublimer sort of clownishness and ill-manners. Genius is cosmopoli-tan."[49] If the cosmopolitan is characterized as a positive absence of lo-cal attachments, then who better to transcend the petty boorishness of national affiliation (all those "ill-manners") and who better to become the "citizen of the world" than the ex-slave just escaped from Maryland? "I have," says Douglass, "no end to serve, no creed to uphold, no govern-ment to defend; and as to nation, I belong to none." It is precisely this contemporary sense of "genius" in America that permits the ex-slave to translate his marginal status into an intellectual advantage, the impossibility of citizenship ensuring he could never be seduced by that same "clownishness" of nationality no white intellectual can finally escape. And this is so, however much James Jackson Jarves insisted at the time, in defiance of calls for an indigenous culture, that "no invidious nationalism should enter into art. The true and beautiful are as free and universal as the air we breathe." In other words, the ex-slave's attenuated affiliations—Douglass's "Aliens are we in our native land"—are transvalued into the requisite credentials of the "intellectual," the public figure who has always assumed the posture Andrew Ross describes as "alienated dissent and social disaffiliation." Thus Irving Howe can boast that for the New York intellectuals of the 1950s, "Alienation was a badge we carried with pride."[50]

In Pauline Hopkins's novel *Contending Forces* (1900), it is perhaps the fact that the black characters seem always on the brink of enfranchisement and disenfranchisement, on the edge of being, in the words of Sappho Clark, "aliens in the very land of our birth"—or, later, "an alien people, without a country and without a home"—that allows them to become, along with the novel's Will Smith, "wealthy cosmopolitans." Hopkins's characters are released into a world of English humanitarian culture that is, at least in part, about its "culture," an oddly decorous society of benevolent lords where British English is set against a coarse Southern vernacular, where black politics thrive at the Canterbury Club of Boston, and where black preachers preach in Prince Albert coats. How peculiar to hear Hopkins's Dora speak with perfectly British inflections for no good reason; she has never left America but is "well, not very tired, mummy dear" after all the "tidying up," with her impertinent *mummy's* and *ta-ta's* pointing to a heightened formality that is neither just a straining, Anglophilic pretense nor a class accessory of being "well-bred" but also evidence, we might say, of a "negative capability" for national identification.[51] It is deeply emblematic of Dora's intelligence that she seems somewhat uncertainly "American," so susceptible to British courtesies and, in this respect, keenly proficient at allowing other national traits to overcome those that are nominally her own.

The black elite of *Contending Forces* enjoy a world of affectations that in many ways prefigure the wider "range of socially transmitted options" that Appiah links to "the freedom to create oneself" as an intellectual; indeed, in fashioning her Harvard-educated Will Smith on

W. E. B. Du Bois, Hopkins helps to solidify the arguments of those who claim this model of the black intellectual—never fully naturalized, often worldly in scope and manner—as an invention of the later nineteenth century.[52] But I would suggest that these tropes of global citizenship, and this language of a traveling intellectualism, were well in place in antebellum America and, in real ways even more pronounced, because the valorization of wide-ranging minds—of minds on the loose—is strangely literalized in a world where these slaves *were* on the loose. The language of "intellectualism" in the period even looks like the language of antislavery, with its professed universalism and ecumenical thinking and its value on wide receptivity. When *Frederick Douglass' Paper* says that Harriet Beecher Stowe's travel writings from Europe are both "free . . . from egotism" and "as free from moroseness as from sectarianism," it means that her writings are thoughtful—"genial, racy, witty, humorous, sportive, sparkling, frank, observing," and so on. It is also easy to see how such a particular form of large-mindedness, of freethinking, resonates for this paper with the same lack of chauvinism that drives its cause: indeed the paper cites Stowe as saying, of her English tour, that "the sublime spirit of foreign missions always is suggestive of home philanthropies, and that those whose heart has been enlarged by the love of all mankind are always those who are most efficient in their own sphere."[53] Consider C. M. Kirkland's sense, just then, that all Americans in Britain had "unconsciously endowed the whole nation with something of Shakespeare's universality—the opposite of mean and narrow prejudice." Had these black abolitionists (consciously) endowed Britain, and their travels to Britain, with this same generosity of spirit—this same Shakespearean breadth ("who," writes William Wells Brown, "has better known the human feelings than Shakespeare?")—but to other, political effect?[54] In any case, there is something a bit shrewd in suggesting that prejudice is the opposite of cosmopolitanism, when cosmopolitanism is so tied to this world of English botany, books, and peers, and even more useful when the logic of this is pulled out to its most confounding corollary, which is, namely, that bigotry is less intelligent.

The Chivalry of Antislavery

What the black cosmopolitan does in pursuing the cause in conversation with the peerage and at tea with Tennyson is to analogize antislavery to a world of high sociability and extreme politesse that, like antislavery itself, has little patience for narrow souls and the rudeness of local ways. How does abolitionism become a *kind* of cosmopolitanism, its own version of a transatlantic genteel culture? When Brown says, "I had eaten at the same table as Sir Edward Bulwer-Lytton, Charles Dickens, Eliza Cook, Alfred Tennyson, and the son-in-law of Sir Walter Scott," he is invoking an American dream of English civility and manners that has everything to do with class. Take the case of the "Cosmopolite" who observes for *Frederick Douglass' Paper* each month how all the "resorts of wealth and fashion" seat "colored gentlemen" in the boxes, or how at the "aristocratic music hall," the "black amateur can take his seat beside the white professor of *la belle science.*"[55] All this talk of blacks in Britain, where antislavery is the cause célèbre and duchesses are blasé on the arms of ex-slaves, seems determined to elicit, from white abolitionists, a degree of social envy, making figures like Brown and Douglass representative not just of moral dignity and political influence but also of ready access to aristocrats. In suggesting that antislavery feeling is as British as the monocle, blacks abroad isolate a vulnerability, one based on fears of American declension and of "Culture" gone to seed in the New World, fears exploited by James McCune Smith in the *Anglo-African Magazine* when he laments the historical "decline of [English] manners and mental cultivation" in Puritan America. Such arguments make it seem that Americans will turn to abolitionism if only to regain this refinement, as if antislavery is just one more aspect of British decorum to be appropriated, however it comes, like the American in the *Life* cartoon who takes his stiff, high hat to the theater when he has a crush hat at home, "because it is the fashion in England" (fig. 26). If antislavery, as *Douglass' Monthly* insists, is "The True British Feeling," then how lucky that such Americans as Sumner are "prejudiced in favor of England."[56]

No one considers abolitionist feeling more the sign of a purely British class status than Ward, who in *The Autobiography of a Fugitive Negro* claims, "The middling and better classes of all Europe treat a black gentleman as a gentleman. Then step into the American colonies, and you will find the lowest classes and those who have but recently arisen there from, just what the mass of Yankees are on this matter. Also, the best friends the Negro has in America are persons generally of the superior classes and the best origins" (31). Or again later, "so far as my experience goes (and that is considerable), the *British gentleman* is a gentleman everywhere, and under all circumstances. Therefore, in every

FIGURE 26. "High Hat." *Life* (May, 5, 1886).

town in Canada, I see what I saw in but few and exceptional cases in the States—viz., that among gentlemen, the black takes just the place for which he is qualified, as if his color were similar to that of other gentlemen—as if there were no Negro-crushing country hard by—as if there were no Negro-hating lower-classes in their midst" (106). Ward observes a kind of color blindness among the elite that lets gentlemen prefer black gentlemen as readily as any other, that confers all the distinctions of class without respect to race, which only the "lowest" seem to heed; not even Europe's "middling" begrudge accomplished blacks their due, while in America, a little upward mobility still leaves the "recently arisen" beholden to racial hatreds of the rabble. Ward puts Anglophilia to novel social purpose: he provides a language that at once consigns American racism to the working classes while flattering America's better classes for already seeming that much more like the "*British gentleman*," and thus "superior," always, to the "mass of Yankees." If whites in antebellum America, as Eric Lott reminds us, looked to solidify their own class status by "seizing on Jim Crow as a common enemy" and thus engaged in a wide range of performances that offered racist spectacle as a comfort for the anxieties of social difference, here we see a similarly tangled play of race and class allegiance but with a profoundly different end. Ward offers the allure of social difference as what whites have to gain by assuming a "British" liberality on matters of race. A sort of inside out of minstrelsy: another white class formation is encour-

aged around a white response to blacks, only now class depends not on
a racialized burlesque but on a drama of sensibility where benevolent
Anglophiles, with elevating sentiments, spread tolerance all around.[57]

Since Ward so casually, so offhandedly, calls the United States the
"colonies," in the passage above—this is the 1850s!—I would like to
say a word about this brief undoing of independence. In Ward, the nation's class politics are cast in sharpest relief when there is no nation
to consider. Class itself is radically displaced as an aspect of a colonial
tutelage that is both mistaken and anachronistic; England once more
lends the proper standards to its American subjects as a dominant culture that levels even the local elite to mere "colonials." But then again
Anglophilia in Ward is not finally about Britain; it is about how American affectations of Britishness speak to issues of class internal to America, where all the Anglicizing only makes us more aware of ourselves.
Anglophilia is particularly obliging to Ward because it represents the
key to understanding a whole host of antislavery incriminations about
America's relative classlessness. Look at the language he uses when an
American traveler turns down an invitation from "Her Majesty's Sec-
retary of State for Foreign Affairs" to a dinner in honor of Benjamin
Roberts, the president of Liberia:

> With real American feeling, this proud republican dame declined. So do
> all of the class. They choose not to know colored persons of distinction,
> when they might; or, knowing them, they choose to misrepresent them.
>
> I must be allowed to record, just here, the very great delight I had
> in hearing the *real* gentleman and nobleman speak, at the meeting re-
> ferred to, in such terms as they were pleased to use, concerning the
> Negro. (184)

What counts for real American "class" is exposed as rather plainly
bourgeois; this "proud republican dame"—an audacious tag—is so
proud, so précieuse, about her class that the "real" distinction of Roberts passes her by (214). In the meantime, she misses her opportunity
for the *real* society of Lords Harrowby and Shaftesbury, of whom Ward
speaks, noblemen whose ability to "admire" Roberts in a way that was
"common to all lips, as it flowed from all hearts" (214), only shows up
the American's slight as utterly déclassé. We might compare the republican dame to Ward's Duchess of Argyll who is "so thoroughly imbued"
with her abolitionist principles, "it seems to cost her Grace nothing to

be kind, because it is so natural." Ward continues, "I do not wonder . . . that she is a friend of the slave. Her mother, and her noble maternal ancestry for generations, have been so" (214). The duchess need not be "proud" (uppity); she is the heir to benevolence, and her kindness to blacks is as inborn and real as her nobility itself. Her kindness costs her nothing because her nobleness cannot be spent—Her Grace has her grace by nature. At the same time, Ward's anecdotes of republican dames and noble duchesses take on the burden of a guidebook, letting white Americans know that a liberal view of race is *natural* at scenes of *real* English culture; prejudice, Ward seems to suggest, is for the tourists.[58]

If, as Douglass points out in his *Narrative,* the cost of slave owning is finally reckoned as the loss of a "noble disposition"—if his mistress Sophia Auld's progress as a slave owner is marked by her decline from "gentle" to fierce—then antislavery is trading on a discourse of social aspiration.[59] What we see again and again in the abolitionist press is a pitch for the cause that relies, at so many moments, surprisingly little on the plea of morality, for example, or of Christian benevolence, but offers on appeal the American's way into an aristocratic dreamworld of civility that is always, and paradigmatically, British. Who would think that the antiabolitionist's loss of "nobility," in Douglass's terms, is as much about rude character as rude taste and yet that "nobility" is not just way of figuring virtue but of identifying, quite literally, the "nobility," a simple naming of the rank to which antislavery might ascend. "One thing is certain," writes the *Liberator* on the barring of Douglass by Americans from a ship's saloon, "that the first functionaries of her Britannic Majesty would have asked, would have endured no such exclusion, nor would have deemed themselves in the least degraded by such society."[60]

First functionaries indeed: there is such awareness, among abolitionists, of British politeness that it often seems as though tolerance is nothing but British politeness, a rejection of racism on the grounds of bad form. When Douglass tells the *Liberator* from England that he was amazed by "the entire absence of everything that looked like prejudice," he is not so much claiming that the "prejudiced" Englishman is an impossibility in terms but, rather, that no self-respecting Englishman would be caught in the appearance of so mean an affect.[61] The emphasis is on a social theatrics of fine behavior that may or may not reflect an ethical commitment; but these are apparently civilities that

Douglass can live with. Traveling among the British subjects of Canada, Ward writes, "I never saw the slightest appearance of [Negro-hate] in any person in Canada recognized there, or who would be recognized here, as a gentleman. Either that class do not participate in the feeling, or their good sense and good taste and good breeding forbid its appearance" (106). Prejudice or no prejudice, the British are too decorous to show prejudice, in an expedience that removes antislavery from the demands of principle or conscience and makes it the sure expression of cultivated tastes. Abolitionist sentiments become the index to a larger system of class protocols, an attempt to consolidate a genteel consensus by equating the antislavery platform with a primer in British courtesies, hoping to produce, in broad effect, a kind of snobbery toward racism. These black writers are all but goading white Americans to say, "O slavery, how provincial!"

Of course, Ward and Douglass had an easy audience. The deportment of many white abolitionist circles was almost ludicrously high, and to enter these Northern networks of political agitation was to cross over into an Anglicized realm of antislavery salons and antislavery soirees, a realm where the payoff for all the polemic was ultimately social.[62] "There is nothing in this country except antislavery," says Boston abolitionist Edmund Quincy, "that is worth a gentleman's notice."[63] Slavery is condemned through the confirmation of status: nowhere is the privileged carriage of extreme abolition more striking than in the indubitable Brahmanism, the press and lore, that surrounds Wendell Phillips. As bracingly forward in his politics as he was hoary in his style—instructed at Harvard by Edward T. Channing to scorn "vulgar" American speech for the "pure simplicity" of British English—Phillips's courting of support among the elite of British abolitionism (Viscount Morpeth, Baron Brougham) appears the logical extension of his ancestral pursuits, his hiring of professional genealogists, for example, or his search through heraldic tables, to establish his own personal tie to the British nobility. In a letter to his "ma," crowing about the Duchess of Sutherland, about his rounds of confection and conversation with an assortment of earls—"I tattle on all this to show you how far from *vulgar* the *Liberator* would be, ma, in London"—Phillips writes as if abolition is perhaps too fine for America, and if its successes back home have been limited, it is because Americans themselves are too brash.[64]

In describing Phillips, Thomas Wentworth Higginson sees his easy affability—the casual grace of his posture and clubby feel of his speech (dropping *g*'s, says Higginson, "like an Englishman")—as the key to his moral authority. "There was absolutely nothing," Higginson writes, "of bull-dog combativeness; but a careless, buoyant, almost patrician air, as if nothing in the way of mob-violence were worth considering, and all the threats of opponents were simply beneath contempt. He seemed like some English Jacobite nobleman on the scaffold, carelessly taking snuff and kissing his hand to the crowd, before laying his head upon the block." This is not John Brown, with his militancy, prophetic wraths or Spartan habit ("[he] did not go to the college called Harvard," writes Thoreau, and "was not fed on the pap that is there furnished").[65] This is a magisterial brush-off, a high disdain, availing itself of cultural legitimacy at every turn, feasting on Harvard as a way of rarifying the antislavery experience as far more distinguished, socially. "I think he has more culture," writes Emerson, "than his own." It is just this sense of Phillips's *savoir-vivre,* of big as you please breeding, that, for Higginson, separates his abolitionism from even Emerson's:

> He occupied during most of his life the willing position of a tribune of the people; nor was there any social class with which he was unwilling to be, logically and politically at least, identified. Emerson, while thoroughly true to the antislavery movement, always confessed to a feeling of slight aversion to negroes; Theodore Parker uttered frankly his dislike of the Irish. Yet neither of these had distinctly aristocratic impulses, while Phillips had. His conscience set them aside so imperatively, that he himself hardly knew that they were there. He was always ready to be identified with the colored people; always ready to give his oft-repeated lecture on O'Connell, to the fellow-countrymen of that hero: but in these and all cases his democratic habit had the good-natured air of some kindly young prince; he never was quite the equal associate that he seemed. The want of it was never felt by his associates: it was in his dealing with antagonists, that the real attitude came out. When he once spoke contemptuously of those who had dined with a certain Boston club that had censured him, as "men of no family," the real mental habit appeared. And in his external aspect and bearing the patrician air never quite left him.[66]

In Phillips, radical reform is always caught up with aristocratic remove; it takes the fair "prince" to give justice fairly and the historian

Higginson is left with an ingenious mix of leveler and socialite, new ideas and old blood. What do we learn but that the best democrats are aristocrats, that the most exclusive rarely exclude, and that antislavery takes the high-minded judgments of an imperious Brahman who has the right to call compromisers "low"? Phillips's superiority makes him so comfortable with "the people," blacks, Irish, anyone at hand, while Emerson is reduced to bodily discomfort around blacks, and Parker's philanthropies extend only to blacks because the Irish make him cringe. But these are precisely the sort of national insularities and petty bigotries that Phillips's "aristocratic impulses" transcend as if his elevated social position—what allows him to be "like an Englishman"— gives him perspective that is quite literally above where other Americans (Emerson, Parker) can operate with their limited views. Higginson, outspoken opponent of the Fugitive Slave Law and colonel of the Union regiment of former slaves, himself cut enough of a figure to be described as resembling a "cavalier of the Jacobean court" and claimed such direct descent from the English crown he called Elizabeth I his "Cousin Betsy Tudor." [67]

Wendell Phillips and Edmund Quincy were publicly known for parlor games in which they played at being aristocrats, writing garish letters as mock Sir Walter Scotts, turning Latin phrases, and endowing one another with honorific titles. Phillips became "the High Noble Lord, Wendell, Earl Arundel"; Quincy dubbed his wife, Ann, "the Countess"; Phillips addressed Quincy as "Edmund, by Divine Providence Bishop of Norfolk," or as "The Unworthy Scion of the *gens Quinctia*." Abolitionists heard the story of how Phillips, once startled by a noise in his library, turned to look, and there stood Quincy, "in a costume of George II's time—cocked hat, buttons, sack coat and all, and wearing a gold-lace vest to his knees—lace ruffles—lace neckband—rings and a silver-mounted rapier." Phillips saluted him as "Sir Charles Grandison." [68] The appropriative excess shows more than Phillips and Quincy as a "fraternity of two" with Brahman inclinations; it also shows a longing for the social trappings that might accompany political identities that were by definition susceptible to British influence and formed in communication with British antislavery discourse. We might think of these performances of abolitionist "nobility" as lending the movement an eminence that its more scandalous politics seemed to risk; or, perhaps abolitionist class fantasies take on a British tone because an emancipated United States can be dreamed of as more like Britain itself. An observer in the

Liberator goes so far as to blame "schemes" for African colonization on an American wish to resettle blacks elsewhere so as to make room for more immigrating English.[69]

The unequivocal effect of Phillips and Quincy dueling in lace in the parlors of abolitionism presents style as the proof of moral substance. "The gentleman," writes George Calvert in 1863, "is an aesthetic fruit on an ethic stem," which more than suggests that his beauty is fairness and that the just proportion of his parts is like the justness of his relations to others. "A man of small soul can only be a gentleman in a superficial sense," but excellence in conduct, an ease of carriage and sensibility to the beauties and properties of speech is, for Calvert, the bearing of the man who is "uncivil to no one." To what moral and mannerly heights might men attain when the purest elevation of feeling consists in "an aesthetic aura" that may be "more felt than seen" but that at least cannot *not* be intimated by a clean and unaffected demeanor. Just how the "moral freedom" that gentlemen possess in good degree is obvious in their vocal unwillingness to, say, "add an *h* to monosyllables or polysyllables beginning with a vowel, or to interchange a *w* with a *v*" in a grievous lapse of elocution, feels remote only as far as we do not grant with Calvert that immorality itself is an "aesthetic incapacity." Calvert frames for us something on the order of a Kantian analogy between the innately beautiful and the morally good, which has the effect of translating an altogether social category (the gentleman) into a supersensible identity that is less an expression of class prestige than an "indefinable presence" that must certainly precede and rise above it. This revaluation of the gentleman on aesthetic grounds means, moreover, that he must be actively defined against the mere accessories—the "purposiveness," we might say, of his wealth and belongings—and any show of status as the material reflection of desire. It is not just that Calvert's gentleman is no "slave to things," conventionalities, or fashions: he is positively dispossessed of any pretensions toward ownership as such. "He should possess all things as not possessing any," Calvert writes, which remarks both on his lack of vulgarity and on the independence of thought that lets him judge so well. Or as he puts it elsewhere, in a pronouncement whose very grammar testifies to the idealism of his argument, "The gentleman is above all things, free."[70]

But in thoroughly rendering the man of property as the man of benevolence, this same discourse provides an attractive figure for white abolitionists seeking to perform a highly wrought masculinity as the better part of valor. Why should this matter to the cause? Such models of character and individual form had long been associated with a Southern aristocracy already imagining itself as the last ward of honor and virtue in opposition to the modernizing North. Indeed, Calvert celebrates no "gentlemen" with more ardor than he does the Chevelier Bayard and Sir Phillip Sidney, whose legendary knighthoods also provide proverbial models of courtesy, hospitality and excellence for the South's romance of its own chivalry. The appeal to deeds of honor that Phillips and Quincy make, and the presumptions of style that fulfill the wish of the appeal, expropriates a Southern language of chivalry for the antislavery cause. But it does so without at all compromising the symbolic value of such gestures to the caste-ridden orders they recall. These Northern "cavaliers," engaging in the ritualistic games of honor, duty, and sacrifice, look much like the Southern squires of John Pendleton Kennedy's plantation novels or of William Alexander Caruthers, *The Knights of the Horseshoe* (1846), and are no less enamored with the coded displays of gallant style in their evidently utilitarian age. In both cases, the expressions of style are just the point; what feels gratuitous (even frivolous) about chivalry—elaborate games and costumes, imperial heroes, bettings and darings, unnecessary combat—are also supreme manifestations of disinterest that become the signature in the social realm of a politics that respects the dignities of form. Pure distinctions of class and breeding are conditioned on nothing; they do not so much aspire as express and communicate. They are free to communicate an ease that extends courtesy and kindness without risk to themselves. Aesthetic freedom "engenders distance vis-à-vis necessity" in a way that allows the style of cavaliers to double as an objective distance from the world of political and economic need on which their gentility is, of course, conditioned but over which they can now magnanimously preside.[71]

In his travel narrative *Aristocracy in America* (1839), German-born Francis Grund reports on the acutely Southern attachment to its own imagined chivalry. That this chivalry often stands as an apology for slavery makes its adaptations by Northern abolitionists seem torturous, but no less clear. "If the tendency of wealth in the north, is towards an aristocracy of money" as one Southerner in Grund's travelogue insists, "the aristocracy of the Southern states, founded on birth and education, is a sort of offset to it, a means of preventing the degeneration of the high-minded democracy which once swayed the country, into a vulgar oligarchy of calculating machines without poetry, without arts, and without generosity." Perhaps not surprisingly, the Southern elites with whom Grund converses portray slavery as the epitome of a "high-minded" paternalism, with "planters not fearing the power and politic influence of slaves," and so all the more free to "treat them generally with humanity and kindness." But the familiar rhetoric of beneficence that Grund recounts—indeed, few defenses of slavery are more common in the antebellum United States—is only one aspect of the South's deep commitment to genteel virtues and to "honor" as nothing less than a medium for social relations. In contrast to the North's "spirit of exclusiveness," which enforces the pursuit of self-interest and demands conformity without community, the South at once manages to avoid practices of "intoleration" and to deny the "arbitrary distinctions [that] refer only to fortune." There is, or so Grund's informants suggest, nothing so coercive and illiberal as the performative expectations of republican manners and egalitarian politics; the lack of an expressive style in the social exchange between classes speaks to a lack of affection, and the ascetic streamlining of conduct only makes for more naked displays of antagonism. Without the "freedom of intercourse" that rank and titles actively enable, American liberty remains an abstraction. "How often did I wish myself in England," one of Grund's Southerners admits, "where I might be permitted to have an opinion of my own, and express it, without suffering in the consideration of my friends and the public!"[72]

It is too much to suggest that an envy along these lines can wholly explain either the theatricality or extent of abolitionist self-fashioning as distinctively Yankee variations on the Southern cavalier. After all, the associations between Southern chivalry and slave power were a familiar feature of antislavery rhetoric, at least in part because such pretensions were so readily pathologized. When Representative Preston Brooks caned Charles Sumner on the Senate floor for insulting the "honor" of his South Carolina kinsman, Senator Andrew Butler, the chivalric code that left Sumner a cripple had already figured prominently in the debate that prompted the attack (fig. 27). In a speech against Kansas's admission to the Union as a slave state, Sumner mocked Butler for believing himself to be a "chivalrous knight"—"with sentiments of honor and courage" gleaned from countless books of chivalry—when he served no damsel but "the harlot, Slavery." Nor should we forget,

SOUTHERN CHIVALRY— ARGUMENT versus CLUB'S.

FIGURE 27. "Southern Chivalry: Argument versus Club's," 1856. Courtesy of American Antiquarian Society.

as William Taylor has shown, that many images of the South's plantation society circulated throughout the North with significant currency in response to the broad transformations we associate with the Jacksonian moment. The resurgence of an aristocratic ideal based in popular images of plantation society is, for Taylor, one of the great ironies of this period and marks a pointedly conservative response to the period's modernizing mix of increased ethnic immigration and more democratic politics.[73]

Still, insofar as chivalry in the 1830s through 1850s was also coded as the perfect marriage of social grace and civic virtue, we can at least begin to understand just how an antislavery ethics of progress and benevolence was indulged in an aesthetic based on courtly rites of privilege and distinction. If "good-will towards the inferior" comes naturally with aristocratic status, a claim on exactly this contested sensibility seems anything but eccentric to the cause of abolition. To imagine antislavery in the trappings of knight-errantry is at once to ritualize the movement's politics of benevolence and, even more conspicuously, to make a certain manner of radicalism along racial lines into a surprising sign of traditionary status and sensibility. Recalling Phillips's commencement address at Harvard, which included a pointedly Tory defense of England's peers, one fellow student declared him "*least likely* to give the enthusiasms and labor of his life to the defense of popular rights."[74] But it is precisely this transposition of aristocratic bearing and reformist ideology that not only lends an aesthetic poise to the laboriousness of political agitation but serves to inoculate antislavery against claims of incorrectness or to gentrify the movement away from prior associations with the uncomfortably middling.

When Harriet Martineau toured the United States in the 1830s she discovered something different in the Boston elite. Anglophiles still, the society that "Lafayetted" Martineau for her Englishness—"lion-hunters," she calls them, with their "flatteries and worship"—regretted her abolitionism as an unfortunate oddity of their otherwise venerable guest. Their homage, she says "was no more related to myself, in fact, than to the heroine of a dream."[75] The best of Beacon Hill, the Hancocks, Hopkinsons, and Otises who "received and entertained" Martineau with their unmistakably American "enthusiasm" were, at the same time, memorably chasing away British abolitionist George Thompson; his 1835 visit inspired the leading papers to call out "men of property and stature" for what amounted to an unlikely aristocratic mob facing down an untimely abolitionist "rabble." Martineau tells us, "eminent scholars and thinkers of the country" revealed their preferences no less clearly, "sneering" at the antislavery controversy "as 'low' and disagreeable, and troubling to their repose." In Martineau's account of her American travels, we see the Boston elite at war with themselves; their urge to toast her British refinement is never reconciled with their unwillingness to take on her politics. Their Anglophilic enthusiasm is not simply hypocritical, since Americans who must preserve their status by closing ranks against antislavery radicalism are the same Americans who acquire status by associating with British society in the first place—society that just happens to be known, in America, as resolutely antislavery. To offend Martineau is to risk some measure of class prominence but so too is any truck with her vigorous support of racial reform. What results is an enabling blindness to her British abolitionism that allows her "Britishness" alone to command that much more respect, in part because Martineau's politics seem to be the only aspects of her demeanor that are not entirely exclusive: Martineau's "aristocratic friendships," Maria Weston Chapman notes, "were better known than her democratic sympathies." Chapman adds, "there was not an eminent statesman or man of science, not an active politician or leading partisan, not a devoted philanthropist, not a great jurist, nor university professor, nor merchant-prince, nor noted divine, nor distinguished woman in the whole land who did not pay homage." [76] Chapman's eminent Americans may disagree with Martineau over the "sore point" (Martineau's term) of antislavery; still, she is courted with "idolatries" familiar to "most English celebrities." Anglophilia offers Martineau inoculation against her own convictions; it lets antebellum Boston socialize with the best of Britain, while keeping that country's more "democratic" ideologies at bay.

Bostonians, says Henry Adams, "always knelt in self-abasement before the majesty of English standards." [77] By the time Wendell Phillips and Maria Weston Chapman began to organize for abolition from the parlors of their "Boston Clique," by the time William Lloyd Garrison sought out the British aristocracy on his grand antislavery tour (where the Duchess of Sutherland especially "bewildered his republican faculties"), American abolitionism had a thing to prove. I am not saying that when Wendell Phillips calls his opponents "men of no family" he is specifically addressing a Boston that sees antislavery as "low" or pointing out that *this* particular abolitionist's great-great had been a passenger on the *Arabella* with the Winthrops and is squarely in an all-Harvard line. But antislavery is, by the 1840s and 1850s, seeking a kind of social status; Phillips's dismissal alone may be the cornstarchy airs of a born aristocrat, but understanding where "the cause" stood during Martineau's visit does help us think about why so much abolitionist writing a decade later is unapologetically expended on society, sociability, and Englishness. Antislavery gains respectability by confronting an older elite on their own turf—if Martineau finds Bostonians false and toadying, then Chapman, Phillips, and Quincy will be more English than these Anglicized nobs. Listen to Chapman describe the Boston establishment, during Martineau's visit, as so many spurious hams who simply fail to be convincingly English: "She [Martineau] came with a social prestige to the showy dwellers of Atlantic cities. These were the persons whose ambition, or rather lack of genuine self-esteem, was shown by their efforts, in humble imitation of the obnoxious class distinctions which the best Englishmen think the least worth perpetuating, to keep up among themselves dim traditional notions and literary illusions unrecognized by the land at large." [78]

Too many "showy" Americans with insecurities: Chapman's accusations of dim distinctions and dimmer pedantries stand in sharp contrast to her Englishmen's largess and play nicely off other claims that the most naturally English Americans are abolitionists. Higginson reminds his readers of the time when, "as Edmund Quincy delighted to tell, an English visitor pointed out to George Ticknor two men walking down Park Street, and added the cheerful remark, 'They are the only men I have seen in your country who looked like gentlemen.' The two men were the abolitionists Quincy and Phillips, in whose personal aspect the conservative Ticknor could see little to commend."[79] The old elite confronts the abolitionist fashionables with Anglophilic propriety that still looks to England for its gentlemanly standards; but theirs is an England as hidebound as that of Edwin Arlington Robinson's poor Miniver Cheevy ("Miniver loved the days of old / When swords were bright and steeds were prancing"). Robinson's "child of scorn" is the most parochial New Englander; it is this same embarrassing narrowness that the Englishman warns against in letting crusty Ticknor know that while Bostonians seem backward, these abolitionists are more in the swim.[80]

The Sociability of Antislavery (and Diversions of Reform)

It is worth emphasizing that abolitionism gives political license to the same range of American idolatries that Martineau fends off. Whites in the antislavery movement have a waggish affinity for Britain, and the right politics only allow for the more perfect pursuit of their British diversions. The politics are the point, of course, and I do not undersell them, but they can also become the occasion to "lion hunt" by these other means, to visit Martineau's home on Lake Windermere where, as Chapman remembers, one could amble across a "charming variety of heath and shrubbery, and green fields" all the way to Wordsworth's house (and all in the name of antislavery), or sit with Lady Byron amid the choicest statuary and paintings of London after a day's session at the Antislavery Convention. To be sure, the abolitionist's excursion to the Knoll, Martineau's Tudor estate—"overgrown to the very eaves" with climbing roses—is fair homage to abolition, and when Chapman is not peeking over the terrace into Matthew Arnold's house, or pawing the Knoll's pretty objects (the silver almanac from Mr. Darwin, the ebony papeterie from Ms. Nightingale), she remembers that it is in this house, at *this* library table, that such famous "moral business" was done.[81]

As a way into the celebrated grounds, the extended drawing rooms, parks, and halls of the "best English," antislavery is, for all its high earnestness, never too far from British amusements. For Charles Sumner, writing to George Sumner, the work of antislavery and the fascinations of Britain go together like "law, literature, society" and a morning's tea: "I think that everywhere the antislavery sentiment will get real strength. The odious Fugitive Slave law furnishes an occasion for agitation. It has shocked the people of New England. . . . I have had a pleasant day or two with Prescott at Peperell, and he has told me of his English pleasures." [82] When Stowe visits Playford Hall, the residence of British abolitionist Thomas Clarkson, her admiration of Clarkson for his antislavery is so bound up with her admiration of Clarkson for his Englishness, it is almost as if (and bear with me) she's admiring *antislavery* for its Englishness, and Englishness for its pleasantness, in a way that seems to declare the humanitarianism of a day's rambles at Playford Hall. "Playford Hall," she says, "is a thing peculiarly English, and Thomas Clarkson, for whose sake I visited it, was as peculiarly an Englishman,—a specimen of the very best kind of English mind and character, as this is of characteristic English architecture." [83] Abolitionist sentiment gets so absorbed in the object world of old England, in the appropriateness of fondling Martineau's tea caddies because Martineau did, or traipsing on George Thompson's carpets, that after awhile, it seems positively a public service for Stowe to let antislavery readers know that Clarkson's house is, indeed, the oldest *fortified* house in all of England and "the only one that has water in the moat." Antislavery in Britain has the same cult of place, the same fetishistic appeal for the American as Bath's spas or Shakespeare's house—"My birthday," cries Sumner, "in the birthplace of Shakespeare!" [84]

Abolitionists could be shameless, in fact, looking around, in the words of Ann Phillips (wife of Wendell), "à la Yankee" for any tokens of real Britain, for Sir Walter Scott's pen (on the desk of Maria Edgeworth) or a traveling lock of "Highland Mary's Hair," and, most of all, for any keepsakes of British antislavery itself. Most famous are accounts of American women, during the London Antislavery Convention, madly swarming and snipping at the mane of the venerable Clarkson for a lock of his hair as souvenir: so desirous were the ladies to each have their own that James Mott recalls fears that the abolitionist would go bald ("never mind," says Clarkson, "shear away"). [85] And here is the otherwise solemn Ann Phillips on the little objects Thompson picks out for the Boston Antislavery Fair: "His hands unfold the papers . . . and he says there that blue basket is my taste, that green pincushion with the white fringe is my choice, this little Scotch thistle also. Think, you will see the things he has handled!"[86] A young Sumner himself travels through Britain with fantasies of filching: "Again in town and in this glorious apartment," he says of the Athenaeum Club, "where I look upon the busts of Milton and Shakespeare, of Locke and Burke, of Bacon and Newton! It was not long since I saw Bulwer writing here; and when he threw down the pen he had been using, the thought crossed my mind to appropriate it and make my fortune by selling it to some of his absurd admirers in America."[87] If Bulwer Lytton's pen was not prize enough for Sumner, he returned to America in a mackintosh— materially improved by a London tailor and "looking rather English"— while carrying a stack of commemorative Exchequer tallies from the reign of George III.

Would it be impolitic to say that, for all their moral seriousness and reforming zeal, these abolitionists are, nonetheless, having fun? Take Wendell Phillips on Boston meetings to discuss the Fugitive Slave Law. Antislavery has all the international intrigue of a gothic thriller—the conspiratorial drama, the exploit, the deep thrilling mystery of men hiding, whispering, the diverting opportunities for plot: "The long evening sessions—debates about secret escapes—plans to evade where we can't resist—the door watched that no spy may enter—the whispering consultations of the morning—some putting property out of their hands, planning to incur penalties, and planning also that, in case of connection, the Government may get nothing from them—the doing, and answering no questions—intimates forbearing to ask the knowledge which may be dangerous to have—all remind me of those foreign scenes which have hitherto been known to us, transatlantic republicans, only in books."[88] Phillips has a way of aestheticizing the experience of abolitionism, of marking it off, socially and discursively, from more "vulgar" affairs. He allows his politics to revive again and again a "transatlantic" community of mutual interests and shared associations, a "sensis communis," to borrow language from David Shields, of clubby cosmopolitans in which talk of antislavery is exactly like the friendly talk of books.[89] Phillips writes of the Underground Railroad as if it were the *Scarlet Pimpernel*, derring-dos smuggling out slaves like French aristocrats, playing their roles in a way that only select groups of readers can grasp. There is little doubt that, in this one letter at least to British

abolitionist Elizabeth Pease, Phillips is allowing himself certain pleasures, not in antislavery per se—though philanthropy brings its own
joys—but in the genteel fellowship he seems to gain *through* antislavery.
A common ground of political understanding is arrived at through a
common cultural vocabulary; Phillips asks Pease to make sense of his
work with fugitive slaves through an intimate gesture that says rather
that both of us, "transatlantic republicans," read the same books.

There are several cultures of American abolitionism, but the one I
am speaking to seems always to involve a stylized community of convivial elites where one's manners and conversation, one's worldly amusements and cultivated "English" ease, become the very sign of proper
politics. William Lloyd Garrison's letters home from his 1846 British
mission so casually maunder between his lectures for the Anti-Slavery
League, on the one hand, and his excursions with Frederick Douglass
to Vauxhall gardens (or to watch "extraordinary feats of horsemanship"
or to tea services with the ladies of Edinburgh), on the other, that when
Garrison finally tells his friend Richard Webb that he and Douglass
are having a "royal time" of it, it is not exactly clear what this means. A
royal time, of antislavery? And yet antislavery is defining itself through
sophisticated tourism, through the ability—the ideological right—to
move freely amid the entertaining and affluent circles of the British
gentility because antislavery is what—along with horsemanship and tea
tables—the gentility do.[90] There is, throughout the writings of Americans abroad, a social index to abolitionism; the movement's success may
at times be measured by just how diverting it is. While there was work
to be done in the salons, clubs, and drawing rooms of Britain, enlisting
nobles in the cause, soliciting contributions for antislavery fairs and bazaars, showing aristocrats just how respectable ex-slaves could be with a
bit of British freedom, there are also festivities that seem to link British
affability and good cheer to a sense of common humanity. At least, a
ready bonhomie is made emblematic of a political disposition that favors the broadest reforms and the most encompassing commitment to
progress. Abolitionism is the final word in British collegiality, which is
why Maria Chapman's *Liberty Bell* lets us know that the secretary to the
Hibernian Anti-slavery Society "is always at leisure for the promotion
of any good thing" with "a good word for every good man." Antislavery
appears to be less rigorous ethic than relaxed hospitality. *The Liberty
Bell* continues, "Though his heart is Irish it beats for the world . . . and
neither sect, party, nor geographical boundary, confines the spheres of

his efforts for the happiness and welfare of his fellow men."[91] Christian fellowship is recast as British cosmopolitanism, and pity the dull, ignoble American with more national ties.

The pages of the *Liberator* especially describe the movement's currency amid the more desirable elements of British society so as to provoke an anxious discomfort at the plain fact of being American, antislavery or no; our nationality becomes a social stigma, or unseasonable faux pas, because once again, America is not embarrassing because it has slavery; America is embarrassing because, having slavery, it is not quite British. Abolitionist writing makes recourse to American worries that the work of civilization is happening elsewhere, that Europe will continue to answer all our claims of progress with a resounding snub. Thus Parker Pillsbury writes in the *Liberator:*

> There is no place, perhaps, except Liverpool, where we are, as a nation, much better known than in Bristol; and yet, in all that large city, I could not find a single American newspaper. By the politeness of my friends, my name was entered at all the large reading rooms and athenaeums in the city, and not one of them receives a single newspaper from my country. I told some of the librarians that the United States had become quite a neighborhood, and were in many places, particularly on the coast, getting *pretty thickly settled*. I spoke of Boston, New York and Philadelphia as becoming places of considerable importance, and recommended them to become better acquainted. Some of them laughed. . . . Many of the British people regard us as a nation of barbarians and savages. Why should they not?[92]

Pillsbury's ironies—which are themselves pretty thick—fall flat when pitched to a British dismissal of American progress he himself endorses at the slightest provocation. There is not much to a nationalism that crumples into shame before the world-historical judgment of a librarian in Bristol, and abolitionism counts on such moments of insecurity. The *National Anti-Slavery Standard* also reprints its share of London attacks on American parochialism, and these provide not only occasions for self-punishment but also the chance to extend abolition's social appeal. "It struck me," writes one author, "that the manners of Americans were deficient in real dignity," with much the same diagnosis we hear delivered by Douglass or Ward, inviting us to identify against ourselves and our national pretensions. We see our conduct as we now know others see it, "abrupt, rude and offensively boastful."[93] And if the English are "too apt to assert, as an undeniable fact, that 'the Americans are ungentlemanlike,'" the final judgment is even more condescending because the only thing this author will concede is that English expectations are, oh, always a bit high: "We have, I admit, set up for ourselves a standard of refinement and *savoir faire* very different from anything we are likely to meet with in the United States."

Abolitionists in England operate at a level of society that is open only to Americans who have somehow ceased being American, whose nationality has become so attenuated that antislavery itself serves as their primary means of belonging abroad. A report in the *Liberator* describes a proposal "to question every American clergyman who may visit England, on his conduct regarding the Fugitive Slave Law," a proposal that is designed not only to isolate and to "mortify" but also to excise from the ranks of English institutions—the pulpits, parlors, and courts—any pro-slavery "misfits" who might try to pass among the nicer classes: "It is proposed by some influential persons in England, that every American visitor shall be excluded from society, unless he can satisfy his questioners that he is an anti-slavery man."[94] This sense of abolitionism as an entry visa—"I was excluded from society as an American, and could be admitted into it only as an anti-slavery man"—informs the transatlantic aspirations of Americans in the movement, who gain access to a British world that insists on antislavery but is always about much more than antislavery.

If abolitionist sentiment is the price to be paid for affiliation with a particular rank of British culture, at the expense, it would seem, of baser ties to America, we might think of the Boston and Pennsylvania antislavery fairs and bazaars as capitalizing on this will to associate. The fairs offered a ritualized form of consumer experience that was, at the same time, sanctioned by antislavery's larger promotion of British things. There, under the direction of Maria Chapman, the self-named "grand dame of antislavery," Americans could purchase British goods for the abolitionist cause, making the acquisition of British manufactures into a moral act with antislavery handkerchiefs, antislavery stationary, antislavery wafers, antislavery samplers for the walls of reform parlors, and antislavery earthenware (so that Americans may "silently preach abolitionism to their guests by the simple process of furnishing their tables"). Both fund-raisers and society events, the bazaars allowed a desire for foreign commodities to be gratified and even celebrated

as politically motivated—"think antislavery, act British"—so that abolitionists could attribute the success of the fairs (which become the chief
source of funding for the American Antislavery Society) to the very
Britishness of the goods.[95] In a letter to Richard Allen, Charles Lennox
Remond jokingly admits that the Boston Female Anti-Slavery Society
"is more anxious & zealous & interested for the timely arrival of the
Boxes" filled with housewares, than for his arrival in person. William
Wells Brown describes how "Honiton lace" and other British products,
"elegant and fashionable articles of wearing apparel, fancy-work, draw-
ings, autographs, etc., sent from Dublin, Cork, Edinburgh, Perth, Glasgow, Bristol, [and] Leeds" will surely be "the greatest attraction" of the
1850 Philadelphia Anti-Slavery Bazaar.[96] "Everybody," writes Margaret
Fuller, "is running to the Anti-Slavery Fair, said to be full of beautiful
things from England. I wish I could go and buy."

Chapman's circulars are bristling with British merchandise—wax
fruit, cut paper birds, old books, shells of Great Britain (scientifically
arranged), Edinburgh fish-woman dolls, a "Great Waxen Victoria in
royal robes," boxes of Bartlett's celebrated needles from Ireland—and
other "rich" goods to attract abolitionists of "social rank & respectability." In 1844, one could buy any number of *petits objets* for the drawing
room, "in great abundance and *bien recherché*"; an elegant table cover
"wrought for the Fair by Harriet Martineau"; pictorial and musical
note and letter paper, "comprising castles and cathedrals, abbeys of
England"; watercolors of "English cottage subjects, by English ladies";
sofa covers, throat shields, dressing gowns, foot cushions, bell pulls,
"all knitted and netted and wrought by English and Irish friends of
the cause." One could also purchase autographs from "almost all the
Literati, Nobility, and Philanthropists of England," including, but not
limited to, "Sir Humphrey Davy, Doctor Parr, Wilberforce, Humboldt,
Clarkson, The Duchess of Sutherland, Queen Adelaide, Moore, Camp-
bell, Peel, Charlotte Smith, The Howitts, Carlyle."[97]

In the acute fascination with British objects, abolition's political
economy fades slowly into abolition's dream work. The tours suggest
the semiotic excess that Barthes makes central to the allure of fashionable commodities, which let us "intoxicate ourselves on images,
identify ourselves oneirically"; though even this argument seems too
timid by half when read against the discourse that surrounds antislavery.[98] There is the need to move product on the cause's behalf, but also
the desire to materialize an Anglophilic fantasy in which American

consumers, enthralled by British goods, can make a nation in better taste. Here again is Chapman, describing the National Anti-Slavery Bazaar of 1846:

> The world is like the sea-anemone: any part of it, however small, has the capacity of becoming a complete model of the whole; and truly and well does this little world in Faneuil Hall show forth a larger one, affording a perfect illustration of the whole Anti-Slavery cause that in its turn typifies the great moral movement of this age, of which it is the vanguard. . . . Make the round of the Hall a second time, to take note of the foreign contributions, which eclipse the home department in variety and beauty. Like that "spiritual theory of another life," which supposes one set of existences within another, like the drawers of a desk, we find England, Scotland, and Ireland, occupying the spaces between New-York, Massachusetts, and Missouri.[99]

An "anemone" that is a synecdoche for advancing civilization—it certainly counts for semiotic excess. Moving goods is moral movement in this phantasmically "united kingdom" where we should all make efforts to own our sympathies. Her symbolic delirium notwithstanding, Chapman communicates her message clearly enough: the "world" of stylized ethics and politicized refinement to which antislavery aspires, is finally tangible in America—we can hold it in our hands and it feels exquisite. British commodities, like relics from a holy land, give promise of "another life" beyond this nation still dominated by the slave power and, what is more, still inadequately supplied with "net-flowers from Bristol," "ornamental glass-work from Manchester" and "brooms and brushes from Hatfield." "Who," Chapman asks, "is sufficient to catalogue them all?"—questioning the limits of her own grasp on this spectacularly British object world. "The absent can never know what they lost."

This is all ripe language, to be sure, but it also helps us understand aspects of these events that are not quite so apparent amid the "spiritualizing" of trinkets and stationery. The antislavery fairs and bazaars cater to an Anglophilic lust for fashionable things, which in turn suggests a great deal about Britain's crucial role in what might be called the social anthropology of American abolition. If Barthes's account of "the fashion system" offers insight into the fairs' dizzying rhetoric, Georg Simmel's essay "Fashion" seems ultimately more useful for gauging their significance, especially in its description of how imports from abroad can maintain group identity at home *through* their "foreignness." "The exotic origin of fashions," writes Simmel, "seems strongly to favor the exclusiveness of the groups which adopt them. Because of their external origin, these imported fashions create a special and significant form of socialization, which arises through mutual relation to a point without the circle." But it is why such imports "socialize" us that warrants our attention: "This motive of foreignness, which fashion employs in its socializing endeavors, is restricted to higher civilization, because novelty, which foreign origin guarantees in extreme form, is often regarded by primitive races as an evil." Thus while "the savage is afraid of strange appearances," Simmel adds, a truly civilized society "transforms this affectation into its very opposite."[100] Refinement involves a taste for the foreign; "exotic" objects confirm social exclusiveness by distinguishing "higher civilizations" from those that can not move past local preferences or know the allure of difference. The foreign tastes of society's "vanguard," recalling Chapman's term, thus separate them from the ruder masses with every acquisition from abroad and every imported purchase.

Although antislavery, I should emphasize, makes for a curiously retrospective "vanguard": that so much of what the fairs put on sale is saturated with an "Englishness" that tends to the "olde," gives the impression of cosmopolitanism shot through with nostalgia for any available piece of a tradition that once belonged to us. As ratifications in the marketplace of America's Anglophile tastes, these bazaars imply a curiously reenacted economy of colony and metropolis, a return to the logic of the Stamp Act where our purchases help to realize our allegiances toward Britain. *Vanity Fair,* commenting on the American willingness to "subject" ourselves to British styles, goes so far as to call for a new abolition aimed at "slaves of fashion," with their "collars of the Byronic persuasion" and compulsion for "the latest, newest, and most *recherché*." The magazine suggests that "the expiring Abolition party"—this is 1862—should "rise from its bed of ashes and get up a new cry—the Emancipation of the Swell."[101] Yet, to repeat, my point is not that white Americans became devoted consumers of British goods because Britain had abolished the slave trade earlier in the century or because Wilberforce was a moral icon; rather, antislavery's transatlantic appeal enjoyed the benefits of a thriving interest in anything of British culture but, particularly, in those aspects that could be mimicked and performed as one's own.

I ought to clarify. Not all abolitionists paid respects to Britain, and not all respects are devotional. Abolitionists could be famously critical of the British class system, and even those who courted the most sympathetic elites did not put British policy above reproach. Britain's own offenses do make the pages of the abolitionist press and are liberally compared to American slavery—poverty, low wages, and dispossession, the same crimes that Chartism takes on, do vie with, if not diffuse, charges of American oppression. "If we have slave-representation," writes the *Anti-Slavery Standard,*

> they have an hereditary monarch, a house of peers and an established church. If we have Slavery, have they not a starving manufacturing and agricultural population? We have Repudiation, to be sure, but they have the national debt and the tithe system. If they point to the horrors of our internal slave trade, we in return tell them to look at the oppressions of their own coal-mines. If they upbraid us with our treatment of the indian tribes, the answer is ready, Hindostan and China. The Institution of Lynch-law we admit, but plead as a set-off the disturbances in the manufacturing districts.[102]

For every few pages on the homely charms of the English cottage, a reprint from the *Democratic Review* comes along that takes us inside to see instead overpopulation, poor rations, too little fuel, depressed spirits, and a "whole chattel estate, including the apparel of man, wife, and children" that "could not be sold for ten dollars."[103] Maria Chapman's *Liberty Bell* runs at least one polemic against British "subjection" to the queen and Church in which all Britons are slaves because all Britons are subjects—even the antislavery champions of the Old World are "vassals" in disguise: "The colossal Brougham is but a vassal. He is but a *giant* subject. Wellington is a *subject.* He conquered Bonapart, but he has to do homage at the foot of a British girl. He wears her collar on his ducal neck. And the mighty O'Connell, whose genius measures the earth, and whose voice 'agitates' it,—he is the subject of that same British damsel. He owes her allegiance and fealty. Her will is his law."[104] Protests against slavery do fan out, occasionally, to protests against royal prerogative and Irish enclosures; abolitionists do find misgovernment elsewhere, and a few notable ones, including William Goodell of the *Emancipator,* see antislavery as a radical critique of all aristocracies of wealth. Labor and agrarian reformers William West and George Henry Evans each has a series of letters in the *Liberator* comparing "wages slavery" with chattel slavery and detailing the starvation of Irish cottagers.[105]

Yet a lion's share of the time, abolitionist critique of Britain sounds more like concession than conviction. I'll grant you Britain's poor and laboring classes, they seem to say, but might we not suffer these a little, choose our fights?—and Britain is so charming besides. Here is Sumner to his brother George:

> Those who know my opinions know that I saw and felt the plague-spots of England as much as anybody. The government is an oligarchy,—the greatest and most powerful in the history of the world. There is luxury the most surprising side by side with poverty the most appalling. I never saw this in England, I never think of it now, without a shock. I pray for some change,—in peace,—by which this constant injustice may be made to cease. But because these things are so, should I therefore condemn all the people? Should I fall foul, like another Smelfungus, of all that is beautiful? . . . But should I not love my friends? Should I not love those minds that have enriched our common language with their high fancies, their glowing thoughts, their learned expositions?[106]

The English aristocracy certainly has its faults, but seeing that, seeing that the very class that extends its philanthropies to America has withheld them from home, should we not, as *Frederick Douglass' Paper* writes, "try and love England a little?" These are not excuses—the infringements are disturbing and real—but England has, you will allow, "played a great, and, upon the whole a *good* part in the historical drama of the world. Shakespeare was English, and how he loved his country! and what a country must that be which a Shakespeare, with such a tender, jovial heartiness, could love! Milton was English, and spent his best days proudly in her service. Charles Dickens is English."[107] And if some of England's best seem uncharitable, are they not, too, in their own quaint and characteristic way, forgivably English? Look at how the *National Anti-Slavery Standard* saves Carlyle:

> About Anti-Slavery, he is unbearable, and about every philanthropic effort. He scoffs with cruel glee at all abolitionists, and all blacks. He disparages Toussaint, denies his attributes, and chuckles at his thick lips in the portrait. Though all this is true, and though it is true that he is not amiable, nor practical, that he is fit only to write his grand ideas, which

are so eminently needed, it is also true, though one can hardly believe it, that he is the most lovable soul you can meet. His feelings are all against his tongue, and he does not know what to do with his sympathies and emotions, impracticable being that he is. . . . He is an inspired idiot, who is to be listened to reverently.[108]

Racism, in Carlyle, is funny and cranky—the British are so awkward showing their feelings and they sound off in such peculiar ways; but, writes this author, Carlyle's "sayings against Anti-Slavery are of no consequence." They have no bearing on "the charm of his purity." [109]

At times, abolitionists offer more subtle pleadings for Britain, some of which even seem to replay, in another idiom of class, apologies for slavery in the United States. It is not that these abolitionists are blind to the rural and industrial poor, but that their circumstances are acknowledged and indulged in ways that echo certain arguments at home. Harriet Beecher Stowe writes, "I do not doubt of there being suffering and misery in the agricultural population of England, but still there are multitudes of cottages, which are really very pleasant objects . . . [with] a flower garden attached to each." [110] Poverty, sure, but it has its simple pleasures when suited to the picturesque rusticity one finds in England—miserable but floral. If Frederick Douglass is "utterly astonished" to find people "who could speak of the singing, among slaves, as evidence of their contentment and happiness," Julia Griffiths has little problem accepting how "thoroughly happy the people looked" at a harvest celebration in Alveston, where villagers, "marching to the sound of music," made "rural offerings" of their labors.[111] Black abolitionists are no less taken with what William Wells Brown describes as the "sanctity and picturesque beauty" of the English agricultural landscape: "The very laborer," he writes, "with his thatched cottage and narrow slip of ground-plot before the door, the little flower-bed, the woodbine trimmed against the wall, and hanging its blossoms about the windows, and the peasant seen trudging home at nightfall with the avails of the toils of the day upon his back—all this tells us of the happiness both rich and poor in this country." [112]

When Samuel Ringgold Ward describes the "cheerfulness of the operatives" at factories in Manchester this is, in part, a strategy of abolition; blacks in Britain tried to distinguish chattel slavery from the mix of social ills, afraid of insulting their working-class audience by calling them slaves—an audience whose "heartiness and enthusiasm" for the cause was "something glorious" (*Douglass' Monthly*)—and afraid, too, of diminishing the response to slavery itself. Douglass especially tends to remind readers that there is, finally, no slavery in Britain, that there are worse evils and lesser evils and that broadening the sense of slavery to include any number of oppressions removes "in some measure the horror with which the system had hitherto been contemplated."[113] Ward worries that any attention to English or Irish workers gives far too much to apologists of slavery who then may claim that even the British wage laborers "are worse off than our slaves." So this goes some way toward explaining just how Ward sees fit to describe the "comfort and cleanliness" and overall "elegance" of the British working class, enjoying their holidays as they can "with their wives and sweethearts"—he would, in other words, "*rather* spoil the parallel between British free labour and the American slave!" (167). Still, British caste is something abolitionists hardly confront; Brown's "peasant" trudges home but under the burden of plenty and to a cottage that sounds, in his narrative, uncannily like the "small mean-looking" birthplace of Shakespeare.[114]

Even those abolitionists who come to Britain with decidedly antiaristocratic tendencies, who arrive, for example, at the London Antislavery Convention, with work to do but a certain avowed distaste for the pomp surrounding it, find their own Britain to rhapsodize. Lucretia Mott may profess to be an unwilling tourist; the jottings from her 1840 visit are elliptical and efficient—went there, did that—and unsentimental where other visitors fawn. Morning services at Windsor Chapel are stagy and "ridiculous." She sees Shakespeare's grave but "forgot to weep," while husband James Mott stood on it ("quite a profanation"). They maintain a sober sense of British privilege with Lucretia remarking that the poor are surely "robbed to supply the luxury" of country seats, while James is more cynical at castles: "Windsor Castle is one of the many monuments of the extravagance and folly of the English nobility and aristocracy which oppress the laborer, by taking from him in the shape of impost and taxes, so much of his earnings as to leave but a scanty subsistence for himself. We met with scarcely any who appeared to see the effect of the large palaces and parks on the population."[115] But, then again, it is Lucretia Mott who is spotted with the rest of them snipping at Clarkson's head, who may find Britain "miserable" but delights to find herself in the house of Mills—"overlooking Milton's garden and the house of Bentham"—where she takes, as souvenirs, ambiguously "ancient relics" and strands of "Bentham's hair."[116] Bentham's hair, Clarkson's hair: Lucretia Mott, for all her sobriety, loves British radicalism with the same fetishizing abandon and idolatries that mark what she sees as a specifically undemocratic response to royalty. These steady democrats adore nonetheless; choosing Burns's house, maybe, over Eaton Hall, or O'Connell over Victoria, their politics simply focus their flatteries; in the abolitionist press, Americans who criticize the English, worship the Irish with the same touristic, Anglophilic susceptibility. A "Portrait in Paddy Land" in the *Anti-Slavery Standard* describes a day with Hannah More: "I am by no means learned," the author qualifies, "in the mysteries of a lady's toilette, that is, so far as the particular names of the various articles of dress are concerned." (He gratifies his correspondents still: "On her head she wore what was called a high mop cap, with an ample bordering of lace, nicely placed, and tied with a monstrous bow under the chin. On her hands she had black cotton gloves, with long sleeves, the tips of the fingers having been cut off").[117]

In Lucretia Mott's journal we see how the most strident antislavery gets absorbed in the displaced social pleasantries of Americans on tour—these abolitionists are not on holiday from antislavery, but they have staged a holiday *of* antislavery. Mott's description of her weekend in the Highlands is typical: "pleasant conversation" with George Thompson is set against the popular rituals of her excursion—rowing across Lake Katrine with a paid guide, who passes spots mentioned in Scott's *The Lady of Lake,* all the while reciting *The Lady of the Lake,* and later walking with Thompson across Scott's grounds to meet the widow of Scott's trusty servant (who lets them drink from the cup of Scott's son). Antislavery *is* pleasant—down Loch Lomond thirty miles to breakfast, then tea, off to castles with Thompson before the antislavery meeting, and, the next day, plenty of gooseberries, a reading of Robert Burns "in broad Scotch" for their amusement, and the adjourned meeting of the Emancipation Society on "the Elevation of the working classes." Abolition is the pursuit of British civilities, and so when Mott meets a Georgia slave owner on the banks of the river, the chitchat that ensues is no less about politics than Ward's "escape" from Holyrood House but a politics strangely caught up in the value of sociability:

> Top of Coach to Melrose—Georgian Planter in company tried to convince us the slave was better off than the working man in England and Ireland—not succeeding—begged off—as he did not want the pleasure of his day's ride destroyed as it was in Ireland by talking on that subject—

seemed to like our company—asked us to join with their party to Abbots-
ford. . . . Thence to Dryburgh Abbey—rode in two carriages—crossed
the Tweed in a small boat—rowed over by the Georgia man—was glad to
do what he could to bring us over to the *other side*. Abby laughed at him
for having such a company of Abolitionists under his charge—long walk
after getting over—plenty of cherries in the enclosure—lagged behind
to eat, while the girls were hastening to sentimentalize & gather flowers
over Scott's grave—beautiful ivy over the ruined window—climbed up
narrow staircase to top of ruins—gathered blue bells & a heap of pretty
posies.[118]

The opposition is, quite literally, on vacation; Southern planter and
Northern abolitionist play out their differences in this Highland tableau where political sides are so many sides of the Tweed. The planter's
pro-slavery sentiments are never more harmful than Carlyle's; they are
finally the byplay of this mutually enlivening moment, of abolition, ruins, and posies at Dryburgh Abbey.

This gentility is finally as central to the appeal of antislavery as emancipation or at least as widely pursued by all Americans enjoying these
more polite, more leisurely, forms of society that make up Britain's
imaginary domain. British sociability, raised to such heightened and
codified registers, comes to define an idyllic social landscape in which
the movement feels comfortably at home. A retreat to Lake Katrine
or the Tweed—with abolition lodged squarely in a sense of Scott—is
anything but diverting; all abolitionists were doing it, and it is precisely
this kind of Anglophilic ritual that gets us back to the strategies of
the movement. Abolition wants what Lake Katrine seems to promise:
a world in which human interest is tied up with "pleasant conversation," where higher culture—this civilized, socialized, *British* culture—
becomes the grounds for a wider understanding.

In *Ellen's Isle* (1870), African American painter Robert Duncanson gives
us the same Lake Katrine (fig. 28). The image depicts an unspecified
moment of scenery from *Lady of the Lake*—its diffusing light, harmonizing landscape, its warm blurry glow of sun skimming Lake Katrine and
two skiffs moving, in any which direction, through all the atmospheric
brown—it all conspires to, what has proved to be for critics, a very remarkable stasis. If this picture is not sheerly derivative, if this black
painter is doing something other than facilely imitating the luminist

FIGURE 28. Robert S. Duncanson, *Ellen's Isle, Loch Katrine,* 1871. Gift of the Estate of Ralzemond D. Parker. Photograph © 1985 The Detroit Institute of Arts.

landscapes of, say, John Frederick Kensett, then surely he must be (to cite David Lubin's use of Henry Louis Gates) "signifyin'."[119] This is, after all, a Reconstruction-era painting that recalls Duncanson's Civil War visit to Scotland—it may look serene, the argument goes, but the topography here, even the use of Scott, must have worked subversively. Lubin, in particular, tries to read *Ellen's Isle* for signs of "Afro-cultural themes": a body of water, a crossing to shore (other critics, too, say this recalls the River Jordan, crossings to freedom); and since *The Lady of the Lake* begins with a great Scottish stag hunt, could African Americans, asks Lubin, have possibly "entertained such a description of the hunt without being reminded of an escaped slave chased through the woods?" Readings of the painting like to look past its Britishness, and while I agree with Lubin that this is more about black Americans than it seems, Duncanson's subject is not a kind of Highland masquerade for slavery, nor must his *The Lady of the Lake* be allegorical to be *about* slavery, nor need we get beyond the veil of Scott's hazy, anodyne scenery to find something "more meaningful."[120]

For while "nothing would seem more irrelevant to the problem of Reconstruction-era African-Americans than a sixty-year-old Scottish romance in iambic tetrameter," I would say that nothing is more meaningful for the black artist abroad, that this *is* a crucially black—and politically black—subject because it is so, shamelessly, British. This is not because, as Lubin suggests, a "denial is also an affirmation"—in denying, that is, that this idealized, preternaturally peaceful "wish-landscape" does not exist in 1865 or 1870, Duncanson is defiantly evoking the social realities that do. I think that Lubin and others rather undersell Duncanson's imitations of Scott. Like the poem itself, Duncanson's picture gives us amid the conflicts and hazards of war (in Scott, the war is impending between Highland and Lowland clans) too much scenery, too vivid (glossy) a view of Lake Katrine, too fine a sense of place. In the poem, we have an overwhelming reproduction of landscape, which makes it more Scottish guidebook than melodrama:

The Summer dawn's reflected hue
To purple changed Loch Katrine blue;
Mildly and soft the western breeze
Just kissed the lake and stirred the trees.[121]

In Duncanson, it is the favoring of location to any adventure in the boats, the pre-Raphaelite urge toward the details of ecology, in the foreground, and the sensibility to blend them in the rest. Such connoisseurship in the midst of the fray, such moments of aesthetic preoccupation and decent delight with what is, really, beside the point makes Duncanson's painting, like the reading of Scott's romance, a genteel pleasure. *Ellen's Isle* is not racial mimicry: it is a black artist reaching, by all accounts, "the peak of his powers," the height of his talents, by reproducing this superbly British world in which all drama is absorbed in cultivated tastes.[122] Britain is the subject of an appropriative and canny reproduction whose ironies are rarely aimed at what is represented, and to equate this British world with any common "whiteness" is to miss the emphatic distinctions that antebellum Americans made between their own tradition and the better one overseas. Duncanson's work is exemplary of a wider identification with Britain that abolition elites, both black and white, performed as much for each other, in mutual tribute, as against America. The honors accorded Britain are at the expense of an America that is nowhere to be seen; but in paying Britain tribute, Duncanson also assumes that these honors are his to bestow, and this is where, I would argue, the painting's class politics come into focus.

In presenting *Ellen's Isle,* his "chef d'oeuvre," as a gift to Sumner, Duncanson points to his own intimacy with a British society that he knew Sumner admired, one as much about antislavery—about the fact, for example, that Duncanson could be there, painting, in 1865—as about guided tours of Scott's estate. Think of Duncanson, says Moncure Conway, "think of a Negro sitting at the table with Mr. and Mrs. Alfred Lord Tennyson, Lord and Lady of the Manor, and Mirror of Aristocracy, and so forth." [123] Lake Katrine is a place where the best civilization meets the best racial politics, where no vulgar intolerance can prevent an artist like Duncanson from taking in the beauty of a scene.

Years later, at the height of the Harlem Renaissance, Du Bois has a similar response to Scott's poem:

> In the high school where I studied we learned most of Scott's "Lady of the Lake" by heart. In after life once it was my privilege to see the lake. It was Sunday. It was quiet. You could glimpse the deer wandering in unbroken forests; you could hear the soft ripple of romance on the waters. Around me fell the cadence of that poetry of my youth. I fell asleep full of the enchantment of the Scottish border. A new day broke and with it came a sudden rush of excursionists. They were mostly Americans and they were loud and strident. They poured upon the little pleasure boat,—men with their hats a little on one side and drooping cigars in the wet corners of their mouths; women who shared their conversation with the world. They all tried to get everywhere first. They pushed other people out of the way. They made all sorts of incoherent noises and gestures so that the quiet home folk and the visitors from other lands silently and half-wonderingly gave way before them. They struck a note not evil but wrong. They carried, perhaps, a sense of strength and accomplishment, but their hearts had no conception of the beauty which pervaded this holy place. [124]

Du Bois makes a pilgrimage to Lake Katrine and is in heaven, "in after life," and heaven looks a lot like Duncanson's painting. There is romance on the water, quiet ripples, a sense of timelessness, and then rude Americans bring the times back in, strident and rushing, aggressive, with drooping cigars and salivating lips and all levels of inharmonious cawing. They strike notes "not evil but wrong": the problem with Americans is not that they're bad; they're off-pitch. Not immoral, but inappropriate. Their manners fall flat. And for Du Bois, the black American is as uniquely qualified to learn this as he is to learn Scott by heart. Powerful Americans, "full-fledged Americans," are vulgar and ugly and "you realize this," he says to the NAACP, "sooner than the average white American because, pushed aside as we have been in America, there has come to us not only a certain distaste for the tawdry and flamboyant but a vision of what the world could be if it were really a beautiful world." [125] Because blacks have been "pushed aside" in America, because they are forced to be, to recall Hopkins, "an alien people" without a home, they are indeed citizens of the world. They look back from Britain, like Duncanson in exile in 1865, or Du Bois from his heaven on the lake, and see America for what it is—harsh, pretentious, provincial, and, most of all, in very poor taste. Blacks are de facto cosmopolitans, and they offer white Americans this vision from afar of an idealized, civilized world in which the highest cultural accomplishment is a likeness to Britain.

Black Anglo-Saxonism

It is not so much that African Americans went abroad in search of means to elevate and refine the race but that their extensive travels chart an American dislocation of social improvement, a progress toward respectability that already codes respectability *as* English. Du Bois's remark that he may "sit with Shakespeare and he winces not," just begins to remind us that almost any gesture toward intellectual authority involves a subtle transaction with a received notion of "American," whether black or white, that is able to recognize its native genius only through dramas of Anglicization.[126] Black refugees in British schools, writes the *Liberator,* "are upon a footing of perfect social equality, having formed friendships as fast, and been received into the best company as freely, as though their features were of the most perfect Caucasian mould, and their cheeks were untinged with a shade of ebony. The most stiff-necked English aristocrat, and the haughtiest European despot, know nothing of prejudice of color." Intellectualism and aristocracy are cheek by jowl; the "Home and Colonial School" in London, where William Wells Brown's daughters attend, owes its stature—despite its politics—to its swollen roster of accumulated grandees: "No American can sneer at the school as plebeian, or because it is supported only by fanatical English abolitionists and philanthropists. Among its members are the Queen, Prince Albert, the Princess Teresa of Oldenburg, the Duchess of Gordon, Sutherland and Beaufort, the Earl of Derby and several hundred peers, peeresses, bishops, baronets, members of

Parliament, clergy, magistrates and merchants." [127] Black abolitionists become both benefactors and stewards of a rarefied Englishness that then serves in the United States as a shared intellectual culture. But black incarnations of American Anglophilia also suggest a perspective on intellectualism that looks ahead to such figures as C. L. R. James and Edward Said: classless "aliens," to borrow a term that Said himself borrows from Matthew Arnold, removed from strong feelings of nationhood and, for exactly this reason, better able to preside over a "common heritage"—a global culture—left behind by the West and best grasped from the position of fugitive or diasporic remove. [128] Thus Samuel Ringgold Ward leaves an antislavery paper in Cleveland named the *Alienated American,* to found his own publication, the *Impartial Citizen.* [129]

If, as Stuart Hall notes, for most diasporans, the return to the homeland is metaphorical, existing in an "imaginative geography" and so offering a sense of belonging that depends on an experience of collective displacement, then the temporary, invented "motherland" that black abolitionists locate in Britain similarly serves. [130] In such works as Joshua McCarter Simpson's antislavery lyric "Queen Victoria Conversing with Her Slave Children"—to be sung to the music of "Come, Come Away"—antislavery's transatlantic logic is rehearsed as a shrewd and maudlin melodrama of renewed custodial affections:

QUEEN

O come, come away, my sable sons and daughters,
    Why linger there
    In dark despair?
    O come, come away!
On Erie's northern banks I stand,
With open arms and stretched out hands;
From tyrant Columbia's land,
    O come, come away?

SLAVES

O, mother Victoria, why do you thus torment us?
    Do you not see
    That we're not free,
    And can't come away?
We're watched by day and chained by night
Both robbed of liberty and right;

While crushed by the oppressor's might
    We can't come away.

QUEEN
O come, come away, my sable sons and daughters,
    Your galling chains
    Now rend in twain
    And come, come away.
Here in my province still is room,
And I will give you if you come
A long, free and happy home,
    O come, come away![131]

Simpson's "slaves" are of course rescued after "mother Victoria" can "tease no longer" and welcomes her African American progeny. The scene plays quite close to a version of Freud's "family romance," where children conjure an alternative past in which they are born of royalty; it recalls the paternalistic language of slavery but makes available a new dependence that is honored and even loved. The tropes of paternalism are now estranged and pointedly made foreign—with all these mother queens, fatherlands, and sable sons—in a way that allows ex-slaves to imagine themselves as perfect "subjects." Suddenly blacks are touting their fitness *as* subjects; in these abolitionist texts, blacks again and again seize on the opportunity to define their condition as a "subject people," but in a transvaluation of terms for blacks abroad, it is the ability to be good "subjects" that finally lets African Americans become proper Englishmen. As Ward says, "The black man is a lover of freedom, a loyal subject, an industrious man" (120). Or later, "I felt more than ever grateful to God that it is my lot, and the lot of my children, to be and remain subjects of the British Crown. . . . Who can blame a Negro for loving Great Britain? Who wonders that we are among the most loyal of Her Majesty's subjects?" (219). Surely not ex-slave Benjamin Drew, who feels compelled to affirm that most fugitives in Canada are "good 'subjects' in the English sense of the word."[132]

Accounts of blacks as faithful subjects help a white audience to distinguish these particular abolitionists from other insurgent strains of the movement; these are not Nat Turners, but blacks who see themselves as everywhere involved, in Britain and the United States, with antirevolutionary feelings of loyalism. Brown, watching a royal procession, notes approvingly a crowd that seems to "beam with delight," conflating political obedience with familial affection: "I had a full view of the queen and all who followed in the train. Her majesty—whether from actual love for her person, or the novelty of the occasion, I know not which—was received everywhere with the greatest enthusiasm. One thing, however, is certain, and that is, Queen Victoria is beloved by her subjects." [133] "We acknowledge," says Daniel Alexander Payne, of the A.M.E. Church, in 1856, "Her Majesty, Queen Victoria, as our rightful sovereign, possessing supremacy over all the British Empire as it exists in Europe, Asia, Australia, North America, South America, the West Indies, and other islands of the ocean." [134] Abolitionism becomes a variation on a traditionary discourse that conserves rituals of hierarchy, which in turn lend dignity and status to the cause. At the same time, there is nothing less demeaning to the abolitionist's white audience than a slavish ingratiation toward Britain. The ex-slave is still scolded and chastened but here, says Ward, is why: "The Earl of Shaftesbury bade me call upon him as often as I pleased. Upon one occasion his lordship shook me by the hand, saying 'God Bless You, my good friend! Call again, when you can.' On another occasion he rebuked me for not having called more frequently" (206).

What does it mean for ex-slaves to enact these ritualized shows of deference? They do not just affirm the social hierarchies but respectfully submit to them. The coercive restraints of slavery are removed but only to make way for spontaneous affective identifications with a dominant power that now manages to inspire obedience. Certainly it seems plausible to see such behavior as the calculative strategy of a movement that would sanction reform only within the legitimating structures of stable social authority. Freedom may be gained, but the interdependence of a system in which blacks play a humble part is also harmoniously secured. That such deference may be given freely makes no less troubling the fact that ex-slaves have been habituated to give it, and one feels caught between reading their gestures as either the reiterations of false consciousness or, more optimistically, mere show. Eugene Genovese reminds us that there is a considerable degree of dissemblance involved in the acts of willingness to obey; seemingly docile slaves turn violent, and there are too many historic outbreaks of unrest to see any deference to a traditional authority as a simple expression of gratitude. [135] We adamantly would not want to say that, in these abolitionist endorsements of the British class structure, we have the signs of a deferential personality that was born of slavery, or that ex-slaves were more ritualized into the ingratiating acts that paternalistic institutions reward. Their deference remains interpretable as a tactic because we neither want to nor are able to extricate these shows of subjection from the antislavery movement's difficult relationship to black power.

Still, there seem to be moments of sincerity within the show, when paying respect acknowledges the self-respect of both parties. There is enough in the deference to suggest, at least as it rhetorically unfolds, that the ritual may be gratifying outside the expressions of obligation. Loving Queen Victoria or loving the Earl of Shaftesbury endorses a kind of social authority that in these poems and narratives will always be the greatest guarantor of personal liberty traditionally conceived (in Britain of course) as a form of civic virtue. To serve a benevolent queen suggests only the restraint necessary to preserve individual freedoms, while the alternative is what Matthew Arnold calls "doing what one likes" and is much closer to the evils of the slave system in which too many liberties create anarchy. Fugitive slave Austin Steward opposes "the outstretched arms of an English Queen" to the tyrannizing chaos of personal power in the South:

> When our ministers of the gospel, are sent back to us from the South, clothed with a coat of tar and feathers; when our best and most sacrificing philanthropists are thrown into Southern dungeons; when our laboring men are shot down by haughty and idle Southern aristocrats, in the hotels of their employers, and under the very eye of Congress; when the press is muzzled and every editor, who has the manliness to speak in defense of Freedom, and the wickedness of the slaveholder, is caned or otherwise insulted by some insignificant Southern bully; and when at last, our Mr. Sumner is attacked from behind, by a Southern, cowardly scoundrel, and felled senseless on the floor of the Senate chamber, for his defense of Liberty,—then, indeed, may Northern men look about them![136]

As Arnold would say, "there is nothing so very blessed" in doing as one likes when it leads to insults on reason and sense; for him, "mere freedom" is the "worship of machinery" while the "principle of authority" is sweetness and light. It is such classical theories of political authority that the abolitionists' deference comes to stage in the willing renunciations that let them recognize the humanity of a queen. Choosing to respect royalty becomes a spectacular experiment in republicanism and not least because it confers "virtue" on its subjects. But not just virtue, culture, too, in Arnold's sense—as a project of human perfectibility through growth and reason, which is often only realized when we defer as we can ("then," he says, "we have got a practical benefit out of culture"). For even before Arnold, ideas and habits of temperament that linked human progress and grace to specifically British forms of authority could make the affections for "mother Victoria" on the part of ex-slaves seem less compromising to a project of reform.[137]

At the extremities of black Anglophilia we find that even a discourse of racial Anglo-Saxonism could be put to work for the antislavery cause. Sometimes this means an indulgence in genealogical beliefs of black "consanguinity" with Britain. William Wells Brown's fond memories of being "at home" in his English "father-land" are writ large by the *Anglo-African Magazine*'s claim that there is no African race, miscegenation having left American blacks no option but to seek their rightful "family privileges" among their "loving brethren" in Britain: "*Fratres patrueles,*—" it writes, "the Anglo-Saxon, and the Congo negro!" Indeed, the whole project of this first black magazine in the United States, published in 1859, announces a much bolder version of abolition's transatlantic ties by incorporating the facts of miscegenation and intermarriage into an operative defense of black affinities for England. "Because," the magazine writes,

> some of our fore-parents, one or two hundred years ago, were brought from Africa, does it prove *us* to be Africans, and our posterity such, forever? Must we, of all people, be excepted from claiming and adopting that simple christening, which nativity always confers? Is there anything so particularly blessed in color, or anything so essentially great in Africa, that we must never clothe ourselves with our proper citizenship, but make haste to give aid to the enemy, by acting as if we never could become naturalized, even by birth, anywhere outside of the tribe-boundaries of the African Continent? The poet Wordsworth, in his "Intimations of Immortality," sings,

> "The soul that rises with us, our life's star,
> Hath had elsewhere its setting,
> And cometh from afar."[138]

Because all Americans are finally from somewhere else—emigrants and exiles mixing their Old World ancestries with their new (Anglo-Saxons, Anglo-Africans)—we have a choice. Why Africa, asks the author, or America alone, when our identities are so various, "hybrids" of historical truths and biological accidents? It is an argument that enlarges on an increasingly popular scientific racialism, with its images of polygenesis and dissipated "mongrel" breeds, by emphasizing instead a more amenable hybridity, one based on Romantic notions of a self that evolves in constant motion away from where it starts, whether in the innocence of childhood or the "tribe-boundaries" of Africa. It is strangely because of racial biology that blacks in America can argue for elective feelings of belonging; Anglo-Saxonism, as an inherited option, allows blacks to take liberties with their points of origin. Racial memory lets African Americans recollect a past that, like one of Wordsworth's intimations, shapes the present while being largely generated in the present—patrimonies that, if real, are no less imaginatively reclaimed. James Clifford describes something akin to these "traveling" theories of racial practice: identities are modeled on the most "ex-centric" cases, where the possibilities of mixture weigh more heavily than fixed traditions and where crucial languages of self-definition take their inflections from abroad.[139] Here is Steward, writing from Canada:

> How many pure Africans, think you, can be found in the whole slave population of the South, to say nothing of their nativity? . . . If the All-wise God, who has created of one blood all nations of the earth, has designated their blood to commingle until that of the African is absorbed in that of the European,—then it is right, and amalgamation of all the different races should be universally practiced and approved. If it be right for the Southern slaveholder, to cruelly enforce the mixture of the races, to gratify his lust, and swell the enormity of his gains, certainly it cannot be wrong to amalgamate from choice and affection.[140]

So if conventional racial theories saw white Americans as the heirs to British civilization, ushered in by the westward course of empire, abolitionist William G. Allen puts blacks, too, in the British line: "[I] differ," he writes in *Frederick Douglass' Paper*,

> with Mr. Mann in regarding the colored people of this country as an *African* race, in contradistinction from any other. The colored people of this country are essentially a *mixed* race. Already more than half

Anglo-Saxonized, it will not take Henry Clay's two hundred years to make them *wholly* such. At this moment, there sits at my side a young man of two-thirds Anglo-Saxon blood: now, since he is to be designated by either the term African or Anglo-Saxon, what propriety or scientific accuracy is there in calling him an African, since Anglo-Saxon blood predominates? . . . by the African race, I do not mean the colored people of this country.[141]

In trying to solve the "puzzle" of Douglass's literary style—to account for the rare polish of writing that allows him to equal if not surpass the most celebrated "wonder[s] of the British literary public"—James McCune Smith decides that the "versatility of talent which he wields, in common with Dumas, Ira Aldridge, and Miss Greenfield, would seem to be the result of the grafting of the Anglo-Saxon on good, original, negro stock."[142] Smith refutes any racialist claim that miscegenation dissipates the "better" influences of Anglo-Saxon heredity; Douglass's mixed blood lends a retrospective inevitability to his successes in Britain, for he is not now, as an intellectual, proving himself as a black American, so much as recovering a British status that was already his by birth.

We find in 1860 *Vanity Fair* mocking black claims to English blood ties: what the "indignant colored brother" sees as a black in line for the British throne, or "De New Prince 'er Wales," the white lampoon sees as a racial aberration, as fantastic and unfathomable as Barnum's "What-Is-It?" (fig. 29).[143] But it is telling that the attack on black pretensions in the cartoon implicitly treats cross-breeding as a form of degeneration, which results in a kind of tawdry hybrid whose freakishness is as wrong as any claim of royal blood on its behalf. For the antislavery rhetoric of black hybridity does not so much deny that race is finally biological but, rather, insists that biology, if taken to its logical extreme, is on the movement's side. When even abolitionists admit the cultural superiority of the racially Anglo-Saxon, their arguments become a way of conceding that the "science" of race itself can provide a model of inheritance that both trades on powerful assumptions about the meaning of white identity and yet baffles the integrity of that identity from within. What the *Anglo-African Magazine* describes as the "incalculable intermixture of races since the beginning of time" amounts really to the sense of one, infinitely combined, terminally jumbled race, a kind of scientific correlative to the cosmopolitan himself who, as Whitman might say,

HOW THE BOYS TAKE IT.

White Boy.—MY EYES! CHARCOAL, SEE HIM! WHAT IS IT! A G'RILLA?
Indignant Colored Brother.—G'RILLA MUCH, YA—AS! DON'T YOU SEE IT'S DE NEW PRINCE
'ER WALES? SHA—A—AW!

FIGURE 29. "How the Boys Take It," *Vanity Fair* (August 11, 1860), 84. The Library Company of Philadelphia.

can "assimilate all" but is finally nothing in particular. "If we would individually exalt as far as in us lies, our simple humanity," says the *Anglo-African,* "and feel less concern that an *African* humanity . . . should be perpetuated to the end of time, we might rely confidingly on our manhood alone." Yet this twist on the universally "human" allows a way of returning to racial Anglo-Saxonism on strictly cultural grounds—that is, to the extent to which race provides a vehicle for the transmission and expression of cultural distinction, blacks should necessarily be included as blood relations within a larger Anglo-Saxon enterprise. How else could blacks in the April 1840 issue of the *Colored American* join Tocqueville in welcoming "the impulse of the British race in the

New World," or let Harriet Beecher Stowe boast in *Frederick Douglass' Paper* that "our very life-blood is English life-blood. It is Anglo-Saxon vigor that is spreading our country from Atlantic to Pacific, and leading on a new era in the world's development?"[144]

What do we make of such a conspicuously color-blind Anglo-Saxonism? There is something in it for everyone. It does not supplant racial biology but works beside it to create a language of cultural achievement and fellowship that even blacks can opt into. In this respect, the Anglicizing rhetoric of black abolitionists recalls a more mongrel sense of Anglo-Saxon "blood" that had long stressed the biological consequence of a national history of invasions and conquests. From Defoe's scabrous celebration of the "Het'rogeneous Thing" that is "The True-Born Englishmen" to Matthew Arnold's writing on the mixed ethnicities of Britain in his *Study of Celtic Literature,* we see depictions of a vigorous, polyglot identity—historically and biologically determined by the inevitable miscegenation of Roman, Teuton, Celt, and Norman—that resonates with an antislavery discourse that seems to relish how impossible it is to make a fetish of Anglo-Saxon purity.[145] The essence of English identity is simply a composite of the inherited traits and dispositions of the races that have conquered, colonized, and plundered, or been plundered, to make the British nation what it inherently is, although the nineteenth century increasingly emphasized the persistence of an Englishness that remained triumphantly inviolate despite an Anglo-Saxon history of amalgamation. Both the first formations and most distinctive expressions of English culture thus are reconstructed to reflect less the legacy of many ethnic mixings, than the transmission of one particular ethnic ideal. And while we might expect black abolitionists to avoid such valorizing racial histories of Anglo-Saxon heritage, their response instead suggests a willingness to entertain the fantasies of Anglo-Saxonism so long as its imagined potency bodies forth in their "English" blood as well.

Abolitionists, to put it plainly, seem ready not only to acknowledge but actively to pursue the implications of treating racial identity as the arbiter of culture. If we may say these black abolitionists are aspiring to rise above race, it is only by way of rhetorically grounding their arguments on the fatefulness of racial biology. Far from a scandal to the politics of antislavery, their arguments make the morality of racial progress depend completely on the belief that race not only counts but also patterns human character in the most pervasive and intrinsic ways. The cosmopolitan black abroad, aspiring to belong to Anglo-

Saxon culture across the color line, quite frequently transcends race as an identity by making it a fact of life. At the very least, black abolitionists faced racial chauvinism with more latitude than we might think; there are strategic moments in which the supremacies we would take for white are enlisted on behalf of slaves who have no rub with the imperial prerogatives of Britain and who invite, to the United States and beyond, exactly the forms of "progress" and "civilization" that Anglo-Saxonism can preach. "Spite [*sic*] of our national independence," writes Douglass, "a common language, a common literature, a common history, and a common civilization makes us and keeps us still a part of the British nation, if not a part of the British Empire. England can take no step forward in the pathway of a higher civilization without drawing us in the same direction. She is still the mother country, and the mother, too, of our abolition movement."[146] Because it involves the refining, cultivating British taking their nobility west, there is such a thing as good Anglo-Saxonism, and good particularly for blacks. Brown, after hearing a British lecture titled "The Rise and Spread of the Anglo-Saxon Race," is so impressed with the speaker's "witty, keen and gentle" style, with his "*high, capacious powers*" and his "language of the drawing room," he all but invites the British to colonize more nations that, like America, would closely resemble themselves. Here is an excerpt of the lecture in Brown's narrative:

> [The Americans] have, in fact, no literature; we don't want them to have any, as long as they can draw from the old country; the feeling is kindly, and should be cherished; it is like the boy at Christmas coming home to spend the holidays. Long may they draw inspiration from Shakespeare and Milton, and come again and again to the old well. Walking down Broadway is like looking at a page of the Polyglot Bible. America was founded in a great thought, peopled through liberty; and long may that country be the noblest thing that England has to boast of.
>
> Some people think that we, as a nation, are going down; that we have passed the millennium; but there is no reason yet. We have work to do,—gold mines to dig, railways to construct, &c. &c. When all the work is done, then, and not till then, will the Saxon folk have finished their destiny. We have continents to fill yet.[147]

The grand rhetoric of a rising, spreading Anglo-Saxon race is rehearsed as a charming familial scene in which the fatherland gives his American "boy at Christmas" the best of literature as so much stocking stuffer. America's lack of culture is attributed, at least implicitly, to its diversity, and it might come as something of a surprise that Brown takes his stand alongside the Englishman's position of superior remove from a "polyglot" America that—though "the noblest" product of British imperialism—remains a Babel without a voice of its own. Elsewhere the speaker puts it plainly: "The Americans are a nation without being a nation." In rehearsing this sentiment for his abolitionist readers, Brown calls for a totalizing Anglo-Saxonism that can rise and spread its Shakespeares and Miltons through mongrel continents but an Anglo-Saxonism that does not yet include—is far too civilized to include—America.

Certainly for white abolitionists, racial Anglo-Saxonism could be rescued for the cause. The Anglo-Saxonism that Daniel Walker Howe describes among American Whigs as "more cultural or ideological than genetic" can also be found in the work of abolitionists who saw their social mission as an ancestral legacy and Old World errand.[148] The abolitionist press often declares a prehistory of the movement that, antedating West Indian emancipation or the politics of British Whigs, draws from the genealogical pot of Saxons, Ivanhoes, and Puritans to inspire such lines as these (in the voice of an Englishman): "Our fathers and *your* fathers bore / The spirit stirring strife of yore, / Our shores flung on your welcoming shore, / The patriot-pilgrims' sail: / And ye are worthy of the name, / And the bright ancestry ye claim; / The same the sire—the sons the same— / Hail! brothers! hail!" The *Liberty Bell* writes that "the first Abolitionists were the immortal pilgrims," which provides at once faith that antislavery is the manifest destiny of a specifically Anglo-Saxon fight for liberty and an excuse to fill pages with poems about "the spirit of olden times," "Broad Forth's old Saxon barony," or "Norway's fiords." "Thy patriots are our own, Sons of the Saxon race," says a "Voice from the Old World" in Chapman's gift book.[149]

For abolitionists, the passage to freedom is the course of Anglicization: in Lydia Maria Child's story, "The Black Saxons," also printed in the *Liberty Bell,* not only is the spirit of Saxon freedom under Norman occupation virtually reborn in a group of slaves during the American Revolution, but their insurrection involves a series of tactical alliances with Britain itself and thus reveals that true "republican sympathies" can be realized only if we all, black and white, "join the British."[150] In the story a slaveholder reads a history of how the Norman Conquest put the Saxons "in base subjection," but his absorption in tales of "free-

souled Harolds," and "fair-haired Ediths" is interrupted by slaves asking for "passes" to attend a prayer meeting. Just as he grasps that this
meeting is a ruse for planning a slave revolt, he is "arrested by a voice
within" that sings "the lively ballad of Robin Hood" and puts his own
slaves' plot in "incongruous association with his spontaneous sympathy for Saxon serfs." The slaveholder finds in medieval lore a typology
of Saxon rights and liberty that leads directly from Wat Tyler to "Big-
boned Dick," a slave leader, while skipping over the Revolution and its
"founding fathers." An Anglo-Saxon legacy is passed down from medieval Britain to blacks slaves, but American Revolutionaries are outside
of this line where no "pretexts of selfishness" or "apologies of sophistry"
can save them. Later, the allegorical echoes of Robins Hoods as blacks
are strenuously made literal. After hoping that British troops land and
help the insurrection, a slave tells how freedom might be attained regardless: "Maybe de British land, and maybe de British no land," he
says, "but tell you sons to marry de free woman, dat know how to read
and write; an you tell you gals to marry de free man, dat know how to
read and write; and den by'm bye, you be de British *yourselves!*" Blacks
finally gain freedom through literacy where the civilizing act of reading makes them more than the equal of American whites—it makes
them British.

In the 1852 novel *Uncle Tom in England; or, A Proof That Black's White*,
an "Echo" to *Uncle Tom's Cabin*, written in England and reprinted that
same year in the United States, two of Stowe's minor characters, Susan
and her daughter Emmeline, join with fugitive slave Thomas Brown
(the new "Uncle Tom") on a long, difficult trip to England where they
are finally freed and educated (fig. 30). The publisher's advertisement
to the American edition shows a black hand and a white hand reaching toward each other in some cosmic space, like Michelangelo's Adam
and God, beneath the title that floats high in bubbly clouds of black-
and-white letters to show how something can be black *and* white, like
print itself. Uncle Tom dies and goes to England, and in England he is
white. Like Du Bois's "after life" on the banks of Lake Katrine, "Uncle
Tom" has an afterlife, too, in Britain: as a sequel. Tom's story, says the
copy, "is absorbing, chaining the attention of the reader with a wonderful power," and indeed the play on captivating things, on slavery
and British literature both, is "echoed" in the text where a young slave,
Tom's son, is so fascinated by British poetry he "was constantly repeat-
ing certain sonnets which he had committed to heart." In England, the

FIGURE 30. Publisher's advertisement, *Uncle Tom in England; or, A Proof That Black's White* (New York: A. D. Failing, 1852). The Library Company of Philadelphia.

narrative tells us, black is white because "there is no natural disqualification of the black population, which should deprive them of the right to enjoy equal political and social privileges with ourselves." In fact, for most of the characters in the novel these social privileges are high— some go to college and become "polished scholars," others contribute "articles of merit to the best English magazines," while young Tom moves through aristocratic circles with his "poetical turn of mind." [151]

Of course, other British privileges are harder to gauge. The clouds of heaven on the frontispiece are belching from the factories of London; there is a sense of Engel's white working class that, in the novel's words, is "blackened by filth" and very nearly slaves themselves. There is a fringe presence of Chartism in the book, and the American reprint can at times turn this back on Britain—where *white* may be *black*—or on the antislavery English, who have ills of their own to reform. Still, for *Uncle Tom in England,* fellowship with the British, including the British working class, is a united Anglo-American effort to end oppression wherever it is and also the lesson of the frontispiece that takes its cues from "Uncle Tom": " '*Then we must make common cause,*' said uncle Tom, '*and help each other!*'—and the dark hand seized the white with a nervous grasp, and held on with brotherly earnestness." It may also take its cues from Stowe herself, who, approaching her "English brethren" with "a kind of thrill and pulsation of kindred," places the "civilizing" work of antislavery in light of "the proud remembrance of centuries of united Anglo-Saxon history." Soon enough, England appears less full of smoggy factories and more as a refinery, "polishing" Americans who like Uncle Tom "had to come across the Atlantic for the cultivation of his mind" and the good of his "common cause." [152]

In the novel, black is also white because Thomas Hanaway, a white American who manumits Uncle Tom, and Rosetta, a black African poet living in England, marry in the end, in a moment of miscegenation that finally stands in for all the transatlantic, transcultural communing. And my point is not that racial Anglo-Saxonism disappears in abolitionist texts (far from it) but that it, itself, gets refined and clarified to exclude conveniently and that sometimes what it excludes from all this marching civilization is the United States itself. Ward, for example, denounces Anglo-Saxons as racist in a way that simply does not implicate the British: "My opinion is, that much of this difference between the Anglo-Saxon on the one and his brother Anglo-Saxon on the other side of the Atlantic is to be accounted for in the very low origin of early American settlers, and the very deficient cultivation as compared with other nations, to which they have attained" (31). In Ross Posnock's essay "Du Bois, Fanon, and the 'Impossible Life' of the Black Intellectual," he quotes Du Bois as he boasts in 1920 of his Negro, French, and Dutch blood, but "thank God! no 'Anglo-Saxon.' " Posnock tells us that Du Bois here is placing himself outside a dilemma of black identity that has, on the one side, Douglass's aspirations to a humanism unqualified by race—he wants to be "a man simply"—and, on the other, Martin Delany's black nationalism (he thanks God "for making him a *black man*").[153] But Du Bois, in choosing not to choose between possibilities, to be many things at once, may be a man and a black man, and French and Dutch, but must isolate himself from Anglo-Saxonism, which represents not one ethnicity but the most essentializing of all ethnicities—the gospel of eugenics and immigration quotas. This Anglo-Saxonism is the opposite of the "cosmopolitan multiplicity" Du Bois is after, but so, for Posnock, is Douglass's humanism and "pseudo-universalism" that are as rigid in their way because they never let him be simply "black." But I would say, rather, that black abolitionists, including Douglass, flaunt their hybridity, and even flaunt Anglo-Saxonism, and there is a way in which being specifically, politically black, at the time, can have a lot to do with an embracing sweep of English humanism. And say also, that the Englishness of antislavery speaks to the degree in which abolitionists could pursue, in the forms and fetes of English life, a set of voluntary kinships and useful affiliations that history made difficult.

Which brings me back to "the importance of being English." In Oscar Wilde's play, characters go about inventing new relations—a few incredible, invaluable relations (a brother named Earnest, a permanent invalid called Bunbury)—to buy themselves freedom and mobility. With connections everywhere, they move easily through social circles, never obliged to stay in one world, because there is always a different one calling, shifting their identities with every move and "philanthropy" as they "wend their way" across a landscape of English drawing rooms, in London, Tunbridge Wells, and Shropshire.[154] Abolitionists maintain fantastic ties in England and enjoy the benefits of these ties. All along they save grace in the process. They invent, in America and abroad, a world where sociability is maximized, where ethics are lost in civilities, and where philanthropy is keenly cultivated. They dream up new relations so that they, too, may go to London whenever they choose.

CHAPTER FOUR

The Anglophile Academy

College was not made for study.
—*Harvard Magazine,* March 1858

The whole frame of things preaches indifferency.
—RALPH WALDO EMERSON, "Experience"

The Social Life of College

Those who remember James Russell Lowell's years as a professor at Harvard agree that "he liked to have someone help him idle the time away, and keep him as long as possible from his work." While Lowell lived, writes William Dean Howells, "there was a superstition which has perhaps survived him that he was an indolent man," which Howells does little to deny in his own reminiscence of visits to Cambridge in 1865 when Lowell had talked with him through the evenings. "No doubt," says Howells, "I was impersonally serving his turn in his way," meaning simply that he served Lowell's willingness to turn from his work for nights of conversation. Lowell would light his pipe and from the depths of his chair invite Howells to "all the ease [he] was capable of in his presence." But Howells was shy: the professor made him conscious, he says, of an "older" and "stricter" civilization than his own, so that conversing together in the study he was aware that Lowell's "[democracy] denied the equality which mine affirmed" and that all of the casualness of the evenings just made more obvious the authority that could naturally occasion it. Lowell was so easy himself: if Howells felt the need to disagree with the professor on matters of literature or the law, this gave Lowell pleasure, too, since he delighted "in the whimsicalities of others" just as much as in his own. Lowell was a man of strenuous convictions, but, if he was fond of you, he suffered you. When he condescended, Howells says, his eyes were "beautiful."[1]

Describing William James some years later, George Santayana finds a similar affability unsettling: "I was uncomfortable in William James's presence. He was so extremely natural that there was no knowing what his nature was or what to expect next; so that one was driven to behave and talk conventionally, as in the most artificial society. I found no foothold, I was soon fatigued." Emerson writes that "we thrive on casualties. Our chief experiences have been casual," but it would be a while before Santayana would adopt a manner that registered enough comfort and belief in, as he puts it, "the existence of this absurd world" to be as offhandedly agreeable to it as James seemed to be at Harvard. Instead, Santayana feels a little like Howells does when, after coming to live in Cambridge himself, Lowell would appear at his door and ask him to go walking around town and through the meadows and salt marshes on its outskirts to talk about poetry and every inch of "old Cambridge." Lowell would tease Howells at any sign of affectation or exuberance, but it was never too serious, which was the point, and this left Howells without much footing either for all the topics of positive reform he would have liked to take up after the war and also, so to speak, for the breadth of ground they covered each time across neighborhoods and, conversationally, across literature, which fatigued him. "It was," says Howells, "that serious and great moment after the successful close of the Civil War when the republican consciousness was more robust in us than ever before or since; but I cannot recall any reference to the historical interest of the time in Lowell's talk. It had been all about literature and about travel," and, then, of course, about the college and Cambridge too. It was not that Lowell had no investment in the historical moment but, rather, that his moral response seemed to depend on not laboring under the embarrassment of any seriousness about it. "I recall but one allusion," Howells writes, "to the days when he was fighting the anti-slavery battle."[2]

But Lowell's detachment, in these anecdotes, is something more than what Bourdieu calls a "seriousness without the 'spirit of seriousness'" or an experience of the world freed from urgency that marks, among genteel classes, the possibility of an intellectual life. Lowell's "reluctance from the political situation" is, for Howells, the cast that his anxiety takes and his recourse to sociability marks another, finer way of signaling his true investments. Though no doubt evidence of Lowell's "growing conservatism," such behavior suggests a commitment, for Howells at least, to pleasures and communications that are themselves "civic" at their core because they are conditioned on a deep regard for whoever is most immediately present. He wished you to agree with him, Howells writes, "but he did not wish you to be more of his mind than he was himself." That is, you should not so much defer to his opinions as to the beautifully calibrated logic of social interplay that suggests his opinions matter less than the degree to which they could be best realized in the circumstances of your company. The style of conversation that lets Lowell dramatize the nonchalance of his politics is precisely what confirms their secondary status, for it is the very strength of his commitment to the appeal of things as they are that is reflected in his seeming incapacity to subscribe to anything so abstract as a position or ideology when faced instead with the occasion for talking or walking in Cambridge.[3]

"The poet," writes Lowell, "is always the man who is willing to take the age he lives in on trust, as the very best that ever was." He likes, for example, "the friendly manner" in which Shakespeare "received everything that came along," which suggests his ability both to register the eccentric nature of human affairs and to "enchant" the fact of their eccentricity. "What a present man he was," says Lowell, speaking of Shakespeare's discovery that the "passing moment is the inspired one," which explains why "he planted a Mulberry tree in Stratford the very year it appeared in England."[4] Shakespeare's business, he says, "was with men as they were, not with man as he ought to be,—with the human soul as it is shaped and twisted into character by the complex experience of life, not in its abstract essence, as something to be saved or lost." The quality that Lowell nominates to admire is also what he seems to have projected on his walks with Howells: Howells comes to define Lowell just the same as Lowell defines Shakespeare, for the delight he took in reproducing the sentiments of "man in society as it exist[s]" without questioning the right of society to exist as it did. There is both a reverence and an irreverence in Lowell's belief that the "secret of poetry is . . . to be alive now." It is pitched against theories and philosophies that do not love enough of the reality of the world as to not try to "save" it.[5]

So what Howells learns about the professor in Cambridge is that his indifference to politics attends from a profound engagement with the world as it most concretely appears to him and that such indifference shapes, in turn, a style of engaging with the world that is genial and tolerant to a fault. When Lowell says that Shakespeare "was essentially

observer and artist, and incapable of partisanship," he means that the
artist should be attentive to all things but few ideas. He celebrates, for
example, the fact that Shakespeare was not born into the period of
political and religious conflict that Milton was because "his whole nature was adverse" to the convictions it would bring, and indeed Lowell
spends a good deal of his time with Howells chiding him for his idealism. "They are men yet unborn," says Lowell, "who live in the future."[6]

This might help explain Lowell's posture of disregard for his own future, too. As Howells reminds us, he was famously lazy, "wasting himself
in barren studies and minor efforts instead of devoting his great powers to some monumental work worthy of them."[7] "Lazy quotha," says
Lowell of the Harvard faculty, when, as a Harvard senior in 1838, they
suspended him for truancy: "I have n't dug, 't is true, but I have done
as well." If there was a lack of accomplishment in the career, there was
much success in how he lived it out, and most of those who remember
him at Cambridge, both as a student and as Smith Professor of Belles
Lettres, agree that his manner at the college helped it assume the character of pure style that would come to be called "Harvard style," but
we will return to this later. What delighted Lowell's colleagues was his
primary belief in the solidness of society and being bound to it. He was
social rather than transcendent, and so, if Lowell had "done as well"
at college without working, it was because doing well acknowledged a
fine way of navigating through the particularities of life at Harvard,
having "chosen," he says, "what reading I pleased and what friends I
pleased."[8] "The formalities of academic work were of little concern to
Lowell," writes his biographer Horace Scudder, so as a professor, years
later, he "turned lecture and recitation hour into a *causerie*." Scholastic
exercises yielded to personal reminiscences until time was up: Lowell,
glancing at "a time-piece that was as idly whimsical as its owner," would
bow and leave and the students went away "complacent over the evasion
of work," though also sometimes "stirred, quickened in their thought."
There was knowledge, imagination, and wit, but they were far too undisciplined to be vexed by the pretensions of a purpose. When Lowell
gave Howells the first chapter of a novel he was attempting to write,
Howells praised it; "but I shall never finish it," Lowell said. He sighed,
as he "laid the manuscript away, to turn and light his pipe."[9]

There is a style of character at Harvard in the mid-nineteenth century,
and Lowell is a good example of it. Maybe he learned from his professor,

Henry Wadsworth Longfellow, who arrived at the college when Lowell
was a sophomore and who preceded him in the Smith Chair. Society is
"impossible to avoid" at Harvard, says Longfellow, "people here are too
agreeable to let a man kill himself with study"—though he seemed to
find more time for it than Lowell. Casual and sentimental in class, and
playful outside it, Longfellow was devoted to a relaxed manner that was
not just an extension of his professorial role but synonymous with the
social imperative that made him the model of a professor in the first
place. Recalling Longfellow with his undergraduates, Edward Everett
Hale writes: "He would talk with them and walk with them; would sit
with them and smoke with them. You played whist with him if you met
him of an evening." [10] If such fraternizing was a priority at Harvard—
where, as Hale points out, Longfellow was instrumental in "breaking
that line of belt ice which parted the students from their teachers"—it
was also recognized as an increasingly crucial part of academic life at
colleges and universities throughout the east. Professors hosted dancing parties and invited students to their homes (President Quincy held
fortnightly levees in his drawing room), all speaking to the estrangement of higher learning from the strictures of the curriculum. The success
cess of college, as described in student newspapers or remembered later
by alumni, was associated with the miscellaneous acquisition of knowledge over four years of wasting time, so when Henry Adams confesses
"he knew nothing" after graduating from Harvard in 1858, this could
only mean that he passed through Harvard admirably. If his "education
had not yet begun," it was also the case that the absence of anything
resembling an "education" as we might think of it—programmatically
coherent and inclined to methodology—was exactly what college had
provided. [11]

  "Harvard College," Adams writes, "was a negative force and negative
forces have value": desultory and superficial, the content of the knowledge he acquired left no impressions but no biases either. It was a kind
of education degree zero that ran him through "libraries of volumes
which he forgot even to their title-pages," but at least Adams could appreciate how readily he got through them, and "in truth hardly any
Boston student" took his education seriously, and none of them seemed
sure that even the presidents of the college "took it more seriously than
the students." What the student got from college, in other words, "was
the habit of looking at life as a social relation," and if the habit did no
great good, it still, writes Adams, nearly always led to "a life more or

less worth living." In fact, it is a commitment to the flexibility of a "life more or less" that Harvard instills: a life that does not apply its energy with close economy but tolerates the loss of time, money, and effort in favor of the delights of amateurism and the willingness to live together comfortably with the little we know. The informality of the faculty offered something of a correlative to the lessons that made Longfellow and Lowell so memorable to their students; which is to say, the dilatory pleasures of the university that they embodied and enshrined were never far removed from the particular ideology of academic status they performed. They helped shape a philosophy of intellectualism that patterned both its daily routines and larger objectives on the affection of both faculty and students for those pleasures that would keep their minds inspired, while also completely disengaged. Henry Adams left college with an absence of positive beliefs and useful information, but in their place he acquired the "mental habits" that made him responsive to a style of education that came to prefer its triviality.[12]

So, to repeat, there was a style at Harvard in the mid-nineteenth century that performed in the social realm an affective doxa for the practice of intellectualism in the academy. Or, said differently, there was a way of being at college that was manifest in an attentiveness to the character one assumed there and that character expressed, in turn, a faith in the pedagogical beliefs of the college. The college believed in aimlessness: this suggests the emerging shape of what we now know as Arnoldian humanism and its defense of the liberal arts but also the more fugitive ends of lounging, lazing, smoking, conversing, and doing as one pleased that gave the acquisition of knowledge at the college its particular manner. To the degree that these expressed the investment of higher learning in nonutilitarian values, we are reminded of any number of arguments about the anxious place of the college in an increasingly professionalized world. Asked in the 1850s what a university is, Lowell answered, "a place where nothing useful is taught." "I hope the day will come," he continued, "when a competent professor may lecture here for three years on the first three vowels of the Romance alphabet and find a fit audience, though few." Still, neither the specific character nor the full extent of academic style can be explained by accounts of the opposition between aspirations of the college and the rise of the modern research university nor between the aesthetic disposition of liberal arts and the practical ends that made literary study for Lowell by the end of the century "too much of a study and too little a pleasure." To treat the emergence of an academic style in America as just a reaction formation within a familiar analysis of higher learning is not only to neglect the fascination of style itself as a means of historical response but also to assume that the distinctive character of college was ultimately determined by what it wanted to stave off. If we grant, however, that "style is properly speaking a germinative phenomenon," as Barthes writes, and so read closely for signs of how it develops and, more important, what it produces, then the ritualized and symbolic devotion to college life that we find in antebellum America begins to look rather different; we see an encompassing attention to the details of collegiate practice that celebrates even the small manners of lifestyle for how they reveal both the provenance and ambitions of the academic type.[13] That type was recognizable to collegians then—as it is to us now—for its pretensions to Englishness.

James Russell Lowell, says Howells, "was in love with everything English and was determined I should be so too." Few remember Lowell's years at Harvard without noting that he possessed the distinctive bearing, posture, diction, pronunciation, and usages without which, in Bourdieu's words, "all scholastic knowledge is worth nothing," and Howells (lingering in the "effort to materialize his presence") insists he acquired these in England. When Lowell returned from London, he wore the top hat that would later be called the "Harvard hat" (fig. 31). His frock, cane, and pipe completed a fashion that suggested how, in the words of the *Harvard Crimson,* "[the Harvard man] must be as Britannic as possible." Howells says, too, that, while Lowell volunteered that the English aristocracy was as corrupt as any, he liked its "disciplined and obsequious society" and modeled his own on it. He preferred the English way of speaking and declared that the best English in the United States was spoken in Cambridge. "And so it was," writes Howells, "when he spoke it." Of course, Lowell had not fully acquired the style in London, since the character of the college was well enough set by the time he was an undergraduate to have learned his Englishness there: Longfellow, describing himself as a professor in the 1830s, already wore a "broad-brimmed black hat, black frock-coat, a black cane," did not study at night, and smoked "most of the time"— all deliberately Anglophilic, he admits, and typical of the faculty then. Edward T. Channing, Boylston Professor of Rhetoric and Oratory, had a similar deportment and, as we will see later, taught his students to speak with English accents. "I do not know," writes Hale of Lowell, "how

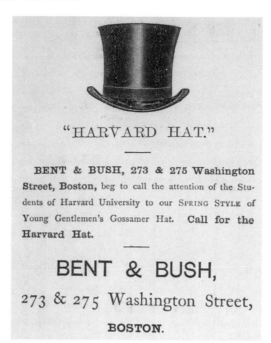

FIGURE 31. "Harvard Hat," advertisement, *Magenta* (June 18, 1875), ii. Courtesy of American Antiquarian Society.

much his clear, simple, unaffected English style owes to Channing, but I am quite sure that he would have spoken most gratefully of his teacher."[14]

But the Englishness of university life in the nineteenth-century United States extends beyond such individual performances of style and manner, though these are altogether crucial within a series of broader transformations that aimed to make schools like Harvard into more complete and socially elaborate institutions. Where American colleges in the years immediately following the Revolution were sites of frequent uprisings and student revolts—reflecting, many argue, the utterly subordinate status of undergraduates subject to the strict authority of the faculty—what emerged in the antebellum decades is a determined investment in the social life of the university, evident both in new student-faculty relations and in the iconography of attachment and belonging that came to signify the very essence of the college years. With the curriculum requiring only a fraction of their time, antebellum students could indulge—and be indoctrinated in—a system of diversions, from literary societies, fraternities, and intramural sports to rituals of celebration and dress, that helped to define the elements of student identity in forms familiar to us today, but in few ways resembling what had come before. These decades brought the rise not only of student clubs and societies but also of organized college sentiment: the first yearbooks, college reunions, college songs, and college novels (and the published memoirs of college that inspired them). Commencement became an important ritual then, as did other school-specific events with processions and regalia that codified one's identity as a "Harvard man" or "Princetonian," but in all cases, as constitutive of one's college institution.[15]

The anthropology of this identity is part of my concern in this chapter, but I am also interested in the broader calculus that made it possible for college in America to function as an institution of social identity in the first place; for it is our assumption that college life should, of course, possess a distinctive character that remains a primary legacy of this period. To say that this character is English is to recognize more than a predictable logic of refinement that saw Britain as a reservoir of tradition and prestige: a deliberately Anglophilic academy was not simply an accessory of class distinction in all the ways made popular by twentieth-century iconographies of "pleasantly blasé and casually critical" students, who, like F. Scott Fitzgerald's Amory Blaine, are "lazy and good-looking and aristocratic—you know, like a spring day."[16] Rather, it is the idea that colleges should predispose us to love colleges, and the social life of the institutions they promote, which is the most acutely English aspect of the academy. Or at least this chapter suggests that the inclination toward the social in colleges borrows from a sense that Englishness as such can provide an exemplary case for the best possible relationship between college and society. And then, it suggests, too, that an attachment to this fantasy—and to all the forms and rituals in which it is made material—shapes not only the particular class structures that begin to thrive in antebellum colleges but also the intellectualism that shows itself with special vividness in respect to the humanities and literary studies. Anglophilia in the academy is certainly about English affects, but these affects are about the deeper purchase Anglophilia has on antebellum understandings of what humanistic knowledge might accomplish in a democracy. Insofar, then, as American academics demonstrated their devotion to English culture as the expression of their academicism, they rendered higher learning as an implicit aspiration toward an English character, the absorbing nature of which I explore here.

The first college novel in America is about the death of the scholar. In Nathaniel Hawthorne's *Fanshawe,* published in 1828, the eponymous hero, "a hard student and a good scholar," works himself to death, while his friend Edward Walcott's "derelictions from discipline" lead to "a life of long calm bliss." There are two kinds of student at Harley College, where the novel takes place: Fanshawe, who "scorned to mingle with the living world or to be actuated by its motives" and Walcott, who prefers society and who convinces us by the end that, in the shady retreats of a college in New England, "study is pleasant," but "idleness delicious." Set eighty years in the past at a college modeled on Bowdoin College, where both Hawthorne and Longfellow graduated in 1825, *Fanshawe* has none of the gravity of the character it kills off but much of the jauntiness of Walcott, whose "youthful follies" were "something perhaps approaching to vices," like Hawthorne's own juvenile work that embarrassed him. Hawthorne published *Fanshawe* anonymously and concealed its authorship the rest of his life, burning the copies he could. But just as Walcott, an erstwhile poet, never regrets that he "left no name behind" him, Hawthorne's college novel is not meant for posterity; it is written as a romance of students at play (perhaps even begun as Hawthorne's own diversion at Bowdoin) and practically announces its triviality in the choice of pleasure over work (of Walcott over Fanshawe) that becomes a convention of the college novels that follow it. "I doubt," says a reviewer of a college novel in 1924, "if an undergrad is worth a novel." [17]

In *Fanshawe,* the ailing student and the handsome student compete for the affections of Ellen Langton, who is the ward of Doctor Melmoth, the president of Harley. The novel, like most later college fiction, stages a conflict between the isolation of the academy and the world of capital outside it, except that in Hawthorne this is wildly desublimated: so, into the college yard comes a vicious pirate with designs on Ellen's inheritance. He abducts her and hides her in a cave, while Walcott and Doctor Melmoth chase them through the woods on horseback. But it is Fanshawe who finally confronts the villain, finding Ellen in the cave and guiding her to freedom up the edge of a cliff with the enemy close behind. Pursued within feet of the summit, the scholar stands firm, and (when the adventurer falls backward to his death down the precipice) Fanshawe wins the affection of the girl, as these things go. Fanshawe, though, does not marry her: convinced that he will die young from a passion for study so arduous that it does, in time, kill him, the scholar renounces his love and returns to his books. "Your life will be long and happy," he tells Ellen, which it is when she marries Walcott.[18]

A generation passed before the college novel became a recognizable genre, and it was not until midcentury when, in response to the popularity of books about undergraduate life at Oxford, especially Cuthbert Bede's *Mr. Verdant Green* series (1853, 1854, 1857) and Thomas Hughes's *Tom Brown at Oxford* (1861), that American novels about academic life followed in earnest. Most of these were published just after their authors' graduation, usually from Harvard, and include William Washburn's *Fair Harvard* (1869), Frederick Loring's *Two College Friends* (1871), George Henry Tripp's *Student-Life at Harvard* (1876), Mark Sibley Severance's *Hammersmith: His Harvard Days* (1878), Charles Macomb Flandrau's *Harvard Episodes* (1897), and the anonymous *Lloyd Lee: A Story of Yale* (1878). But the early examples of the genre and Hawthorne's novel in particular signal the special pleasure these works take in announcing that what college best teaches is, in the words of one Harvard paper, how not "to cast aside the pleasant habit of indifference"—to study, to accomplishment, to money (which students spend), to politics, and finally to the consequences of such indifference for a life past college.[19] In *Fanshawe*, Edward Walcott does not save Ellen because to save her or not has consequences, and the chivalry with which he approaches her rescue contains too many elements of sport and play to be of much use to her future or to his. As Walcott looks for Ellen, with Doctor Melmoth at his side, the sociability of their adventure together (student and professor), and all the trust, friendship, challenges, and darings involved in the primary impulse to set out in the woods on horseback takes on a fullness of significance that is not about saving her. The immediate play of the forms of rescue has its own stakes: at least Melmoth and Walcott get so involved in the game of capturing the villain that their belief in the game provides a margin of distance from the urgency (Ellen, dead or alive in a cave) that occasions it. Melmoth, freed for once from his duties as a scholar and as president of the college, abandons himself to the moment of the chase, so that what he is chasing after is lost to the pretext for displays of enjoying it: "Alas, youth! These are strange times," observed the president, "when a Doctor of Divinity and an under graduate set forth, like a knight-errant and his squire, in search of a stray damsel." Walcott, "whose imagination was highly tickled by Doctor Melmoth's chivalrous comparison," pursues the conceit and needless to say that all the couple's "most valiant" methink-ing and betake-ing of themselves here and there, and girding themselves with "lances" to get the girl, does not effect so much as Fanshawe who purposively scales a cliff. Their seriousness, to return to Bourdieu, lacks the spirit of seriousness that Fanshawe enacts, but as such it suggests a new relation between the student and the professor and to the culture that inclines them to amuse themselves offhandedly as a knight and squire, while a girl is really abducted and while, less urgently (but still), "a learned treatise, important not only to the present age, but to posterity" is left, says Melmoth, "unfinished in my study." Like the Harvard undergraduates that the *Crimson* describes as "indifferent" to achievement, Melmoth and Walcott "do not labor up the mountain because they choose to entertain themselves with dulcimer and harp in the valley below."[20]

"Culture," says Bourdieu, "is what remains when you've forgotten everything."[21] The collegian who survives *Fanshawe* takes little from college when he leaves it, but this does not "create any very serious apprehensions respecting his future welfare" as a "gentleman." In other words, Walcott does not have culture as Fanshawe has Latin or Greek; what he has, following Bourdieu, is "a *relation* to culture," and this means that his style and general bearing afford a sense of ease that does not require any knowledge in particular for him to presume his way through a cultural exchange. If one measure of "distinction" is the ability to be casual with what you both do and do not know, then the "natural grace" of Walcott's manners—"improved by early intercourse with polished society"—give him a decided advantage over Fanshawe and his anxious dedication. Fanshawe, notwithstanding, strives to learn at the expense of society and still worries that his efforts are inadequate to the work of being learned: "He had climbed but a few steps of a ladder that reached to infinity," Hawthorne writes, and "he had thrown away his life in discovering, that, after a thousand such lives, he should still know comparatively nothing." Such futility is morbid and captures the strained determination that is the consequence, for Bourdieu, of not knowing "how to play the game of culture as a game." The largely "rustic" students at Harley College—many of whom seem "but recently [to have] left the plough, to labor in a not less toilsome field"—have few claims to higher learning based on their class or status, and though Hawthorne does not specify whether Fanshawe emerges mysteriously from their ranks, he is nonetheless consumed by a devotion to his studies that sets him apart from such "models of fashion" as Walcott.[22] The signature of the emerging academic style that interests Hawthorne—and of course Bourdieu as well—is a curious disregard for knowledge as the outcome of education. Students learn instead how best to indulge and refine their own relations to each other and to the faculty in an environment where intellectual pursuits are not the object but the occasion for sociability. This is why Walcott's futile chase earns him the happy rewards of Fanshawe's strenuous heroics; to the degree that college life, as Hawthorne sees it at this early moment in its literary history, is imagined to have any real purpose, it is to instill a faith in ritual displays of character that are isolated from results. While Fanshawe sets off alone to save the day, Walcott and his favorite professor ride through the woods in stylized abandon, doing little but confirming their attachment to each other and to the symbolism of their pursuit. What does their chase prove? Nothing much. It's academic.

The American college was not college as Hawthorne knew it at Bowdoin eighty years before, when *Fanshawe* takes place. The rise of free time at college was a late eighteenth-century innovation, and then still, most of the student activity we associate with the high-collegiate style of the progressive era did not appear until after 1830, including fraternities and organized sports (intramural at first). If students of the eighteenth century were subject to the severe discipline of a clerical faculty, and the rigorous schedule of study and declamations it enforced by college law, in the nineteenth century they had considerable autonomy. Rules were relaxed and schedules were flexible; recitations and preparations took only a fraction of student time and new leisure allowed for extracurricular pursuits. The student riots and revolts against college authority, defining the period after the Revolution (and in emulation of it), finally ended; the last great rebellion at Harvard was in 1834, followed "by a revolution in higher education" that protected and encouraged student freedoms. An old system of punishment and public chastisement was replaced with one based on a series of "marks" or demerits; students could now calculate how often they might behave irresponsibly without consequence and then did so that often. A student at Amherst College wrote into his college paper in 1853, "As I thought it advisable to begin with my dickey in good season, I neglected prayers to-night, and suppose that, consequently, I have added eight to my thirty-two marks, and thereby filled up the measure of my iniquity for the present term . . . you know the love of a tall, stiff, exquisitely setting dickey, with a flourishing neck-tie, has always been one of my besetting sins." [23]

So the years Hawthorne attended college mark the beginning of, what Roger Geiger calls, "the rise of the student estate," with its new emphasis on the collective experience of campus life over the regime of the curriculum.[24] Hawthorne sets his novel well before this, at a moment when punishing models of authority held students to strict standards of behavior and rigorous forms of intellectual discipline. That Fanshawe, whose values accord perfectly with this older college style, is introduced as doomed from the beginning is certainly an index to Hawthorne's historicizing point of view; it is the emergence of a new collegiate culture, embodied in Walcott's ease and relish for society, that Hawthorne locates squarely in the middle of the eighteenth century, where it does not belong. This has the effect of making *Fanshawe* into a speculative archaeology of Hawthorne's present, and so as much an exercise in pathology as in romance. The college novel, as I said, comes to life only with the scholar's death. And Walcott's long and happy future with Ellen suggests the ascendancy of both another sort of college and another sort of relationship to college as an experience. Where Fanshawe is entirely scholastic—beholden to an intellectual aesthetic that would atavistically return the college student to the rigors of the monastery—Walcott is perfectly adapted to enjoy the "modern" university, which offers a wider range of academic pleasures and, more important, which is conceived of as an interlude along a conventional trajectory that leads to nothing more sublime than graduation. It is the difference between the academy as a calling and the academy as a phase to be adored in retrospect but not taken too seriously because at its best it nurtures one's diversions.

Hawthorne's displacement of Fanshawe's story onto a bygone past only reproduces, in an extreme and heightened form, the striking anachronism that comes to structure undergraduate culture in the nineteenth century. College, as we will see, is deeply invested in producing nostalgia for college. Insofar as undergraduate experience is thus predicated on a version of Fredric Jameson's famous "nostalgia for the present," the fact that Hawthorne sets *Fanshawe* in the colonial past is also telling.[25] Walcott is at Harley College, "rather than at one of the

English Universities, to the expenses of which his fortunes would have been adequate." The phrasing here suggests that Harley serves as a fit alternative to Oxford or Cambridge because, as Hawthorne imagines it, it is already emulative of such English institutions. Indeed English universities had changed in the eighteenth century: their monastic character gave way to a newly affluent student culture, reflected in its elegance, fashion, and leisure. The rise of student societies, clubs, and "common rooms" cultivated the pleasures of debating and drinking, while the old scholasticism appeared provincial compared with the sociability of students with nothing to do. As Sheldon Rothblatt writes, "Late rising, long walks, lengthened periods of dining, evenings spent in drink, pranks and practical jokes . . . are evidence of a condition in which learning and study were secondary."[26]

Walcott's insistent will to leisure and dilettantism make him the image of a figure quite familiar in nineteenth-century U.S. accounts of English student life and associate him broadly with the kind of easy amateur who, in contrast to the Puritanical, driven American, "plays the great complicated absorbing game of life for the sake of the game." My point, though, is not that Hawthorne patterns Walcott solely to evoke this English type but, rather, that Walcott's proximity to England, in a novel set when "America" was itself defined by this proximity, allows for precisely the kind of "compensatory importation" that Jameson describes.[27] Fanshawe dies and in his place what flourishes is an academic style derived from an American preoccupation with Englishness. Nowhere is the significance of this style more visible than in Walcott's collegiality with Dr. Melmoth, who not only licenses his flights from study but who sincerely enjoys them, too, for the idea of sociability they ritualize. Hawthorne may mourn Fanshawe's passing, but the very existence of his novel suggests that, like Walcott, he knew how to capitalize on the opportunities for extracurricular diversion that were enshrined in U.S. colleges as an aspect of their Anglophilia.

In *A Collection of College Words and Customs* (1851), Benjamin Homer Hall, who compiled it "during the leisure hours" of his senior year at Harvard, defines the act of "cramming" as the power of "filling the mind with knowledge hastily acquired for a particular occasion, and to be forgotten when the occasion is past." Cramming, if we look back to the verb "to cram," from which it comes, is "peculiar to the English

Universities." As is "to cut," meaning, of course, "to be absent from; to neglect," lectures, recitations, and so on, as they say "at the University of Cambridge, England," creating the need "to cram" later. "Skinning," too, "Cantabridgically" speaking (that is, "according to Cambridge" in England) may be a fine solution for the student who chooses not to spend college "digging" (applying oneself) or "grinding" (at work), but "borrowing another's ideas and presenting them as one's own" (plagiarizing). The student who most desperately tried "to dead"—to be a complete failure in his recitations "by doing that hardest work of all, nothing"—received the honor of the "Wooden Spoon." Adapted from a tradition at the English universities, the Wooden Spoon was conferred on the student who ranked last of all in his class. At Yale, the ceremony took place at the end of junior year, where, after a series of burlesque dissertations and disputes, the hero ascended the stage for the delivery of the Wooden Spoon, a very large spoon with his class and rank carved on it. The president of the class (probably its poorest scholar) rose with becoming dignity and bestowed the honor of the ladle in Latin, so far as he was able. All sang: "But do not think our life is aimless; / O no! we crave one blessed boon, / It is the prize of value nameless, / The honored, classic WOODEN SPOON." The collegians involved were encouraged to be "bosky," or just a little drunk, "in the cant of the Oxonians." [28]

In William Thompson Peters's illustrated tale, *The College Experience of Ichabod Academicus* (1849), Ichabod gets the Wooden Spoon. Returning to college his junior year, after a "rustication" [*Brit.* suspension), Ichabod buys a coat from an English tailor, cultivates a mustache, loafs, parades the streets, falls in love, resigns his love, crams for exams, and bears off the Wooden Spoon. His senior year, he goes on a vacation spree, tricks gullible freshmen, discards his books, plays billiards, buys new clothes, gets visited by a creditor—all part of the process by which he "emerges from his chrysalis state, and blooms in Senior dignity" until commencement when the story ends (fig. 32). Such is the bildungsroman of the young man at college: the "country boy," like George Henry Tripp's hero in *Student-Life at Harvard,* catches "something of the polite indifference" of his "chum" (*Brit.* roommate) and learns to trifle away his allowance, patronize a tailor, play cards, smoke a cigar, cut prayers, and cut lectures. "That these purposes did not constitute the object for which he came to college, he knew," but the modes of dress and deportment, the "debonair good-fellowship" of the hero's chums

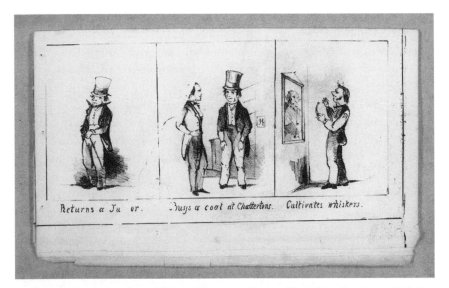

FIGURE 32. Illustration from William Thompson Peters, *The College Experience of Ichabod Academicus;* illustrated by William T. Peters, and dedicated to their brother collegians by the editors, H.F.P. & G.M., 1849. Courtesy of American Antiquarian Society.

and, also, their "easy spending of money and their peculiar grace" are "the growth of habit" and take four years to acquire. "Eton," says Tripp, "could not acquire them in a day," and neither could the country boy who at last, by senior year, becomes, in the society of his chums, "somewhat *blasé*," which is to say that his self-realization as a student, at Harvard, for example, in Washburn's *Fair Harvard,* gives him a "repose of manner in pleasing contrast to his former effervescence." [29]

This is the "Senior's Soliloquy," years later in the *Harvard Lampoon:*

Degree, or no degree, that is the question:
Whether 't is better for our peace of mind to grind,
Evolving from the seething brain a plan
And power to cast off all the base conditions of our course,
Or to take refuge in our high prerogative,
And, with a haughty indolence, keep cutting to the end.
To lounge, to laze, and by protracted sprees induce
The headache, and the thousand natural shocks
The Stomach's heir to. To smoke, to yawn, to roll with idle fingers
The slender cigarette, and aimless leaning out the open window
Gaze adown the Yard.

Lyman Bagg writes, in his memoir of college at midcentury, that cheating was largely tolerated at Yale, which would need to be the case if the "careless boy-man" he observes there—or the yard gazer we see above at Harvard—was, in Bagg's words, to be conscious of "the peculiar and delightful life about him." As John Kirkland, president of Harvard from 1810 to 1828, writes of his own college years, "The imputation of a plodder was deprecated above all things; so we used to spend the day in pleasure. . . . I wasted much time, much money, some virtue and some health."[30] We can go a distance toward understanding the tributes to idleness by recalling, as Ronald Story does, that the student body at Harvard sharply gentrifies after 1830. For a wealthier and more homogenous student population, with fewer rural undergraduates and growing "town and gown" friction, shows of leisure may be read at least in part as expressions of class privilege in a straightforward way. We find faculty and administrators (and the Harvard Corporation that governed them) bearing witness to the "elevated tone" of the college's changing demographic, and both Quincy and Edward Everett, his successor as Harvard president, take steps to ensure that such indolence appeared genteel enough. Under their administrations, students began to dine on china and used silver embossed with college arms. They stabled their horses for riding and paid servants to draw their baths. And, when regulation dress was discontinued in the 1840s, students pursued high fashion: with top hats, beaver hats, canes, shooting jackets, English walking coats, boots, gloves, and the intimate, indebted relation to tailors who kept them outfitted ("the correct thing," says the *Crimson*, of tailors, "is to let the bill run, and not pay it at all"), Quincy could proudly assure the class of 1845 that they were the "best-dressed" he had seen (according to Lowell who remembered it).[31] But the insistence on privilege is also the means of registering an academic attitude toward work that makes a freedom from the necessity to do any broadly distinguish both the everyday routine and the intellectual character of college life. The determination to appear not to work, familiar as a mark of status for many characters in, say, Edith Wharton or Henry James, means that studying is the scandal that undergraduates conceal. "In their studies," writes a contributor to the Williams College magazine, "they despise the daily plodding in a path marked out for them by any faculty, however wise or learned. Go to the rooms of these persons, and if they are at study when you knock, they will quickly lay aside the great book, and take up a novel." At the same time, student slack—or at least, hiding the acquisition of knowledge, in Bourdieu's sense, by not learning in public—communicates a degree of critical taste alongside its denial of purpose. Thus undergraduate "loafing" is distinguished from "the vulgar street-corner and bar-room form of this refined enjoyment," as the Harvard *Magenta* puts it, because students, in not working, indulge in "the graceful and elegant passing of one's time." So they make "vulgar" both the less elegant passing of time but also the usefulness of not simply passing time.[32]

The *Lampoon*'s would-be Hamlet helps to clarify the stakes of such a claim. For while there is obviously something "princely" in the speaker's disregard for striving and utter void of work ethic, the burlesque also captures a dimension of what recommends Hamlet, at least according to T. S. Eliot (Harvard '10), as a likely "study for pathologists." For Eliot, Hamlet is a figure suffering from a "bafflement at the absence of objective"—caught up in the "buffoonery of an emotion which can find no outlet in action"—and we might say that this alienation from any actual purpose is precisely what the "Senior's Soliloquy" indulges and transvalues. This pastoral romance of the "Yard" wants, in the broadest possible appropriation of Hamlet's own existential joke, to refuse a future that demands that young men apply themselves with consequence and decision. A version of Eliot's "buffoonery" is here their "high prerogative": like Shakespeare's famous college student, home from school at Wittenburg, "How weary, stale, flat and unprofitable / seem to [them] all the uses of this world!"[33]

"Ye Harvard Studente," lazing, reclining, smoking, observing, conversing: a *Lampoon* cartoon shows him in all the postures of a summer's day within and outside the dormitory that it calls "ye Palace of Indolence" (fig. 33). He cultivates a lassitude that by now, in 1875, was widely described as "Harvard Indifference," in part because the term had been in use for a generation at least, but more immediately because the *Crimson* and *Advocate* were debating it in a series of articles that excited "more warm discussion in College circles" than any others that year (thus making the *Crimson* "skeptical as to the real existence of that indifference" it otherwise assumes). "As I said before," writes the *Crimson*, "the majority of fellows here don't take any interest in athletics, don't care for politics, don't read, won't study." The *Advocate* describes "a carelessness in regard to the world in general": boys of nineteen are "as blasé as [men] of forty" and so on the field and in the classroom and "in every phase of college life," they neglect the things "with which

FIGURE 33. "Manners and Customs of Ye Harvard Studente. Ye Palace of Indolence; or, Holworthie upon a Summer Afternoon," *Harvard Lampoon* (June 22, 1876). Courtesy of American Antiquarian Society.

[they] are immediately concerned." Politics are treated with contempt or, at least, the life of politics is followed, in the *Nation* especially, "as if it were something unconnected with ourselves." But the *Crimson* defends this "condition of college," which is also the impetus to its "culture," as an active refusal and moral response: "This indifference—to keep the more general term—is usually supposed to result from a precocious and unerring insight into the realities of things, and a moral and intellectual nature of too high a 'tone' to take any interest in the vulgar and short-sighted struggles of the external world." [34]

There are two points here, and one seems more interesting than the other. The desire to remove college life from the world outside invokes a long tradition of fears about the fate of status in a democracy, especially one distinguished by its marginal investment in the meaning of intellectual practice. In 1861, a Williams College student warns his fellow students not to soil themselves, for example, in "the muddy stream" of politics: "There are those who believe," he says, "it would be better for students to live in entire ignorance of all political subjects, and that,

at the end of their course, if they should go into the world as unacquainted with everything of that nature as though they had spent the
time in a foreign land, their conditions would be far better."[35] It is not
difficult to see such language as a gesture of class affectation, nor to
understand the nature of the compensation that it offers in which the
academy is saved from feeling powerless by making the powerful seem
abject.

But it is a second point suggested by the *Crimson* that makes "Harvard indifference" into something more than the presumption of an
elite believing that what bores it does not matter. The indifference, says
the *Crimson*, comes from "a precocious and unerring insight into the
realities of things," which is a considerable claim. The students writing
for the *Crimson* respond to liberal editorializing with a defense not of
their politics but of their epistemology; a "blasé" lack of interest in a
world of stands, reforms, and partisan agendas is, in truth, a deeper
and more profound attention to—which is as much to say, a willing
and more contemplative acceptance of—the world at large. We might
readily enough see through these niceties and find them troubling—
coincident, as they are, with the end of Reconstruction, to name just
one matter of concern to the *Nation* that students could expressly ig-
nore. But to do so is to reproduce the instrumental logic to which the
Crimson answers with this oddly affecting bit of undergraduate philosophy in the first place. There is a politics to such political "indifference," and it entails a largely conservative position on any number of
concerns. Thus, Edward Everett Hale, looking back at Harvard from
late in the century, writes, "Let it be remembered that the whole drift
of fashion, occupation and habit among undergraduates ran in lines
suggested by literature. Athletics and sociology are, I suppose now, the
fashion in Cambridge. But literature was the fashion then. In November when the state election came round there would be the least possible spasm of political interest, but you might really say that nobody
cared for politics. Not five 'men' in college saw the daily newspaper. My
classmate William Francis Channing in 1838 would have been spoken
of, I think, as the only abolitionist in college."[36]

But in the context of nineteenth-century Harvard's academic culture, and that of eastern colleges more generally, the disavowal of
politics as anti-intellectual is neither an excuse to take conservative
positions nor a complete failure to acknowledge the place of politics
in American society. "Harvard indifference" is best understood as an

aesthetic rather than a position: it offers itself as an intuitive engagement with the "realities" of a complex and actual world. Politics, on the other hand, reduces reality to precepts that one chooses between; it sacrifices the miscellaneous givenness of society to "short-sighted" and theoretical wagers on its future. At times, such "unerring insight" may begin to look like blindness: "Little interest is taken in politics in college," writes the *Harvard Magazine* in 1860, a moment at which it would certainly take a bit of calculated denial to remain above affairs of state.[37] But Harvard students take comfort in their belief that living comfortably with the little they know and do is a reflection of their intellectual commitment to society as it is for them at college. Harvard students, in other words, do not broker what is here now against what they or others may make of it later: the practice of being a student is more consuming than that and, besides, it takes a kind of maturity ("precociousness") to understand that any vocabulary of change, including politics, is more or less narrow-minded compared with the desultory ideas of things as they appear outside a dormitory window on a lazy afternoon, so why bother?

"Literature was the fashion then": Hale recalling Harvard in the 1840s is a moment worth revisiting because it all but blames the lazy politics of undergraduates on their literary enthusiasms, and this is something likely never to be said again. Hale's comment makes more sense when we remember that literature, especially in the antebellum period, was only slowly being integrated into the curriculum as one of the first subjects to be offered in a new elective system. As Gerald Graff reminds us, in colleges where only a few faculty, including Lowell and others, were teaching European literatures in a belletristic way and where "English" still meant lessons in elocution and rhetoric, literature was principally an extracurricular pursuit. (In a send-up of a secret society in the *Williams Quarterly Magazine,* the members of the Ineffable Idleburians Club convene for "strictly literary" purposes.)[38] Which is to say that students were only starting to be able to show their indolence by *not* studying literature along with the other fields they neglected. Indeed for many students, as Hale suggests, reading literature, and engaging in the diversions of a literary culture, was an identifying ritual of their stylized lack of commitment to any discipline. But the flourishing of literary societies, offering informal opportunities for undergraduates to hone their tastes and also publishing magazines where students could practice criticism for an audience of fellow "idleburians," seems to have meant the very opposite of what standard theories of the public sphere would lead us to expect. So the expressions of a literary sensibility do not prepare the way for political and rational reflections; literary feeling is too tolerant and capacious. "As we survey our table," writes the Union College magazine of its contributors in 1862, "we are forcibly impressed with the fact, that 'war' is not the only subject of consideration among students. Never have the contributions been so copious, and may we not say so purely literary?" "Politics," laments one Rutgers student in 1861, "is the forbidden tree, in this Eden of literature." [39]

"I am not idle when I sit at my window on an indian summer noon": a writer for the *Harvard Magazine* does nothing more than experience doing nothing at his window, and the value of his idleness is what he registers with it. At the Idleburians literary society, members may "boast of their indifference to all learning and usefulness," but, the magazine warns, we should not mistake indifference for "sluggishness." Do not be surprised, it says, to see the Idleburians years after leaving college, "shooting themselves, one after the other, like so many sky-rockets," to the heights of literary genius and fame. For these college magazines, literary culture is what indifference creates. Or, rather, indifference is staged as an alternative to the disciplines of college, and of the world beyond college, and offers the appeal of what literary culture offers as the academy defines it at midcentury: a commitment to feelings over abstraction and complexity over didacticism. The literary style, writes David Simpson, "[restrains] the emergency of any radical vocabulary," because it does not like the explicitness of beliefs. It prefers what T. S. Eliot prefers when he says that Henry James has "a mind so fine that no idea could violate it," suggesting an immediacy of perceptions that cannot be defined in principle.[40] In the mid-nineteenth century, literature becomes the place where an antipathy to systems can be redeemed as valuable to higher education. A *Crimson* response to the *Advocate*'s critique of "Harvard indifference" helps us see how this value is assessed: the "divided energy" that characterizes the collegiate sensibility is nothing less than the celebration of experience in its "heterogeneous complexity" and in its "diverse and indiscriminate forms." Indifference is the way of life for students who choose to "sip the sweets of various flowers," and it is also, with a little pruning of the rhetoric, a nascent version of what will be come to be a primary defense of liberal education in the later nineteenth century and of course the twentieth as well.[41] Harvard indifference, when translated from a style to a curriculum, is an ethic of the liberal arts that remains a secret sharer in so many of our contemporary arguments on behalf of literary study.

The Sincerity of Dilettantes

"Briefly," writes the *Crimson*, "are we not indifferent from superficial thought, and superficial from desultory attention, divided energy, want of definite purpose, and laziness? A laziness fostered, it is true, by a little *dilettante* culture."[42] The question asked and answered here evokes a familiar story about the institutional character of the humanities as it was practiced in U.S. universities in the antebellum period. Though not always championed in such flagrant terms, the experience of the dilettante, moving freely across topics and interests, was consonant with the spirit of the humanities at large. At Harvard, for instance, where the idea of the generalist professor, as Gerald Graff reminds us, was all but invented and, then, enshrined in college lore, the pedagogical aesthetic of faculty like Longfellow or Lowell involved the casual display of literary knowledge, delivered with great enthusiasm. What was not germane to this style of literary instruction—indeed, what was antithetical to both its classroom presence and intellectual priorities—was a methodology of approach to the range of literary topics as they impressed themselves on the critic's imagination. The antipathy to method, about which Graff and Simpson have written powerfully, helps to ensure that literary studies in America develop along lines divergent from, and often anxiously resistant to, the emphasis on formalism and research that comes to define the discipline of literature later in the nineteenth century. Professors of literature, in the dominant mode of Lowell, favored an impressionistic approach to texts. Hostile to general theories, they lectured through anecdotes and examples. They celebrated, to paraphrase Simpson, understandings of "the mutually incommensurable details" of social and psychological experience that the texts seemed to communicate to common sense. So, as models for experiencing the range of impulse captured in the texts, and the speed with which such energies could shift in tone and feeling, it was not the role of the professor to prove his mastery over them. The professor's work was to demonstrate responsiveness and succeeded best when it engaged with the immanent eccentricities—and the charm, humor, and variety—of the literature itself. Anything more abstract risked an estrangement from the palpable attractions of the material. "Students prefer a course with a dilettante," writes Irving Babbitt, drawing on his experience at Harvard, for he is "freer to devote himself to being clever and entertaining."[43]

Of course more than the entertainment value of the dilettante was at issue: the preference for such a relaxed relationship to knowledge suggested a more elaborate commitment to a style of character. A dilettante makes modest claims and, then, delights in the style that attends from his modesty. (The "Harvard style," says a student paper, is "elegant," while lacking "force and vigor.") But the modesty of the dilettante has pretensions, too, because as the expression of a commitment to variety and complexity, it also expresses ambivalence toward a democratic character that Tocqueville and others were defining as deeply attached to the possibilities of simplicity. "Democratic nations," says Tocqueville famously, "are passionately addicted to generic terms or abstract expressions."[44] But the dilettante, as he is described at the colleges, does not generalize. He proceeds inductively and in a miscellaneous way, collecting the knowledge that forms the basis of more humble impressions. He likes surprises and excludes nothing, while mastering nothing. He dislikes ideology, which presumes that truth comes in a handful of propositions, because there are too many sentiments that vitally bind him to other points of view. In the same fashion, the generalist at the lectern does not hypothesize but recalls what he has read and done and passes on the sensibility that has been shaped by these experiences. What he performs is less of an embodiment of impersonal authority and more of an engagement with the discrete events and prior twists of fate that situate him before the classrooms of students with whom he shares the more personal histories of his intellect. He has no theories he can pass down to a future generation, but he can at least instill a faith that the concrete facts of social life, registered with special clarity in the works he has read, will form his students as they have formed him. Where theory fails, he learns to comprehend the power of tradition.

At a moment when people thought about such things as national characters, this professorial manner and the forms of learning it encouraged were understood to be profoundly English. The "English mind," writes Henry Adams as he experienced it in 1863, is "eccentric, systematically unsystematic and logically illogical." This was also how the English characterized themselves, as Stefan Collini and Simpson have argued eloquently; conceiving of their specific cast of mind as an amalgam of Baconian inductiveness and Lockean sensationalism, English intellectuals articulated a "national philosophical identity" that championed intuition over method and empiricism over theory. Asserting the priority of the particular and local, a distinctly English intellectual position was articulated in contrast to such figures as Condorcet, who represented France's excessive worship of theories, or Kant, who represented Germany's excessive faith in complete systems. If, after the 1790s, a priori claims of universal knowledge seemed to be the property of revolutionaries, the British, following the example of Burke, instead declared "the rights of immethodical thought and expression, presenting them as the rhetorical incarnation of a free and liberal society itself imagined as uniquely British." At the same time, the German love of metaphysics and pure reason seemed like an assault on English common sense grounded in institutions and in the example of practices over time. "I beg leave to throw out my thoughts, and express my feelings, just as they arise in my mind, with very little attention to formal method": so Simpson quotes Burke to show just how resistant the voice of Englishness could be to the single-mindedness of methods. The stylistic analogue to this "revolt against theory" is what Simpson identifies in Burke's "discontinued way of writing": his reflections on the French Revolution especially confront the forthright ideas of a political order with an associative and "literary" response. Instead of didacticism and epitome, we have contingency and repetition, and this is much like the "vagabondage of intellect and sensibility" that, for Irving Babbitt, defines what the dilettante enjoys.[45]

As Perry Anderson suggests, the centrality of empiricism to English thought produces "a deep instinctive aversion to the category of the totality," which is another way of describing the antipathy to theoretical abstractions that impresses Americans in their accounts of Englishness. What Adams and others observe is the intensity with which the English have faith in "the thick, coarse actuality" of their English world, as Lionel Trilling puts it. "England," writes Emerson in *English Traits* (1852), "is the best of actual nations. It is no ideal framework." Why can't the English be idealists? Because, Emerson says, they are too conditioned by the reality of their society, "as if, having the best conditions, they could not bring themselves to forfeit them." Emerson attributes the English "skepticism of theory" to the legacy of Locke for whom "the meaning of ideas is unknown": there are objects, senses, and feelings but the "understanding" Locke inspires, and which becomes "the measure, in all nations, of the English intellect," accepts the world only as it works in practice. In "high departments," says Emerson, the English became "cramped," preferring to gather "mountains of facts, as a bad general wants myriads of men," thinking that what is the most forceful is the most evident. The English, in other words, make an "unconditional surrender to facts"; they "do not occupy themselves on matters of general and lasting import, but on corporeal civilization, on goods that perish in the using." The English mind "turns every abstraction it can receive into a portable utensil, or a working institution" and while it "shrink[s] from generalization," it holds all it gains. This means that while it forsakes the "lofty sides of Parnassus," it accommodates everything that its world has in it as an appreciable aspect of that world. England, writes Emerson, is "stuffed full." [46]

In a discussion of "dilettantism," which is also a discussion of Englishness, Henry Adams likens the English mind to "the London drawing-room, a comfortable and easy spot, filled with bits and fragments of incoherent furnitures, which were never meant to go together, and could be arranged in any relation without making a whole, except by the square room." His sense of the English mind, containing a collection of things, like a room that is slowly furnished, gives a materialist sense of character (the English are what they have) that is also firmly Lockean (how, asks Locke, does the mind come "to be furnished?").[47] For the empiricist, knowledge is not abstract of course: the mind is stacked with all the impressions it acquires, so that knowing becomes an act of possessing. Adams tells us that what the empiricist has to go on are the tastes that guide his experience, for while "philosophy might dispute about innate ideas till the stars died out in the sky," about tastes no one "has the right to doubt." Least of all, he continues, "the Englishman, for his tastes are his being; he drifts after them as unconsciously as a honey-bee drifts after his flowers, and, in England, everyone must drift with him." So the Englishman's empiricism is a style and not a theory; he is drawn, says Adams, to books, science, or art (or hunting or horse racing) not through his conceptions of them but his feelings for them. His involvements are "scrappy" and "fragmentary": he accumulates experiences and knowledge in an eccentric way and "for the sake of eccentricity itself," the only caveat being, for Adams, that perhaps in the end the English are right in thinking that there are no general ideas and that "history, like everything else, might be a field of scraps, like the refuse about a Staffordshire iron-furnace." If one must resign oneself to decline and fall, so to speak, on "a golden dust-heap of British refuse," Adams says that at least one can expect to do so with a degree from Oxford.[48]

For both Emerson and Adams, there is a moral quality of character that proceeds from this taking of "the world as it goes." It is what Lionel Trilling, following Emerson, calls "sincerity" and sees as an expression of the obedient relationship to reality by which the English measure themselves. "Their practical power," writes Emerson, "rests on their national sincerity. . . . They are blunt in saying what they think, sparing of promises, and they require plain dealing of others." In calling it as it is, the Englishman adheres to things as they are, the implication being, for Emerson and Trilling, that the person who accepts his situation as a necessary condition of his life "will be sincere beyond question." The "indubitable thereness" of the English, in Trilling's words, is decidedly conservative; the English meet reality without imagining otherwise and without pretending otherwise, and this is what sincerity is. They devote their energy to registering the world as it looks to them now; the bluntness is the form that their empiricism takes, and it is moral in its way. The English do not lie or misrepresent. They do not theorize ("rushing into the savage wilderness of *isms*," as Lowell says Americans do). The Englishman "understates, avoids superlatives, checks himself in compliments," while the American, we learn from Francis Grund, is "apt to overdo things": "We are either too lavish in our praise or too severe in our criticism. We always deal in superlatives." The English "avoid pretension and go right to the heart of the thing. They hate nonsense, sentimentalism and highflown expression" (Emerson); but Americans "vent their pomposity from one end of a harangue to the other" (Tocqueville). The English, says Henry Adams, are "bluff, brutal, blunt," and, being pleased to speak plainly, presume nothing.[49]

If this kind of distribution of national traits suggests the "character of a closed system, in which objects are what they are *because* they are what they are," then Edward Said's account of how nations mythologize nations describes just what Americans do. In the antebellum academy, such constructions of the English mind shape not only a style of learning but also a more general understanding of what college achieves: an ethics complimented by a declared commitment to the facts of common sense. The English, writes a student in the *Williams Quarterly*, "will dig and plow in the fields of literature but hate theories and generalizations. . . . I wish our American students might learn of English students, and cease to think that the development of our mental powers is the sole object of their existence."[50] The wish, in other words, is for considerably more of *existence* than the life of the mind to which the literary life is opposed, at least in these remarks from a review of *English Traits*. For the empiricist, it is the immersion in the realities of the world, and in the details that texture our experience of it, that defines human nature by rejecting any abstract idea of the self. "Self-realization through society," as Trilling puts it, is a recurring trope of English sincerity and a logic of character that is deeply foreign to the a priori authenticity of the individual that is later associated with R. W. B. Lewis's "American Adam," to give just one example.[51]

It is also deeply foreign to models of humanistic learning that, later in the nineteenth century, flourished within the modern research university as it came increasingly to reflect the influence and prestige of German academic practices. The example of John Hopkins, as Graff and others have shown, inspires a series of transformations that remake both the style and conduct of higher learning, placing a newfound emphasis on the protocols of specialties and the systematic organization of knowledge into disciplines with their own languages and methods. In the context of this academic culture, with its emphasis on expertise, the ability to acquire knowledge by intercourse and conversation, or even the inclination to peruse knowledge as an enthusiast would, becomes a disobedient response to what the research university demands. But in the antebellum years, as professors of literature and languages and also future college presidents began the ritual of postgraduate training in Germany (George Ticknor, Edward Everett, and Lowell are only a few of the many who studied in Göttingen), their form of approach to knowledge remains distinctively English despite the subjects they learn. They explore the conceptual heights of German philosophy, for example, with considerable skepticism. Ticknor calls Fichte and Schelling "unintelligible idealists," who live "entirely isolated from the world." He castigates the "vehement exertion" of German thinkers who are intent on having all knowledge "reduced to philosophical systems." And the Germans, he says, have bankrupted the Kantian tradition by making a fetish of the difference between ideas and sensations (that is, between their understanding of life and their experience of it). In contrast, there are the "practical" English—Locke, Hartley, and Priestly—who embrace the world "psychologically," which is Ticknor's way of naming the mix of response, intuition, and feeling to which American scholars aspire. "In

England," Ticknor continues, "the man of letters must be more or less a practical man," while in Germany he is "a pure idealist or theorist," and Ticknor likes to be realistic.[52] So even when American professors become students in Germany, they come to see culture, like the "Anglo-maniacs" in Germany who Adorno despises, not "as a separate sphere of the objective mind" but "as a form of empirical existence."[53]

"American literature," says a Yale student magazine, "is not Germanic, but Anglican development. . . . Our philosophy and logic are based rather on the solid English substratum of Bacon and Locke, than on the dreams of Fichte."[54] As Franklin Court points out, the rise of formal literary studies in America not only preceded the period when Germanic models enjoyed their greatest prestige within higher education but, more important, coincided with a pervasive turn to British models for understanding the nature what it meant to be a critic. Court identifies a specific fascination with Scottish commonsense philosophers, beginning early in the century: the principles of an experiential practice in works by Francis Hutcheson and Thomas Reid were crucial to Edward T. Channing, for example, who came increasingly to insist that oratory and rhetoric be taught by way of first-hand engagement with primary works instead of their abstracted versions in textbooks. Hugh Blair's *Lectures on Rhetoric* was immensely popular in antebellum America, as were any number of works that could be associated with a broadly British style of criticism that aimed to please and persuade by appealing to common understanding. The Scottish moral philosophy behind these texts argues that an inherent sense disposes us to approve of what is beautiful and good; moral judgments are derived not from reason but from the preferences of taste, and so we learn to trust our aesthetic responses as the best indications of virtue. Thus when criticism became a part of the curriculum—by 1811, Columbia had courses designated specifically as "criticism"—it is no surprise that students were instructed to understand that the proper judgment *of* a text is all but indistinguishable from a feeling *for* a text.

An affective hermeneutics was the natural extension of an emotive theory of ethics, which is an elaborate way of saying that early nineteenth-century academic criticism saw good reading as good feeling, and vice versa. A rigorous analysis could not demonstrate genius as convincingly as an intense reaction to the most vivid aspects of a work. The emphasis, in other words, was less on language's ideas than its effects, so that a critical appreciation of how language moves us, so to speak, became the imperative for literary practice. Reading literature was an immersion in the experience of literature, and criticism was a communication of the *sense* of that experience. "We inhale knowledge," a Williams College paper declares, "by breathing a literary atmosphere." John Kirkland, president of Harvard from 1810 to 1828, is eulogized for a similar approach to understanding: "By a sort of literary intuition he got at what the author meant, and what his book was designed to teach.—And is not this, after all, the true learning?"[55]

This suggests a mode of reading that is, to put it mildly, indifferent to the claims of hard study as the epitome of intellectual practice. "He had, too," says Kirkland's biographer in 1840, "the faculty of getting all the good out of a book by rapidly turning over its leaves and running his eye over its pages without reading it in course from beginning to end." The "universality of [Kirkland's] studies, freeing him as they did, from all pedantry and narrowness of mind," invokes the sensibility of the antebellum dilettante but suggests something, too, of the specific forms in which literary practice survived within the far more disciplined university that emerged in the decades following the Civil War.[56] As a scholarly pursuit grounded in common feeling and the impulsiveness of taste, criticism represented an increasingly tenuous paradigm for humanistic study: distinguished from more specialized languages of scholarship, criticism emphasized a respect for the total experience of reading as an "insight into the realities of things," to return to the *Crimson*. This is not to say that nineteenth-century academic "critics" were always set in opposition to the development of literary studies as a discipline along German lines, nor that more recent champions of literary criticism as such are right to long for a return to some prior moment before "theory" when American academics were not beholden to the complications of French and German thought. The allure of criticism reflects an investment in a more traditional intellectual style that trades on its residual status within the division of mental labor structuring the modern university from the nineteenth century on. As an academic idiom that insists on common sense and affect as essential features of its nonmethodology, criticism's institutional appeal depends on the belief that it is always giving way to the latest theories and their transactional approach to human knowledge.

Where in the present age can we find, asks Lowell, "the strange sense of the sense escaping things?" Shutting his eyes, he says, "in certain speculative directions," he finds solace in the intimations of reality that his readings provide, suggesting how literature offers a retreat from the difficulties of pure reason.[57] Posing the obscurantism of the profession against the humanism of belles lettres, Lowell reverts to an empiricist discourse that treats literary culture as the affirmation of reality, just as British epistemology and style claim to engage with the world completely. Indeed, belletrism in the academy, with its cultivated show of feelings and its embrace of common sense (as both a rhetoric and an aesthetic) presumes a kind of Anglophilia even when it does not announce—or know—its provenance. To make this claim is to argue that the practice of belles lettres in America was not just occasionally inflected by the conventionality and custom that Simpson and others associate with a British intellectual tradition; rather, American belletrism was so deeply shaped by this tradition that its character remains apparent across a range of partisan positions, from the apoliticism that Howells observes in Lowell, to more recent attempts, from a decidedly left perspective, to make any brand of abstract, academic discourse seem complicit with modern bureaucratic rationality, or worse.[58]

We need not assign a definitive politics to belletristic criticism in order to appreciate the stakes on which it was practiced in the nineteenth century and continued in a variety of twentieth-century incarnations. Criticism is both a demonstration of, and enthusiasm for, the diverse power of literature to capture something of the "variousness, possibility, complexity and difficulty" that Trilling prizes and that Leon Wieseltier confirms of him when he says that his "criticism was a long search for the sense of reality, and a long tribute to it."[59] The ability of belletrists to indulge in the immediacy of reading is the proof of their own sensibility and the best evidence of their commitment to a reality that they may not fully understand but still feel very much. The Britishness of American belles lettres is resonant not only in this sentimental preference for spontaneous reaction over systematic method but, more generally, in the deferential attitude toward reality that such a preference redeems. By translating an anxiety about the place of literary culture into a more encompassing nostalgia for a society of greater sensibility, literary academics can fantasize about a new purpose and direction for their profession that relies on its diminished sway within the modern university; criticism functions as the means by which faculty and students preserve the sense of a moment, as Lowell puts it, before "analysis is carried into everything." Thus as early as the 1840s, Kirkland is mourned at Harvard for embodying a bygone day when literary appreciation was an intuitive concern and when learnedness was as eclectic and inconsistent as the nature of the world that made it possible. All of which may help to explain why the anachronism of Kirkland's approach to reading is also remembered as an aspect, in Edward Everett's words, of his "pure English style."[60]

Lowell tells us that when Wordsworth says "books are a real world," he was thinking of "such books as are not merely the triumphs of pure intellect, however supreme, but of those in which intellect infused with the sense of beauty aims rather to produce delight than conviction, or, if conviction, than through intuition rather than formal logic." Speaking of the life of the mind, Lowell describes the images that every one of us can summon up "to the tiny shadow-box of the brain" through the work of memory and imagination. He does not call this work invention (even when Donne or Wordsworth do it), but the expression of *realities*. "Am I wrong," he asks, "in using the word *realities*?" Art confirms life by apprehending the spirit or essence of it, which is another way of saying again that, for Lowell, art is a form of "common sense."[61]

Emerson makes a similar claim later in his career, in "Experience," when the idealism for which he is famous seems to him like compensation for a reality he can never really know, being too volatile and changeable. We are idealists, he says, when we do not "find reality." Dreaming of his dead son, who he cannot meaningfully mourn, Emerson discovers that there is no "lasting relation between that intellect and that thing," but, of course, he prefers "that thing"—which in this case, is his lost son, who all the acts of thinking and dreaming can never make real for him. Emerson finds consolation in the feeling that we might approximate a sense of the "real nature" of the life and the people that are left for us, treating them, he says, "as if they were real; perhaps they are." As if we should use our imagination to accept the moments we are in, so far as we are able, not thinking too hard about them and not trying to change them ("enough of the futility of criticism"). We use our imagination, that is, not to "postpone and refer and wish, but do broad justice where we are, by whomsoever we deal with, accepting our actual companions and circumstances." The creed that Emerson says he has settled into is less stoicism than a reaction to all of the "referring" and "wishing" that mark the speculative practices of his earlier work and that, finally, produce no understanding. Emerson rebels against even the "noblest theory of life" because the "splendor of the promise of the times" too often "ends in headache" and leaves him no closer to feeling the "sharp peaks and edges" of reality, for contact with which, he says, he would even accept the cost of losing his son. If our relations to each other are "oblique and casual," then the answer, for Emerson, is to "give a reality" to what we find and ask no questions: "The great gifts are not got by analysis." Between the "cold realm of pure geometry and lifeless science" and that of simple sensations is poetry and understanding instead.[62]

At last, poetry is sincere and so is Emerson in "Experience." "I have set my heart on honesty," he says. His literary pursuits are there to attest to "the clangor and jangle of contrary tendencies" in a life he no longer tries to determine. Literature does not lend itself to philosophies but to the "love of the real" and to the world that Emerson calls the "mid-world," where we do not look ahead or back but "set up the strong present tense." Too many things, says Emerson, "are unsettled which it is of the first importance to settle;—and, pending their settlement we will do as we do." That doing includes just about all we can do; "dedication to one thought is quickly odious," and Emerson tells us how he moved from reading Montaigne to Shakespeare, to Plutarch, Bacon, Goethe, and so on, each time believing that he should never need another book and each time tiring of his conviction. Still, Emerson tells us, that he "will never read but the commonest books": he reads to delight in what other readers already read, suggesting, of course, that there are no further truths to find and no transcendent truths ("do not craze yourself with thinking, but go about your business anywhere"). "Everything good," he continues, "is on the highway," by way of saying that the best experiences are the common ones, and the best knowledge is the knowledge that we are poised to share. Emerson finds comfort, in other words, in the empiricist resignation that life's chief good is for people "who can enjoy what they find"; we have, after all, "no more root in the deep world" than it seems, and so the art of life is to "live amid surfaces" and to "skate on them well."[63]

Of course, this comfort becomes tiresome, too: the moments of idealism and vision return, as B. L. Packer points out, "whether we want them to or not" and, these visions of transcendence are also within the range of one's nature and response to "experience."[64] Emerson claims in "Montaigne" (1850) that the skeptic, who sees the "yawning gulf" between our ideals and our "shabby life" will also have the "poise and vivacity" to admit them both in turn, since our beliefs will change with our moods. He likes Montaigne because he has a certain and intelligible way of not deciding, of seeing plainly that he cannot see enough to assert one thing at the expense of another, and so his *Essays* "are an entertaining soliloquy on every random topic that comes into his head." They are frank and abundant; "like the language of conversation transferred to a book," the essays "smack of the earth and of real life, sweet, or smart, or stinging" without abstracting or refining too much. "I weary of these dogmatizers," writes Emerson, and then, without a pause: "I tire of these hacks of routine, who deny dogmas." At least, in the writings of Montaigne (and presumably of Emerson, too), there is "much to say on all sides." With the opinion that we are only "superficial tenants of the globe" and should act accordingly—enjoying and confirming the variety and superficiality in which we live everyday in any case—Emerson's late conservatism turns him into a dilettante.[65]

Is this what Howard Mumford Jones means when he says, in an introduction to *English Traits,* that "Emerson was an Anglophile?"[66] Certainly *English Traits* is aware of the limitations of a nation whose "scholars have become un-ideal": "There is a cramp limitation in their habit of thought . . . and a tortoise's instinct to hold hard to the ground with his claws, lest he should be thrown on his back." They hold hard to reality—"for they feel no wings sprouting at their shoulders"—but at least, says Emerson, they see the "poor best" they have got, which is just what he sees in them (the poor best *we* have got, "the best of actual nations"). The book, then, wants nothing more nor less than to avail itself of "the epitome of our times" and does so in the diversified expression of the manners, habits, abilities, beliefs, and learning that together amount to a sense of the "genius" of the English. The travelogue Emerson writes is as miscellaneous and copious as the English he describes and, yes, Anglophilic for the ways in which it is finally alert to all the details and glad to be literal with them. The English, Emerson writes, may lack an ability to speculate about the future, "but they read with good intent, and what they learn they incarnate."[67] One could argue, then, that the English in *English Traits* already know the lessons of "Experience": that life, as Emerson puts it, is not "intellectual or critical, but sturdy"; that "to fill the hour" is the greatest happiness; and that the "practical wisdom" that lets us fill the hour however we can (with Montaigne or Shakespeare maybe) "infers an indifferency" from objections to the futility of our doing it. In this regard, there is nothing for Emerson that is more characteristically English than being satisfied and engrossed within the present moment as it comes to be.

The empiricist temperament of the English inoculates them against any metaphysics that would otherwise defer reality in hopes of finding better. Or put differently, to understand the value of experience is to understand not only that it is, as the saying goes, its own reward but also that it is the only reward we can expect to have. "Let us know what we know, for certain," he writes in "Montaigne." "What we have, let it be solid and seasonable and our own." The mode of thought that Emerson affirms in "Experience" is already "English" along these lines: "Common-sense is a rare as genius,—is the basis of genius, and experience is hands and feet to every enterprise." [68]

What does it mean to link genius to common sense? This is not Wordsworth's idea of genius as the agent of originality and inspiration: "Genius," Wordsworth says, "is the introduction of a new element into the intellectual universe; or, if that not be allowed, it is the application of powers to objects on which they had not before been exercised, or the employment of them in such a manner as to produce effects hitherto unknown." In any case, the only proof of genius is "what was never done before," but, in Emerson, the man of genius invents nothing. [69] His mind is both the best incarnation of the world as he knows it and the medium that gives expression to its common culture. So the greatest genius, writes Emerson in *Representative Men,* is "the most indebted man," perfectly hospitable to the practical wisdom and knowledge of his times and also "not afraid or ashamed to owe his originality to the originality of all." He takes knowledge wherever he finds it—his powers of thought are "genial" in that way—and if he is remembered by a future age it is only as the sincere "recorder and embodiment of his own." The genius is against a spirit of innovation and is distinguished, as Emerson says Shakespeare is distinguished, more by his "range and extent, than by originality." Genius consists, he says, "in not being original at all; in being altogether receptive; in letting the world do all, and suffering the spirit of the hour to pass unobstructed through the mind." [70]

Shakespeare in Emerson has the "negative capability" that he has in Keats for being passive and receptive to the influence of existence as he encounters it and for being "in uncertainties . . . without reaching after fact and reason." Keats is a great believer in the "Indolence" of contemplation, as he calls it—in letting the world work on you without working on it. "I was led to these thoughts," Keats writes in a letter to J. H. Reynolds, by "the beauty of the morning operating on a sense of Idleness"—and we may remember all the student reveries claiming that idleness is productive as such ("I am not idle when I sit" idle at my window and so forth) and that may, in fact, have been influenced by Keats.[71] But in Emerson, the indolence of the intellect is also what guarantees its conventionality; a genius is "a heart in unison with his time" and the best manifestation of it. The genius "finds himself in the river of the thoughts and events, forced onward by the ideas and necessities of his contemporaries." All thoughts are borrowed thoughts: the genius moves beyond the awkwardness of this fact to acknowledge that the best of what he does is "no man's work, but came by wide social labour." He is bound to society, and the literary productions that arise from his avowal have a primary sincerity that Emerson calls "earnest" and "sweet."

Emerson tells us that Shakespeare felt entitled "to steal from the writings of others," and thus plagiarism becomes an argument for fair or common use. A good Englishmen, Shakespeare values traditions and precedents: he knows the world (and all that the world has written) by heart and likes to be faithful to it. Here at last, writes Emerson, "is perfect representation," by which he means both Shakespeare's lack of originality and the universalism by which he powerfully registers the thoughts of humanity without any imposition of his will. "Give a man of talents a story to tell, and his partiality will presently appear," but the genius, continues Emerson, "has no peculiarity, no importunate topic; but all is duly given; no veins, no curiosities: no cow-painter, no bird-fancier, no mannerist is he." Shakespeare, says Emerson, "has no discoverable egotism." Most other accounts of Shakespeare's genius insist on the point that Emerson repeats, that "there is not a trace of egotism" in it. "He seems to have been without egotism," writes George Calvert in 1879.[72] Henry Hudson, describing Shakespeare's mind, in his *Lectures on Shakespeare* (1848), says that the "perfect absence of Shakespeare from his own pages, makes it difficult for us to conceive of a human being's having written them." Instead, the "vital powers" of his mind that encompass the earth in its "multitudinous unity" let us see everything but his own image, or else, "like the sunlight which always takes the precise form and color of the object it shines upon," his image in other things. Genius is what makes Shakespeare "the soul of his age," and "representative" of it, which is just the way Emerson describes him. For Hudson, too, genius gives Shakespeare the capacity to be "common"; at a moment when "perhaps the growing lust of originality is the worst of all guides to truth," his art is simply the "sensuous, organic embodiment of ideas, emotions and conceptions."[73] "We do believe," writes the *American Whig Review* of Shakespeare in 1847, that "sound *common sense . . .* was in him." At least, says the magazine, he does not ask us to "assume as existing a *sense* which is not *common.*" Shakespeare is not particular, and the assimilative powers of his genius that make his work, in Hudson's words, "the very abridgment and eclecticism of humanity" also make it utterly not his own. Lowell describes Shakespeare's work as the expression of "the grand impersonality of Shakespeare."[74]

Who would have thought that Shakespeare's plagiarism could be so celebrated? In an essay called "Plagiarism: An Apology for the Last Comer," the *American Whig Review* describes what it is like for a reader to come across a passage that he knows is plagiarized: "He at once gives it the greeting of an old and cherished friend; the vacant expression flies from his countenance, and sparkling eye and animate gesture testify to the pleasure that thrills through the whole man. With awakened interest, he is tempted to read further. . . . Does he think of chiding the writer of the book as a plagiarist? Not at all, but instead would heap thanks upon him for his efficient service in the cause of the Muses." When the *Whig Review* claims that Shakespeare "merge[d]" himself "entirely in the mass of humanity," it means that he was unoriginal, and it means it as a compliment. His genius is both appropriative and conservative—it "shuns novelties and cleaves to old familiar objects"— and, indeed, it is the nature of genius "to *love* what we have long known, and to love it the more the longer we have known it." So it follows that "high genius is practically and essentially conservative, and discovers no such worth in abstractions and theories."[75] In his essay "Shakespeare Once More" (1868), Lowell tends to agree that the poet is essentially an "observer": "The passions, actions, sentiments, whose character and results he delighted to watch and to reproduce, are those of man in society as it existed; and it no more occurred to him to question the right of that society to exist than to criticize the divine ordination of the seasons." Coming of age in a period before religious speculation— before, that is, the "centre of intellectual interest" was "rather in the region of thought and principle and conscience than in actual life"— Shakespeare, says Lowell, "was not run away with by the hobby of any theory." Rather, his attempt to "search every nook and cranny" of human life and to communicate its "complex experience" makes Shakespeare, for Lowell, profoundly unoriginal. It also makes him "so thoroughly English." He is, writes Lowell, "a representative Englishman," which is finally what he seems to be for Emerson, too, and not least for the delight he takes in watching and reproducing the eclectic cast of society and its "thousandfold interests." The delight in the pursuit matters because without it (without what Emerson calls "cheerfulness") no man can be a genius, "for beauty is his aim." "Beauty, the spirit of joy and hilarity, he sheds over the universe": the genius is nothing less— and, for Emerson, blessedly nothing more—than the amateur.[76]

Were Harvard students geniuses? They were amateurs, of course, and certainly they were plagiarists, or at least, they claimed to be in a culture that equated idleness with intellectualism. Benjamin Homer Hall's insistence on the extent of "skinning"—borrowing another's ideas and presenting them as your own—suggests that what was good enough for Shakespeare was good enough for students at college. "Shakespeare was a great plagiarist," asserts a Bowdoin magazine article approvingly. A Dartmouth paper's "Recipes for Making a Composition" seems cribbed from Hudson's account of Shakespeare's practice and adapted for student use: "When a subject is announced don't trouble yourself to think about it, but go to the library and run over the catalogue . . . then with a pen in hand, transcribe here and there a pithy well-tuned phrase . . . if a passage be so elegant as not to admit of alteration without injury, it is better to copy it literally." Like Lowell and others who admired Shakespeare for his ability not to invent ideas but to rehearse them as he finds them, this anonymous Dartmouth writer sees such borrowings as the index to a kind of authenticity that cannot follow from originality. "The above prescriptions," the paper concludes, "are in perfect agreement with the ends of composition, which word derived from *con* and *pono* signifies a putting together—whether of one's own thoughts or another, it doesn't matter." The genius of plagiarism, as it is discussed, condoned, and celebrated in college newspapers, lets students avoid work, while respecting the standing record of accumulated knowledge and expression that suggests they need never work again. The plagiarist, after all, trades on the power of precedent and received authority. To make the case for plagiarism, then, as writers in college papers often do, is to acknowledge that both education and imagination are constituted socially and best practiced in the pleasing context of others. It is not the most uplifting challenge, ethically, but it speaks nonetheless to the values of an intellectual style resistant to "that spirit of innovation so rife at the present day." Worried over the "mania for originality" that is bringing "restlessness and inquietude" to campus, a Wesleyan paper argues that "true originality consists in no such far-fetched efforts. If we mean by the term, a power that *creates* entirely new and independent ideas, it is a vain chimera; there exists no such power." The charm of college life is that it need not subscribe to this particular illusion but can afford to be more realistic (even commonsensical) about the limits of ingenuity: "All thoughts, worthy to be so named, are but combinations of preconceived ideas . . . the only creations of mind are the endless and various combinations of those things which already exist." [77]

The Englishman, writes Bliss Perry from Harvard in 1904, is "an amateur born and bred," while defining the amateur for the way "he passes through the university with the minimum of industry" and also for "his inveterate faith in the superiority of the rule of thumb." The amateur, in other words, is both idle and conservative, accomplishing little because he has world enough and time. He is against the drudgery of "methodical instruction" because he is for the "amateur's ideal life," in which he can be versatile and responsive to the variety of things but also casual toward them because, "after all, it is not a vital matter whether he succeed or fail." [78] Emerson's own faith in the superiority of amateurs rests squarely on this devotion to "experience" itself, which amateurs find irresistible because they are not alienated from it and because, in any case, they would find it boring to be so. Describing himself, as a professor at Harvard, George Santayana says that he "accepted having feet, ugly and insufficient as they may be," sounding much like Emerson when he rejects too much analysis to say that experience is the "hands and feet" of every enterprise. "I believe," writes Santayana, "compulsorily and satirically in the existence of this absurd world; but as to the existence of a better world, or of hidden reasons in this one, I am incredulous or rather critically skeptical." So Santayana rejects "systems of philosophy" and adopts "aesthetics" as his "specialty" but, it turns out, that the point of his chosen discipline is to be as discursive and undisciplined as possible. "I consciously continued my readings as an amateur," he says, and then later, "so superficial was my study." When the Harvard *Magenta* describes the kind of "superficial knowledge" that was "becoming so common at Harvard," it shows some concern for the "fashion of trying to get a general idea of all elective studies, rather than an accurate knowledge of a few." And thus culture at college comes to be "the ability to talk on any subject readily and fluently enough for five minutes or perhaps a quarter of an hour, to know a little music, a little science, a little Greek, a little mathematics, and a little of fifty other things; that is, not to know them at all." [79] Which returns us to Emerson's lesson that superficial knowledge may be all we have, so we might as well learn to enjoy it.

The English Accent

Why do some academics talk like they do? In America, where does the English accent come from? The association of English accents with the professorate is such a commonplace of popular representations—think of John Houseman's linguistic superciliousness in *The Paper Chase* or Richard Burton's intermittent brogue in *Who's Afraid of Virginia Woolf*— that it seems hardly worth mentioning except as a fascination with those class performances of intellectuals that seem to invite suspicion, even in examples of "serious" culture. The fact that figures of repressive academic authority in almost any Hollywood comedy set on a college campus invariably speak with a British accent further suggests the extent to which the famous terms of Richard Hofstadter's argument about American "anti-intellectualism" still flourish, making it both customary and convenient for a certain style of professor to always appear a bit like a foreigner. Of course, the academic John Lithgow played throughout the nineties on *Third Rock from the Sun* was quite literally an alien: who else on campus today would be so enunciative? In contemporary America, then, it is not quite the case that people with "Oxford" accents, as Bourdieu suggests, "have the power to discourage the intention of discerning what they are 'in reality'": rather, such accents are all too easily offered up as shows of haughtiness, anxiety, or delusive grandeur. There is less "unconscious reference to their class distribution" and more overt burlesque of their class pretension. [80] Perhaps not every incarnation of an academic Englishness is subjected to this treatment, but even when more gently ironized or tacitly admired, the intimation of a fundamental inauthenticity comes to surround almost any American who talks like *that*.

Hollywood's explanation for this way of speaking need not be seconded to acknowledge that English accents are a fact of academic life in reality and that their history reflects a series of attitudes toward the expression of intellectualism and how it sounds. How *does* intelligence sound? "The distinction to a delicate ear is very marked," writes Richard Grant White in 1871, though it is often a difference of pitch alone.

Even when the pronunciations are the same, the pitch of the English accent, says White, is higher, and "more penetrating" than the American accent, and the inflections are more varied—"because they more frequently rise"—suggesting that Americans who speak like Americans have a monotone.[81] Then, everything depends on the sound of the *a* in words such as "glass," "father," and "pastor," where the *a* alone is the surest indication of social culture. What better mark of education than the "full, free, unconscious utterance of the broad *ah* sound of *a*," opening the throat and lungs to give the voice roundness and depth? The American student, states a Harvard paper in 1875, returns from three months in England, pronouncing "all his a's in broad alphas," because only students with less cultivation give *a* the throaty sound of *aw* or the thin, flat sound of "anatomy," as if it were formed in the nose. American nasality, says Andrew Peabody in 1855, overlabors the vowels and neglects the consonants, so that what is most pleasing in the "refined" accent of Englishmen is the recognizable presence of *g* in words ending in "ing." But then, Englishmen are also much more casual about the ends of words, meaning, for Jacob A. Cummings, author of the popular *Pronouncing Spelling Book* (1819), that it is not sophisticated to take final syllables so seriously as Americans who always seem to prefer "gardens" to "gar'dns" and "pardons" to "par'dns."[82]

By the 1820s a "college pronunciation" was becoming recognizable at Harvard and other eastern universities: it liked contractions and broad *a*'s. Those predisposed to this pronunciation called it "clear and pleasant" and looked for the choices of pitch, emphasis, tone, volume, and pace that seemed to mark it as both simply English and, in the words of the *North American Review* in 1857, "a leading test of intellectual culture." Edward T. Channing's voice, says the magazine about his "readings out loud," exemplified a taste for "English style" that could be found to a remarkable degree in "the speaking and writing of those who have been educated at Harvard."[83] And Lowell, of course, spoke the "best English" in Cambridge along these lines. But the English accent, as both a set of pronunciations and a vocal effort at modulating, phrasing, and pausing so as to sound English, was not a de facto diction that evolved from British colonial English among New England's more patrician classes. At Harvard, beginning in the 1820s, an American sense of "English" English was conceptualized and codified, and soon after adopted across a range of curricular initiatives that helped to make this particular way of speaking into a signature effect of higher learning.

As students began to deliver English orations, alongside Latin ones, and as English declamations and forensics became part of the institutional culture of the college, so did special lessons on voice, enunciation, and delivery. Channing, as professor of rhetoric and oratory, did not simply demonstrate how one should speak in his flexible recitations of Shakespeare at the lectern; he taught students how to form the vowels and declaim from the chest and also how to land on the correct syllables so as to maintain the "purity and elegance of style" that stood as "a breakwater against the tides . . . of misleading fashions" in American language. The voice, writes Channing, "in order that its full compass of expression may be known, and that it may be capable of giving the best utterance, needs cultivation, vigilant study and many experiments." So students, says Edward Everett Hale, would sit "physically, at his side" and listen to him read their own themes, an exercise intended at once to reveal any language that departed from a "purity and simplicity in the English style" and to allow them to experience this style in Channing's own oral performances.[84] With an emphasis on the dignity of plain English speech—well-paced and pleasingly sounded—Channing, along with such professors as Edward Everett and Cornelius Felton, served both to inspire and to inculcate through the aesthetic appeal of the linguistic standards they performed.

Edward Everett Hale claims that Channing "deserves the credit of the English of Emerson, Holmes, Sumner, Clarke, Bellows, Lowell, Higginson, and the other men whom he trained," whose English, in turn, "did more credit to Harvard College, I think, than any other of its achievements" for the thirty-two years in which Channing worked there. More than rehearsing a series of object lessons in the superior use of language, Channing comes to represent a Harvard ideal that makes the acquisition of his rhetorical manner, including the English accent it entails, central to the reproduction of academic character itself. "Mr. Channing carried his deportment forward," explains his cousin, Richard Henry Dana, Jr., in his introduction to Channing's *Lectures on Oratory* (1856), "until its relative influence was so great that excellence in it became essential to honors and high rank, and neglect of it incompatible with continuance in college at all."[85] So when Hale says that he does not know how much of Lowell's "clear, simple, unaffected style he owes to Channing" but that Lowell certainly would have spoken "gratefully of his teacher," the point is to suggest that the power of Channing's example was sufficiently pervasive at Harvard that Lowell need not have acquired his English accent from Channing to have had it all the same.

Years later, William Dean Howells is quite sure of the provenance of his own accent when he remembers that *his* teacher, Lowell, was a "stickler for the best diction" and corrected his "erring Western" ways.[86]

In the early nineteenth century, two sets of dictionaries and spellers competed for authority within the educational system. Noah Webster advocated for linguistic nationality and programmatic reform; his dictionaries actively sought to standardize an American or federal language. Joseph Worcester's *Dictionary of the English Language,* alternatively, followed British spellings and upheld London pronunciation as the model for Americans to imitate. Each side in the conflict had strong partisans on college campuses, with Yale favoring Webster, who was from Connecticut, and Harvard permitting only the use of Worcester, a Bostonian, among its students. The appeal of state pride notwithstanding, Harvard was firmly committed to Worcester's positions on both the particulars of pronunciation and orthography and the assumptions guiding his representation of the English language. In wanting to keep "English" English as the model for American usage, Worcester was perfectly in line with the preferences of Channing and other professors who were insisting that Americans must learn to speak more like British subjects to be Harvard students. Indeed, when the *Atlantic Monthly* weighed in on the "dictionary wars" in 1860, Worcester was named the winner, which especially makes sense since Lowell was the magazine's editor. In addition to his own dictionaries, Worcester helped to popularize John Walker's *Critical Pronouncing Dictionary,* first published in England and famous for adhering to British pronunciations even in its American editions. In a "Letter from Noah Webster" published in a Wesleyan student paper in 1842, Webster himself confirms that "Walker intended to give the fashionable pronunciation in England" to "our children or their teachers." Those who wished the same also recommend Walker and Worcester, including Goold Brown, whose series of grammar books set out to guide students toward language based on "common sense" and who advocated a turn from Webster toward English pronunciation and orthography.[87]

The terms of Worcester's victory are particularly revealing in respect to the intellectual culture I describe because they show not only how, by 1860, the English accent was pedagogically encouraged at Harvard but also how that accent flourished alongside an ideology of language and use that was itself coded as English. The American accent that Webster hoped to define, and eventually to institute, through an elaborate set of linguistic rules was far more prescriptive than the English accent taught at Harvard and enshrined in Worcester's dictionary. Thus, Webster's effort to standardize American English as it was commonly pronounced and, then, to bring orthography into line with pronunciation—ideally omitting superfluous and silent letters (writing "laf" for "laugh" or "blud" for "blood")—was only part of his more encompassing project to devise, from the varieties of everyday language, fixed principles for how words should look and sound. It was not that Webster had no interest in common use but that this interest was temporary; Webster might have listened to how Americans spoke but only in order to codify what he heard as a set of abstract linguistic laws for all Americans to follow. Just as federal laws bind individual states of the union, to borrow Webster's own political analogy, a federal language embraces linguistic difference by transcending it. The vagaries of use give way to the universal norms that the dictionary prescribes, and though Webster grounded these norms in common expression (in American English, for example, instead of British English), his dictionary ultimately aimed to dictate and unify that expression. In contrast, common use as employed in Worcester's dictionary, is not the raw material for rules of correctness but, instead, a stubborn fact of language's own life that resists correctness. Or as an author in the *Atlantic Monthly* writes, Webster "evidently thought the business of a lexicographer was to *regulate,* not to *record,*" while Worcester "has aimed to give us a true view of English as it is, not as he himself may have wished it should be or thought it ought to be."[88] Thus, Worcester's determination to look to England is not just more conservative because it gives priority to precedent over an abstract idea of linguistic nationality but because it proceeds from the assumption that language should exist only as the world has made it.

"A true view of English as it is": if Worcester wins over Webster, it is because the *Atlantic Monthly* disdains reform. Webster, one might say, thinks too hard about language; "attempting to force his peculiar notions upon the world in his Dictionary, instead of confining them to his Preface," he sacrifices the vitality of speech to the grandeur of his principles. The "besetting sin" of American diction is that it reduces the complexity of pronunciation to a system of pronunciation as it is devised by a language specialist. "The average American tries to pronounce too distinctly," says White in his book *Everyday English* (1880); "he is conscious about his syllables." For White, the effect is, in a word, "unlovely," because to pronounce words according to how they are spelled or even how they should sound is to care more about principles of pronunciation than style, and it is simply less lovely, for example, to care if one makes it through all the syllables of Worcester's name so as to not call him "Wuster," as the English might. American speech is so constrained by rules, it is tone deaf. "Strong, clear, healthy, living speech" is not the gift of people who must "be correct or die," and so if the demands of style suggest that on any given day it sounds better to walk through a "gar'dn," and swallow the ending, we might remember, as Henry Alford puts it in *A Plea for the Queen's English* (1863), that "very often we cannot have exactness and smoothness together."[89]

In *Words and Their Uses* (1870), White suggests that the best language is formed by custom not by rules and that if English has a claim to this distinction it is because, in its strongest, living form, it is a grammarless tongue. Without the cases, genders, and tenses that encumber other languages, English is not one of those languages, says White (citing Sir Phillip Sidney), for which "a man should be put to schoole to learne his mother tongue." Instead, words in English "are formed into sentences by the operation of an invisible power," by which White means that the "right uses" of English are not always determined by "correct uses." Thus, White gives us a series of amateur essays about the "fitness of verbal expression" as it is determined by "intuition" and "taste"; "any excursion into higher walks of philology," he says about his book, "is transient and incidental." Good English is only a good sense of English, and for White no one has a better sense of it than Lowell, whose diction, he says, perpetuated and enriched the language as it used to be (before Americans started trying too hard), and to whom he dedicates his book. The vocal variations of tone and emphasis, the endless powers of adaptation through which the meanings of sounds are made, are not learned here in principle. Instead, "language is generally formed by indirect and unconscious effort," while all the bookism and rules of American speech create "stilted nonsense" and an indelicate dispensation of language that is ultimately rude for being so labored. "Those who speak the best English are those who take no thought as to their speech," but, for Americans, speaking is a self-conscious process, so what is lost is the casualness and naturalness of caring less. When White insists that the "free, unconscious utterance of the broad *ah* sound of *a*" is the sign of social culture, he also suggests that spoken language is the product of social experience and not phonetic arrangement. Is it any surprise that White is accused of Anglophilia? Not only does he believe that "in so far as it deviates from the language of the most cultivated society in England it fails to be English." He believes that what makes English sound English is its indifference to the ways it should technically behave; "usage in the end makes language," as it adjusts and responds "to the law of life" in which it lives.[90]

One cause of poor elocution, writes Edward Channing, "is studying to speak well; for it supposes that natural impulse is insufficient, that the ear is an inadequate judge of sounds."[91] When the Harvard student acquires the Harvard accent, he does more than pronounce his broad alphas. He develops "a studied stammer" (the *Magenta*) and pauses more, like he thinks the English do.[92] To him, the English seem less worried about being lexical:

1ST CANTAB[RIDGIAN]. Aw,—what happened to the First Trinity at the Centennial race?

2ND CANTAB. "Close jacked up," they say.

1ST CANTAB. Aw,—yaas. Fagged out, I suppose, had to shake hands with so many people before the race.

CHORUS. "Aw,—waw.[93]

The Harvard student with the Harvard accent uses contractions and, sometimes (if one can't bother to say the words), shortens them into diminutives. When students refer to the *Harvard Lampoon,* it is fondly called "Lampy." Conjunctions can be lost and so can pronouns, prepositions, auxiliaries, and articles. One does not trouble to specify that the boatsman who lost the race "had to shake hands" when one knows, "aw,—yaas," that it was the boatsman. Could he have won if he did not shake hands? Could have done. The Harvard student also strings words together, since some words are weaker than others and might be swallowed. When a college proctor tells a sophomore in the *Lampoon* not to make a formal call because he smells like tobacco, the student replies, "*Whyhicnotoleboy?*" Don't care about stressing each syllable the same (or arriving with a hint of weed on you), *so why the heck not, old boy?*[94] Then slang, too, "becomes natural to him," says the *Harvard Magazine* in 1858, "and takes place without any effort on his part," though it takes a considerable amount of learning by sophomore year to make his language seem effortless.[95]

"A consciousness of self," says Channing, "forever prevents the full, lively manifestation of self," and so, in speech, "the tones should be spontaneous and sincere." Let them gradually acquire, he continues, "that arresting power which marks the colloquial manner" because the best speaker—the speaker with the most "power," that is—sounds "familiar." To the effect of sounding casual, emphasis is of primary importance, because speech as it naturally is has timing and connectedness, and if all words are pronounced in full and none are weak they will lack what Channing sees as the "natural impulse" behind how we talk and hear. Thus the Harvard student who transcribes the Harvard style as the hallmark "of oral dignity and of English style" is sure to instruct his readers in the rhythms of reading aloud.[96] A "correspondent," writing in to the *Lampoon* about a masquerade, stresses his words eccentrically to play on the critical sense that the Harvard accent is most admirable for its emphasis: "My costume was that of a *patient waiter* of the present century, but I was most decidedly a *loser*, for some man with more taste than scruple preferred *my* fur-lined London checkered Ulster to his own shabby coat. But what *was* the loss of my coat compared with the loss of my *heart?*"[97]

Richard Grant White suggests that only one syllable per word be stressed, lest we commit the Americanism of bleating out every last noise, which is both an act of vulgarity and an act of pomposity for all its enunciative rigidness. White gives the example of a policeman he heard describing "an *institootion*" for girls who have "deviated from the paths of *rectitood*," where the policeman's words were right enough but failed in tone. Henry James would say they failed in "tone-standard," expressing a similar view as Channing and White in his 1905 address, "The Question of Our Speech," delivered to the graduating class of Bryn Mawr College. Rejecting the scientific study of language, James urges his audience to accept the "the question" of how to pronounce English as a question of faith. It is, in other words, only a sort of faith and trust in a sense of sound that protects our pronunciations from "the ugly, the flat, the thin, the mean, the helpless" noises that conspire to make us "as little distinct as possible from the grunting, the squealing, the barking or the roaring of animals." Let the demonstration of how we should speak proceed, he says; "let the demonstration abound, let it be as vociferous as it will, if you will only meanwhile hug the closer the faith I thus commend to you." Americans lack nothing but "tone," but without it their vox Americana is as bad as bad manners and as bad as barking, while the English articulate "the innumerable differentiated, discriminated units of sound and sense that lend themselves to audible production, to enunciation, to intonation."[98] The English accent, as James and Channing see it, is complex, irregular, and inflected; it rises and falls according to the manner in which it is used. The English accent disengages human sounds more casually and flexibly, while the American accent is an "expulsive orotund" that never adapts. It is for reasons along these lines that advocates of a British pronunciation think, like Goold Brown, that Webster was "wrong" when he "resolved to spell all words exactly as they are pronounced" (because each word might be pronounced in so many ways on so many occasions). It is also why James believes that the nature of the inelegance of our language is that, in America, English is "disjoined from all the associations, the other presences, that had attended her," meaning that pronunciations are so formal and rote they have ceased to be developed socially.[99] Insofar as James believes that pronunciations convey meaning through pitch and tone, they have ceased to be social.

It is not enough, writes Ebenezer Porter in his *Rhetorical Reader*, for a student "to speak his words distinctly and fluently, and 'mind the stops.'" If this were the case, then "careful" readers would be "good readers," but it is apparently more the case that students who have learned to read aloud do not know "*how* to read" with inflections, modulations and emphases, though Porter hopes to guide them.[100] For Channing, teaching seniors at Harvard, the point of elocution is to confirm the social nature of speech, in which the "best speakers obey the received varieties of language." The best speakers, that is, understand, as White suggests, that the mastery of English "has come to them from association, from social and intellectual training, and from an acquaintance with the writings of the best authors" and not from linguistic principles and, certainly, not by complying with spellings in dictionaries. Pronunciation of the English language, writes Brown, "is confessedly very difficult to be mastered. Its rules and their exceptions are so numerous, that few become thoroughly acquainted with any general system of them. Nor, among the different systems which have been published, is there any which is worthy in all respects to be accounted a STANDARD." Instead we should "appeal to custom," and, by custom, he suggests only the accumulated experience of how sounds might sound and the sense of them we can gain by listening. For such armchair grammarians, the English accent at least comes closest to acknowledging the contingent, undisciplined, nature of words responding to the diversity of occasions they announce.[101] So we could say that the Englishness of the English accent is not about the distinction of its sound but the indistinction. "On the whole," says Dana of Channing's taste in language, "he was a wide liker. He was not fond of fault-finding. He was no martinet. Wherever he saw sincerity, earnestness, and power, no man made larger allowances for faults," suggesting, too, that wherever language is faultless it is probably less sincere in its inflections. "Courses of doctrine and style" were "most distasteful to him," but otherwise, Channing's taste in elocutionary style is accommodating and includes speech that is mostly wrong. Lowell's taste seems similar when he celebrates Shakespeare's language for the freedom of its missteps: Shakespeare, he says, "found a language already to a certain extent *established,* but not yet fetlocked by dictionary and grammar mongers,—versification harmonized, but which had not yet exhausted all its modulations, nor been set in the stocks by critics who deal judgment on refractory feet that will dance to Orphean measures of which their judges are insensible." Dancing on refractory feet (poetic pun intended), the "living tongue" of Shakespeare is sensible to the extraordinary measures that language takes to give voice to "every subtilest fibre of feeling." The "comparative uniformity" of other dramatists is less refractory but less "true." [102]

"The tones should be spontaneous and sincere": Channing's notion of how words should sound returns us to a model of language that is also English for how it signifies, appealing to context to keep language faithful to the immediacy of common use and direct expression. In contrast to an American style that is neither natural at the level of the phoneme nor genuine at the level of semantics, the best English is distinguished, above all else, by the ease with it acknowledges that there is something contingent in every utterance and that there is little to be gained by striving for a language that is abstracted from the traditions that have formed it. Thus one reason why "Americanisms" are to be loathed is that, by definition, they mark the failure of a shared collective ground on which English is most broadly understood; more troubling still, Americanisms reflect not just deviations from the precedents of English usage but a rhetorical estrangement from reality as well. Our English means much less precisely because it tries to do too much with words.

In *Words and Their Uses,* White calls these Americanisms "affectations" and warns against all the euphemizing and hyperbolizing that abuses sense and is "insufferable to ears." Americans "*extend* an invitation," instead of just inviting someone to dinner or asking someone to dinner, but, in Shakespeare only the "pompous, pragmatical Malvolio" says, "I extend my hand to him." "If you are going to bed," says White, "say so, should there be occasion. Don't talk about retiring": "retiring" is an Americanism. And unless a man is a crown prince "it is well for him to have a house or home, where he lives, not a place of *residence,* where he resides." Everything in America that is satisfactory, says White, is "splendid" or "perfectly splendid"; and Andrew Peabody agrees that Americans commit offenses against taste when they use "*splendid* for *pretty, magnificent* for *handsome, horrid* for *unpleasant, immense* for *large, thousands* or *myriads* for any number greater than *two.*" "Don't," writes Oliver Bunce in his book, *Don't: A Manual of Mistakes and Improprieties,* misuse the word "elegant" "if you wish to avoid Americanisms." "Don't say 'an elegant morning' or an 'elegant piece of beef.'" "Don't say anybody or anything is *genteel.* Don't use the word at all. Say a person is 'well-bred' or a thing is 'tasteful.'" "Don't use terms of endearment when you do not mean them." Consider, says Bunce, "the waste."[103]

It is better not to use "pretentious metaphors," says White, "which have broken out all over the place," insisting that some things are other things and not irreducibly themselves. Saying, for example, that candidates for the presidency run "campaigns" is "indefensible bombast" that sees elections as military victories and violates the tone and sense of public discourse "enough to make one sick and sorry." Not only do Americanisms render everyday experience as figuratively inflated, they treat language itself as a system of arbitrary signs that possess no natural relation to their use. If the best sort of English expresses, with as little strain as possible, the incommensurable reality of a world where things are what they are, then there can be no greater failure of both sense and style than indulging in language that overstates and compares. But this is just how Americans are said to sound, and we might think of Channing's elocutionary preferences or Lowell's literary tastes as responding to the same problem of a nation that has forgotten how to speak because it works too hard at making words sound new. "I feel the rage of simile upon me," says Charlotte in Royall Tyler's *The Contrast,* a play whose very title works to indict her American predilection for making equivalencies between all things, and aggrandizing them in the process.

The American way of speaking becomes a cliché in the antebellum period, and college students take great pleasure in exploiting it. A sketch in an early Harvard paper comparing New York unfavorably with England apologizes for the comparison: "I must needs ask forgiveness for expressing this partiality, since I do it willfully; knowing that comparisons are generally 'odorous,' particularly Yankeeish, and decidedly condemned by [me]." A mock dialogue in a Yale paper about the difference between English and American universities has the Englishman qualify, "We Englishmen don't deal in comparisons; we are generally inclined to take things pretty much as we find them." [104] Which returns us, in its way, to college "indifference," where an "unerring insight into the realities of things" seems at last to justify the English accent, as well as the unwillingness to innovate too much or to say too much or say it hard. Is such Englishness among students, including the casualness involved in sounding English, just a phase as short-lived as college? "A Western enthusiast," says the *Crimson,* "would liken our temporary passivity to the falcon's poise in the air before his unerring swoop." But, it adds, "a Harvard indifferentist rejects—*the simile.*" [105]

Pomp and Circumstance; or, How to Be a Chum

Once more I would like to return to the point that the last student revolt at Harvard was in 1834 and that what followed was "a revolution in higher education" that encouraged student freedom and pleasure. Nothing better marks U.S. college life at the end of the eighteenth century than the vast number of student riots and rebellions against the oppressive measures of the faculty: fires in administration buildings, vandalism, theft, attacks on college chapels, emetics in the drinking water, random pistol fire, and boycotts of classes.[106] And then, with the waning of clerical domination and the relaxing of discipline (giving students more autonomy and leisure, in all the ways we have seen), the rebellions began to end. At least in reality, because, as Steven Novak and others suggest, the rebellions seemed to continue in unreal ways, so that legitimate protest came to motivate emptier rituals of protest. "What happened," says Novak, "is that the student revolt became a tradition," so that well after the most volatile period from 1788 to 1808, riots occurred every four or five years at a fairly regular pace ("a college education," he says, "was incomplete without one").[107] To think about rebellions being something of a campus routine is already to raise questions about the nature of the disruptive energies they unleashed;

like any ritualized assault on order and authority, there is reason to see the violence of such uprisings as a rite of passage within the institutions more than an attack on them. We need not fully subscribe to the skepticism we have learned from Bakhtin, Foucault, and others to be wary of the liberatory impulses behind these later incarnations of the college riot, which are as much inspired by the presumed right to riot as by any actual outrage.

In any case, after 1834, there were no major student disturbances, in part because an increasingly secular and professionalized faculty encouraged student culture and in part because student culture itself changed. The rise of literary societies early in the century and the rise of the fraternities that supplanted them as an organizing principle of student life coincided with the end of the revolts largely because, as critics argue, they inoculated against unruliness by preserving the spirit of unruliness as play. The first fraternity was founded at Union College in 1825, and by the 1840s fraternities had spread to most New England colleges; the initiation rites, the pledges of secrecy and brotherhood, and the rhetoric of high purpose provided students with a compensatory social system of trust and mutuality. They also ritualized a culture of pranks and mischief against the hierarchical structures of the college that became, in effect, a systematic part of how that hierarchy operated. Student misconduct may have evoked the era of rebellion, but the elaborate, empty forms it took as a series of annual rites within a college, tended rather to confirm the student's place within the academic community; such codified acts of misconduct not only asserted the collective identity of the students who performed them but also made participation in these ceremonial dramas central to the college experience itself.[108]

It was not just fraternities that encouraged students to see the college years as motivated by rituals of association. The idea that social bonds define the aim of academic life, apart from any sense of intellectual attainment (as Hawthorne's Fanshawe learns too well), was reinforced across a range of newly vital college practices. Secret societies flourished in the period and represented a particularly ornate version of a widespread will to join; here, the drama of membership took on an arcanum of rites—iron doors and padlocks, meetings in "tombs," passwords and solemn oaths—that encouraged loyalty through private languages and symbolic acts. Other forms of group identity were far easier to come by as students turned out for displays of mischief that

THE BURIAL OF CALCULUS. Page 271.

FIGURE 34. "The Burial of Calculus," from Elijah Kellogg, *The Whispering Pine; or, The Graduates of Radcliffe Hall* (Boston: Lee & Shepard, 1872), 271. Courtesy of American Antiquarian Society.

became ritual holidays of the school year. While some of the events evoked a past history of unrest, their tone was relaxed and juvenile, suggesting how inconceivable any outbreaks of real violence had become. At Princeton, the students barricaded the entrance to North College and called it their "Barring-Out Spree"; they broke into the registrar's room and destroyed last year's grades. They got access to the college bell and rang it. At Yale, sophomores performed the custom of the "Burial of Euclid," in which, after a year of calculus, they assembled ("secretly for fear of the Faculty") and staked a heated poker through a copy of Euclid; then laying the smoking book on a bier and covering it with a pall, the corpse ("i.e. the book") was carried in slow procession, "with the moaning music of the flutes and fifes . . . to the open grave or funeral pyre" (fig. 34). So the author of *Sketches of Yale College* (1843) describes the rite marking the end of the "terror" that is calculus one's sophomore year. The ceremony that let students linger on the eulogium of Euclid usually devolved into great hilarity and, then, onto the next event in the academic calendar that had been passed down, "from time

immemorial," meaning since it had begun a few years earlier. Sometimes the events involved dragging horses into recreation rooms or, at
Harvard, hazing freshmen on "bloody Monday night" or, at Princeton,
"Smoking Freshmen," by filling their rooms with cigar smoke. "Every
college has a language of its own," write James Henry and Christian
Scharff in their 1853 memoir of Princeton, *College as It Is,* suggesting
that colleges seem to operate through the same principles of symbolic
coding and ritual solidarity as the secret societies themselves.[109]

It is during the antebellum years that Americans began to understand, in the words of a Harvard paper, "that college is not college when
shorn of its societies."[110] The idea that "social culture," as the paper
puts it, should be the aim of one's collegiate years is a central legacy of
the period and so, too, the sense that college is defined by the particular character of its social life, apart from its curriculum. These are assumptions that come so naturally to us today that it is only in the face of
serious challenges to them that we are reminded of their contingency;
thus when John Guillory or Bill Readings point out that universities,
in a more efficient future, will be able to do business without worrying
too much about the role of culture, they help to underscore the fact
that universities need not be cultural institutions in the first place.[111]
But this was not the case in the antebellum United States, where the
distinctive culture of the academy was valued for how it taught students
to identify with their institutions as sites of feeling and tradition. As
the experience of college became at once more ritualistic in spirit and
more sentimental in tone, matriculation took on the drama of a virtual
initiation into the rites of being a student. That college symbolism still
functions largely in this way (where every school has its slang, its icons
and personalities, and its hallowed ground for mischief) is testimony to
the lasting power of the academic culture that emerges before the Civil
War. In these years, colleges began to adopt school songs and school
colors and established not only formal athletics (the first Harvard-
Yale crew race was in 1852) but also a whole series of observances that
marked the year with moments to reflect on, and deepen, the emotive
bonds between students and institutions. The more ornate and socially
comprehensive culture that flourished at college had students reveling
in the native practices of their respective schools, all the better to make
sure that future Yalies would remain distinct from future Princeto-
nians. In rendering college life as an expression of what Lévi-Strauss
might term "the science of the concrete," these rituals suggest a style

of acculturation that communicated the meaning of a social system through an immersion in its daily presence; these customs reproduced the general character of the academy as a "metonymical order" or set of specific acts that were transmitted across generations and rehearsed as forms of loyalty to the institution.[112] One could say, then, that the crucial transformation in the social structure of the American college is the growing awareness that the college exists essentially as a social structure. So the elaborate world of ritual allows for students to live out their commitments to their friends, fraternity, class, and institution in terms that also emphasize their reverence for the principle of belonging to an institution. Academic culture inspires devotion to the social life of academic culture and, just as certainly, to the belief that respect for institutions lets students feel more deeply toward the other, fellow students that institutions make.

When antebellum students dedicated themselves to the customs of undergraduate life, and when they chose to identify themselves through the ritual behaviors that being, say, a freshman or an upperclassman entailed, it was in open imitation of the English. The English student worshiped forms and within the social space of the school that may have taught him almost nothing (but "taught it very well") these forms enacted his inclusion in the culture of the institution that had him speaking, dressing, and comporting himself in certain ways. Americans were fascinated: the iconography of the social life of school as it appeared to be in England circulated in correspondence from abroad, in copies of Charles Astor Bristed's *Five Years in an English University* (1852) and, most of all, in the American editions of Thomas Hughes's *Tom Brown's School Days* and its sequel, *Tom Brown at Oxford*. *Tom Brown's School Days*, about public school life at Rugby under Thomas Arnold (father of Matthew Arnold), was especially welcomed by college readers, who followed the adventures of Tom through his sixth-form year, "with a kind of pleasure rarely experienced before in the perusal of a book."[113] Athletic, and not at all serious, Tom arrives at the gates of Rugby to a world of games and sports, of "hot and ruddy students" usually back from boating or from strenuous walks in the foothills. The big boys at Rugby "sit round and drink beer," and all the students tour the quad singing "vociferous songs" about their school and football matches and, sometimes, about the British Empire, like "The Siege of Seringapatum," and so forth. Tom also finds at Rugby a stratified class system in which sixth-form boys preside over time-honored ceremonies of singing, drinking, and hazing and in which he is forced to "fag," or wait on other boys of a higher form or class, until the following years when the lower forms fag for him. In the second half of the novel, the headmaster gives Tom care of a younger student, George Arthur, who is frail, effeminate, and smart and who Tom protects from bullies and teaches to be "a jolly good fellow." Arthur teaches Tom to study and pray, and in time, the "chums," help each other to develop into young gentleman who do their homework and excel on the cricket team, and all by the design of Arnold who had "chummed" them to begin with. "There is not a 'twinge of indigestion,'" writes the Williams College paper, "in any part of the Rugby system: chapel, cricket-plate, schoolroom, four-course race, all bloomed with a healthy and vigorous English boyhood." [114]

Arnold's tenure as headmaster of Rugby, from 1827 to 1842, marks what Ian Baucom calls "an event in the discourse of Englishness," in which Arnold's famous style of educational authority contributes to the shape of England's cultural identity abroad. Arnold made strict adherence to the disciplinary routines of school into the equivalent of submission to a moral code; his systems of "fagging" and "prefecting," in which older students policed younger students as a prerogative of their seniority, allowed boys to internalize and reproduce the headmaster's authority as both a ritual of hazing and a reinscription of his idea of order. As the "national pedagogy" of Victorian England, the image of the student fashioned by Arnold's training—so acclimated to the rules and rituals of society that self-discipline is his second nature—enshrined the virtues of an English education as both the prerequisite for and the product of imperial rule. [115]

But what did Americans learn from Tom Brown? When college newspapers claim, after reading his story, that "the public schools of England are much more akin to the colleges than to the public schools in the U.S.," they suggest that the structure of relations between classes at Rugby is much like the progress from freshman to senior year at Harvard. The extent to which the experience of college is projected onto the social apparatus of the English school speaks to the attraction for American students of Tom Brown's journey from a rustic youth to a figure who dramatically embodies an institutional ideal. Tom Brown's *bildung* evolves within what we might call, again following Lévi-Strauss, the "systems of transformations" that are made possible only by the Englishness of his education: Tom learns reverence toward the institution in which he develops as a social being, and this reverence helps him know, in turn, how bound he is to society and how determined by its particulars. The emphasis is not on the knowledge that is instilled in him but on the anthropology of form and ritual through which he learns to "hero-worship" Arnold and to love Rugby and regret leaving it as he departs for Oxford and presumably, then, his "corner of the British Empire." The students at Rugby understand that getting smarter is not as good as simply getting better by virtue of being fashioned by their school. Rugby creates character, and as the president of Amherst said at midcentury sounding much like Thomas Arnold, "character . . . is of more consequence than intellect." Thus, Americans imagine the appeal of an Arnoldian education in terms similar to those of Lytton Strachey when he claims that from Arnold, "we have come to believe that an English schoolboy who wears the wrong clothes and takes no interest in football is a contradiction in terms."[116]

Thomas Hughes teaches that a student arrives at a better version of his character through socialization into the life of his institution. This is a thoroughly English notion if there ever was one, since, in Emerson's words, the English were thought to be (in the best sense) "the most conditioned men." If their relation to society "is one of obedient service and inner reverence" (Trilling), then to say, as Strachey does, that English schoolboys are what they wear is simply to say that they saw their characters as the fulfillment of such outward forms and not the other way around.[117] Tom does not just leave Rugby, he loves it, and Hughes makes a point of returning him to his school years later to mourn the death of Arnold, who embodied the laws of the institution to which Tom was, and still is, loyal.

At both Rugby and the antebellum college the primary means of socialization was the class system. Just as Ichabod Academicus, who arrives at college a "verdant Freshman," becomes a "blood-hard Soph" and "spooney Junior" (meaning, idle) and blooms at last in "Senior dignity," Rugby students under Arnold's tutelage emerge as "gentlemen," in Strachey's words, who worship "good form." The Rugby model helped articulate how a class system provided for taxonomic difference among student ranks and, just as powerfully, social cohesiveness within the institution. Each class knew its place, along with its manner, walk, posture, and dress, so that the practice at Harvard, for example, of wearing a badge on one's sleeve to denote one's class (called a "crow's foot" for the shape it resembled) became redundant about the time it fell into disuse in 1850. "We presume no one who has ever been 'over the course,'" editorializes a Williams College paper, "has failed to notice certain distinguishing characteristics of the four classes in College." "The *symptoms* are never-failing—indubitable," the paper says about the "manners and physiognomy in indicating a student's position in College": there is the "self-sufficient swagger," and the "sort of dignified, pitying contempt upon his younger and less fortunate companions," which we take to be the stance of the sophomore (but do not really know, since the author just assumes we do). There is the freshman with his short jacket (no tails), who looks downcast and the junior (we assume it's the junior) with a "*negligé* air" who does not feel above his classmates because he has been around too long not to see the folly of caring. The senior is more composed than the junior; he "lounges" rather than revels and, as a "gentleman," speaks with an "air of cordiality" toward underclassmen, who he patronizes and gives unsolicited advice. On the whole, continues the author, in his address, "you are well pleased" with the senior and "look forward with longing, yet almost despairing, gaze for the time" when you can be one too. "Here we are seniors," writes George Henry Tripp in *Student-Life at Harvard*. "The dignity comes in time, and sits easily and gracefully on our shoulders. We are the college." [118]

Like new students at Rugby, freshmen had to be taught the social characters of the school, and it was the role of upperclassmen both to instruct them in a symbology of class and to represent its logic as the very teleology of their four years at college. Indeed, the prerogatives of being upperclassmen depended on their ritualistic interactions with the classes below them and not, simply, because a sort of deconstructive shorthand signified sophomores as "not freshmen" in a system where these distinctions referred to nothing outside their own formalities. Rather, students defined themselves to one another by showing deference: freshmen learned how to respect upperclassmen, both as a rite of passage in their development and as a means of learning what they would need to know as seniors, when it would be their turn to be respected for all the ways they then embodied the "dignity" of the institution. Seniors *were*, after all, the college, to return to Tripp.

The hazing that these rituals involved was carefully distinguished from the "Freshman Servitude" that prevailed in the colleges a century before, in which members of the upper classes treated freshmen as inferiors and generally abused them. (President Quincy's *History of Harvard* describes how the government of the college codified "freshman servitude" as a set of rules—"no Freshman shall speak to a Senior with his hat on," "all freshmen . . . shall be obliged to go on any errand . . . for any of his Seniors," and so on.) These customs, writes Benjamin Homer Hall in the 1850s, appear "at the present day strange and almost unaccountable," as do other "outward tokens of respect" formerly required of the students by the college officers, including "making obeisance" to one's seniors by standing up in their presence and keeping quiet until spoken to. But while "Freshman Servitude" was abolished, its "ancient customs of subordination among the classes" still maintained "a part of their power over the students," which meant there was no end to the means used by sophomores, especially, to torment the freshmen. To them was allotted, writes Hall, the duty of preparing each freshman, "by a due induction into the mysteries" of the college "for the duties of his new situation," which most often comprised "fagging" for upperclassmen. At Yale, they called the practice "Tutoring Freshmen," so where "Freshman Servitude" disappeared as a law, its archaic forms were retained as rituals that served pedagogically, insofar as they "tutored" freshmen in the traditions of the class system around which the college's social life was built. As no more nor less than a ritual, the hazing was not actually about what freshmen would do—getting out of bed at midnight to find alcohol for sophomores, and so on—but about the expressive act of hazing as a symbolic initiation into the college at the moment when freshmen were no longer servants in any real sense. Tutoring freshmen, in other words, revived freshman servitude as a symbolic practice to teach that participation in the rituals of the institution affirms and renews one's place within it. Thus "tutoring" depended on the power of the ceremonial acts of tutoring: a sophomore at Yale is described as "seated solemnly in his chair of state, arrayed in a pompous gown, with specs and powdered hair," awaiting the approach "of the awe-struck subject." Everything that can increase "his sufficiently reverent emotions, or produce a readier or more humble obedience, is carefully set forth" until the freshman approaches the sophomore (usually waiting in the shadows of the room) "with no little degree of that terror with which the superstitious inquirer enters the mystic circle of the magician." [119] Of course, none of this is at all serious, and the freshman, who is not actually in "servitude," knows it. Still, the practice preserves a relation to the serious, in Durkheim's sense, so that playing at these symbolic forms of behavior by sophomores and freshmen consecrates the experience of being in college with the high ritual of that experience; it dramatizes college as a traditionary institution that survives, at least in part, through its theatrical games. Freshmen learn to recognize the figure that is cut by the dignity of the sophomore, and their deference is instructive for the figure they hope to cut a year later.

Why should colleges have traditions? The shared rituals of student life—from campus lingo and styles of dress to official convocations and commencements—transmit the culture of the college to successive classes and encourage loyalty to, and spirit for, one's school. But why have school spirit anyway? In the antebellum years, colleges began to adopt school colors (and the organized sports in which colors were worn). After 1836, students at Harvard had a school song, "Fair Harvard," and each graduating class also wrote a class song to its tune. Harvard instituted yearbooks ("class books") in the 1820s, along with annual reunions and other practices that encouraged former students to memorialize their attachments to each other and, more important, to the college itself. "Class Day," marking the formal end of the year, became an important festival for both current and former students, with processions and parades in honor of the college, led by the class marshall, and the communal singing of the class ode. In 1828, Harvard erected a monument to its namesake, John Harvard, in tribute to a school, "safe, from the vicissitudes to which all else is subject," and so the founding father was adored along with the alma mater he established. On the one hand, cultivating bonds of feeling that lasted beyond graduation codified a sense of identity among alumni, who were then encouraged to patronize their institutions. Such school loyalty could be financially beneficial and was part of a larger campaign for elite involvement at a time when the elite were increasingly in control of eastern universities. That said, the fact that alumni became more important to colleges (attending Class Day "with throbbing hearts and glowing lips" and then giving money) only partially explains the rites of institutional emotion and allegiance around the image of alma mater. The alumni associations, forming in the three decades after 1820 "to advance the reputation and interests of our Alma Mater," were also the legacy of a new emphasis on institutional loyalty and devotion as signature affects of undergraduate identity. Thus, as Grace Greenwood watched the Harvard graduating class of 1848 sing "Fair Harvard," forming a circle of garlands around an old elm, then singing "Auld Lang Syne" (and crying out together, "Harvard!"), she is so overcome with their feelings for their college that, she says, "an involuntary prayer sprang to my lips, that they might prove true to *Alma Mater*, to one another, to their country, and to Heaven."[120]

At a moment of increasing secularization at colleges in America, with Harvard in particular, as one student paper writes, "[leaning] towards infidelity," the dedication to college rituals at their most ornate and ornamental allows for the experience of enchantment, not just within, but *by* the social logic of the institution.[121] The practices that enshrine loyalty and school spirit as central to the developmental function of college are those that borrow most liberally from the symbology and conceptual power of high ceremony, which makes the socializing process of the institution into an object of intense belief and, even, awe. It is not just that one remembers one's institution with reverence, but that a love for alma mater translates an affectionate regard for one's years at college into an aesthetic response toward the institution as such. The object of the reverence thus solicited and performed remained expressly secular and social, which also finally distinguished it from Thomas Arnold's educational approach, which enshrined Christian principles as its first priority. Indeed we could say that the social life of college in America began in earnest where the centuries of religion left off, so when Santayana says he believes "compulsorily and satirically in the existence of this absurd world," he means also that his lack of faith inspired a devotion to his place within it. In any case, college was simply not college without the high formalism of its ritual observances, processions, music, caps, and gowns and the increasingly lavish ceremonies that consecrated its end.

It should come as no surprise that such symbolic practices evoked the iconography of Oxford and Cambridge and were described in great detail by Bristed, Hall, and others: "At the English universities," writes Hall, "there are few objects that attract the attention of the stranger more than the various academical dresses worn by members of those institutions." The rituals and regalia at once distinguished an English educational tradition and an English social practice—both of which Americans found attractive for their shared commitment to the aesthetic possibilities of institutional belonging. In the complex formality of English colleges, Americans saw the expression of a specifically English structure of feeling much like what Perry Anderson calls the "mystagogy towards institutions, for which England has won an international reputation."[122] Colleges, according to the English model that Americans had observed, relied on ritual to cultivate a style of loyalty that was less the product of an abstract allegiance to an institutional ideal than a response to the mystique of institutional authority and to the emotional rewards of seeing it performed. When Edward Everett, as president of Harvard, lead the Class Day processional of students "in his Oxford hat and gown," at least one observer noted that he was "a man of most imperial presence . . . grand in form," which is to suggest that the collective making of a student body depends in part on the artistry with which the college ennobled its appearance.[123] School spirit finally asked students to revere all the local acts and material forms that embodied—indeed, which quite strictly speaking, fetishized—the traditions that distinguished the character of the institution as a social system. Loving college as a site of ritual and ceremony becomes a way of paying tribute to the socializing power of tradition, which in turn represents the socializing routines of college life (the affiliation into classes, fraternities, and groups of friends) as the most consecrated ground within the culture of higher education. More important, the rituals that signified school loyalty (being "true" to alma mater)—because they testified to the countless ways that institutions could condition and solidify the personal bonds of individuals belonging to them—comprised a lesson in how the Englishness of college allowed students in America to feel closer to one another.

The process of formation through social influence by which students like Tom Brown and Arthur realize themselves in the company of fellows is reproduced in the culture of the antebellum college, and indeed there was nothing more English than the affect of relations known as "chumship." Taken from the English word for roommates, "chums" were no more or less than that, but the idea that each student's character is bound to another student's character (who also may happen to share his bed, meals, and pipes) meant that the "habit of looking at life as a social relation" that college cultivated (for Henry Adams to "no good" end) was cultivated through the bonds of chums. "My Chum," writes a student at Virginia in 1859: "I have been united with another who stood to me in that mysterious relationship, for better, for worse, as it has been called, 'college wife.'" When Adams says of the social life of college that it "cultivated a weakness which needed no cultivation," and means by this that it did not help "to make men of the world," he also means in part—or lets us infer in part—that such a socializing, domesticating culture made so many "wives" of men. "Chums rub against each other," continues the student, "and being that general polishing process which we undergo in leaving home and entering the world . . . [my chum] had a great influence on my character." So chums rubbing against each other (to polish their characters, as it were) made for enough of a community of men, with "a sort of effeminate dependence upon one another," that such a "glowing feeling of common brotherhood shut out from the world" would shut it out quite happily. The "young fresh students" with "warm beating hearts, in bosoms bounding with affectionate impulses" were in no rush, writes one paper, toward any prospects after college and especially those that were "peculiarly obnoxious" respecting "*matrimonial affairs*" so long as they remained associated with their chums, smoking, talking, and lazing around. Indeed, says the *Harvard Magazine,* "were it possible for us, when we become bachelors (laureate) to enjoy all the comforts of a Holworthy room, chum included, I doubt whether many of us would ever be induced to change this certain happiness of single blessedness." Oh to be bachelors laureate and bachelors at the same time, keeping "green and fruitful such a love for our College friends as inspired the *Lycidas* of Milton and the *In Memoriam* of Tennyson." No wonder William Dean Howells wrote of Lowell that "of women he had an amusing diffidence . . . he would rather not have had them about." [124]

Neither would the young Amory Blaine in F. Scott Fitzgerald's *This Side of Paradise,* who is defined early on by his aversion to girls and whose story is the legacy of nineteenth-century stories about the exhilarations of chumship ("She slipped her hand into his, her head drooped against his shoulder. Sudden revulsion seized Amory"). The fact that the presence of chums is conditioned on the absence of women is at once suggestive and misleading. Certainly it is worth noting that the same decades that witness these outpourings of male friendship and attachment at college witness, too, the first calls for coeducation (and protests against it); that the bonds between chums are deeply, energetically homosocial thus makes perfect sense insofar as they depend on college remaining a "paradise of bachelors," as Melville might say, where women are not just irrelevant but antithetical to this dream of fraternal comforts and pleasures. But if women are technically absent, it is also the case that all the chums make for a pointedly effeminized culture of men. Like Melville's "bachelors," the fact that "household comfort was the grand trait of the affair" suggests that this is a model of homosocial community that wants to reproduce at least some of the values associated with the sex it excludes. The more sentimental and plaintive expressions of students' desire for their chums court a language of romantic deference to masculine vigor and charm: "Chum is six-two. I am five-two; Chum is handsome, Chum is a master of dancing." One gets the decided impression that this diminutive admirer is ready to take the floor with his "chum," and there is no mystery just who will lead; then again, since this comes from a piece entitled "In Bed," one gets more than just dancing.[125] At such overripe moments of sexualized sentiment, the practice of being a chum seems an episode within a history of homoerotics on campus, with the example of Walter Pater and his circle at Oxford looming especially large.

"Lovely spring morning, windows open, birds singing. Dog '77 and chum enjoying life": so the *Lampoon* sets a scene of two chums, reclining together, exhaling, smoking, cutting—but as they say, this is life and they are enjoying it nicely (fig. 35). "What we call friendship," writes the *Harvard Magazine,* "is nearer love," and while we cannot say for sure if this is a scene of love, tired as chums seem—one leg up and

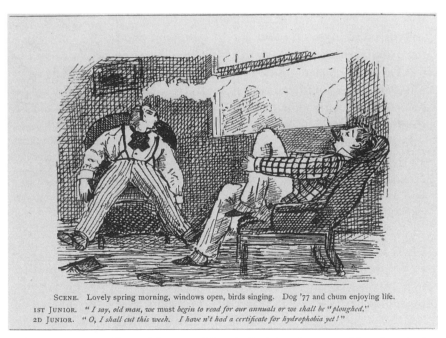

SCENE. Lovely spring morning, windows open, birds singing. Dog '77 and chum enjoying life.
1ST JUNIOR. " *I say, old man, we must begin to read for our annuals or we shall be "ploughed."*
2D JUNIOR. " *O, I shall cut this week. I have n't had a certificate for hydrophobia yet!* "

FIGURE 35. Cartoon, *Harvard Lampoon* (May 18, 1876), 92. Courtesy of American Antiquarian Society.

the others spread eagle—it at least evokes the sentiment for which another paper cries out, "Student-sympathy! Oh! It is a glorious thing." College is not about studying but about learning to do it or not with chums, which is why the same paper says that "together with the first offerings on the altar of learning are poured the glowing libations on the shrines of student-sympathy."[126] Chums share a special bond to each other that lends feeling and force to their ties to the school that brought them together; though devoted to all the aspects of college that would appear most removed from the process of education itself, their relationship is nonetheless powerfully academic. Whatever we call the emotion that students affect when they become chums, there is no mistaking that it is a form of "triangular desire," in René Girard's classic sense, that depends on an "impulse toward the object that is ultimately an impulse toward the mediator." Simply put, students show their feelings for college by showing their feelings for each other. The figure of the chum—as idealized friend, faithful companion, and substitute mate—exemplifies the very social logic of the institution not by making young men want to study but my making them want to belong. "Students move and act in bodies—by impulse," writes the Union College paper. "There is a reckless abandon."[127]

When Trilling writes that "the person who accepts his class situation, whatever it may be, as a given and necessary condition of his life will be sincere beyond question," he does not have college students in mind and does not intend class to mean freshmen as opposed to sophomores.[128] But in making this claim on behalf of the English—whose institutional aesthetic informs the world of American college just as surely at the level of affect and play as it does at the level of high ritual and ceremony—his argument applies much the same. What Americans do not learn until college is what Trilling says the English know as second nature: that we finally feel at home only in the society we teach ourselves to love.

Coda: Education and Nostalgia

In 1805, five years after his graduation from Harvard, while studying in Rome, Washington Allston painted his self-portrait (fig. 36). Against the moldering wall of a Roman ruin, the artist looks at the viewer with the half-smile of the Mona Lisa, his face softened by the incandescent light (from the moon, maybe) and by the golden bow he wears, and the downy curls that frame his eyes. It is all very androgynous, as

FIGURE 36. Washington Allston, *Self Portrait*, 1805. Photograph © 2008 Museum of Fine Arts, Boston.

David Bjelajac points out, in the nod to Leonardo and in the gentleness that etherializes the figure of the artist and makes him beautiful. Allston poses in a melancholy way, suggestive of dignity, and one can only guess how much he is insisting he has grown on the Italian tour five years past his "senior dignity" at Harvard. We think of Harvard because, against the flat black velvet of his coat, beneath another bow, Allston has pinned his Phi Beta Kappa key, and it shines much more than the little jewel at his chest and more than the golden bow beneath his face.

Bjelajac describes the golden key as a kind of "solarized seed that generates the painting's angelic ascent," by which he means that the emblem of Allston's Harvard education suggests the source of the repose and contemplation we find in the artist in the painting. Hanging by the navel, the little golden "seed," is certainly generative of something, and Bjelajac sees it as representing the "alchemical process of self-cultivation" (or *bildung*) from a student into a gentleman.[129] If there is a language of magic in the portrait it takes its cues from the secret society that contrived the key and that linked an appreciation for philosophy and the arts to the arcane rituals and symbols that it derived from Masonry. Phi Beta Kappa's elite membership of students was brought toward illumination and knowledge by way of blindfolded initiation ceremonies and occult practices. Thus, for Bjelajac, the solemn intelligence of Allston's portrait is revealed through the unspoken mysteries of his art.

It is fascinating how Allston carries the little key with him when he was already making a name for himself in London, where he studied with Joshua Reynolds, and in Rome, where he befriended Coleridge most famously. The little symbol of his education tied to a bow is the sensible sign of his pedigree but also of the bonds of fraternity and affiliation he carries with him even into the solitary scene of the artist among the ruins. In portraits, we can use these emblems, and if Allston really felt the need for us to know he went to Harvard, then he has included a little sign of it. But here, I would agree with Bjelajac that the key in the picture gives us more than knowledge of Allston; it gives us a mystification of his knowledge and its work in the painting. The key is the key to the picture, which puts the young artist at the start of his career in a kind of secret temple, with the sense of mystery that would attend it in the moonlight and with the secret society's key suggesting that the painting itself might be a sort of initiation rite into the world of artists and men. A German critic reported, after all, that almost everyone who saw the painting in Allston's studio in Rome found it striking—it was his first notable piece. So we are learning about a new artist on the scene, and, in consideration of this, the artist has preserved for us the link between learning and mystery that he would have experienced as a member of Phi Beta Kappa at Harvard, dedicated to "Friendship, Morality and Literature," but not without a considerable amount of arcana and awe.

Freemasonry, on which Phi Beta Kappa modeled itself, believed in the connection between epistemology and ritual. If the object of Masonry was to "make better and happier the human race" through a moral education, it tried first to impress the minds of its members with the power of ritual acts. "We are creatures of sense rather than intellection," writes a Mason in 1827, with the idea that such an emblematic education as the fraternity offered could appeal to the intellect by appealing to the imagination. So the wonder, magic, solemnity, and fear that marked a member's initiation, for example, could be seen as a Lockean exercise in learning the values of Masonry through a powerful experience of it. If the fraternity, in other words, was to be "the great instrument of civilization," as it hoped, then an empirical feeling for its greatness would be the first step toward creating the devotions of brotherhood. Moral pedagogy followed institutional awe, and so the symbols, ceremonies, rituals, and languages that best engaged the attention of the members could also best cultivate the virtues of their character. But only if their minds were "properly imprest with the importance of the institution," as one member put it.[130]

In Allston's painting, the Phi Beta Kappa key stands as a symbol for his Harvard education but also for his belief in symbols as such. Five years past college, he wears his loyalty to it, and to his society within it, as a symbol on his navel and the portrait of the man, alone with his shadow in an evacuated space is incomplete without it. Allston's self-portrait is a romantic image of the artist against the dreamscape of a ruin, but he has preserved this *punctum* detail of the key; and it is the single, identifying token within an idealizing picture that puts the artist either somewhere important within the place of history or else somewhere outside it. If Romanticism embraces particularism, as Naomi Schor suggests, it does so finally to transcend it by flattering the details as an essential part of the whole.[131] So the key in the painting is not an ornament *on* the portrait of the artist (or a status symbol alone) but a synecdoche for the portrait. What Allston recalls from the void is a conception of the artist as closely tied to the institution that has made him and the small umbilical-like matter at the navel seems to suggest that the portrait owes its conception to the force of the experience that the symbol represents. Allston is reproducing the symbol of his education in the symbolic realm of his art and, then, suggesting that the power of that institution for him is also the power of the aesthetics we feel as we look at his portrait.

But as a memento of his college years, the key that hangs from Allston's coat is also nostalgic—an intimate souvenir of the social life of Harvard. College is over, but the key brings it back as a fetish, and the melancholy of the portrait in the moonlight suggests a private moment of contemplation that is redolent of nostalgia, too. Like the class books that alumni put on their shelves and the songs they sang on Class Day—

"Fair Harvard! thy sons to thy Jubilee throng"—the key recalls college as a lost place of belonging from which the "sons" of alma mater set out, as individuals and artists, with tokens of their experience tied up in bows and with the sentimental promise of reunions (which, incidentally, began to happen each year anyway). College nostalgia was invented in the first decades of the nineteenth century, and if Allston, says one classmate, "paid no more attention to our college studies than was necessary," he is nonetheless, in this romance of the artist alone in his temple, preserving a material piece of college as a lost society and as a cult of memory whose central rite was the forgetting of individual distinction and the commitment to being a "high fellow" (as Allston's classmate tells us he was). This is the charm of college (the little charm) that Allston carries with him.

"I have not much cause, I sometimes think, to wish my Alma Mater well, personally," writes Emerson years after graduating Harvard. "I was not often flattered by success, and was every day mortified by my own ill fate or ill conduct. Still, when I went today to the ground where I had had the brightest thoughts of my little life and filled up the little measure of my knowledge, and had felt sentimental for a time, and poetical for a time, and had seen many fine faces, and traversed many fine walks, and enjoyed much pleasant, learned, or friendly society,—I felt a crowd of pleasant thoughts, as I went posting about from place to place, and room to chapel." [132] The familiar iconography of the college catalog, with students under trees with volumes of poetry testifies "to a sentimentalized idea of teaching as pastoral romance"; thus Gerald Graff and Michael Warner describe the nostalgic turn to the "preprofessional" faith in college as an idyllic community. They warn against forgetting that such idylls compensate for the antivalues of capitalistic production and utility; humanistic study, after all, was never immune to their incursions, if only in the way it at times suggested the prerogatives of a leisured class.[133] But Emerson, in returning to college to feel "sentimental for a time and poetical for a time" is also celebrating his education as nostalgia for the little he knew and for the diminished moments of walking, socializing, and being poetical in just the way his "little life" let him in the specific locale of Harvard (though, personally, how glad he is the mortifying years are over, so he can). The idealizing gesture is not what remembering college is about any more than what being at college was about; so Emerson feels sentimental about returning to the place where he had once "felt sentimental."

College produced nostalgia for college: Emerson, "posting about from place to place," in and across the yard, feels perhaps, as one Class Day poet writes, "emotions for Alma Mater too deep for the tongue" or, at least, pleasant enough and not worth articulating, since college was a waste when he really thinks about it.[134]

By 1840, the Harvard "yard" was demarcated by a quadrangle of trees and fences, a process of enclosure that President Kirkland completed for good after 1870 with iron gates and brick walls. College would be picturesque, a pastoral yard framed by trees at some remove from Cambridge Common, and students would be attached to their sense of place.[135] They declared themselves the "adopted sons" of alma mater (like English students did) and spoke of their institutions by poetical appellations, like the "classical shades," and so forth, of Harvard. They thought that being on campus in autumn sounded like this: "How often have we at such times carried along with us our little, well-worn pocket edition of Coleridge's poems and read aloud till we fancied the tree and stones listened, and the brook ceased its music to hear the sweeter melody of verse." College is "a fairy-like place," says one author for the *Harvard Magazine:* recollecting stories of Joseph Addison's famous "walks" through Oxford as a student, he describes the "romantic air" of the "peculiar locality" of college, good for walking, conversing, and feeling strongly for college. Thus the pictures of Harvard in this period reproduce the romantic localism of pastoral conventions—the college as a retreat from the town, framed by trees and an immediate landscape and then, at a safe middle-distance, small clusters of students talking or reading, or else students pictured alone with canes, strolling and taking in views (fig. 37). The undergraduate, says one paper, ought to "invest with interest, every permanent object about the building and grounds, however unlikely, however minute, and make them all the subject of Poetry, of *Song.*"[136]

The new buildings on campus around this time were modeled on English institutions, but it was the structure of feeling toward these buildings and the yard that seemed especially English. Venerating the campus recalled an English style of sentiment toward social space not just in the elaborate devotion to particular sites of belonging but in the way this devotion suggested that it was the experience of place that most dramatically enacted a proper respect for tradition. The "old world relics" among which the "modern Englishman lives," suggests the *Harvard Magazine* in 1858, attach him "to the institutions of his fathers"

FIGURE 37. "Quincy View of Gore Hall," 1840, Hamilton Vaughan Bail, *Views of Harvard: A Pictorial Record to 1860* (Cambridge, MA: Harvard University Press, 1949), plate 55. Courtesy of American Antiquarian Society.

and "so with a hundred customs here—they own their power not to themselves but to their associations" with "some tree or room or building." If Harvard and Yale represent, according to the *Magazine*, "the two strong-holds of conservatism in this country," it is in part because they are quite literally constructed to be spaces that charm with the "power which old places and things possess" and with an image of practices that belong to another time but are preserved on the grounds of the college precisely because they give meaning to the present. The language of English pastoralism is so readily transposed onto the language of college nostalgia because both of these traditions exist, as Raymond Williams would say, to imprint "lost relations and lost certainties" on a particular landscape. Such languages finally owe their force to the urgency with which their retrospective claims can speak to the aspects of a changing world that is "at once dissolved and recreated in images which carry the meanings and yet compose a way of seeing that suppresses them."[137] This is why the rather obvious fact that the Harvard Yard is not the English countryside presents little problem for those most committed to misremembering their years at college as worth loving for their Englishness. What makes for the affecting "conservatism" of college is that it derives entirely from a fiction of the institution that does not need to be believed in order to be adored.

For Henry James, returning to Harvard in flight from the modernity and diversity of New York, the palpable feeling in the yard "was the instinct not to press, not to push on, till forced, through any half-open door of the real." In the yard, one could "cultivate the idyllic, for the social, for the pictorial illusion, by every invoking and caressing art" because the space of college makes both possible and metaphoric— possible because metaphoric—an aesthetic distance from society that is also an experience of learning to belong to society by way of the "illusion" that gives it shape and meaning. In "the land of the 'open door,'" as James describes the nation of immigrants where he, too, has just arrived after decades in England, the college yard stands apart as "an admirably interesting example of the way in which the formal enclosure of objects at all interesting . . . immediately establishes value." "The enclosure," he continues, "may be impressive from without, but from within it is sovereign; nothing is more curious than to trace in the aspects so controlled the effect of their established relation to it. This resembles, in the human or social order, the improved situation of the foundling who has discovered his family or of the actor who has mastered his part." There is no way to assess the value of the "enclosure" without recognizing that this pastoral fantasy is loved to a significant degree for all that it keeps out: Harvard is "the place inaccessible . . . to the shout of the newspaper, the place to perambulate, the place to think, apart from the crowd." But it is not simply the case that James finds comfort in a logic of reaction and retreat; if his nostalgia evokes an anxiety about an America that no longer feels like home, it also evokes a sense that, for this famously "restless analyst" at least, "there was scarce an impression of local life at large" that did not somehow "play into" his reflections from within the confines of the college yard. No sooner is James safely inside the consecrated space of Harvard than he is mentally venturing out, "to Ellis Island" and "the ceaseless process of the recruiting of our race, of the plenishing of . . . foreign matter into our heterogeneous system." James, of course, is of two minds about the "ubiquity" of immigrants, and for every moment when he seems to castigate the effects of their "infusion," there is another when he celebrates their "heritage" as it resists the pale contrivances of culture in America. His response to Harvard Yard anticipates this ambivalence. The power of the yard compels attachment and acculturation; it provides a model for "social order" that feels as natural and familial as an "established relation" but is formalized and rehearsed as a part. The pastoral space of college may even be capable of teaching strangers how to act and get along (or so the drift of associations to Ellis Island suggests). The yard reveals the "genius loci" of college, inviting us to revisit the time and place of our own social becoming "against the picture of proportions and relations overwhelmingly adjusted," wherein the sense of becoming is already felt to be an aspect of the traditionary "order" of things.[138]

The "sovereign" aesthetic of education, which dialectically embraces retrospection and futurity, shapes a moment of pastoral reverie in James that draws on an Anglophilic iconography of both college and the social order that college reproduces. A variation on this aesthetic patterns Samuel Morse's *Allegorical Landscape of New York University* (1835–36), a similarly intense and motivated fantasy of college life that looks to academic culture as a homogenizing counterbalance to the "heterogeneous system" of American democracy—and here, James's exquisite ambiguity gives way to a more pronounced conservatism (fig. 38). While running for mayor of New York on the Native American ticket, having just published *Imminent Dangers to the Free Institutions of the U.S.* against Catholics and immigrants, Morse imagined New York University (NYU) as a luminous fantasy at sunrise, where Washington Square

FIGURE 38. Samuel F. B. Morse, *Landscape Composition: Helicon and Aganippe (Allegorical Landscape of New York University)*, 1836, accession no. 1917.3. Collection of The New-York Historical Society.

is a landscape of lavender and yellow and where all the elements of the picturesque (the framing tree, Gothic buildings in the middle ground, figures in togas) are in harmony with the dissolving illusionism of the scene. Painted at the time of the opening of the new University Building, designed by Alexander Jackson Davis in the English Collegiate style and pictured at the left, *Allegorical Landscape* suggests that the new city college (founded in 1831) can be understood in archaic terms: Athena stands on the near side of the lagoon and heralds the dawn of the institution as a recovery and translation of traditionary forms. It is a scene of illumination that works visually and ideologically from the perspective of a "west" defined through the inheritance that it accepts by looking east (to the sunrise, that is). New York University was a good subject for a picture of the future, with its progressive attitude toward science, engineering, and practical arts and its commitment to educating an ecumenical student body from the urban middle class.[139] But that class is not pictured here: Morse's painting finds the promise of the college not in the vitality of its students and faculty (which he joined) but in the symbolic grandeur of the institution and in an organic vision that admits no sign of change but a formulaic dawn. Given Morse's reactionary politics, the dramaturgy of acculturation that James powerfully locates within the yard is more troubling here because it makes thinkable the effect of assimilation. There is obviously a lot that Morse represses to pattern education on nostalgia, and it is possible to see in his denials something of the politics that, later in the nineteenth century, informs efforts to deny college admission to immigrants, minorities, and Jews. The Anglophilia that Jerome Karabel finds as a shaping influence at Harvard and elsewhere lies behind exclusionary practices by suggesting that college is not about its intellectualism but about the perpetuation of a culture and a "character." Reverence for the life of the institution is a form of Anglophilia that only the imperialism of Anglo-Saxonism could insure.[140]

But the beauty of college in Morse also returns us to the symbolic expressions that students were taught to love as an effect of their acculturation into college, and thus I end this book somewhere near where I began: with a scene that reflects a radical investment in how institutions look when they are enchanted by and imagined within an aesthetics of nostalgia and loss. Morse's landscape of NYU is, after all, nothing less than Morse's *House of Representatives* (fig. 1, p. xvi) "transplanted outside," as Paul Staiti points out and as it becomes irresistible to see in the emptiness at the center of the painting marked by the well of the lagoon and by the structures of the buildings that frame it. The lagoon imitates the circular composition of the seats in the *House*. The escarpment at the right is a viewer's gallery for figures in the back. The University Building is where the Speaker's chair is, flanked by a pedestal that preserves the function of the column in the *House*. The figure of Athena is silhouetted, with her back to us; like the doorkeeper, she raises an arm to the brilliant light at the center of the scene made "incandescent" by it. Thus Morse's picture of NYU is "allegorical" for a model of the state that, in turn, appears to retain the shape and the atmosphere of college. At the same time, Morse would no doubt want us to see how his picture of the *House* was informed from the start by a longing for objects of reverence that college teaches us to admire. The moment of civic becoming remembers its past with a transitive fondness for the places that lay claim to its legacy.

"I speak of Old Cambridge," writes James Russell Lowell in 1854 of his undergraduate days and beyond, "and it was essentially an English village, quiet, unspeculative, without enterprise, sufficing to itself." Naming his estate Bromley Vale, after an English country seat, Lowell tried to preserve his vision of life at Harvard as it was, "so genial, so courtly." It felt "charmingly rural," he says. "Commencement preserved all the features of an English fair" and the president of the college wore a square cap that "recalled Oxford and Cambridge." A country village needs a country churchyard, and so Lowell is sure to include college memories of wandering among the graves in Mount Auburn Cemetery, founded in 1831 as "America's first garden cemetery," and also credited as its first public park. Like Capability Brown's English landscape gardens, Mount Auburn placed classical monuments in a rugged "picturesque" terrain with ponds, groves, and hills; it was a place, writes Joseph Story at its dedication, where one could find solace in "melancholy meditations."[141]

The refuge of the dead also happened to be the resort of choice for Harvard students who nicknamed it "Sweet Auburn," after Goldsmith's "Deserted Village," and thus inspired its name. "Show me a place," says Lowell as a student in 1837, "so sweet as that most delightful of spots, 'sweet Auburn.'"[142] Dispensing with the more formal geometries of French landscape design in particular, Mount Auburn invited its visitors to linger for moments of reflection and reverie and to experience, in short, all the sense of a place that offered the aesthetic pleasures of nature on the consecrated grounds of the dead. Harvard students left their studying to roam among the relics, but their retreat, like Allston's artist in the ruined temple, was not so much a departure from their life at college as its apotheosis. College was where Americans could learn that the memories they enshrined in symbolic form were the substance of who they were. The nostalgia that students like Lowell indulged at Mount Auburn was not, despite the markers of English style and tradition, about some return to a mythic past that Americans had long since abandoned. What made Mount Auburn "sweet" was that it provided a place for students to imagine their commitment to college as hallowed and sacred, especially when they happened to be stealing away from it. Mount Auburn both extended and naturalized the place of piety: amid a landscape mingling emblems of reverence with picturesque scenes, students learned that they already inhabited a world of tradition and that its character was felt as an emotional response to the sites that they had shared. "I lead a somewhat studious life," Longfellow writes in 1837, "and take long solitary walks through the green fields and woodlands of this fair neighborhood. Yesterday I was at Mount Auburn, and saw my own grave dug; that is, my own tomb. I assure you, I looked quietly down into it, without one feeling of dread. It is a beautiful spot."

This may be untimely morbidity for a rising star in the academy who was just thirty, a professor at Harvard, and some forty-five years from the grave. Still, Longfellow's melancholy is perfectly in keeping with the academic style this chapter has sought to explore; one says such things to help feel what it means to be part of an institutional culture that is designed to outlive one's self, no matter how prominent (or well published). The social life of college transforms these isolated moments of melancholy and introspection into the collective expressions of academic culture. The "beauty" of Longfellow's letter, then, is not that he is so sanguine about the prospect of death but that he appears already to know that it is the fate of any professor to survive only insofar as his presence continues to haunt the college grounds. Thus I find it apt that Longfellow signs off by inquiring after his predecessor as chair of belles lettres and promising that his strolls through the cemetery are not taking too much time from his work in the classroom: "Where is Mr. Ticknor now? When next you meet, salute him from me. Tell him that the lectures of his successor commence in two days from this date." [143] It is the nature of things for professors to come and go; college allows for this plain fact of history to appear as a noble procession of scholars bound to each other by the strength of their mutual devotions.

This may well be a fantasy that our own institutional present renders even more of an anachronism than it already was for Longfellow and Lowell, Emerson and Hawthorne, Channing, Ticknor, Everett, and all the anonymous students for whom the experience of college depended on a version of the traditionary culture that has been this chapter's concern. That said, it is harder than we might think to escape the memorializing aesthetic of college that remains a primary legacy of the nineteenth century; to imagine, after all, that the university is somehow "in ruins" is to give every campus its own claim to Sweet Auburn's appeal, its own aura of half-forgotten icons succumbing to time, its own sadness and quietude about the lost relations and certainties that are finally the point of college nostalgia. If American Anglophilia in part explains the shape this nostalgia most often takes, it can also help us acknowledge its power and continuing hold. To admit that this dream life of college refers to an image of academic tradition that was never quite ours to begin with is to begin to suggest why it matters: the historicized character of college gives students and faculty a way to pay their respects to all the feelings that draw them to knowledge, which quite often is best treasured in forms that do not necessarily translate to the world that awaits them once campus is left behind. "The past is dead, is death itself," Trilling writes, "but for that very reason it is the course of order, value, piety, and even love. If we think about education we wonder if perhaps there is not to be found in the past that quiet place at which a young man might stand for a few years, at least a little beyond the contemporary problem that he is told he can master only by means of attitudes and generalizations, that quiet place in which he can be silent, in which he can *know* something."[144] It is not just that Trilling associates the deliberate anachronism of college with the essence of its intellectual appeal; he associates college itself with a set of emotions and epistemological claims that should strike us by now as transcendently English in ways that perhaps only Americans could find so affecting. We learn what we want from the experience of such imaginary places without ever believing they are real.

Notes

Preface

1. Hannah Arendt, *On Revolution* (New York: Penguin Books, 1963), 130.

2. Slavoj Žižek, *The Ticklish Subject: The Absent Centre of Political Ontology* (New York: Verso, 1999), 136. For more on the individual portraits, see Helen Cooper, *John Trumbull: The Hand and Spirit of a Painter* (New Haven, CT: Yale University Press, 1982), 76–81.

3. Alexis de Tocqueville, *Democracy in America,* ed. Phillips Bradley, 2 vols. (New York: Vintage Books, 1990), 1:199.

4. Ernesto Laclau, *On Populist Reason* (New York: Verso, 2005), 105; see Paul J. Staiti's chapter on the painting in *Samuel F. B. Morse* (New York: Cambridge University Press, 1989), 71–101.

5. See Samuel F. B. Morse, *Imminent Dangers to the Free Institutions of the United States through Foreign Immigration* (1835; reprint, New York: Arno Press, 1969); Morse to Jedidiah Morse, August 6, 1812, and Morse to Jedidiah Morse, November 1, 1812, Morse Papers, Library of Congress. See also Staiti, *Morse,* 21.

6. From letters to his parents as cited in Samuel Irenaeus Prime, *The Life of Samuel F. B. Morse, LL.D., Inventor of the Electro-Magnetic Recording Telegraph* (New York: D. Appleton & Co., 1875), 36, 45–46, 60, 62.

7. Ibid., 65; as cited in Edward Lind Morse, ed., *Samuel F. B. Morse: His Letters and Journals,* 2 vols. (Boston: Houghton Mifflin Co., 1914), 1:54.

8. Edward Shils, *Center and Periphery: Essays in Macrosociology* (Chicago: University of Chicago Press, 1975), 160.

9. As cited in Prime, *Life of,* 63.

10. Laclau, *Populist Reason,* 71.

11. E. L. Morse, ed., *Morse,* 1:80 and 110.

12. See Staiti, *Morse,* 84–89; and William Kloss, *Samuel F. B. Morse* (New York: Henry N. Abrams, 1988), 75.

13. Staiti, *Morse,* 91.

14. Claude Lefort, *Democracy and Political Theory*, trans. David Macey (Minneapolis: University of Minnesota Press, 1988), 17.

15. See Sigmund Freud, "The Return of Totemism in Childhood," in *Totem and Taboo* in *The Complete Psychological Works of Sigmund Freud,* trans. and ed. James Strachey, standard ed. (London: Hogarth Press, 1953–74), 13:100–161.

16. Prime, *Life of,* 123.

17. Shils, *Center,* 130; Slavoj Žižek, *For They Know Not What They Do: Enjoyment as a Political Factor* (London: Verso, 1991), 272.

18. Samuel F. B. Morse, *Lectures on the Affinity of Painting with the Other Fine Arts,* ed. Nicolai Cikovsky, Jr. (Columbia: University of Missouri Press, 1983), 70.

19. Clifford Geertz, *The Interpretation of Cultures: Selected Essays by Clifford Geertz* (New York: Basic Books, 1973), 443.

20. Laclau, *Populist Reason,* 70.

21. The term "Anglophilia" was not commonly used until late in the nineteenth century, but the first known uses of "Anglomania" or "Anglomany," as an aesthetic, disposition, or indisposition (and also "Angloman," as one who has it), appear tellingly during the Constitutional debates in Thomas Jefferson's correspondence, usually to describe the Federalists. See, for example, his letter to James Madison, December 20, 1787 (*The Republic Letters: The Correspondence between Thomas Jefferson and James Madison, 1776–1828,* ed. James Morton Smith [New York: W. W. Norton, 1995], 1:513) or his letter to John Adams, November 13, 1787 (*The Adams-Jefferson Letters,* ed. Lester J. Cappon [Chapel Hill, NC: Omohundro Institute of Early American History and Culture and University of North Carolina Press, 1987], 212). Jefferson writes to French philosopher Constantin-François Volney that he awaits the day when "[Anglomany] yields to Americanism" (*Memoir, Correspondence, and Miscellanies from the Papers of Thomas Jefferson,* ed. Thomas Jefferson Randolph [Charlottesville, VA: F. Carr, 1829]).

22. Henry James, *A Small Boy and Others* (New York: Charles Scribner's Sons, 1941), 87–88, and 81.

23. Walter Benjamin, *Illuminations: Essays and Reflections,* ed. Hannah Arendt, trans. Harry Zohn (New York: Schocken Books, 1968), 222.

24. Giorgio Agamben, *Homo Sacer: Sovereign Power and Bare Life,* trans. Daniel Heller-Roazen (Stanford, CA: Stanford University Press, 1998), 18, 6, and 11.

25. Arjun Appadurai, *Modernity at Large: Cultural Dimensions of Globalization* (Minneapolis: University of Minnesota Press, 1996); David Cannadine, *Ornamentalism: How the British Saw Their Empire* (New York: Oxford University Press, 2001); C. L. R. James, *Beyond a Boundary,* introduction by Robert Lipsyte (Durham, NC: Duke University Press, 1993); Tom Nairn, *Enchanted Glass: Britain and Its Monarchy* (London: Vintage, 1998).

26. Theodor Adorno, *Minima Moralia: Reflections from Damaged Life,* trans. E. F. N. Jephcott (London, Verso, 1996), 189.

27. David Harlan, *The Degradation of American History* (Chicago: University of Chicago Press, 1997), 188.

28. Shils, *Center,* 312, 277.

29. The quote is from Elizabeth Fries Ellet, *Domestic History of the American Revolution* (New York: Baker & Scribner, 1850), 90, 95.

30. Georg Simmel, *On Individuality and Social Forms,* ed. Donald N. Levine (Chicago: University of Chicago Press, 1971), 129, 133–34.

31. Shils, *Center,* 277.

32. Emerson, *English Traits* in *Essays and Lectures* (New York: Library of America, 1983), 811; see esp. Lionel Trilling's chapter "Society and Authenticity" in *Sincerity and Authenticity* (Cambridge, MA: Harvard University Press, 1972).

33. William Shakespeare, *Richard II,* 2.1.45–46, in *Complete Works of Shakespeare,* ed. David Bevington (New York: HarperCollins, 1992), 735; Ian Baucom, *Out of Place: Englishness, Empire, and the Locations of Identity* (Princeton, NJ: Princeton University Press, 1999), 3–40.

34. Bhabha, "Signs Taken for Wonders," in *The Location of Culture* (New York: Routledge, 1994) 113.

35. Benedict Anderson, *Imagined Communities: Reflections on the Origin and Spread of Nationalism,* rev. ed. (London: Verso, 1991), 141.

Chapter 1

1. Elias Canetti, *Notes from Hampstead,* trans. John Hargraves (New York: Farrar, Straus & Giroux, 1998), 13; Ralph Waldo Emerson, "The American Scholar," in *Nature: Addresses and Lectures* in *Essays and Lectures* (New York: Library of America, 1983), 71.

2. F. O. Matthiessen, *American Renaissance: Art and Expression in the Age of Emerson and Whitman* (New York: Oxford University Press, 1941), vii; see also Robert E. Spiller et al., eds., *Literary History of the United States* (New York: Macmillan, 1948). For recent examples, see Sacvan Bercovitch, ed., *Cambridge History of American Literature* (New York: Cambridge University Press, 1994); and Emory Elliott, ed., *Columbia Literary History of the United States* (New York: Columbia University Press, 1988). Two useful articles chart how pervasive this consensus has been in American literary criticism: Gene Wise, " 'Paradigm Dramas,' " in American Studies: A Cultural and Institutional History of the Movement," *American Quarterly* 31, no. 3 (1979): 293–337; and Donald Pease, "New Americanists: Revisionist Interventions into the Canon," *boundary 2* 17, no. 1 (Spring 1990): 1–37.

3. "Ode to H.R.H.," *Harper's Weekly,* September 22, 1860, 596; "The Prince of Wales in New York—Splendid Military Display—Vast Concourse of People—Immense Enthusiasm," *Frank Leslie's Illustrated Newspaper,* October 20, 1860. See also, "The Prince in America," *New York Observer and Chronicle,* October 18, 1860, 334. For details of the visit overall, see Kinahan Cornwallis, *Royalty in the New World; or, The Prince of Wales in America* (New York: M. Doolady, 1860); and Gardner D. Engleheart, *Journal of the Progress of H.R.H. the Prince of Wales through British North America; and His Visit to the United States, 10th July to 15th November, 1860* (London, 1860).

4. Edmund C. Stedman, "The Prince's Ball," pt. 3, *Vanity Fair,* October 20, 1860, 196.

5. "Domestic Intelligence," *Harper's Weekly,* October 27, 1860, 679; "The Royal Ride up Broadway," *New York Herald,* October 12, 1860; Stedman, "The Prince's Ball," 197.

6. "In Snobbery, Waspishness Takes a Stingingly Ugly Turn," *Chicago Tribune,* February 28, 1990; "The Prince in Philadelphia," *New York Herald,* October 11, 1860; "The Prince and the Ladies," *Harper's Weekly,* October 13, 1860, 644; "Will the Prince of Wales Marry an American?" *Harper's Weekly,* August 18, 1860, 514; "The Prince in New York," *Vanity Fair,* October 27, 1860; "The Prince among the Ladies," *Harper's Weekly,* November 3, 1860. See also "The Prince of Wales," *Saturday Evening Post,* October 20, 1860; "The Prince of Wales Matrimonially Provided For," *Chicago Tribune,* November 12, 1860, 3; "A Dream—the New York Belle's Courtship and Marriage with the Prince of Wales," *Harper's Weekly,* October 20, 1860, 672; and the fictional story by Mary Martin, "The Prince of Wales at Pennytown," *Godey's Lady's Book,* December 1860, 526.

7. "Visit of the Prince of Wales—Our Concluding Pictures," *Harper's Weekly,* November 3, 1860, 689; "Anecdotes of the Prince," *Vanity Fair,* November 17, 1860, 253. *Vanity Fair* also featured a weekly column detailing Albert Edward's American travels, called "Prince-of-Walesiana." It ran from September 8 to October 20.

8. Michael Kinsley, "What an Extraordinary Thing for a Chap to Say: The American Writer Michael Kinsley Defends This Country against Dr. Carey's Harsh Strictures," *Sunday Telegraph,* April 10, 1994, 33.

9. "Intercepted Correspondence," *Harper's Weekly,* October 20, 1860, 663 and 658. *Littell's Living Age* speaks of "the adulatory scribblers who chronicle every word the prince utters, and the precise number of times he sneezes" (November 3, 1860, 320). See also, "How the Prince of Wales Travels," *Cincinnati Commercial Gazette,* September 28, 1860.

10. There are at least two Winslow Homer illustrations that reference the prince, *Thanksgiving Day, 1860—the Two Great Classes of Society* in *Harper's Weekly* for December 1, 1860, in which his feathers appear in the background, and *Welcome to the Prince of Wales* on the front page of *Harper's Weekly,* October 20, 1860. I am grateful to Roger B. Stein for pointing out one and helping to identify the other.

11. George Templeton Strong, *The Civil War,* vol. 3 of *The Diary of George Templeton Strong,* ed. Allan Nevins and Milton Halsey Thomas (New York: Macmillan Co., 1952), 52.

12. In Cornwallis, *Royalty in the New World,* 249. The letter was widely reprinted in local papers. I cite it here from the *New York Herald,* July 12, 1860. See, for example, "Queen Victoria and President Buchanan," *Littell's Living Age,* September 8, 1860, 614; and "The Visit of the Prince of Wales," *Saturday Evening Post,* July 21, 1860, 3.

13. "The Prince in New York," *Vanity Fair,* October 27, 1860, 208; "The Prince of Wales," *Nassau Literary Magazine,* October 1860, 90.

14. David Waldstreicher, *In the Midst of Perpetual Fetes: The Making of American Nationalism, 1776–1820* (Chapel Hill: Omohundro Institute of Early American History and Culture and University of North Carolina Press, 1997), 51. The contemporary references are to "The Prince Denationalized," *New York Herald,* October 25, 1860, 2; and Strong, *Diary,* 50. For a good discussion of the role that

such "spontaneous" associations and popular rituals of consent played in the early United States, see Gordon S. Wood, "The People Out-of-Doors," in *The Creation of the American Republic, 1776–1787* (New York: W. W. Norton, 1969), 319–28.

15. "Our Welcome to the Prince—Arrival and Reception of Victoria's Son in the Metropolis," *New York Herald,* October 12, 1860; "The Renfrew Ball," *Boston Daily Evening Transcript,* October 19, 1860; "Prince's Day in New York—Its Political Significance," *New York Herald,* October 13, 1860; Cornwallis, *Royalty in the New World,* 174; "Our English Visitors—the Display on the Detroit River," *Chicago Tribune,* September 22, 1860. The *Herald* writes, for example, that "Richmond, for its size, carried away the palm in the enthusiasm of its inhabitants, so much indeed as to cause grave men to remark that what was intended for respect had boiled over into adulation" (October 11, 1860); the *Baltimore Sun* describes thirty thousand people in St. Louis "packed and jammed in the seats and along the promenades of the amphitheater" (October 2, 1860); and so on. See also, "Incidents of the Prince's Visit. His Interview with Harriet Hosmer— the Boston Reception," *Chicago Tribune,* October 26, 1860. The *Herald* describes a "struggle" with no stakes in its account of the prince and the "ladies": "The struggle is now amongst themselves. It is a sort of internecine conflict, a social strife, in which all the contestants are equally skillful" (October 10, 1860, 4).

16. Edgar Allan Poe, "The Masque of the Red Death," in *Selected Tales,* ed. David Van Leer (New York: Oxford University Press, 1998), 129.

17. "The Visit of the Prince of Wales," *Baltimore Sun,* October 5, 1860.

18. "Reception of the Prince of Wales—a Democratic Jubilee—New York Out of Doors," *New York Daily Tribune,* October 12, 1860; Cornwallis, *Royalty in the New World,* 176; see also "The Prince of Wales' Tour," *Littell's Living Age,* October 27, 1860, 254–56; "The Scene in Broadway," *New York Herald,* October 12, 1860, 3; and "The Prince of Wales in the United States," *Littell's Living Age,* December 1, 1860, 547–48. Walt Whitman remembers the Prince of Wales's parade down Broadway, in his 1860 poem, "Year of Meteors" (*Leaves of Grass, 1891–1892,* ed. Sculley Bradley and Harold W. Blodgett [New York: W. W. Norton & Co., 1973], 239):

> Songs therefore would I sing, to all that hitherward comes would I welcome
> give,
> And you would I sing, fair stripling! welcome to you from me, young prince
> of England!
> (Remember you surging Manhattan's crowds as you pass'd with your
> cortege of nobles?
> There in the crowds stood I, and singled you out with attachment;).

I am grateful to Mark Maslan for calling this passage to my attention.

19. "Reception of the Prince of Wales—a Democratic Jubilee—New York Out of Doors," *New York Daily Tribune,* October 12, 1860.

20. Fred Somkin, *Unquiet Eagle: Memory and Desire in the Idea of American Freedom, 1815–1860* (Ithaca, NY: Cornell University Press, 1967), 131, 136, 140.

21. "The Renfrew Ball," *Boston Daily Evening Transcript,* October, 20, 1860; "The Prince of Wales Visit: The Philosophy of the Reception in the British Provinces and the United States," *New York Herald,* October 25, 1860. *Littell's Living Age* writes, "The Prince of Wales has been the object of enthusiastic applause from thousands who pride themselves on the knowledge that the establishment of royalty among themselves is impossible" (December 22, 1860, 758).

22. *London Times* as quoted in "The Prince's Reception," *New York Observer and Chronicle,* November 15, 1860, 366.

23. "The Prince of Wales Tour," *Littell's Living Age,* December 22, 1860, 758. For the press's response to Prince William Henry's visit to the American colonies in 1781, see Frank Moore, *Diary of the American Revolution, from Newspapers and Original Documents,* 2 vols. (New York: Charles Scribner, 1860), 2:387–88.

24. "The Visit of the Prince," *Monthly Religious Magazine and Independent Journal,* December 1860, 367; "The Prince of Wales' Visit—the Philosophy of the Reception in the British Provinces and the United States," *New York Herald,* October 25, 1860; Alexis de Tocqueville, *Democracy in America,* ed. Phillips Bradley, 2 vols. (New York: Vintage Classics, 1990), 2:106.

25. "Reception," *New York Daily Tribune,* October 12, 1860; "Prince's Day in New York—Its Political Significance," *New York Herald,* October 13, 1860. My understanding of the language of popular self-government is informed by Robert H. Wiebe, *Self-Rule: A Cultural History of American Democracy* (Chicago: University of Chicago Press, 1995); and Edmund S. Morgan, *Inventing the People: The Rise of Popular Sovereignty in England and America* (New York: W. W. Norton, 1988).

26. Harriet Beecher Stowe, "The Prince," *Liberator,* November 24, 1860; Anderson, *Imagined Communities,* 7.

27. Karen Halttunen, *Confidence Men and Painted Women: A Study of Middle-Class Culture in America, 1830–1870* (New Haven, CT: Yale University Press, 1982); John F. Kasson, *Rudeness and Civility: Manners in Nineteenth-Century Urban America* (New York: Hill & Wang, 1990). See also Edwin Harrison Cady, *The Gentleman in America: A Literary Study in American Culture* (Syracuse, NY: Syracuse University Press, 1949); and Tamara Plakins Thornton, *Cultivating Gentlemen: The Meaning of Country Life among the Boston Elite, 1785–1860* (New Haven, CT: Yale University Press, 1989).

28. "Every American Descends from a Redcoat," *Harper's Weekly,* October 13, 1860, 647.

29. "The City Dining the Prince," *Harper's Weekly,* August 25, 1860, 530; "Who Shall Dance with Him?" *Harper's Weekly,* September 15, 1860, 578.

30. Stedman, "The Prince's Ball," 196; Strong, *Diary,* 3:51; "How to Receive the Prince," *Harper's Weekly,* September 8, 1860, 562. See also "Artemus Ward Sees the Prince of Wales," *Saturday Evening Post,* October 20, 1860, 8.

31. Richard L. Bushman, *The Refinement of America* (New York: Random House, 1993).

32. "Prince's Day in New York—Its Political Significance," *New York Herald,* October 13, 1860.

33. J. Hector St. John de Crèvecoeur, *Letters from an American Farmer and Sketches of Eighteenth-Century America,* ed. Albert E. Stone (New York: Penguin Books, 1986), 68; "Baron Renfrew in Richmond," *Richmond Enquirer,* October, 9, 1860.

34. Peter D. Salins, *Assimilation, American Style* (New York: BasicBooks, 1997), 99; Nairn, *Enchanted Glass,* 178, 183; Adrian Peracchio, "Why Yanks and Brits Never See Eye to Eye," *New York Newsday,* January 24, 1993, 38; Geoffrey Wheatcroft, "London Diarist," *New Republic* 202, no. 11 (March 12, 1990): 46.

35. See Reginald Horsman, *Race and Manifest Destiny: The Origins of American Racial Anglo-Saxonism* (Cambridge, MA: Harvard University Press, 1981); David R. Roediger, *The Wages of Whiteness: Race and the Making of the American Working Class* (London: Verso, 1991), Alexander Saxton, *The Rise and Fall of the White Republic: Class Politics and Mass Culture in Nineteenth-Century America* (New York: Verso, 1990); Dana D. Nelson, *National Manhood: Capital Citizenship and the Imagined Fraternity of White Men* (Durham, NC: Duke University Press, 1998). On the Irish, see Cornwallis, *Royalty in the New World,* 195; "The Prince of Wales," *Liberator,* September 21, 1860, 151; "The Irishmen and the Prince of Wales," *Chicago Tribune,* November 19, 1860, 2; "The Visit of the Prince of Wales," *Monthly Religious Magazine and Independent Journal,* December 1860, 367. See also coverage of Corcoran's refusal to march in the parade in *Irish News,* September 8, 1860, 344, and of Corcoran's trial in the *Irish-American,* April 27, 1861, 2. Charges against Corcoran were dismissed in the wake of the secession and war.

36. "The Visit of the Prince," *Monthly Religious Magazine and Indepdendent Journal,* December 1860, 367.

37. Toni Morrison, *Playing in the Dark: Whiteness and the Literary Imagination* (New York: Vintage Books, 1992), 16; Cornwallis, *Royalty in the New World,* 205–6.

38. "What the Prince Did and Saw at Richmond," *New York Herald,* October 10, 1860, 4.

39. "Baron Renfrew in Richmond," *Richmond Enquirer,* October 9, 1860; "Prince of Wales in Richmond," *New York Herald,* October 8, 1860. For the African American response to the prince's visit in both the United States and Canada, see "The Prince and the Colored People's Address" and "Colored People's Address," *Liberator,* September 28, 1860, 1; "Address of Colored Citizens of Boston to the Prince of Wales," *Liberator,* December 31, 1860, 210. I return to the black response to the British monarchy and to the language of loyalty in chapter 3.

40. "Reception of the Prince of Wales—a Democratic Jubilee," *New York Daily Tribune,* October 12, 1860. In the meantime, the *Southern Literary Messenger* claims that the South saw the visit as a national event and blames the Northern press for politicizing it: "The reporters of the Northern papers availed themselves of this occasion to display that insane malice which is so characteristic of a certain class at the North, and which our Union-loving Southerners are striving to appease by apologizing for Lincoln" (November 1860, 394). On the "crowd symbol" and its significance for the psychology of national identity, see Elias Canetti's "National Crowd Symbols," in *Crowds and Power* (New York: Farrar, Straus & Giroux, 1984), esp. 169–71.

41. "The Prince's Visit to Washington," *New York Herald,* October 17, 1860, 10. See also "The Prince of Wales at Richmond," *Chicago Tribune,* November 28, 1860, 3; "The Prince of Wales in Richmond," *Christian Observer,* October 11, 1860, 163.

42. "The Visit of the Prince of Wales—the Chivalry," *New York Daily Tribune,* October 10, 1860. See also "The Prince of Wales Invited to Visit the South," *Saturday Evening Post,* September 29, 1860, 6.

43. "Our Welcome to the Prince—Arrival and Reception of Victoria's Son in the Metropolis—Half a Million on Broadway," *New York Herald,* October 12, 1860; "The Character and Suggestiveness of Baron Renfrew's Visit to the President and the Tomb of Washington," *Baltimore Sun,* October 4, 1860; "The Reception in New York—The Ball in the Metropolis," *New York Herald,* October 10, 1860. The *Herald*'s headline, "The North against the South End," appears on October 20, 1860, 10.

44. "The Scene in Broadway and the Park before the Arrival of the Prince; the People Waiting on Royalty," *New York Herald,* October 12, 1860, 3. For more on the prince's visit to Mount Vernon, see the *Baltimore Sun* cited above and "The Prince's Visit to Washington's Tomb," *Littell's Living Age,* November 3, 1860, 320.

45. Strong, *Diary,* 3:44; Stowe, "The Prince," *Liberator,* November 24, 1860.

46. "Singular, if True," *Vanity Fair,* October 20, 1860, 203.

47. "The Visit of Ralph Farnham to the Prince," *Liberator,* November 2, 1860, 176; "The Prince Meets Ralph Farnham," *Harper's Weekly,* October 27, 1860, 679; "Departure of the Prince" [on Farnham], *New York Observer and Chronicle,* October 25, 1860, 342.

48. "Local Matters: Arrival of Lord Renfrew and Suite in Baltimore, and His Departure for Washington," *Baltimore Sun,* October 4, 1860. For the "Young America" movement, and just how comical this allusion might have seemed, see Edward L. Widmer, *Young America: The Flowering of Democracy in New York City* (New York: Oxford University Press, 1999), 183.

49. See Horsman, *Race and Manifest Destiny.* Contemporary references are to "The Visit of the Prince of Wales; the Historical Significance of the Event and Simultaneous Commotions in Europe; the American Union, etc.," *Baltimore Sun,* October 5, 1860; "Reception of the Prince," *New York Daily Tribune,* October 12, 1860.

50. Horsman, *Race and Manifest Destiny,* 65; Roland Barthes, *S/Z: An Essay,* trans. Richard Miller, preface by Richard Howard (New York: Hill & Wang, 1974), 119–20, and Barthes, *The Pleasure of the Text,* trans. Richard Miller (New York: Hill & Wang, 1975), 56; "The Prince of Wales in New York—a Remarkable Day," *New York Herald,* October 12, 1860.

51. "The Visit of the Prince," *Baltimore Sun,* October 5, 1860.

52. For "emblems of fraternal union," see "Prince's Day in New York—Its Political Significance," *New York Herald,* October 13, 1860; for "ties of consanguinity," see "Prince of Wales in New York," *New York Herald,* October 12, 1860. For coverage of Southern secession, besides coverage of the prince's visit, see, for example, "Revolution of the South: Arming in Virginia—the Crisis to Come before the Inaugu-

ration of President," *New York Herald*, October 23, 1860, 4; or descriptions of the Union Torchlight Parade in the *Herald*, October 24, 1860.

53. "Reception of the Prince," *New York Daily Tribune*, October 12, 1860. For a description of children in Boston singing, "God Save the Queen," see "A Pleasant Picture," *Brooklyn Circular*, October 25, 1860, 155.

54. "The Prince of Wales," *Philadelphia Saturday Evening Post*, October 20, 1860; "The Prince's Reception in Montreal—Observations and Views of a Washington Lady on the Subject—Loyalty and Costume on the Occasion—Wane of Loyalty in the United States," *Baltimore Sun*, September 4, 1860. The motto on the prince's crest and arms, *Ich Dien*, or "I serve," also inspired reflections on the virtues of national loyalism. "With human instinct," writes the *Nassau Literary Magazine*, "that principle has gone. . . . How grand now, becomes the allegory . . . to serve and to be subject" (December 1860, 182).

55. "Ode to H.R.H.," *Harper's Weekly*, September 22, 1860, 596.

56. "America to the Prince of Wales," *Boston Daily Evening Transcript*, October 17, 1860; "Prince of Wales at Washington's Tomb," *New York Herald*, October 27, 1860, 4; for "Revolution at the South," see p. 2 of this issue.

57. "Lines to the Prince of Wales," *New York Herald*, October 27, 1860, 4; for "Revolution at the South," see p. 2.

58. The Holmes poem appears without a title but is described as an "international ode" in the *Boston Daily Evening Transcript*, October 17, 1860. An article in a Brooklyn paper makes a similar analogy between Christian piety and monarchical devotion: "We are not sure but that the latent veneration for Kingship, so long repressed in the American mind by the influence of Democracy, may have asserted itself a little, and that the effect will be good. For, after all, there is something in human nature which harmonizes with the monarchical idea; and Democracy, unless it is allied to something higher—to the absolute monarchy of Theocracy—will never achieve the development of perfect humanity" ("The Prince of Wales," *Brooklyn Circular*, October 18, 1860, 150).

59. "Our Offer to the Prince," *Vanity Fair*, September 1, 1860, 116; "The Prince of Wales Visit," *New York Herald*, October 25, 1860, 2. And see Rufus Choate, "Speech 'on the Political Topics Now Prominent before the Country,'" delivered at Lowell, MA, October 28, 1856, in *Addresses and Orations of Rufus Choate* (Boston: Little, Brown, & Co., 1891), 440.

60. "Victoria," *New York Mirror*, July 14, 1838, 23.

61. "The Coronation," *New York Mirror*, August 11, 1838, 59.

62. "The Reginamania," *New York Mirror*, March 31, 1838, 315; "Queen Victoria's Hat," *New York Morning Herald*, June 21, 1838; see also, "The Victoria Fever," *Democratic Review* 6 (July 1839), 74–76.

63. Žižek, *For They Know Not What They Do*, 48; Nairn, *Enchanted Glass*, 48. For historical perspective, see Ernst Kantorowicz, *The King's Two Bodies: A Study in Medieval Political Theology* (Princeton, NJ: Princeton University Press, 1957); and John Neville Figgis, *The Divine Right of Kings*, introduction by G. R. Elton (1896; reprint,

New York: Harper Torchbooks, 1965). For a wonderful reading of the material and sublime functions of monarchy, see Bill Brown on Mark Twain's *The Prince and the Pauper* in *A Sense of Things: The Object Matter of American Literature* (Chicago: University of Chicago Press, 2003), 40–41.

64. Nathaniel Parker Willis, "Jottings Down in London," *Corsair,* August 17, 1839, 361; Nairn, *Enchanted Glass,* 48; Ralph Waldo Emerson, *English Traits* in *Essays and Lectures* (New York: Library of America, 1983), 831, 811; Perry Anderson, *English Questions* (London: Verso, 1992), 31. For more on the historical understanding of British empiricism, see Nairn, *Enchanted Glass,* 93–98; David Simpson, *Romanticism, Nationalism, and the Revolt against Theory* (Chicago: University of Chicago Press, 1993); and Jules David Law, *The Rhetoric of Empiricism: Language and Perception from Locke to I. A. Richards* (Ithaca, NY: Cornell University Press, 1993).

65. Shils, *Center and Periphery.*

66. Willis, "Jottings Down in London," August 31, 1839, 394. The "grasshopper on the steeple" likely alludes to the famous grasshopper weathervane on top of Boston's Faneuil Hall. The weathervane itself was designed to recall a "grasshopper" on top of the London Royal Exchange.

67. Shils, *Center and Periphery,* 162.

68. Ibid., 160; Walter Bagehot, *The English Constitution,* ed. Paul Smith (1867; reprint, Cambridge: Cambridge University Press, 2001), 34–67; the phrase "brilliant to the eye" is from Bagehot, *Economic Studies* (1880), as cited in Christopher Herbert, *Culture and Anomie: Ethnographic Imagination in the Nineteenth Century* (Chicago: University of Chicago Press, 1991), 138; David Cannadine, "The Context, Performance and Meaning of Ritual: The British Monarchy and the 'Invention of Tradition,' c. 1820–1977," in *The Invention of Tradition,* ed. Eric Hobsbawm and Terence Ranger (Cambridge: Cambridge University Press, 1983), 119.

69. Bagehot, "The Monarchy and the People," as cited in Cannadine, "The Context, Performance and Meaning of Ritual," 119; Cannadine, "The Context," 109; Hobsbawm, "Introduction: Inventing Traditions," in *The Invention of Tradition,* ed. Hobsbawm and Ranger, 1.

70. See Cannadine, "The Context," as well as his *Ornamentalism;* and Margaret Homans, *Royal Representations: Queen Victoria and British Culture, 1837–1876* (Chicago: University of Chicago Press, 1998); see also Vernon Bogdanor, *The Monarchy and the Constitution* (New York: Oxford University Press, 1995); Clifford Geertz, "Centers, Kings and Charisma: Reflections on the Symbolics of Power," in *Culture and Its Creators: Essays in Honor of Edward Shils,* ed. Joseph Ben-David and Terry Nichols Clark (Chicago: University of Chicago Press, 1977), 150–71; Philip Ziegler, *Crown and People* (Newton Abbott: Readers Union, 1979); Sean Wilentz, ed., *Rites of Power: Symbolism, Ritual and Politics since the Middle Ages* (Philadelphia: University of Pennsylvania Press, 1985). John Plunkett's recent book, *Queen Victoria: First Media Monarch* (New York: Oxford University Press, 2003), suggests that Cannadine and others who focus on Victoria's symbolic role in the empire have downplayed both the populist invention of the monarchy during the first half of her reign and the "imaginative potency" of this popular appeal, apart

from the pageantry that comes later. The book is also informative on just how news of Victoria in the British press during these years helped to mobilize a radical opposition.

71. Cannadine, *Ornamentalism*, 46.

72. Roland Barthes, *Empire of Signs,* trans. Richard Howard (New York: Hill & Wang, 1983), 3.

73. Horace Greeley, *Glances of Europe, in a Series of Letters* (New York: Dewitt & Davenport, 1851), 96; Caroline M. Kirkland, "Detached Thoughts about England," *Sartain's Magazine,* February 1849, 127. Of course, the queen remains just as fascinating to Americans as the prince. Take this June 1, 1991, letter to the editors of the *Washington Post* on the response to Elizabeth II's American tour: "Washington, get a grip! I can't believe people are upset because your paper's columnists poked a bit of fun at the queen. The War for Independence ended two centuries ago—why is the queen such an object of devotion here?"

74. Anderson, *English Questions*, 43, 31.

75. Brendan McConville has recently and provocatively shown a similar colonial attachment to the monarchy in America, before the Revolution. With the prevalence, after 1688, of imperial rituals and royal celebrations in the colonies— rituals in which Parliament had no symbolic role—"the monarch apart from the Parliament became the primary and common imperial link, the empire's living embodiment" (*The King's Three Faces: The Rise and Fall of Royal America, 1688–1776* [Chapel Hill: Omohundro Institute of Early American History and Culture and University of North Carolina Press, 2006], 8). At the same time, the new power of the Parliament in England meant royal rites played a far smaller role at home, creating an "imperial paradox" that anticipated the structure of the empire in the nineteenth century in which "the imperial fringe's enthusiasm for Protestant monarchy contrasted sharply with the metropolitan center's apathy toward the monarch" (50).

76. The foreign correspondent of the *Evening Star,* "Twiddle-Twaddle about the Queen," *New York Mirror,* April 21, 1838.

77. Walt Whitman, "Song of Myself," in *Leaves of Grass,* ed. Bradley and Blodgett, 28; James Gordon Bennett, "The Farewell," *Morning Herald,* May 1, 1838.

78. Willis, "Jottings Down in London," July 27, 1839, 313; "Scene in Broadway," *New York Mirror,* May 26, 1838, 383.

79. Sarah Orne Jewett, "The Queen's Twin," in *The Country of Pointed Firs and Other Stories,* introduction by Marjorie Pryse (New York: W. W. Norton & Co., 1981), 203, 207, 206.

80. Ibid., 207–8.

81. Ibid., 205. For the relationship between aesthetics and the ethics of citizenship, see especially David Lloyd and Paul Thomas, *Culture and the State* (New York: Routledge, 1998); and Terry Eagleton, *The Ideology of the Aesthetic* (Oxford: Blackwell, 1990).

82. "To Queen Victoria; Written Immediately after Her Accession to the Throne," *Southern Literary Messenger* (June 1839), 369.

83. Benjamin, *Illuminations*, 222.

84. From *Memoirs of Thomas Sully,* cited in Edward Biddle and Mantle Fielding, *The Life and Works of Thomas Sully* (1921; reprint, New York: Da Capo Press, 1970), 55.

85. Review of *The Republican Court; or, American Society in the Days of Washington,* by Rufus W. Griswold, *North American Review* 81, no. 168 (July 1855): 38; George Perkins Marsh, "Address" in *The New England Society Orations,* ed. Cephas Brainerd and Eveline Warner Brainerd (New York: Century Society, 1901), 1:412; William Wordsworth, *The Prelude* (1805), ed. Jonathan Wordsworth, M. H. Abrams, and Stephen Gill (New York: W. W. Norton, 1979), 48.

86. "Mr. Sully's Portrait of the Queen," *Corsair,* June 15, 1839.

87. "The Astonished Painter," *Godey's Lady's Book* 19 (November 1838): 193; also cited in Carrie Rebora Barratt, *Queen Victoria and Thomas Sully* (New York: Metropolitan Museum of Art, 2000), 62.

88. From *Memoirs of Thomas Sully,* 53.

89. Edmund Burke, *Reflections on the Revolution in France,* ed. J. G. A. Pocock (Indianapolis: Hackett Publishing Co., 1987), 67.

90. See Sigmund Freud, "The Sexual Aberrations," in *Three Essays on the Theory of Sexuality,* trans. James Strachey, introduction by Steven Marcus (New York: Basic-Books, 2000), 19–21.

91. From *Thomas Sully's Journal* as published in Barratt, *Queen Victoria and Thomas Sully,* 142.

92. Freud, "Sexual Aberrations," 20.

93. Žižek, *For They Know Not What They Do,* 267; Claude Lefort, *Democracy and Political Theory,* trans. David Macey (Minneapolis: University of Minnesota Press, 1988), 17.

94. Wendy Greenhouse, "Imperiled Ideals: British Historical Heroines in Antebellum American History Painting," in *Redefining American History Painting,* ed. Patricia M. Burnham and Lucretia Hoover Giese (New York: Cambridge University Press, 1995), 263–76. For more on the analogy between the English Civil War and the American Civil War, see William R. Taylor, *Cavalier and Yankee: The Old South and American National Character* (Cambridge, MA: Harvard University Press, 1979).

95. *The Last Soirée of Charles II* is lost, but a photograph of it is reprinted in Barbara S. Groseclose, *Emanuel Leutze, 1816–1868: Freedom Is the Only King* (Washington, DC: National Gallery of Fine Arts, 1975), 54. The painting is also described in "Foreign Correspondence," *The Crayon* 4, no. 3 (March 1857): 89.

96. Groseclose, *Emanuel Leutze,* 20, 53–54.

97. Geertz, "Centers, Kings and Charisma," 168. My reading of the painting attends from David Lloyd's and Paul Thomas's use of Friedrich Schiller's *Aesthetic Education* to discuss the role of spectacle and theater as an "exemplary state apparatus" (*Culture and the State;* see, esp., 55–65). I also draw on Joseph Roach's sense of both the legacy of the idea of the king's two bodies and the process of "surroga-

tion" that compensates for symbolic loss (*Cities of the Dead: Circum-Atlantic Performance* [New York: Columbia University Press, 1996]; 38–39).

98. John Brewer, *The Pleasures of the Imagination: English Culture in the Eighteenth Century* (New York: Farrar Straus & Giroux, 1997), 6–8.

99. Geertz, "Centers, Kings and Charisma," 168; Bagehot, *English Constitution*, 37.

100. Bagehot, 37; Friedrich Schiller, *On the Aesthetic Education of Man, in a Series of Letters,* trans. Reginald Snell (New Haven: Yale University Press, 1954).

101. Francis J. Grund, *Aristocracy in America* (1859; reprint, New York: Harper & Brothers, 1959), 56; *Queen Victoria's Memoirs of the Prince Consort* (New York: Harper & Brothers, 1868); Sarah Josepha Buell Hale, *Manners; or, Happy Homes and Good Society All the Year Round* (1868; reprint, New York: Arno Press, 1972), 6; "Queen Victoria," *Southern Literary Messenger* 18, no. 3 (March 1852): 187, 191, 192. See also "The Betrothal of Victoria," *Ladies' Repository,* vol. 27 (November 1867); and Grace Greenwood, *Queen Victoria: Her Girlhood and Womanhood* (New York: J. R. Anderson & H. S. Allen, 1883).

102. "Queen Victoria," *Ladies' Repository,* no. 13 (April 1853); Elizabeth Fries Ellet, *The Queens of American Society* (Philadelphia: Porter & Coates, 1867), ii. Also see Ellet's *Court Circles of the Republic; or, The Beauties and Celebrities of the Nation* (Philadelphia: Philadelphia Publishing Co., 1869).

103. Ellet, *Queens,* ii.

104. Daniel Huntington's *The Republican Court in the Time of Washington, or Lady Washington's Reception Day* was inspired by Rufus Griswold's popular book, *The Republican Court, or American Society in the Days of Washington* (New York: D. Appleton, 1855), for which it served as the frontispiece in later editions. I am working from an 1867 color engraving of the image by A. H. Ritchie. For critical response, see *New York Daily Tribune,* October 21, 1865, 9, as cited in William M. S. Rasmussen and Robert S. Tilton, *George Washington: The Man behind the Myth* (Charlottesville: University Press of Virginia, 1999), 221.

105. Henry T. Tuckerman, *Book of the Artists: American Artist Life* (1867; reprint, New York: James F. Carr, 1966), 323. My sense of "collective effervescence" here derives from Émile Durkheim, *The Elementary Forms of Religious Life,* trans. Carol Cosman, introduction by Mark S. Cladis (New York: Oxford University Press, 2001), 171.

106. Tuckerman, 329, 332.

107. See Howard Jones, *To the Webster-Ashburton Treaty: A Study in Anglo-American Relations, 1783–1843* (Chapel Hill: University of North Carolina Press, 1977); Martin Crawford, *The Anglo-American Crisis of the Mid-Nineteenth Century, 1850–1862* (Athens: University of Georgia Press, 1987); and Ephraim Douglass Adams, *Great Britain and the American Civil War,* 2 vols. (New York: Longmans, Green & Co., 1925). Frank Thistlethwaite, *The Anglo-American Connection in the Early Nineteenth Century* (Philadelphia: University of Pennsylvania Press, 1959); H. C. Allen, *Great Britain and the United States: A History of Anglo-American Relations, 1783–1952*

(New York: St. Martin's Press, 1955); Robert H. Ferrell, ed., *Foundations of American Diplomacy* (Columbia: University of South Carolina Press, 1968). The rapport between Webster and Ashburton is also described in Howard Jones and Donald A. Rakestraw, *Prologue to Manifest Destiny: Anglo-American Relations in the 1840s* (Wilmington, DE: Scholarly Resources Inc., 1997).

108. See, esp., Crawford, *Anglo-American Crisis,* 106–33.

109. Daniel Greenleaf Thompson, *Politics in a Democracy: An Essay* (New York: Longmans, Green, & Co., 1893), 4.

110. See Walter L. Arnstein, "Queen Victoria and the United States," in *Anglo-American Attitudes: From Revolution to Partnership,* ed. Fred M. Leventhal and Roland Quinault (Burlington, VT: Ashgate, 2000), 94; Thomas Paine, "The Rights of Man," pt. 2, in *Thomas Paine Reader,* ed. Michael Foot and Isaac Kramnick (New York: Penguin Books, 1987), 275; Dallas as cited in Beckles Willson, *America's Ambassadors to England, 1785–1929* (New York: Frederick A. Stokes, 1929), 297–98.

111. Buchanan on the queen as "gracious and dignified" and "without blemish," as cited in Arnstein, "Queen Victoria," 93, 95; Everett on British government, as cited in Willson, *America's Ambassadors,* 241; Buchanan on court dress as cited in Arnstein, "Queen Victoria," 94. See also Philip Shriver Klein, *President James Buchanan: A Biography* (University Park, PA: Pennsylvania State University Press, 1962), 228–29.

112. Bagehot, *English Constitution,* 37.

113. Ibid., 37, 41.

114. George M. Fredrickson, "The Doctrine of Loyalty," in *The Inner Civil War: Northern Intellectuals and the Crisis of the Union* (Urbana: University of Illinois Press, 1993), 138, 141, 150. See also Horace Bushnell, "The Doctrine of Loyalty," *New Englander* (July 1863), 560–81; and Henry Dutton, "Loyalty and Disloyalty: Interpreting the Constitution," *New Englander* (April 1863), 316.

115. George P. Putnam, *The Tourist in Europe* (New York: Wiley & Putnam, 1838), 90; Shils, *Center and Periphery,* 198–99.

116. "A Day of Excitement," *New York Mirror,* 5 May 1838, 359.

117. Rufus Choate, "Address on the Fourth of July" (1858), 497; "The Preservation of the Union" (delivered in Faneuil Hall, November 26, 1850), 401; "The Position and Functions of the American Bar as an Element of Conservatism in the State" (delivered in Cambridge, July 3, 1845), 156, all in *Addresses and Orations.* For more on Choate and Whig culture, see Jean V. Matthews, *Rufus Choate: The Law and Civic Virtue* (Philadelphia: Temple University Press, 1980); Daniel Walker Howe, *The Political Culture of American Whigs* (Chicago: University of Chicago Press, 1979); Michael F. Holt, *The Rise and Fall of the American Whig Party* (New York: Oxford University Press, 1999).

118. Matthews, *Rufus Choate,* 85; Ralph Waldo Emerson, "Historic Notes of Life and Letters in New England," in *Lectures and Biographical Sketches,* vol. 10 of *The Complete Works of Ralph Waldo Emerson,* ed. Joel Myerson (New York: AMS Press, 1979), 326; David Hume. "Of the Origin of Government," in *Essays; Moral, Political,*

and Literary, ed. Eugene F. Miller (Indianapolis: Liberty Fund, 1985), 38–39. For the rhetoric of loyalty and duty as it is used in the military, see Elizabeth D. Samet, *Willing Obedience: Citizens, Soldiers, and the Progress of Consent in America, 1776–1898* (Stanford, CA: Stanford University Press, 2004).

119. Thompson, *Politics in a Democracy,* ix, xii–xiii.

120. See C. L. R. James, *Beyond a Boundary* and Arjun Appadurai, *Modernity at Large.*

121. "St. George's Society, New York. Anniversary Dinner," *Anglo-American* (April 29, 1843): 18–19. The *Anglo-American,* published by A. D. Patterson in New York, sought, as its object, "to uphold and sustain kindly feelings and amicable relations between the two great nations whose emblems are there combined." It continues, "How is it morally possible that . . . the people of these countries should be able to shake off these ties, to renounce this connection, to exhibit a snarling aspect and a hostile attitude, and to hold aloof from that brotherly confidence which so many causes contribute to inspire," 20.

122. Karl Marx, *The Eighteenth Brumaire of Louis Bonaparte,* trans. C. P. Dutt (1869; reprint, New York: International Publishers Co., 1994), 15, 17.

123. "Whipple's *Essays and Reviews,*" *American Whig Review* (February 1849), 167. The essay is a review of Edwin P. Whipple, *Essays and Reviews,* 2 vols. (New York: D. Appleton & Co, 1849).

124. "Whipple's *Essays and Reviews,*" 166; review of *The Republican Court* by Griswold, 45.

125. Anderson, *English Questions,* 20; Freud's discussion of "deferred obedience" appears in *Totem and Taboo,* 13:143–45.

126. Griswold, *The Republican Court,* 16.

127. This seems to revise revolutionary rhetoric as described in Jay Fliegelman, *Prodigals and Pilgrims: The American Revolution against Patriarchal Authority, 1750–1800* (New York: Cambridge University Press, 1982); Edward Everett, "Reception at Hereford" (delivered September 9, 1843), in *Orations and Speeches on Various Occasions,* 4 vols. (1850; reprint, Boston: Little, Brown, & Co., 1883), 2: 472–73.

128. Rufus Choate, "The Colonial Age of New England" (delivered in Ipswich, MA, August 16, 1834), in *Addresses and Orations,* 41–42.

129. Abraham Lincoln, "First Inaugural Address" (delivered March 4, 1861), in *The Portable Abraham Lincoln,* ed. Andrew Delbanco (New York: Penguin Books, 1993), 204. For "silver cords," see Jonathan Prescott Hall, "Discourse, 1847," in *The New England Society Orations,* ed. Cephas Brainerd and Eveline Warner Brainerd (New York: Century Co., 1901), 2:76; Edward Everett's "The Fourth of July" (1858), in *Orations,* 3:645.

130. Daniel Webster, "Second Speech on Foot's Resolution" (delivered January 26–27, 1830), in *The Works of Daniel Webster,* 10th ed. (Boston: Little, Brown & Co., 1857), vol. 3:342.

131. "Peerages and Genealogies," *North American Review* (July 1863), 69; Worthington C. Ford, "American Genealogies," *North American Review* (April 1856), 471.

132. "Heraldry in New England," *North American Review* (January 1865), 186. Nathaniel Hawthorne, "Consular Experiences," in *Our Old Home* (1863), ed. Fredson Bower, vol. 5 of *The Centenary Edition of the Works of Nathaniel Hawthorne,* ed. William Charvat, Roy Harvey Pearce, and Claude M. Simpson (Columbus: Ohio State University Press, 1970–97), 5:6–40; Hall, "Discourse, 1847," 5.

133. Sir Bernard Burke, *A Genealogical and Heraldic Dictionary of the Peerage and Baronetage of the British Empire* (London: Harrison, 1863); James Savage, John Farmer, and O. P. Dexter, *A Genealogical Dictionary of the First Settlers of New England* (Boston: Little, Brown, & Co., 1860–62); William Whitmore, *A Handbook of American Genealogy; Being a Catalogue of Family Histories and Publications Containing Genealogical Information* (Albany, NY: J. Munsell, 1862); Charles Boutell, *A Manual of Heraldry, Historical and Popular* (London: Winsor & Newton, 1863) or, for an American ed., Boutell, *English Heraldry* (New York: Cassell, Petter, & Galpin, 1867); John Collins Warren, *Genealogy of Warren, with Some Historical Sketches* (Boston: J. Wilson & Son, 1854); Isaac Appleton Jewett, *Memorial of Samuel Appleton of Ipswich, Massachusetts, with Genealogical Notices of Some of His Descendents* (Boston: Bolles & Houghton, 1850).

134. Cited in "Peerages and Genealogies," 37.

135. Ford, "American Genealogies," 471.

136. Frederick Law Olmsted, *Walks and Talks of an American Farmer in England* (1852; reprint, Ann Arbor: University of Michigan Press, 1967), 308–10; Ann S. Stephens, *High Life in New York* (New York: Bunce & Brother, 1854), 92.

137. Stephen Spender, *Love-Hate Relations: English and American Sensibilities* (New York: Random House, 1974), 5.

138. I draw on Freud's idea of the "family romance," in "Family Romances" (1909), in *Complete Psychological Works,* trans. and ed. Strachey, 9:235–44, and on *Totem and Taboo;* "Heraldry," *American Whig Review* (December 1845), 624; "Heraldry in New England," 186.

139. Michel de Certeau, *The Writing of History,* trans. Tom Conley (New York: Columbia University Press, 1988), 47.

140. Van Wyck Brooks, "The Wine of Puritans" (1908), in *Van Wyck Brooks: The Early Years: A Selection from His Works, 1908–1925,* ed. Claire Sprague (Boston: Northeastern University Press, 1993), 8; Rev. Thomas Brainerd, "A Day at Stratford-on-Avon," *Sartain's Magazine* (May 1850): 341–42.

141. Rufus Choate, "The Positions and Functions of the American Bar, as an Element of Conservatism in the State" (delivered in Cambridge, July 3, 1845), in *Addresses and Orations,* 156; George H. Calvert, *First Years in Europe* (Boston: William Spencer, 1866), 16.

142. Jacqueline Rose, *The Case of Peter Pan; or, The Impossibility of Children's Fiction* (London: Macmillan Press Ltd., 1984), 44. See also Carolyn Steedman, *Strange Dislocations: Childhood and the Idea of Human Interiority, 1780–1930* (Cambridge, MA: Harvard University Press, 1994); Roni Natov, *The Poetics of Childhood* (New York: Routledge, 2003); and Virginia L. Blum, *Hide and Seek: The Child between Psychoanalysis and Fiction* (Urbana: University of Illinois Press, 1995).

143. Olmsted, *Walks and Talks,* 89.

144. William James, *Talks to Teachers on Psychology and to Students on Some of Life's Ideals* (New York: W. W. Norton & Co., 1958), 73. On empiricism and childhood, see esp. Rose and Gillian Brown, *The Consent of the Governed: The Lockean Legacy in Early American Culture* (Cambridge, MA: Harvard University Press, 2001). See also Brown's "Child's Play," *differences: A Journal of Feminist Cultural Studies* 11, no. 3 (1999): 76–106.

145. Olmsted, *Walks and Talks,* 70.

146. Hall, "Discourse, 1847," 2:76.

147. Michael Paul Rogin, *Subversive Genealogies: The Politics and Art of Herman Melville* (Berkeley: University of California Press, 1983), 33.

148. "Travel in Europe," *North American Review* (April 1861): 550.

149. Brooks, "The Wine of Puritans," 8, 9.

150. Jacob Abbott, *Rollo in London* (Boston: Taggard & Thompson, 1854), 146–47; Brooks, "The Wine of Puritans," 8.

151. Putnam, *The Tourist in Europe,* 107. The Englishness of childhood in America is also taken up by Emerson in *English Traits.* The American, he says, on first visiting England, "finds himself among uncles, aunts and grandsires. The pictures on the chimney-tiles of his nursery were pictures of these people. Here they are in the identical costumes and the air which so took him" (801).

152. Everett's speech appears in part in *The American Speaker; or, Exercises in Rhetorick* (Boston: Cummings, Hilliard & Co., 1826), as cited in Ruth Miller Elson, *Guardians of Tradition: American Schoolbooks of the Nineteenth Century* (Lincoln: University of Nebraska Press, 1964), 121; the citation from the *Hillard Reader* appears in Elson, 123; references to Allston and Paulding in contemporary readers and spellers appear in Elson, 122–23. See also Charles Carpenter, *History of American Schoolbooks* (Philadelphia: University of Pennsylvania Press, 1963). For more on lessons of obedience in antebellum children's literature, see Anne Scott MacLeod, *American Childhood: Essays on Children's Literature of the Nineteenth and Twentieth Centuries* (Athens: University of Georgia Press, 1994). MacLeod writes, "Obedience was the most fundamental virtue for a child to acquire: few stories closed without at least one salute to its importance" (94).

153. On nursery rhymes and picture books, see esp., Gillian Avery, *Behold the Child: American Children and Their Books, 1621–1922* (Baltimore: Johns Hopkins University Press, 1994); Peter Hunt, ed., *Children's Literature: An Illustrated History* (New York: Oxford University Press, 1995); and Gloria T. Delamar, *Mother Goose, from Nursery to Literature* (Jefferson, NC: McFarland, 1987). See also John Absolon and Harrison Weir, *A Treasury of Pleasure Books for Young Children* (New York: D. Appleton & Co., 1853).

154. Samuel G. Goodrich, *Recollections of a Lifetime; or, Men and Things I Have Seen: In a Series of Familiar Letters to a Friend* (New York: Orton & Mulligan, 1856), 312, 314–17; Elizabeth Palmer Peabody, *Lectures in the Training School for Kindergartners* (Boston: D. C. Heath & Co, 1888), 211, and as cited in Brown, "Child's Play," 85.

155. See Edward H. Davidson and Claude M. Simpson, "Historical Commentary," in Nathaniel Hawthorne, *The American Claimant Manuscripts,* in vol. 12 of *The Centenary Edition of the Works of Nathaniel Hawthorne,* (Columbus: Ohio State University Press, 1977), 510; Nathaniel Hawthorne, "The Minister's Black Veil," in *Tales and Sketches* (New York: Library of America, 1982), 381. Several critics have observed Hawthorne's failure to dramatize his narrative sufficiently; see Edward H. Davidson, *Hawthorne's Last Phase* (New Haven, CT: Yale University Press, 1949); Richard H. Brodhead, *The School of Hawthorne* (New York: Oxford University Press, 1986), 67–69; and James T. Fields, *Hawthorne* (Boston: James R. Osgood & Co., 1876).

156. Hawthorne, *American Claimant Manuscripts,* 265–68. This volume includes three unfinished manuscripts on the subject of an American claimant to an English estate, as well as Hawthorne's marginalia and preliminary studies. The first of the untitled manuscripts was published as "The Ancestral Footstep" in the *Atlantic Monthly,* 1882–83; a heavily edited composite text of the other two manuscripts was published by Julian Hawthorne as *Doctor Grimshawe's Secret* in 1882. The volume's "Historical Commentary" contains a useful discussion of the texts' composition, 491–522. All subsequent references will be cited internally.

157. See Edmund Wilson, *Patriotic Gore: Studies in the Literature of the American Civil War,* Norton paperback ed. (New York: W. W. Norton & Co., 1994); Hawthorne, "Chiefly about War Matters," *Atlantic Monthly* (July 1862), 43; and *Our Old Home,* 4. All other references to this book will be cited internally.

158. George William Curtis, review of *The Works of Nathaniel Hawthorne* by Hawthorne, *North American Review* (October 1864), 539–57: "The character of his genius isolated him," says Curtis, "and he stood aloof from the common interests. . . . What other man of equal power, who was not intellectually constituted precisely as Hawthorne was, could have stood merely perplexed and bewildered, harassed by the inability of positive sympathy, in the vast conflict which tosses us all in its terrible vortex" (551–52).

159. Herman Melville, "Hawthorne and His Mosses," in *The Piazza Tales and Other Prose Pieces, 1839–1860,* ed. Harrison Hayford, Alma A. MacDougall, and G. Thomas Tansille (Evanston and Chicago: Northwestern University Press and Newberry Library, 1987).

160. Dicey in *Macmillan's Magazine* is cited by Curtis, review of *The Works of Nathaniel Hawthorne,* 554; Sacvan Bercovitch, *The Office of the Scarlet Letter* (Baltimore: Johns Hopkins University Press, 1991), 104.

161. Strong, *Diary,* 52.

162. Mark Twain, *The American Claimant and Other Stories and Sketches* (New York: Harper & Brothers, 1899), 346.

163. Ibid., 244.

164. Hawthorne points to this kind of purposeful return in an 1864 letter to Fields after the failure to produce his *Dolliver Romance.* It at least suggests that the escape to England might include a confrontation with "reality": "I am not low-spirited, nor fanciful, nor freakish, but look what seem to me realities in the face,

and am ready to take whatever may come. If I could but go to England now, I think that the sea-voyage and the 'old home' might set me all right" (cited in Henry James, *Hawthorne* [New York: Collier Books, 1966], 154).

165. Louisa May Alcott, *The Inheritance,* ed. Joel Myerson and Daniel Shealy (New York: Penguin Books, 1998), 142, 143. Alcott wrote this first, unpublished novel in 1849, at the age of seventeen.

166. Ibid., 12, 74.

167. Nathaniel Hawthorne, *Biographical Stories for Children* (1842), in *True Stories from History and Biography,* vol. 6 of *The Centenary Edition of the Works of Nathaniel Hawthorne,* ed. Charvat, Pearce, and Simpson, 248–49.

Chapter 2

1. George Ticknor Curtis, *The True Uses of American Revolutionary History: An Oration Delivered before the Authorities of the City of Boston, on Monday the Fifth of July, 1841* (Boston: Eastburn, 1841), 3, 4, and 7.

2. Richard Hildreth, *The History of the United States of America, from the Discovery of the Continent to the Organization of Government Under the Federal Constitution* (New York: Harper & Brothers, 1849), 1:iii–v.

3. David D. Van Tassel, *Recording America's Past: An Interpretation of the Development of Historical Studies in America, 1607–1884* (Chicago: University of Chicago Press, 1960), 103.

4. On antiquarianism and new archives, see Michael Kraus, *A History of American History* (New York: Farrar & Rinehart, 1937); Van Tassel, *Recording America's Past;* George H. Callcott, *History in the United States, 1800–1860* (Baltimore: Johns Hopkins University Press, 1970); Clifford L. Lord, ed., *Keepers of the Past* (Chapel Hill: University of North Carolina Press, 1965).

5. On the Whig interpretation of history, especially Sir Lewis Namier's critique of it along these lines, see Gordon S. Wood, "Rhetoric and Reality in the American Revolution," in *The Revolution That Wasn't: A Contemporary Assessment of 1776,* ed. Richard M. Fulton (Port Washington, NY: Kennikat, 1981), 123–45.

6. The figure of the "angel of history" famously appears in Walter Benjamin, "Theses on the Philosophy of History," in *Illuminations,* ed. Hannah Arendt, trans. Harry Zohn (New York: Schocken, 1968), 257–58. See also Benjamin's "Eduard Fuchs, Collector and Historian," in *One-Way Street and Other Writings,* trans. Edmund Jephcott and Kingsley Shorter (London: Verso, 1992), 349–86.

7. John Fanning Watson, *Annals of Philadelphia and Pennsylvania in the Olden Time: Being a Collection of Memoirs, Anecdotes, and Incidents of the City and Its Inhabitants and of the Earliest Settlements of the Inland Part of Pennsylvania from the Days of the Founders,* 2 vols. (Philadelphia: Elijah Thomas, 1857), 2:309–10. Watson published his annals in 1830 and expanded them in subsequent editions though 1877.

8. The phrase "professed historian" is from ibid., 2:279.

9. "It is this idea of continuity," writes George Bancroft, "which gives vitality to history. No period in time has a separate being; no public opinion can escape the

influence of previous intelligence. We are cheered by rays from former centuries, and live in the sunny reflection of all their light" (*History of the United States*, 10 vols. [Boston: Little, Brown, 1834–74], 4:9). On Motley, see David Levin, *History as Romantic Art: Bancroft, Prescott, Motley, and Parkman* (Stanford, CA: Stanford University Press, 1959), 27.

10. "Vague traditions" is Curtis's phrasing (*True Uses*, 9).

11. On the romantic historians as archivists, see esp. Peter Novick, *That Noble Dream: The "Objectivity Question" and the American Historical Profession* (Cambridge: Cambridge University Press, 1988).

12. Watson, *Annals of Philadelphia*, 2:279.

13. Callcott, *History in the United States*, 223.

14. Peter Force, preface to *American Archives: Consisting of a Collection of Authentick Records, State Papers, Debates, and Letters and Other Notices of Publick Affairs*, 9 vols. (Washington, DC: M. St. Clair Clarke and Peter Force, 1837–53); Benson J. Lossing, *Pictorial Field-Book of the Revolution; or, Illustrations, by Pen and Pencil, of the History, Biography, Scenery, Relics, and Traditions of the War for Independence*, 2 vols. (1850; reprint, New Rochelle, NY: Caratzas Brothers, 1976), 1:xxxii. On Ranke, see esp. Novick, *That Noble Dream*, 21–31. See also Hayden White, *Metahistory: The Historical Imagination in Nineteenth-Century Europe* (Baltimore: Johns Hopkins University Press, 1973), 163–90.

15. Bancroft as cited in Levin, *History as Romantic Art*, 27.

16. Thomas L. Haskell, *Objectivity Is Not Neutrality: Explanatory Schemes in History* (Baltimore: Johns Hopkins University Press, 1998), 145–73.

17. Srinivas Aravamudan, "The Return of Anachronism," *Modern Language Quarterly* 62, no. 4 (December 2001): 347; Roland Barthes, *Image, Music, Text*, trans. Stephen Heath (New York: Hill & Wang, 1977), 52–68; Reinhart Koselleck, *The Practice of Conceptual History: Timing History, Spacing Concepts*, trans. Todd Samuel Presner et al. (Stanford, CA: Stanford University Press, 2002), 125.

18. Bonnie Honig, *Political Theory and the Displacement of Politics* (Ithaca, NY: Cornell University Press, 1993), 163, 164, 180.

19. Haskell, *Objectivity Is Not Neutrality*, 150.

20. Watson, *Annals of Philadelphia*, 2:315.

21. James Chandler, *England in 1819: The Politics of Literary Culture and the Case of Romantic Historicism* (Chicago: University of Chicago Press, 1998), 173. Gordon S. Wood suggests that Bancroft's conception of the colonial past as integral to the nineteenth-century did not last. On early efforts to see colonial history as distinct from the rest of American history, see Wood, "The Relevance and Irrelevance of American Colonial History," in *Imagined Histories: American Historians Interpret the Past*, ed. Anthony Molho and Gordon S. Wood (Princeton, NJ: Princeton University Press, 1998), 144–63.

22. Curtis, *True Uses*, 19.

23. Famously attributed to Holmes by Isabel Leighton, "Meet Trouble as a Friend," in *A New Treasury of Words to Live By: Selected and Interpreted by Ninety Eminent Men and Women*, ed. William Nichols (New York: Simon & Schuster, 1959), 46.

24. Benson J. Lossing, *Seventeen Hundred and Seventy-Six; or, The War of Independence: A History of the Anglo-Americans, from the Period of the Union of the Colonies against the French, to the Inauguration of Washington, the First President of the United States of America* (New York: Walker, 1847), 243.

25. Lossing, *Pictorial Field-Book*, 1:79, 1:80, 1:37. See Philip Freneau's epic poem, "America Independent; and Her Everlasting Deliverance from British Tyranny and Oppression" (1778), in *Poems of Freneau*, ed. Harry Hayden Clark (New York: Hafner Publishing Co., 1968), 24–33.

26. Preceding quoted material can be found in Lossing, *Pictorial Field-Book*, 1:81.

27. Quoted in Ellet, *Domestic History of the American Revolution*, 90, 95.

28. See Friederike von Riedesel, *Letters and Journals relating to the War of the American Revolution, and the Capture of the German Troops at Saratoga* (1827), trans. William L. Stone (Albany, NY: Munsell, 1867), 136–37. General James Wilkinson is the first to translate Riedesel's Burgoyne anecdote and cites her in *Memoirs of My Own Times* (Philadelphia: Small, 1816); Lossing cites Riedesel as well in *Pictorial Field-Book*, 1:91. But the anecdote is recounted often. See, for example, Oliver Bunce, *Romance of the Revolution* (New York: Bunce & Brother, 1852), 249; James Thacher, *Military Journal during the American Revolutionary War, from 1775–1783, Describing Interesting Events and Transactions of This Period with Numerous Historical Facts and Anecdotes, from the Original Manuscript* (Boston: Richardson & Lord, 1823), 452; and William L. Stone, *Border Wars of the American Revolution* (New York: Harper & Brothers, 1843), 1:251–52.

29. Maurice Blanchot, *The Unavowable Community*, trans. Pierre Joris (Barrytown, NY: Station Hill, 1988); and Jean-Luc Nancy, *The Inoperative Community*, ed. Peter Connor, trans. Peter Connor (Minneapolis: University of Minnesota Press, 1990), 60. I allude here, with some irony, to Gordon S. Wood's argument in *The Radicalism of the American Revolution* (New York: Vintage, 1991).

30. Riedesel, *Letters and Journals*, 142–43; Ellet, *Domestic History*, 288–90.

31. Alexander Graydon, *Memoirs of His Own Time, with Reminiscences of the Men and Events of the Revolution*, ed. John Stockton Littell (Philadelphia: Lindsay & Blakiston, 1846), 283. See also Stephen Carl Arch, "Writing a Federalist Self: Alexander Graydon's *Memoirs of a Life*," *William and Mary Quarterly*, ser. 3, 52 (July 1995): 415–32.

32. I take Franklin's letter from Thomas J. Rogers, *A New American Biographical Dictionary; or Remembrancer of the Departed Heroes, Sages, and Statesmen of America* (Easton, PA: Rogers, 1823), 167. Franklin never sent the letter, but its frequent appearance in nineteenth-century collections of his work, including the one by Jared Sparks (1836–40), makes it an established part of the antebellum revolutionary archive I am discussing. For a fine treatment of the letter in its contemporary context, see Jay Fliegelman, *Declaring Independence: Jefferson, Natural Language, and the Culture of Performance* (Stanford, CA: Stanford University Press, 1993), 184–87.

33. J. G. A. Pocock, "Classical Theory of Deference," *American Historical Review* 81, no. 3 (June 1976): 522. See James Harrington, *The Commonwealth of Oceana* (1656), in *A System of Politics*, ed. J. G. A. Pocock (Cambridge: Cambridge University

Press, 1992). See also Howard Newby, "The Deferential Dialectic," *Comparative Studies in Society and History* 17, no. 2 (April 1975): 139–64.

34. Georg Simmel, "Sociability," in *On Individuality and Social Forms,* ed. Donald N. Levine (Chicago: University of Chicago Press, 1971), 139.

35. Franklin's advice to a chess player offers a similar sentiment: the "generous civility" that might cause you to "lose the game to your opponent," by offering him advice and correcting his poor moves, lets you win what is better: "his esteem, his respect, and his affection" (from "The Moral of Chess" [June 1779], in *Writings* [New York: Library of America, 1987], 927–31).

36. Ellen Glasgow, *The Woman Within* (New York: Harcourt, Brace & Co., 1954), 233.

37. All quotes of Graydon are from *Memoirs,* 284.

38. "Typical anomaly" is Chandler's phrase (*England in 1819,* 308).

39. Compare Moran's painting to John Trumbull's *Surrender of General Burgoyne* (1826) on the Capitol Rotunda, in which Burgoyne bows to Gates, or to the commemorative medal presented to Gates, as sketched in Lossing's *Pictorial Field-Book,* 1:240, which depicts the surrender much the same as Trumbull.

40. I allude to Susan Stewart's discussion of nostalgia in *On Longing: Narratives of the Miniature, the Gigantic, the Souvenir, the Collection* (Durham, NC: Duke University Press, 1993), 140.

41. William Taylor discovers a similar sentiment in antebellum novels of the colonial period: "Everything—English colonial policy and the improvident savage— must give way before the dynamic tide of European settlement" (*Cavalier and Yankee: The Old South and American National Character* [Cambridge, MA: Harvard University Press, 1979], 216).

42. Watson, *Annals of Philadelphia,* 2:287.

43. Elizabeth Lanesford Cushing, *Saratoga; a Tale of the Revolution* (Boston: Cummings, Hilliard & Co., 1824), 189.

44. Watson, *Annals of Philadelphia,* 2:288. See also John Richter Jones's description of the royal entry into Philadelphia in his novel, *The Quaker Soldier; or, The British in Philadelphia* (Philadelphia: T. B. Peterson & Brothers, 1858), 31–32.

45. Watson, *Annals of Philadelphia,* 2:279.

46. Ibid.

47. John H. Mancur, "La Meschianza," in *Tales of the Revolution* (New York: Colyer, 1844), 320.

48. See L. P. Hartley's novel *The Go-Between* (1953; reprint, New York: New York Review of Books, 2002), 17. David Lowenthal takes this line to describe a new sense of anachronism during the Romantic period in *The Past Is a Foreign Country* (Cambridge: Cambridge University Press, 1985), xvi. Chandler cites both Hartley and Lowenthal in his brilliant discussion of anachronism and historicism's efforts to date a cultural place, (*England in 1819,* 108–9).

49. William Gilmore Simms, *The Partisan: A Romance of the Revolution* (1853; reprint, New York: W. J. Widdleton, 1870), 345–49, passim.

50. Ibid., 443. On Marion's appearance, see also William Gilmore Simms, *The Life of Marion* (New York: Henry G. Langley, 1845), 177–78; and John Frost, *Life of General Marion: Embracing Anecdotes Illustrative of His Character* (Boston: Lee & Shepard, 1868).

51. James Kirke Paulding, *The Old Continental; or, The Price of Liberty* (New York: Paine & Burgess, 1846).

52. Simms, *The Partisan,* 113.

53. On the mezzotint's publication by the Apollo Association, see Mary Bartlett Cowdrey, *American Academy of Fine Arts and American Art-Union: Introduction, 1816–1852* (New York: New York Historical Society, 1953). The painting was later engraved by Currier and Ives.

54. Mason Locke Weems and Peter Horry, *The Life of General Francis Marion, a Celebrated Partisan Officer, in the Revolutionary War, against the British and Tories in South Carolina and Georgia* (1824; reprint, Winston-Salem, NC: John F. Blair, 2000), 141–44, passim; for Simms on Weems's language, see the preface to *Life of Marion.* Weems and Horry's anecdote was recounted frequently in antebellum historical novels and histories of the Revolution; see, e.g., Frost, *Life of General Marion;* Lossing, *Pictorial Field-Book,* 2:565; Paulding, *The Old Continental,* 171; Ellet, *Domestic History,* 228; Rogers, *A New American Biographical Dictionary,* 279–83. Reproductions of Blake's painting appear in, for example, *The Young American's Picture Gallery, with Seventy Illustrations* (Philadelphia: Lindsay & Blakiston, 1856), 66; and the *Boston Miscellany of Literature and Fashion* 1, no. 5 (May 1842): 236.

55. Simms, *Life of Marion,* 176–77.

56. Herman Melville, "The Paradise of Bachelors and the Tartarus of Maids," in *Herman Melville: Uncollected Prose* (New York: Library of America, 1984), 1262.

57. I allude specifically to Benjamin West's 1771 painting. Marion, like William Penn, stands with the English, to the right of half-clad "savages"—with his outstretched arm he also gestures left in an act of diplomacy.

58. Weems and Horry, *Life of General Francis Marion,* 139.

59. Catharine Maria Sedgwick, *The Linwoods; or, "Sixty Years Since" in America,* 2 vols. (New York: Harper & Brothers, 1835), 2:212–14.

60. Ibid., 215.

61. In William Gilmore Simms's romance, *Katharine Walton; or, The Rebel of Dorchester,* about the social life of occupied Charleston, an American officer urges his lover to go to town when he leaves for war: "You sigh Kate; but what the need? . . . you will find yourself in the enjoyment of society, of luxuries, gay scenes, and glorious spectacles; the ball, the rout, the revel, the parade" (New York: Redfield, 1854), 58. In *The Linwoods,* Sedgwick writes, "The gala days of Sir Henry's Clinton's reign in New-York are still celebrated in traditionary fire-side-stories, as a brilliant period in the colonial *beau-monde.* . . . Never, according to the grandmammas, was there such abundance of the elements of a belle's happiness—such music!—such dresses!—so many, and such admirers" (2:86). For more on loyalists and rebels crossing military lines to socialize, see Judith L. Van Buskirk, *Generous*

Enemies: Patriots and Loyalists in Revolutionary New York (Philadelphia: University of Pennsylvania Press, 2002).

62. Diana Treat Kilbourn, *The Lone Dove: A Legend of Revolutionary Times* (Philadelphia: Appleton, 1850), 128. Later in the century Anne Hollingsworth Wharton's *Through Colonial Doorways* (Philadelphia: J. B. Lippincott, 1893), a collection of historical anecdotes from the colonial and revolutionary periods, recalled similar scenes of festivity during the war. "The regular Assembly balls," Wharton writes, "seem to have been discontinued during the War of the revolution, though most of the time there was no lack of gaiety in Philadelphia, especially in Tory circles, as is shown by contemporaneous letters. Miss Franks writes to a friend in 1778, while the British were in possession of the city,—'You can have no idea of the life of continued amusement I live in. I can scarce have a moment to myself'" (217).

63. William Dunlap, *A History of the American Theater* (New York: J. & J. Harper, 1832), 45–46.

64. Graydon, *Memoirs of His Own Time*, 59.

65. For Graydon's politics, see Arch Littell and John Stockton Littell, introduction to *Memoirs*, esp. xvii–xxii; and Arch, "Writing a Federalist Self."

66. Aaron S. Fogelman, "From Slaves, Convicts, and Servants to Free Passengers: The Transformation of Immigration in the Era of the American Revolution," *Journal of American History* 85, no. 1 (June 1998): 43–76; Michael Zuckerman, "Tocqueville, Turner, and Turds: Four Stories of Manners in Early America," *Journal of American History* 85, no. 1 (June 1998): 13–42.

67. See Jesse Lemisch, "The American Revolution Seen from the Bottom Up," in *Towards a New Past: Dissenting Essays in American History,* ed. Barton J. Bernstein (New York: Pantheon Books, 1968), 40. In "The Nature of Deference and Demeanor" (*Interaction Ritual: Essays on Face-to-Face Behavior* [New York: Pantheon Books, 1967]), Erving Goffman distinguishes between deference as an asymmetrical relation and deference as a "sentiment of regard" between equals (58–60).

68. Jack P. Greene, "Society, Ideology, and Politics: An Analysis of the Political Culture of Mid-Eighteenth-Century Virginia," in *Society, Freedom, and Conscience: The American Revolution in Virginia, Massachusetts, and New York,* ed. Richard M. Jellison (New York: Norton, 1976), 14–76; Pocock, "Classical Theory of Deference"; Richard L. Bushman, *King and People in Provincial Massachusetts* (Chapel Hill: University of North Carolina Press, 1985).

69. Robert A. Gross, "The Impudent Historian: Challenging Deference in Early America," *Journal of American History* 85, no. 1 (June 1998), 93.

70. Zuckerman, "Tocqueville, Turner, and Turds," 16.

71. Buskirk, *Generous Enemies*, 85.

72. David Denby, "No Limit: Going Too Far in the Revolution, in Blaxploitation and in Gross-Out Comedy," *New Yorker,* July 3, 2000, 87.

73. Christopher Hitchens, *Blood, Class, and Nostalgia: Anglo-American Ironies* (New York: Farrar, Straus & Giroux, 1990), 180–99.

74. Jamie Malanowski, "The Revolutionary War Is Lost on Hollywood," *New York Times,* July 2, 2000, Living Arts Section, 9. Even Howard Fast, perhaps the most successful historical novelist of the twentieth century who dared to take on the Revolution, tends to villainize not the British but their allies—"the dreaded German Hessians." See *The Hessian* (New York: Morrow, 1972), as well as *The Crossing* (New York: Morrow, 1971), which was adapted for a 1999 film.

75. Caroline Matilda Kirkland, "Detached Thoughts about England," *Sartain's Magazine* (February 1849), 127.

76. David Ramsay, *The History of the Revolution,* vol. 1, ed. Lester H. Cohen (Indianapolis: Liberty Fund, 1990), 27. Cohen describes how these two justifications of the Revolution existed side by side in eighteenth-century accounts: historians hoped to show, on the one hand, how Britain had abused the constitutional privileges of the colonists, who were themselves Englishmen by natural right, and, on the other, how the colonists maintained a separate, parallel culture, alienated from Britain, from the very first American settlements. See Cohen, *The Revolutionary Histories: Contemporary Narratives of the American Revolution* (Ithaca, NY: Cornell University Press, 1980), 131–60; and Arthur H. Shaffer, *The Politics of History: Writing the History of the American Revolution, 1783–1815* (Chicago: Precedent Publishing, 1975).

77. George Washington Greene, *Historical View of the American Revolution,* 6th ed. (Boston: Houghton, Mifflin & Co., 1895), 17, 13. I quote from "Lecture I: Causes of the Revolution" (in *Historical View*), written for the conservative Lowell Institute in 1862.

78. Sedgwick, *The Linwoods,* 1:66 and 2:270.

79. George Washington Greene, "Lecture XI: Literature of the Revolution," in *Historical View,* 358–60.

80. Delia Bacon, *The Bride of Fort Edward: Founded on an Incident of the Revolution* (New York: Colman, 1939), 37.

81. John McClung, *Camden: A Tale of the South* (Philadelphia: Carey & Lea, 1830), 109.

82. Henry C. Van Schaack, *The Life of Peter Van Schaack, Embracing Selections from His Correspondence and Other Writings, during the American Revolution, and His Exile in England* (New York: Appleton, 1842), 166–67. Van Schaack is describing the famous "Mischianza," designed in large part by Major André in honor of Howe in 1778. I will return to this later.

83. McClung, *Camden,* 48. Emerson, *English Traits,* 834.

84. See Jones, *The Quaker Soldier,* 113.

85. An Officer, *Ambrose and Eleanor; or, The Disinherited Pair: A Tale of the Revolution* (New York: Clussman, 1834), 6.

86. An Officer, *Ambrose and Eleanor,* v; Jones, *Quaker Soldier,* 113.

87. The exchange takes place between the staunch patriot Allan M'Lane and the Quaker Caleb Hazelwood, who likes "a little of it," in Jones, *The Quaker Soldier,* 114.

88. Thacher, *Military Journal*, 116. The legend is also commemorated on a plaque erected by the Daughters of the American Revolution in 1903 at Park Avenue and 37th Street in New York. For more on the story, see Charles Monaghan, *The Murrays of Murray Hill* (Brooklyn: Urban History Press, 1998).

89. *Dearest Enemy*, based on a book by Herbert Fields, premiered September, 18, 1925, at the Knickerbocker Theatre in New York. Its plot revolves around an American girl who must choose between her country and her British lover. In the song "War Is War," a chorus of girls swoons over the handsome British officers who have occupied their neighborhood. "Hooray!" they cheer, "we're going to be compromised!" Edward Percy Moran also commemorates the anecdote in his painting, *Mrs. Murray's Strategy* (1908).

90. Baucom, *Out of Place*, 36.

91. David Cannadine, *Ornamentalism: How the British Saw Their Empire* (New York: Oxford University Press, 2001), 128.

92. Baucom, *Out of Place*, 7, 39.

93. An Officer, *Ambrose and Eleanor*, 16–18, 18.

94. Moore's preface claims that these materials from Whig and Tory papers, published during the Revolution, "present to the student of this day the same view the readers of the revolutionary period enjoyed." On the arrival of Prince William Henry, see Moore, *Diary of the American Revolution*, 2:499. Celebrations of the queen's birthday appear on 2:9 and 2:254.

95. James Fenimore Cooper, *The Spy: A Tale of the Neutral Ground* (New York: Penguin Books, 1997), 26 and 32.

96. Lossing, *Pictorial Field-Book*, 2:58.

97. On Carpenter's Hall, Lossing, *Pictorial Field-Book*, 2:58; on the disregard for revolutionary relics, 1:34. The rest I take from his preface, 1:viii.

98. Ibid., 1:35, 1:34, 1:viii.

99. Jones, introduction to *Quaker Soldier*, xxvii–xxix; also 166–67.

100. Elizabeth Fox-Genovese, "Psychohistory versus Psychodeterminism: The Case of Rogin's Jackson," *Reviews in American History* 3 (December 1975): 407–18, quote on 415.

101. Major John André, with the help of loyalist Oliver De Lancey, was architect of the affair, choreographing the pageants and designing the sets, scenery, and costumes. Watson remembers the Mischianza (*Annals of Philadelphia*, 1:279) just as he is describing the kind of historical anecdotes that resist the totalizing narratives of romantic history.

102. Howe is succeeded by Sir Henry Clinton. See Winthrop Sargent, *The Life and Career of Major John André, Adjutant-General of the British Army in North America* (Boston: Ticknor & Fields, 1861), 164–65. James M'Henry writes of Howe's capture of Philadelphia in his novel *Meredith; or, The Mystery of the Meschianza: A Tale of the American Revolution*: "It corrupted the martial spirit of that army by exposing it to the enervating influence of a gay and luxurious city, which, in fact, became the fascinating Capua that rendered the warlike officers of Britain effeminate, and her private soldiers impatient of discipline" ([Philadelphia, 1831], 187–88).

103. André's letter was published in the *Annual Register,* a London magazine, in 1778. Reprinted often in antebellum histories, it became the standard source on the Mischianza. See, for example, Lossing, *Pictorial Field-Book,* 2:97–101, as well as Lossing, *Seventeen Hundred and Seventy-Six,* 259; Watson, *Annals of Philadelphia,* 1:292; Sargent, *Life and Career of Major John André,* 167–77; Thomas Jones, *History of New York during the Revolutionary War, and the Leading Events of Other Colonies in That Period,* ed. Edward Floyd De Lancey (New York: New York Historical Society, 1879), 241–51. See also the facsimile of André's letter as it appears in a "Lady's Magazine" in *American Historical and Literary Curiosities; Consisting of Facsimiles of Original Documents relating to the Events of the Revolution,* ed. John Jay Smith and John F. Watson (New York: G. P. Putnam, 1861).

104. M'Henry, *Meredith,* 240, 225.

105. Sargent, *Life and Career of Major John André,* 178. The address, intended for recitation at the banquet by a "celestial guest," was not delivered because William Howe "wisely forbade" it (177).

106. Mancur, "La Meschianza," 363.

107. Ibid., 365.

108. Ibid., 371.

109. A fascination with the array of military colors and uniforms visible in American cities during the occupation appears throughout nineteenth-century accounts. "There was something," says one novel, "noble and pleasing in the aspect of the British officer, and to [the American's] unpracticed eye there could be nothing more seducing than the grace with which the glittering sword and epaulets set upon his elegant form" (Mary Elizabeth Moragne Davis, *The British Partizan: A Tale of Olden Time* [Macon, GA: Burke, Boykin & Co., 1864], 20).

110. John Trumbull, *Catalogue of Paintings, by Colonel Trumbull; Including Eight Subjects of the American Revolution as Included in Autobiography, Reminiscences and Letters of John Trumbull, from 1756 to 1841* (New York: Wiley & Putnam, 1841), 412. On the anecdote of Small and Warren as it appears in Trumbull's painting, see Graydon, *Memoirs of His Own Time,* 64, and on the anecdote more generally, Richard Frothingham, *History of the Siege of Boston, and the Battles of Lexington, Concord, and Bunker Hill,* 6th ed. (1849; reprint, Boston: Little, Brown, & Co., 1903), 172. For more on the painting, including the comments of Dunlap, see Helen A. Cooper's catalog *John Trumbull: The Hand and Spirit of a Painter* (New Haven, CT: Yale University Art Gallery, 1982), 48–51. Patricia M. Burnham offers an instructive reading of the picture in "John Trumbull, Historian: The Case of the Battle of Bunker's Hill," in *Redefining American History Painting,* ed. Patricia M. Burnham Burnham and Lucretia Hoover Giese (New York: Cambridge University Press, 1995), 37–53.

111. In February 1818, the *Analectic Magazine* published a description of the battle, giving credit to Israel Putnam as the commander of the American troops. In the March issue of *Portfolio,* General Henry Dearborn disagreed and set forth claims that William Prescott had headed the troops. The following month, in the same magazine, General Putnam's son entered the controversy on his father's behalf, and in June, Dearborn published a "vindication" of Prescott's role at the

battle. Daniel Webster later wrote an article for the *North American Review* making the case for Putnam. Consensus seemed to favor Putnam, until historians of the 1840s, cautiously analyzing the evidence, declared for Prescott. Most famous of these is Richard Frothingham, who returns to the debate in his *History of the Siege*. See also Daniel Webster, review of *An Account of the Battle of Bunker Hill*, by Henry Dearborn, and *A Letter to Major General Dearborn, Repelling His Unprovoked Attack on the Character of the Late Major General Israel Putnam*, Daniel Putnam, *North American Review* 7, no. 20 (July 1818): 225–58; and Tassel, *Recording America's Past*, 122–24. The Lossing reference may be found in *Pictorial Field-Book*, 1:550.

112. Lossing, *Pictorial Field-Book*, 1:547; Webster, review of *Account of the Battle of Bunker Hill* and *A Letter to Major General Dearborn*, as cited at length in Frothingham, *History of the Siege*, 204–6.

113. On the historical reasons for why the figure with Grosvenor is not Peter Salem, see especially Sidney Kaplan and Emma Nogrady Kaplan, *The Black Presence in the Era of the American Revolution* (Amherst: University of Massachusetts Press, 1989), 20–24.

114. J. R. Simms, *The American Spy; or, Freedom's Early Sacrifice: A Revolutionary Tale of New York, Founded Upon Fact* (Albany, NY: Munsell, 1846), 38.

115. Lossing, *Pictorial Field-Book*, 1:97.

116. Nathaniel Hawthorne, "Howe's Masquerade," in *Tales and Sketches*, ed. Roy Harvey Pearce (New York: Library of America, 1982), 628–29.

117. Ibid., 638–39.

118. Lossing, *Pictorial Field-Book*, 1:768; Sargent, *Life and Career of Major John André*, 446.

119. The "Ballad of Nathan Hale" appears in Frank Moore, *Songs and Ballads of the American Revolution* (New York: D. Appleton & Co., 1855), 134; Jared Sparks, "The Life and Treason of Benedict Arnold," in *The Library of American Biography, Conducted by Jared Sparks* (Boston: Hilliard, Gray, & Co., 1835), 3:306; Bunce, *Romance of the Revolution*, 179. Here is James Thacher on a similar note: "Whilst almost every historian of the Revolution has celebrated the virtues and lamented the fate of André, *Hale has remained unnoticed, and it is scarcely known that such a character ever existed*" (*Observations Relative to the Execution of Major André as a Spy, in 1780, Correcting Errors and Refuting False Imputations* [Boston: n.p., 1834], 11). C. Edwards Lester writes, "Let us see what England has done for her great men. . . . Even André the Spy was brought across the Atlantic by a solemn act of Parliament, and entombed by the side of heroes and over him breathes the marble of a great sculptor. And where does Hale—the American spy—a loftier and nobler character—sleep? Nobody appears to know except a few brave women of Connecticut, who are building his monument with their needles, and I need not say that every stitch is to our Government a stitch of shame!" (*The Artist, the Merchant, and the Statesman* [New York: Paine & Burgess, 1845], 2:129). On sympathy for André more generally, see the introduction to Caleb Crain, *American Sympathy: Men, Friendship, and Literature in the New Nation* (New Haven, CT: Yale University Press, 2001).

120. As quoted in Christopher Harris, *Public Lives, Private Virtues: Images of American Revolutionary War Heroes, 1782–1832* (New York: Garland Publishing, 2000), 64.

121. Samuel Woodworth, *The Widow's Son; or, Which Is the Traitor: A Melo-Drama, in Three Acts, as Performed at the New-York Park Theatre* (New York: Circulating Library and Dramatic Repository, 1825), 19, 17.

122. Sparks, "The Life and Treason," 153; Bacon, *The Bride of Fort Edward,* 173.

123. Bacon, The Bride of Fort Edward, 151.

124. Appadurai, *Modernity at Large,* 30. On the idea of an ancestral "Englishness," see also Tom Nairn, *Pariah: Misfortunes of the British Kingdom* (New York: Verso, 2002).

125. Tallmadge, as quoted in Sargent, *Life and Career of Major John André,* 369; André served as a drawing master for the son of his Quaker friend Caleb Cope— see Sargent, *Life and Career of Major John André,* 89. On Honora Sneyd, denied to André by "parental authority," see, for example, Jared Sparks, "The Life and Treason"; and Lossing, *Pictorial Field-Book,* 1:766; Henry Peterson, *Pemberton; or, One Hundred Years Ago* (Philadelphia: John C. Winston Co., 1872), 329; Sargent on André's "enterprise" (*Life and Career of Major John André*), 446.

126. Thacher, *Military Journal,* 275; On Hale's last words, George Lippard, *Washington and His Generals; or, Legends of the Revolution* (Philadelphia: T. B. Peterson, 1847), 264–70.

127. For an account of the Congressional debate on Paulding's pension and the public debates that followed, see Sargent, *Life and Career of Major John André,* 461–64; and Lossing, *Pictorial Field-Book,* 1:773–74. The three captors, John Paulding, Isaac Van Wart, and David Williams, were most famously defended by Egbert Benson in his *Vindication of the Captors of Major André* (New York: Kirk & Mercein, 1817), who stressed that their actions should be judged not by their unknowable motives but by their celebrated consequences. For critical discussion, see Robert E. Cray, Jr., "Major John André and the Three Captors: Class Dynamics and Revolutionary Memory Wars in the Early Republic, 1780–1831," *Journal of the Early Republic* 17 (1997): 371–99; Wayne Franklin's introduction to Cooper's *The Spy;* and Ann Uhry Adams, "Democracy, Regionalism, and the Saga of Major André," in *Redefining American History Painting,* ed. Burnham and Griese. Alexander Hamilton's response to André's execution may be found in Sargent, *Life and Career of Major John André,* 370.

128. Washington Irving, "The Legend of Sleepy Hollow," in *The Sketch-Book of Geoffrey Crayon, Gent.,* ed. Susan Manning (New York: Oxford University Press, 1996), 313.

129. Henry Peterson, *Pemberton,* 131, 136.

130. Thacher, *Observations,* 1–15; Buchanan's accusations are found on 6–7 and the account of Washington is on 10. For a reading of André's exhumation and the controversy that ensued, see Michael Meranze, "Major André's Exhumation," in *Mortal Remains: Death in Early America,* ed. Nancy Isenberg and Andrew Burstein (Philadelphia: University of Pennsylvania Press, 2003), 123–35.

131. William Gilmore Simms, "The Epochs and Events of American History, as Suited to the Purposes of Art in Fiction," in *Views and Reviews in American Literature, History and Fiction,* ed. C. Hugh Holman (1845; reprint; Cambridge, MA: Harvard University Press, Belknap Press, 1962), 56, 58; Cooper, *The Spy,* 302.

132. Simms, "Epochs," 56; Homi Bhabha, "Signs Taken for Wonders," 107.

133. Appadurai, *Modernity at Large,* 42.

134. Sarah Orne Jewett, *The Tory Lover* (Boston: Houghton, Mifflan & Co., 1901), 197.

135. Ned Thomas, *Derek Walcott: Poet of the Islands* (Cardiff: Welsh Arts Council, 1980), 21; and as quoted in Bruce King, "New Centres of Consciousness: New, Post-colonial, and International English Literature," in *New National and Postcolonial Literatures,* ed. Bruce King (Oxford: Clarendon Press, 1996), 26. See also Derek Walcott, "The Caribbean: Culture or Mimicry?" in *Critical Perspectives on Derek Walcott,* Robert D. Hammer (Washington, DC: Three Continents Press, 1993), 51–57.

136. Lydia Maria Child, *The Rebels; or, Boston before the Revolution* (1825; reprint, Boston: Phillips, Sampson & Co., 1850), 32.

137. Ibid., 53 and 85; James Fenimore Cooper, *The Pilot: A Tale of the Sea,* in *Sea Tales,* ed. Kay Seymour House and Thomas L. Philbrick (New York: Library of America, 1991), 67; Sedgwick, *The Linwoods,* 2:24; Cornwallis's "dignity" is described in Sargent, *Life and Career of Major John André;* and in Simms, *The Partisan,* 461. Burgoyne appears in Cooper's *Lionel Lincoln; or, The Leaguer of Boston,* ed. Donald A. Ringe and Lucy B. Ringe (Albany: State University of New York Press, 1984), as "the elegant and accomplished" (157).

138. Child, *The Rebels,* 34–49, passim. William Hubbard's history was saved from destruction in the fires at Hutchinson's house by Dr. Andrew Eliot and, later, donated by his son to the Massachusetts Historical Society, which published it in 1815. On the fate of Hutchinson's *History of Massachusetts-Bay,* see Bernard Bailyn, *The Ordeal of Thomas Hutchinson* (Cambridge, MA: Harvard University Press, Belknap Press, 1974), 35; and Kraus, *A History,* 115–17.

139. Child, *The Rebels,* 121; Child on *The Rebels* as quoted in Thomas Wentworth Higginson, *Contemporaries* (Boston: Houghton, Mifflin & Co., 1899), 166.

140. See the "Advertisement" to Jared Sparks, ed., *The Diplomatic Correspondence of the American Revolution* (Boston: N. Hale and Gray & Bowen, 1829), 1:vii–xii.

141. Peter Force, preface to *American Archives.*

142. "The Causes of the American Revolution," *North American Review* (April 1855), 390.

143. See Callcott, *History in the United States,* 50; and Kraus, *A History,* 176.

144. On the imperial historians, see Wood, "The Relevance and Irrelevance of American Colonial History," 151.

145. J. G. Herder, as cited in White, *Metahistory,* 76.

146. Charles Kendell Adams, "Some Neglected Aspects of the Revolutionary War," *Atlantic Monthly* 72 (1898): 177.

147. I derive my sense of Nietzsche on war from Samuel Weber, "Wartime," in *Violence, Identity, and Self-Determination,* ed. Hent de Vries and Samuel Weber (Stanford, CA: Stanford University Press, 1997), 92.

148. John Adams to Thomas Jefferson, July 3, 1813, in *The Adams-Jefferson Letters,* ed. Lester J. Capon (Chapel Hill: University of North Carolina Press, 1987), 349.

149. As cited in Henry C. Van Schaack, *The Life of Peter Van Schaack, LL.D., Embracing Selections from His Correspondence and Other Writings, during the American Revolution, and His Exile in England* (New York: D. Appleton & Co., 1842), 130.

150. Ibid., 300; Peter Van Schaack to John Jay, August 11, 1782, in ibid., 301; John Jay to Peter Van Schaack, September 17, 1782, in ibid., 302–3. My sense of Michelet is derived from White, *Metahistory,* 135–62.

151. Van Schaack to Jay, October 15, 1782, in *Life,* by H. C. Van Schaack, 303; Jay to Van Schaack, June 16, 1783, in *Life,* 307–8.

152. Watson, *Annals of Philadelphia,* 2:315, reflecting on the diary of "a widow lady of respectable character, of tory feelings and prejudices"; Lorenzo Sabine, *Biographical Sketches of Loyalists of the American Revolution, with an Historical Essay,* 2 vols. (Boston: Little, Brown, & Co., 1864), 1:88; Van Schaack to Jay, October 15, 1782, in *Life,* by H. C. Van Schaack, 304–5.

153. George Atkinson Ward, *Journals and Letters of the Late Samuel Curwen, Judge of Admiralty, Etc., an American Refugee in London, 1775–1784* (New York: C. S. Francis & Co., 1842), iii.

154. Sabine, *Biographical Sketches,* 1:515 and 1:442–43. The reluctance to rebel against a "benevolent" monarch that nineteenth-century antiquarians recovered from the archive has recently been confirmed by Brendan McConville in *The King's Three Faces: The Rise and Fall of Royal America, 1688–1776* (Chapel Hill: Omohundro Institute of Early American History and Culture and the University of North Carolina Press, 2006). "Theoretically," he writes, "a loving bond came to exist between every subject and the monarch, a tie that held the empire together" (107). He attributes the Revolution to the frustration of Americans not with the "imperial father" but with a "tyrannical Parliament" that excluded the colonies from full participation in the empire: "The desperate desire for place intensified as the imperial cult of monarchy spread the idea of the polity as a series of ruling fathers headed by a benevolent king. . . . This was one of the first empire's central truths, its strange equation—the ever-growing number of colonists wanted into the empire and wanted more patriarchy until the empire collapsed, a failure that grew in part from their desires" (247, 147).

155. Shaffer, *The Politics of History,* 122; "Sabine's *Sketches of Loyalists,*" *North American Review* (July 1847), 138; Sabine, *Biographical Sketches,* 1:442–43; Bernard Bailyn, ed., *Pamphlets of the American Revolution, 1750–1776* (Cambridge, MA: Harvard University Press, 1965), 1:90, x. See also Gordon Wood, "Rhetoric and Reality in the American Revolution," 138–39.

156. Sabine, *Biographical Sketches,* 1:62–68.

157. Nairn, *Enchanted Glass,* 98, 10.

158. George Chalmers, *An Introduction to the History of the Revolt of the American Colonies, Being a Comprehensive View of its Origin, Derived from the State Papers Contained in the Public Offices of Great Britain*, 2 vols. (Boston: J. Munroe & Co., 1845).

159. "Chalmers's *History of the American Revolution*," *North American Review* (April 1860), 368–93, quote on 370; Sparks's edition of Chalmers is quoted in John A. Schutz, "George Chalmers and *An Introduction to the History of the Revolt*"; and Lawrence Henry Gipson, "George Chalmers and the *Political Annals*," both in *The Colonial Legacy*, vol. 1, *Loyalist Historians*, ed. Lawrence H. Leder (New York: Harper & Row, 1971).

160. Lossing, *Pictorial Field-Book*, 1:126. See especially the introduction to Jon Butler, *Becoming America: The Revolution before 1776* (Cambridge, MA: Harvard University Press, 2000); as well as T. H. Breen, " 'Baubles of Britain': The American and Consumer Revolutions of the Eighteenth Century," in *Of Consuming Interests: The Style of Life in the Eighteenth Century*, ed. Cary Carson, Ronald Hoffman, and Peter J. Albert (Charlottesville: University Press of Virginia, 1994), 444–82; Breen, "Ideology and Nationalism on the Eve of the American Revolution: Revisions Once More in Need of Revising," *Journal of American History* 84 (1997): 13–39; Richard L. Bushman, *King and People in Provincial Massachusetts* (Chapel Hill: University of North Carolina Press, 1985); Wood, *Radicalism of the American Revolution*.

161. Van Schaack, *Life*, 61–62. For a more recent perspective on the American reluctance to rebel, see Mary Beth Norton, *The British-Americans: The Loyalist Exiles in England, 1774–1789* (New York: Little Brown, 1972).

162. Lossing, *Pictorial Field-Book*, 1:126; Moore, *Diary*, 1:169. On the persecution of loyalists, see also Jacob Bailey, *Frontier Missionary: A Memoir of the Life of the Reverend Jacob Bailey* (Boston: Ide & Dutton, 1863). Recent histories include Janice Potter, *The Liberty We Seek: Loyalist Ideology in Colonial New York and Massachusetts* (Cambridge, MA: Harvard University Press, 1983); and Norton, *The British-Americans*.

163. Thomas Balch, ed., *The Examination of Joseph Galloway, Esq., by a Committee of the House of Commons* (Philadelphia: Printed for the Seventy-Six Society, T. K. and P. G. Collins, 1855), 13, 11, 12.

164. On the position of the sitters and the painting's exhibition history, see Helmut von Erffa and Allen Staley, *The Paintings of Benjamin West* (New Haven, CT: Yale University Press, 1986), 571; Allen Staley, "From the New World to the Old," in *Benjamin West: American Painter at the English Court* (Baltimore: Baltimore Museum of Art, 1989), 31–33; and Kenneth Pearson and Patricia Connor, *1776: The British Story of the American Revolution* (London: Times Newspapers Ltd., 1976), 135–36. The quote on James Allen is taken from Pearson and Connor, *1776*, 135.

165. C. L. R. James, *Beyond a Boundary*, introduction by Robert Lipsyte (Durham, NC: Duke University Press, 1993).

166. Lossing, *Pictorial Field-Book*, 1:ix.

167. J. B. Jones, *The Monarchist: An Historical Novel, Embracing Real Characters and Romantic Adventures* (Philadelphia: A. Hart, 1853), 13.

168. Bacon, *The Bride of Fort Edward*, 156, 106, 162, 152.

169. Fliegelman, *Declaring Independence*, 137–44.

170. David Wilson, *The Life of Jane McCrea, with an Account of Burgoyne's Expedition in 1777* (New York: Baker, Godwin & Co., 1853), 38–41. See also Stone, *Border Wars,* 1:183; and Lossing, *Pictorial Field-Book,* 1:160.

171. Lossing refers not only to their violation of Burgoyne's orders but also to Indian desertions from the British cause (*Pictorial Field-Book,* 1:160). See also Robert Sears, *Pictorial History of the American Revolution* (New York: R. Sears, 1846), 252.

172. Stone, *Border Wars,* 1:183. Lossing, *Pictorial Field-Book,* 1:99. See also William L. Stone, "The Jane McCrea Tragedy," *Galaxy* (January–April 1867), 46–52.

173. Wilson, *The Life of Jane McCrea,* 86.

174. In *Our Country* (New York: Amies Pub. Co., 1888), Benson Lossing includes a picture of Jane McCrea falling from her horse after being shot by an American bullet. Her Indian guides stand innocently in front of the horse and look for the perpetrator (2:928). John Warner Barber illustrates a similar version of her death in *Historical Scenes in the United States* (New Haven, CT: Monson & Co., 1827), 40.

175. Bacon, *The Bride of Fort Edward,* 68.

176. Wilson, *The Life of Jane McCrea,* 34–35.

177. Ibid., 74–89, passim.

178. Jared Sparks, "The Life and Treason of Benedict Arnold," in *The Library of American Biography* (Boston: Hilliard, Gray, & Co., 1835), 3:107. See also Samuel Y. Edgerton, Jr., "The Murder of Jane McCrea: The Tragedy of an American *Tableau D'Histoire*," *Art Bulletin* 47, no. 4 (December 1965): 481–92.

179. Stewart, *On Longing,* 135; Wilson, *The Life of Jane McCrea,* 119. For a similar portrait of Jones, see Lossing, *Pictorial Field-Book,* 1:101.

180. Ann Douglas, *The Feminization of American Culture* (New York: Anchor Books, 1977). All citations are from the chapter entitled, "The Escape from History: The Static Imagination," 165–99, passim.

181. Child, *The Rebels,* 129; Sedgwick, *The Linwoods,* 238 and 59.

182. Sedgwick, *The Linwoods,* 59; Lossing, *Pictorial Field-Book,* 1:77. See also Buskirk, *Generous Enemies,* on the issuing of passports to women, 63–68.

183. Sargent, *Life and Career of Major John André,* 151; Moore, *Diary,* 2:387.

184. See Susanna Rowson, *Charlotte Temple,* ed. Ann Douglas (New York: Penguin Books, 1991); An Officer, *Ambrose and Eleanor,* iii. In his novel, *The Refugee,* James Jones describes the ease with which such courtships took place: "During the occupancy of 'York Island by the British, various expedients were resorted to whereby communication might be kept up . . . for the rightly conducting the love affairs of the royal officers" (New York: Wilder & Campell, 1925), 302.

185. James E. Heath, *Edge-Hill; or, The Family of the Fitzroyals: A Novel, by a Virginian* (Richmond: White, 1828), 1:42.

186. Cooper, *The Pilot,* 22 and 416

187. Jewett, *The Tory Lover,* 79.

188. Lossing, *Pictorial Field-Book,* 1:69. Narratives in which the anecdote appears include Ellet, *Domestic History,* 87; Thacher, *Military Journal,* 439; Stone, *Border Wars,* 245. For fictionalized accounts, see Elizabeth Cushing's historical romance, *Saratoga,* 85–89; and James McClung's *Camden,* 2:38–48.

189. Thomas Jefferson, "Declaration of Independence," in *Autobiography* in *The Life and Selected Writings of Thomas Jefferson,* ed. Adrienne Koch and William Peden (New York: Modern Library, 1998), 27; Sedgwick, *The Linwoods,* 2:85 and 2:286.

Chapter 3

1. Alexander Crummell to John Jay, August 9, 1848, in *The Black Abolitionist Papers,* vol. 1, *The British Isles, 1830–1865,* ed. C. Peter Ripley et al. (Chapel Hill: University of North Carolina Press, 1985), 143.

2. Julian Barnes, *England, England* (New York: Alfred A. Knopf, 1999).

3. "Queen Victoria's Birth-day Drawing-Room," *Frederick Douglass' Paper,* June 16, 1854; Samuel Ringgold Ward, *The Autobiography of a Fugitive Negro: His Anti-Slavery Labors in the United States, Canada, & England,* (1855; reprint, Chicago: Johnson Publishing Co., Inc., 1970), 235. Subsequent citations to Ward will be internal, unless specifying a periodical or journalistic source.

4. Review of *What I Saw in London; or, Men and Things in the Great Metropolis,* by David W. Bartlett, *Frederick Douglass' Paper,* June 3, 1852.

5. See Paul Gilroy, *The Black Atlantic: Modernity and Double Consciousness* (Cambridge, MA: Harvard University Press, 1993). While recalling the response of a large number of black abolitionists to Britain, I discuss a somewhat select group from among those who traveled there between 1830 and 1865. These include William G. Allan, Henry "Box" Brown, William Wells Brown, Ellen Craft, William Craft, Alexander Crummell, Paul Cuffe, William H. Day, Martin Delany, Frederick Douglass, Robert Douglass, William L. Douglass, Henry Highland Garnet, Nathaniel Paul, James W. C. Pennington, Robert Purvis, Charles Lenox Remond, Sarah Remond, Prince Saunders, James McCune Smith, and Samuel Ringgold Ward. For a more specific detailing of blacks abroad and the scope of their abolitionist activities, see the introduction to *Black Abolitionist Papers,* ed. Ripley et al.; and R. J. M. Blackett, *Building an Antislavery Wall: Black Americans in the Atlantic Abolitionist Movement, 1830–1860* (Baton Rouge: Louisiana State University Press, 1983).

6. Given that *Frederick Douglass' Paper* had a significantly white audience—much the same as Garrison's *Liberator*—what follows will address how such ascriptions to Englishness not only function within black abolitionist culture but also serve as points of identification with a specifically white affection for England. While my concern here is with the paper's cultural and political interest in England, there were perhaps black readers for whom such ties to the country would ring a more genealogical bell—those of mixed race with quite overt claims on an "old" English heritage or Great Britain as "motherland." These claims point to other aspects of black Anglophilia in the period that I address a bit later.

7. Ward, *Autobiography,* 170. This is not to deny partisanship within the movement but to suggest that the black abolitionist response to Britain is remarkably consistent. While I am focusing on what this meant for antislavery in the United States, others describe how the cooperative organizing and joint work of blacks

in Britain tended to disregard sectarian differences back home, with Garriso-
nians and anti-Garrisonians displaying, in Blackett's words, "a startling degree
of unanimity" (*Building an Antislavery Wall*, 123). For Blackett, "the fact that
black visitors were affiliated with one or the other wing of the moment was of little significance" (119). This point is also pursued by *Black Abolitionist Papers*, ed.
Ripley et al.

8. See, for example, "Lady Jane and Bishop Gardiner," *Colored American*, August
15, 1840; Julia Griffiths Crofts, "Letters from the Old World—No. LXXV," *Douglass'
Monthly*, August 1861.

9. "Journal of Mary Powell," *North Star*, August 24, 1848.

10. "Prejudice against Color," *Frederick Douglass' Paper*, February 2, 1855. Other
examples of this abolitionist interest in a historicized England include "An English Landscape," *North Star*, June 9, 1848; or William Wells Brown's descriptions of
Tintern Abbey in *The American Fugitive in Europe: Sketches of Places and People Abroad*
(1855), in *The Travels of William Wells Brown, including "The Narrative of William Wells
Brown, a Fugitive Slave," and "The American Fugitive in Europe: Sketches of Places and
People Abroad,"* ed. Paul Jefferson (New York: Markus Wiener Publishing, Inc.,
1991), 144–45.

11. William G. Allen to William Lloyd Garrison, "Letter from Prof. Wm. G. Allen," *Liberator*, July 22, 1853, 116.

12. Brown, *American Fugitive*, 188.

13. Frederick Douglass, *Life and Times of Frederick Douglass* (1893), in *Autobiographies* (New York: Library of America, 1994), 929.

14. Douglass takes his name from the hero of Walter Scott's *The Lady of the Lake*.
For a good discussion, see Alasdair Pettinger, "Send Back the Money: Douglass and
the Free Church of Scotland," in *Liberating Sojourn: Frederick Douglass and Transatlantic Reform*, ed. Alan J. Rice and Martin Crawford (Athens: University of Georgia
Press, 1999), 31–55. I return to ex-slaves in Scotland a bit later.

15. Ward describes his family's "deliverance" from slavery at the beginning of
his narrative; see Ward, *Autobiography*, 14–19.

16. Frederick Douglass, *My Bondage and My Freedom* (1855), in *Autobiographies*,
373–74.

17. Ward, *Autobiography*, 235.

18. Edward W. Said, *Orientalism* (New York: Vintage Books, 1978), 72.

19. Brown, *American Fugitive*, 209–16; and Ward, *Autobiography*, 216–17.

20. Charles Sumner, *Memoir and Letters of Charles Sumner*, vol. 2, *1838–1845*, ed.
Edward L. Pierce (Boston: Roberts Brothers, 1893), 41.

21. Julia Griffiths Crofts, "Letters from the Old World—No. LXXVII," *Douglass'
Monthly*, November 1861, 549–50.

22. "Royal Visits to Liverpool and Manchester," *Frederick Douglass' Paper*, October
2, 1851.

23. Sumner, *Memoir and Letters of Charles Sumner*, 2:41.

24. Ibid., 2:15.

25. "Queen Victoria's Birth-day Drawing-Room," *Frederick Douglass' Paper,* June 16, 1854; Nathaniel Parker Willis, "Jottings Down in London," *Corsair,* August 17, 1839, 361.

26. Horace Greeley, *Glances at Europe* (New York: Dewitt & Davenport, Publishers, 1851), 84; Alexander Crummell, *Civilization and Black Progress: Selected Writings of Alexander Crummell on the South,* ed. J. R. Oldfield (Charlottesville: University Press of Virginia, for the Southern Texts Society, 1995), 12.

27. Brown, *American Fugitive,* 221.

28. Harriet Beecher Stowe, *Sunny Memories of Foreign Lands* (Boston: Phillips, Sampson, & Co., 1854); Sumner, *Memoir and Letters of Charles Sumner,* 1:327.

29. George P. Putnam, *The Tourist in Europe; or, A Concise Summary of the Various Routes, Objects of Interest, &c. in Great Britain, France, Switzerland, Italy, Germany, Belgium, and Holland* (New York: Wiley & Putnam, 1838), 175. Catharine Maria Sedgwick writing to the *National Anti-Slavery Standard* from England relates a similar surprise: "Our coachman," she says, "(who, after our telling him we were Americans, had complimented us on our speaking English, and 'a very good English too,') professed an acquaintance of some twenty years standing with Miss Mitford" (April 13, 1843, 180). The comments appear again in Sedgwick's *Letters from Abroad to Kindred at Home* (New York: Harper & Brothers, 1841), 46.

30. "Emma," November 19, 1997, episode of *Ellen,* videocassette ([New York]: A&E Home Videos, 2006).

31. Rufus Choate, *Addresses and Orations,* 6th ed. (Boston: Little, Brown, & Co., 1891), 37; Sumner, *Memoir and Letters of Charles Sumner,* 2:177.

32. Brown, *American Fugitive,* 223; "Trollope's North America," *North American Review* (October 1862): 417.

33. Samuel Ringgold Ward, "Letter from an Englishman," *Colored American,* April 4, 1840; Joseph Story to Charles Sumner, in *Memoir and Letters of Charles Sumner,* 2:10.

34. Letter from William Wells Brown to Wendell Phillips, August 8, 1851, in "A Sampler from the Blagdon Papers," in Irving H. Bartlett, *Wendell and Ann Phillips: The Community of Reform, 1840–1880* (New York: W. W. Norton & Co., 1979), 128; Julia Griffiths, "Letters from the Old World—Number IX," *Frederick Douglass' Paper,* December 7, 1855. Griffiths was secretary of the Rochester Ladies' Anti-Slavery Society. Her column appeared monthly.

35. "The Farewell," *Morning Herald,* May 1, 1838; Emerson, *English Traits,* 785; Ward, *Autobiography,* 175.

36. Sumner, *Memoir and Letters of Charles Sumner,* 2:78.

37. Alexis de Tocqueville, *Democracy in America,* vol. 2, *1840,* ed. Phillips Bradley (New York: Vintage Classics, 1990), 228.

38. Sumner, *Memoir and Letters of Charles Sumner,* 2:78 and 81.

39. James McCune Smith, introduction to *My Bondage and My Freedom* (1855) by Frederick Douglass, in *Autobiographies,* 130.

40. Emerson, "The American Scholar," from *Nature: Addresses, and Lectures,*

NOTES TO PAGES 194–197 ❦ 361

in *Essays and Lectures,* ed. Joel Porte (New York: Library of America, 1983), 54; Smith, introduction to *My Bondage and My Freedom,* by Douglass, 129–30. For a fine discussion of the relationship, in Douglass, between cosmopolitanism, ethical judgment, and civic virtue, see Gregg D. Crane's chapter "Cosmopolitan Constitutionalism," in *Race, Citizenship, and Law in American Literature* (New York: Cambridge University Press, 2002). Crane evocatively links Douglass's universalism, inspired in part by his first trip to England, to his antislavery constitutionalism and belief in higher law.

41. Frederick Douglass, *Life and Times of Frederick Douglass* (1893), in *Autobiographies* (New York: Library of America, 1994), 690.

42. Douglass, *My Bondage and My Freedom,* 370.

43. Smith, introduction to *My Bondage and My Freedom,* by Douglass, 132.

44. See Henry Louis Gates, Jr., *The Signifying Monkey: A Theory of African American Literary Criticism* (New York: Oxford University Press, 1988), 129.

45. William Wells Brown, *The Black Man, His Antecedents, His Genius, and His Achievements* (New York: Thomas Hamilton, 1863), 244; Abigail Mott, *Narratives of Colored Americans* (New York: William Wood & Co., 1875), 47.

46. Sumner, *Memoir and Letters of Charles Sumner,* 2:41 and 65.

47. See Russell Jacoby, *The Last Intellectuals: American Culture in the Age of Academe* (New York: Basic Books, 1987); William Wells Brown, "Letter from William Wells Brown," *Frederick Douglass' Paper,* October 2, 1851.

48. Ross Posnock, "How It Feels to Be a Problem: Du Bois, Fanon, and the 'Impossible Life' of the Black Intellectual," *Critical Inquiry* 23, no. 2 (Winter 1997): 324; Stanley Crouch, as quoted in Robert S. Boynton, "The New Intellectuals," *Atlantic Monthly,* March 1995, 53–67. See Kwame Anthony Appiah, "Cosmopolitan Patriots," *Critical Inquiry* 23, no. 3 (Spring 1997): 617–39; Martha Nussbaum, "Patriotism or Cosmopolitanism," *Boston Review* 19, no. 5 (October–November 1994): 3–6; Ross Posnock, *Color and Culture: Black Writers and the Making of the Modern Intellectual* (Harvard, MA: Cambridge University Press, 1998); Julia Kristeva, *Nations without Nationalism,* trans. Leon Roudiez (New York: Columbia University Press, 1993); Cornel West, "The Dilemma of the Black Intellectual" in *Breaking Bread: Insurgent Black Intellectual Life,* ed. bell hooks and Cornel West (Boston: South End Press, 1991). Nussbaum's *Boston Review* essay leads off an issue devoted to responses and arguments with her position; the discussion provides a useful sense of the central terms in the present debate about cosmopolitanism and nationalism.

49. "Longfellow's *Kavanagh:* Nationality in Literature," *North American Review,* July 1849, 196–216.

50. Douglass, *Life and Times,* 687; James Jackson Jarves, *Art-Hints* (New York: Harper & Brothers, 1855), 18; Douglass, "Speech before American and Foreign Anti-Slavery Society, May 1854," as quoted by Smith, introduction to *My Bondage and My Freedom,* by Douglass, 128; Andrew Ross, as quoted in Bruce Robbins, *Intellectuals: Aesthetics, Politics, and Academics* (Minneapolis: University of Minnesota

Press, 1990), 125; Irving Howe, as quoted in Boynton, "New Intellectuals," 54. See also Andrew Ross, *No Respect: Intellectuals and Popular Culture* (New York: Routledge, 1989).

51. Pauline Hopkins, *Contending Forces: A Romance Illustrative of Negro Life North and South,* introduction by Richard Yarborough (1900; reprint, New York: Oxford University Press, 1988), 125, 385. Dora's Briticisms appear throughout, but the best examples may be found in the section entitled "Ma Smith's Lodging-House," 80–113.

52. Appiah, "Cosmopolitan Patriots," 625.

53. "Extracts from Stowe's New Book: *Sunny Memories of Foreign Lands,*" *Frederick Douglass' Paper,* August 18, 1854.

54. Caroline M. Kirkland, "Detached Thoughts about England," *Sartain's Magazine* (May 1849), 127; Brown, *American Fugitive,* 141.

55. Brown, *American Fugitive,* 227; "Letter from 'Cosmopolite,'" *Frederick Douglass' Paper,* August 31, 1855. See also *Frederick Douglass' Paper,* March 16, 1855. Letters from the "Cosmopolite," or his titular son, "Cosmopolite, Jr.," appear every few months.

56. James McCune Smith, "The German Invasion," *Anglo-African Magazine* (February 1859), reprinted in *The Anglo-African Magazine* (New York: Arno Press, 1968), 45; "The True British Feeling," *Douglass' Monthly,* March 1863, 81; Charles Sumner to George Sumner, July, 6, 1842, in Sumner, *Memoir and Letters of Charles Sumner,* 2:213.

57. Eric Lott, *Love and Theft: Blackface Minstrelsy and the American Working Class* (New York: Oxford University Press, 1993), 137. I take from Lott's chapter, "'Genuine Negro Fun': Racial Pleasure and Class Formation in the 1840s." William Pease, a fugitive slave in Canada, pursues a similar logic when he writes, "Almost all the colored people that I know are doing well. It was so in London, where I stopped a while, and it is so here. There is some prejudice here among the low class of people, but it has not the effect here it has in the States, because here a colored man is regarded as a man" (in Benjamin Drew, ed., *The North-side View of Slavery: The Refugee; or, The Narratives of Fugitive Slaves in Canada Related by Themselves* [Boston: John P. Jewett & Co., 1856], 130).

58. It is worth remembering that Douglass, Crummell, and Ward pursued a particularly decorous course of antislavery in Great Britain, aimed at both noble benefactors and the genteel tastes of their audience. It is perhaps just this manner of polite performance on the antislavery circuit, and its reception by the British elite, that wrought such effects back home. But this is not the whole story of black abolitionists in Britain. A useful counterpoint can be found, for example, in Marcus Wood's discussion of Henry Box Brown who, in his showy antics—spectacular reenactments of his escape from a "box," performed with song, a panorama, and moments of comedy—promoted the cause in Great Britain through a program of popular entertainment and mass response that offended the most "respectable" abolitionists. See Wood, *Blind Memory: Visual Repre-*

sentations of Slavery in England and America, 1780–1865 (New York: Routledge, 2000), 103–17.

59. Frederick Douglass, *Narrative of the Life of Frederick Douglass* (1845) in *Autobiographies*, 40.

60. "Mr. Frederick Douglass and Slavery," as reprinted from the *London Christian Witness* in the *Liberator,* July 2, 1847, 112.

61. I cite this passage from a "Letter" to the *Liberator* included in Douglass, *My Bondage and My Freedom*, 373.

62. I do not propose that all abolitionists were a ready audience. Members of the movement who linked the cause to Protestant revivalism and a larger agenda of moral reform would not have moved in these circles, including, for example, many influenced by evangelist Charles G. Finney. The "proclerical faction" of female abolitionists in Boston—mostly middle-class Congregationalists and Baptists—especially took issue with the "high" culture of antislavery I am describing here. See Debra Gold Hansen, *Strained Sisterhood: Gender and Class in the Boston Female Anti-Slavery Society* (Amherst: University of Massachusetts Press, 1993); and Ronald G. Walters, *The Antislavery Appeal: American Abolitionism after 1830* (Baltimore: Johns Hopkins University Press, 1976), 37–45.

63. Edmund Quincy to Richard Webb, May 23, 1846, quoted in Irving H. Bartlett, *Wendell Phillips: Brahmin Radical* (Boston: Beacon Press, 1961), 103.

64. For Edward T. Channing on "English English," see Ronald Story, *The Forging of an Aristocracy: Harvard and the Boston Upper Class, 1800–1870* (Middletown, CT: Wesleyan University Press, 1980), 112; Wendell Phillips to Sarah Phillips, July 24, 1840, as quoted in James Brewer Stewart, *Wendell Phillips: Liberty's Hero* (Baton Rouge: Louisiana State University Press, 1986), 80.

65. Thomas Wentworth Higginson, *Wendell Phillips* (Boston: Lee & Shepard, 1884), x; Henry David Thoreau, "A Plea for Captain John Brown" (1860), in *Collected Essays and Poems* (New York: Library of America, 2001), 397.

66. Emerson as quoted in Bartlett, *Wendell Phillips*, 192; Higginson, *Wendell Phillips,* xv. George William Curtis's eulogy for Phillips describes him as "a figure of patrician port, of sovereign grace,—a prince coming to his kingdom" (*A Memorial of Wendell Phillips from the City of Boston* [Boston, 1884]). Higginson and Curtis also managed to expropriate a specifically Southern language of "Cavaliers"—one that derived from Walter Scott and insisted, for example, on the likeness of Southern planters to English squires—for the Northern antislavery cause. The descriptions of Phillips, with their reiterated appeal of English ancestry and Cavalier honor, look surprisingly like the aristocratic pretensions of plantation novels. I return to this point later. See William R. Taylor, *Cavalier and Yankee: The Old South and American National Character* (New York: George Braziller, 1961).

67. See Lawrence Lader, *The Bold Brahmins: New England's War against Slavery: 1831–1863* (New York: E. P. Dutton & Co., Inc., 1961), 180–82.

68. As cited in Quincy-Phillips letters, 1848 and 1849, in Stewart, *Wendell Phillips*, 128–30.

69. William Mountford, "A Voice from America," reprint from the *London Inquirer* in the *Liberator*, August 15, 1851.

70. George Calvert, *The Gentleman* (Boston: Ticknor & Fields, 1863). The citations, in order, are from 116, 28, 113, 138, 151, 147.

71. See Pierre Bourdieu, *Distinction: A Social Critique of the Judgment of Taste* (Cambridge, MA: Harvard University Press, 1984), 55.

72. Grund, *Aristocracy in America*, 150, 149, 52, 53.

73. For the story of Preston and Sumner, see David M. Potter, *The Impending Crisis: 1848–1861* (New York: Harper Torchbooks, 1976), 209–11, 220–21; on chivalry in the antebellum South and North, see Taylor, *Cavalier and Yankee;* and John Fraser, *America and the Patterns of Chivalry* (Cambridge: Cambridge University Press, 1982).

74. As quoted in Bartlett, *Wendell Phillips*, 25. How glad Phillips would have been to have seen the movement characterized in the following way by the British press years later:

> Yet, in spite of all that America has done or can do to deface images of self-sacrifice and beauty, there are chosen souls in her own borders who have fulfilled the heroic ideals of the olden time. The Abolitionists of New England encountered great perils when they first set out to redress the great human wrong of negro slavery, and they fought as noble a context against organised iniquity as any knight of ARTHUR's Court. They faced political obloquy, mob violence, loss of limb, sometimes of life, and the falling away of friends and relatives, because they had inherited the old instinct of knights, to lead lives of duty to their fellow-men. . . . Coward souls at the North said, "It will cost much money and many lives to reconquer the South: let them go; let the Republic break up; what is a country to us?" but a chivalry that came down from British ancestors animated the men who followed GRANT, and they kept to their high purpose until the field was won.

(*Daily Telegraph,* January 13, 1890, as cited in *Mark Twain: The Critical Heritage*, ed. Frederick Anderson and Kenneth M. Sanderson [New York: Barnes & Noble, 1971], 162). I am grateful to Amanda Claybaugh for bringing this to my attention.

75. Harriet Martineau, *Harriet Martineau's Autobiography: With Memorials by Maria Weston Chapman* (London: Smith, Elder & Co., 1877), 2:37. The extensive account of Martineau's experiences among American abolitionists is on 2:22–83 of her text.

76. Maria Weston Chapman, "Memorials," in ibid., 3:98–99.

77. Henry Adams, *The Education of Henry Adams: An Autobiography*, ed. Ernest Samuels (Boston: Houghton Mifflin Co., 1973), 19.

78. Chapman, "Memorials," 3:99.

79. Higginson, *Wendell Phillips*, xv.

80. Edwin Arlington Robinson, *Selected Poems of Edwin Arlington Robinson*, ed.

Morton Dauwen Zabel, introduction by James Dickey (New York: Collier Books, 1965), 85.

81. Chapman, "Memorials," 3:260–71. William Wells Brown describes his own response to visiting Martineau's home in *American Fugitive*, 160–61.

82. Charles Sumner to George Sumner, October 22, 1850, *Memoir and Letters of Charles Sumner*, 3:218.

83. Harriet Beecher Stowe, "A Day Spent at Playford Hall," in *Autographs for Freedom*, ed. Julia Griffiths (Rochester, NY: Wanzer, Beardsley & Co., 1854), 279.

84. Stowe, "A Day Spent at Playford Hall," 277; Sumner, *Memoir and Letters*, 2:36.

85. As quoted in Bartlett, *Wendell Phillips*, 62. See also Mrs. S. C. Hall, "Miss Edgeworth at Edgeworthstown," *National Anti-Slavery Standard*, March 2, 1843, 156; "Burns," *National Anti-Slavery Standard*, November 16, 1843, 96; and James Mott, *Three Months in Great Britain* (Philadelphia: J. Miller M'Kim, 1841), 26, as quoted in a note in Lucretia Mott, *Slavery and "The Woman Question": Lucretia Mott's Diary of Her Visit to Great Britain to Attend the World's Anti-Slavery Convention of 1840*, ed. Frederick B. Tolles (Philadelphia: Friends' Historical Association, 1952), 33.

86. Ann Phillips to Maria Weston Chapman, July 30, 1839, quoted in Bartlett, *Wendell Phillips*, 62.

87. Sumner, *Memoir and Letters of Charles Sumner*, 2:34.

88. Wendell Phillips to Elizabeth Pease, March 9, 1851, quoted in Bartlett, *Wendell Phillips*, 154.

89. David S. Shields, *Civil Tongues and Polite Letters in British America* (Williamsburg and Chapel Hill: University of North Carolina Press for the Institute of Early American History and Culture, 1997). Shields's chapter on "metropolitan conversation" is particularly useful here (11–54).

90. The fact that Garrison's "royal time" appears most immediately in the context of a successful antislavery meeting only makes it more intriguing: "On Thursday evening, Douglass and I held a meeting in Kirkcaldy, which was got up in the course of a few hours. Notwithstanding the haste, and that everyone present had to pay for admission, we had six or eight hundred present; and a 'royal time' we had of it." How do we gauge the appropriateness of measuring an abolitionist event by how much it was personally enjoyed? The festivity surrounding American antislavery in Britain is my main concern here. See William Lloyd Garrison, letter to Richard Webb, October 24, 1846, in *The Letters of William Lloyd Garrison*. vol. 3, *No Union with Slaveholders*, ed. Walter M. Merrill (Cambridge, MA: Harvard University Press, Belknap Press, 1973), 442.

91. James Haughton, "A Voice from Erin," in *The Liberty Bell* (Boston: National Anti-Slavery Bazaar, 1842), 70.

92. Parker Pillsbury, "Letter from Parker Pillsbury," *Liberator*, July 28, 1854, 119.

93. Mrs. Houstoun, "American Manners and British Critics," reprint from the *London Athenaeum*, in the *National Anti-Slavery Standard*, February 6, 1845, 144.

94. William Mountford, "A Voice from America," reprint from the *London Inquirer* in the *Liberator*, August 15, 1851.

95. A report of the Eleventh Massachusetts Anti-Slavery Fair says, "The Fair was never before so productive, so attractive and beautiful; and this we owe, in a large measure, to the taste, skill, and liberality of our British coadjutors" (*National Anti-Slavery Standard,* January 23, 1845, 134).

96. Charles Lenox Remond to Richard Allan, November 19, 1841, in *Black Abolitionist Papers,* ed. Ripley et al., 1:100; William Wells Brown, *A Description of William Wells Brown's Original Panoramic Views of the Scenes in the Life of an American Slave, from His Birth in Slavery to His Death or His Escape to His First Home of Freedom on British Soil* (London, 1849) in *Black Abolitionist Papers,* 1:214.

97. "Eleventh Massachusetts Anti-Slavery Fair," *National Anti-Slavery Standard,* December 19, 1844, 115. More general discussion of the fairs may be found in histories of the antislavery movement; see Jane H. Pease and William H. Pease, "The Boston Bluestocking: Maria Weston Chapman," in *Bound with Them in Chains: A Biographical History of the Antislavery Movement* (Westport, CT: Greenwood Press, Inc., 1972); Hansen, *Strained Sisterhood;* Walters, *The Antislavery Appeal.* For Margaret Fuller on the fair, see *The Letters of Margaret Fuller,* vol. 2, ed. Robert N. Hudspeth (Ithaca, NY: Cornell University Press, 1983), 261, also cited in Hansen, *Strained Sisterhood,* 129.

98. Roland Barthes, *The Fashion System,* trans. Matthew Ward and Richard Howard (Berkeley: University of California Press, 1990), 17.

99. Maria Weston Chapman, "The Twelfth National Anti-Slavery Bazaar," *National Anti-Slavery Standard,* January 29, 1846, 138.

100. Georg Simmel, *On Individuality and Social Forms,* ed. Donald N. Levine (Chicago: University of Chicago Press, 1971), 299–301.

101. "Slaves of Fashion," *Vanity Fair* (November 22, 1862), 244. A similar discourse around antislavery and fashion can be found in responses to both British and American "Antislavery Soirées." See "Farewell Soiree to Mr. Frederick Douglass," *Liberator,* April 30, 1847; and "Farewell Soiree to George Thompson, M.P.," *Liberator,* June 27, 1851.

102. "England and America," *National Anti-Slavery Standard,* September 5, 1844, 51.

103. "A Visit to an English Cottage," reprint from the *Democratic Review* in the *National Anti-Slavery Standard,* April 25, 1844, 188.

104. N. P. Rogers, "British Abolitionism," in *The Liberty Bell,* (Boston: National Anti-Slavery Bazaar, 1842), 101–2.

105. As cited in David Brion Davis, *Antebellum American Culture: An Interpretive Anthology* (University Park: Pennsylvania State University Press, 1979), 432. Blackett (*Building an Antislavery Wall*) provides a detailed account of black response to the conditions of the British working class.

106. Sumner, *Memoir and Letters of Charles Sumner,* 2:213–15. Sumner is alluding to Laurence Sterne's name for novelist Tobias Smollett, whose *Travels through France and Italy* is full of complaints for, and resistance to, everything he encounters on the Grand Tour.

107. "John Bull to Fanny Fern," reprint from the *New York Tribune* in *Frederick Douglass' Paper*, July 21, 1854.

108. "Character of Carlyle [Extract from a private letter from England]," *National Anti-Slavery Standard*, June 20, 1844, 20.

109. Ibid.

110. Stowe, "A Day Spent at Playford Hall," 300.

111. Douglass, *Narrative*, 24; Julia Griffiths Crofts, "Letters from the Old World—Number LXXVIII," *Douglass' Monthly*, January 1862, 582.

112. Brown, *American Fugitive*, 160.

113. From the redaction of Frederick Douglass's speech, "Slavery as It Now Exists in the United States: An Address Delivered in Bristol, England on 25 August 1846," *Bristol Mercury and Western Countries Advertiser*, August 29, 1846, reprinted in *The Frederick Douglass Papers*, ser. 1, *Speeches, Debates, and Interviews*, ed. John W. Blassingame, C. Peter Ripley, et al. (New Haven, CT: Yale University Press, 1979), 1:343.

114. Brown, *American Fugitive*, 183.

115. J. Mott, *Three Months*, 12; L. Mott, *Slavery*, 16 and 19.

116. L. Mott, *Slavery*, 33 and 53.

117. "Pen and Ink Sketches of Popular Persons and Places: By a Cosmopolitan: A Day with Hannah More," *National Anti-Slavery Standard*, August 28, 1845, 52.

118. L. Mott, *Slavery*, 68–72.

119. David M. Lubin, *Picturing a Nation: Art and Social Change in Nineteenth-Century America* (New Haven, CT: Yale University Press, 1994), 144–52; see also Joseph D. Ketner, *The Emergence of the African-American Artist: Robert S. Duncanson, 1821–1872* (Columbia: University of Missouri Press, 1993).

120. Lubin, *Picturing a Nation*, 146.

121. Ibid., 146, 148; Walter Scott, *The Lady of the Lake*, in *The Complete Poetical Works of Scott* (Boston: Houghton Mifflin Co., 1900), 173.

122. Lubin, *Picturing a Nation*, 151.

123. Moncure Conway, as quoted in Ketner, *Emergence*, 154.

124. W. E. B. Du Bois, *The Seventh Son: The Thought and Writings of W. E. B. Du Bois*, ed. Julius Lester (New York: Random House, 1971), 2:313. Lubin's mention of Du Bois is quite different in the context of the painting (Lubin, *Picturing a Nation*).

125. Du Bois, *Seventh Son*, 2:313–14.

126. W. E. B. Du Bois, *The Souls of Black Folk*, in *Writings*, ed. Nathan Huggins (New York: Library of America, 1986), 438.

127. "Education of Colored Refugees in England," *Liberator*, January 14, 1853, 7.

128. See Edward Said, "Nationalism, Human Rights, and Interpretation" in *Reflections on Exile and Other Essays* (Cambridge, MA: Harvard University Press, 2003), 413, and Said, *Culture and Imperialism* (New York: Vintage Books, 1993).

129. See "Samuel R. Ward," *Frederick Douglass' Paper*, June 26, 1851.

130. Stuart Hall, "Cultural Identity and Diaspora," in *Colonial Discourse and Post-Colonial Theory: A Reader*, ed. Patrick Williams and Laura Chrisman (New

York: Columbia University Press, 1994), 399. See also Victor J. Ramraj, "Diasporas and Multiculturalism," in *New National and Post-Colonial Literatures: An Introduction*, ed. Bruce King (New York: Oxford University Press, 1998), 214–29. The idea of an "imaginative geography and history" derives from Edward Said's discussion of Gaston Bachelard's *Poetics of Space* to describe the ways in which "by a kind of poetic process . . . the vacant or anonymous reaches of distance are converted into meaning for us here" (*Orientalism*, 55).

131. Joshua McCarter Simpson, "Queen Victoria Conversing with Her Slave Children," in *The Emancipation Car, Being an Original Composition of Antislavery Ballads, Composed Exclusively for the Underground Railroad* (1874; Miami: Mnemosyne Publishing Co., Inc., 1969), 59–63.

132. Benjamin Drew, *The North-side View of Slavery* (Boston: John P. Jewett & Co., 1856), 199.

133. Brown, *American Fugitive*, 102.

134. Daniel Alexander Payne, *History of the African Methodist Episcopal Church* (Nashville: A.M.E. Sunday School Union, 1891), 376.

135. Eugene D. Genovese, *In Red and Black* (London: Penguin Press, 1971), 74. See also Howard Newby, "The Deferential Dialectic," *Comparative Studies in Society and History* 17, no. 2 (April 1975), 139–64.

136. Austin Steward, *Twenty-two Years a Slave, and Forty Years a Freeman* (Rochester, NY: Allings & Cary, 1861), 330.

137. Mathew Arnold, *Culture and Anarchy*, ed. Samuel Lipman (New Haven, CT: Yale University Press, 1994), 55. I should clarify that Arnold's "principle of authority" does not extend to the aristocracy in Britain but to the State. He faults Carlyle for not recognizing that aristocracies, "being by the very nature of things inaccessible to ideas, unapt to see how the world is going, must be somewhat wanting in light, and must therefore be, at a moment when light is our great requisite, inadequate to our needs" (56).

138. S.S.N., "Anglo-Saxons, and Anglo-Africans," *Anglo-African Magazine*, August 1859, 247–51.

139. James Clifford, "Traveling Cultures," in *Routes: Travel and Translation in the Late Twentieth Century* (Cambridge, MA: Harvard University Press, 1997), 25.

140. Steward, *Twenty-two Years a Slave*, 331.

141. William G. Allen, "Letter from Prof. William G. Allen," *Frederick Douglass' Paper*, reprinted in the *Liberator*, November 26, 1852, 190.

142. Smith, introduction to *My Bondage and My Freedom*, by Douglass, 136–37.

143. Though these days, the inclinations of black Americans and British royalty seem to run outside-in. The *New York Times Magazine* writes that Prince Charles, in keeping with Tony Blair's "Cool Britannia," wants a make-over; he is the "new" Prince of Wales, more "down" than dapper—now that Will Smith has abdicated his title of "The Fresh Prince" (Warren Hoge, "The Fresh Prince," *New York Times Magazine* [November 22, 1998], 44).

144. Alexis de Tocqueville, "The Anglo-Americans," *Colored American*, May 16,

1840; "Extracts from Mrs. Stowe's New Book: *Sunny Memories of Foreign Lands*," *Frederick Douglass' Paper,* August 18, 1854.

145. For a discussion of Defoe and other attempts to racialize English identity, see Ian Baucom, *Out of Place,* 15–16. Arnold's sense of Anglo-Saxonism as an impure, cross-bred nationality is cogently examined in Vincent P. Pecora, "Arnoldian Ethnology," *Victorian Studies* 41, no. 3 (Spring 1998), 355–79. For more on how the epistemology of culture can traffic in the biology of race, see Walter Benn Michaels, *Our America: Nativism, Modernism and Pluralism* (Durham, NC: Duke University Press, 1995).

146. Douglass, *Life and Times,* 929.

147. Brown, *American Fugitive,* 184–86.

148. Daniel Walker Howe, *The Political Culture of the American Whigs* (Chicago: University of Chicago Press, 1979), 39; see also Walters, *The Antislavery Appeal.* Reginald Horsman describes a very different Anglo-Saxonism in *Race and Manifest Destiny.*

149. "The American Abolitionists," in *The Liberty Bell* (Boston: National Anti-Slavery Bazaar, 1841), 18; Richard D. Webb, "Memories of the Past," in *The Liberty Bell* (Boston: National Anti-Slavery Bazaar, 1842), 51–58; "Voices from the Old World," in *The Liberty Bell* (Boston: National Anti-Slavery Bazaar, 1847).

150. Lydia Maria Child, "The Black Saxons," in *The Liberty Bell* (Boston: National Anti-Slavery Bazaar, 1841), 19–44, passim.

151. *Uncle Tom in England; or, A Proof That Black's White: An Echo to the American "Uncle Tom"* (New York: A. D. Failing, 1852), 113, 123.

152. See "Extracts from Stowe's New Book: *Sunny Memories of Foreign Lands*," *Frederick Douglass' Paper,* August 18, 1854; *Uncle Tom in England,* 115, 120, 112.

153. Ross Posnock, "How It Feels to Be a Problem," 323–49. For an extended discussion, see Posnock, *Color and Culture.*

154. Oscar Wilde, *The Importance of Being Earnest and Other Plays,* ed. Richard Allen Cave (New York: Penguin Classics, 2001).

Chapter 4

1. William Dean Howells, *Literary Friends and Acquaintance: A Personal Retrospect of American Authorship,* ed. David F. Hiatt and Edwin H. Cady (1900; reprint, Bloomington: Indiana University Press, 1968), 187, 180–81.

2. George Santayana, *The Middle Span: Persons and Places* (New York: Charles Scribner's & Sons, 1945), 2:167 and 155; Ralph Waldo Emerson, "Experience," from *Essays: Second Series,* in *Essays and Lectures,* ed. Porte, 483; Howells, *Literary Friends,* 183, 181, and 186. For more on Lowell's walks through Cambridge, see William G. Morse, *Pardon My Harvard Accent* (New York: Farrar & Rinehart, 1941), 214–17.

3. Pierre Bourdieu, *Distinction: A Social Critique of the Judgment of Taste,* trans. Richard Nice (Cambridge, MA: Harvard University Press, 1984), 54; Howells, *Literary Friends,* 184, 185.

4. James Russell Lowell, "The Function of the Poet" (1855), in *Essays, Poems, and Letters,* ed. William Smith Clark II (New York: Odyssey Press, 1948), 57.

5. James Russell Lowell, "Shakespeare Once More" (1868), in *Among My Books* (Boston: Houghton, Mifflin & Co., 1893), 152; Lowell, "Function of the Poet," 57.

6. Lowell, "Shakespeare Once More," 152; Lowell, "Function of the Poet," 57.

7. Howells, *Literary Friends,* 188.

8. Lowell to G. B. Loring, July 8, 1838, in *Letters of James Russell Lowell,* ed. Charles Eliot Norton (Boston: Houghton, Mifflin & Co., 1904), 1:35. My sense of Lowell, in this context, as "social rather than transcendent" derives from my reading of Howells but also from Lionel Trilling's discussion of Englishness in *Sincerity and Authenticity,* 114. I return to Trilling later.

9. Horace E. Scudder, *James Russell Lowell: A Biography* (Boston: Houghton, Mifflin & Co., 1901), 1:395, as quoted in Gerald Graff, *Professing Literature: An Institutional History* (Chicago: University of Chicago Press, 1987), 40; Howells, *Literary Friends,* 188.

10. Letter from Henry Wadsworth Longfellow to his father, March 22, 1837, in *Life of Henry Wadsworth Longfellow, with Extracts from His Journals and Correspondence,* ed. Samuel Longfellow (Boston: Ticknor & Co., 1886), 1:250; Edward Everett Hale, *James Russell Lowell and His Friends* (Boston: Houghton, Mifflin & Co., 1899), 20.

11. Hale, *Lowell,* 20; Henry Adams, *The Education of Henry Adams,* ed. Jean Gooder (New York: Penguin, 1995), 70. Josiah Quincy was president of Harvard from 1829 to 1845. For the levees he inaugurated at the president's house, and which continued until the Civil War, see Ronald Story, *The Forging of an Aristocracy: Harvard and the Boston Upper Class, 1800–1870* (Middleton: Wesleyan University Press, 1980), 110.

12. In describing Adams's "education degree zero," I allude to Roland's Barthes's idea of "writing degree zero" to "affirm the existence of a formal reality" that aspires to be its own object (*Writing Degree Zero,* trans. Annette Lavers and Colin Smith, preface by Susan Sontag [New York: Hill & Wang, 1997], 5). Adams, *Education,* 62 and 65.

13. Lowell, "Address Delivered in Sanders Theatre, Cambridge, on the Two Hundred and Fiftieth Anniversary of the Foundation of Harvard University" (1886), in *Literary and Political Addresses* (Boston: Houghton, Mifflin & Co., 1904), 192–93; Barthes, *Writing Degree Zero,* 11. On Lowell's sense of the fate of literary study in the modern research university, I quote Gerald Graff and Reginald Gibbons, *Criticism in the University* (Evanston, IL: Northwestern University Press, 1985), 45.

14. Howells, *Literary Friends,* 201, 202, and 204; "On Dress," *Crimson* 6 (September 30, 1875): 9; Longfellow to George W. Greene, August 6, 1838, reprinted in *Life of Henry Wadsworth Longfellow,* ed. S. Longfellow, 293; Hale, *Lowell,* 21. The quote by Bourdieu is from *Distinction,* 91.

15. The best source for these social innovations is college newspapers of the nineteenth century, some of which I cite below. New rituals are also well documented in Benjamin Homer Hall, *A Collection of College Words and Customs* (Cam-

bridge: John Bartlett, 1856). For recent accounts, see Story, *Forging of an Aristocracy;* Graff, *Professing Literature;* and also Roger Geiger, ed., *The American College in the Nineteenth Century* (Nashville: Vanderbilt University Press, 2000); and James McLachlan, "The *Choice of Hercules:* American Student Societies in the Early 19th Century," in *The University in Society,* vol. 2, *Europe, Scotland, and the United States from the Sixteenth to the Twentieth Centuries,* ed. Lawrence Stone (Princeton, NJ: Princeton University Press, 1974), 449–94.

16. F. Scott Fitzgerald, *This Side of Paradise* (New York: Signet Classic, 1996), 52 and 39.

17. Nathaniel Hawthorne, *Fanshawe* (New York: Library of America, 1983), 113, 11, 114, 18, 4. Walcott's "youthful follies" may be found on 11; the quote that follows is on 114. See Isabel Petterson's review of *The Education of Peter,* by John Wiley, *New York Herald Tribune,* March 2, 1924, as cited in John O. Lyons, *The College Novel in America* (Carbondale: Southern Illinois University Press, 1968), xiv. For more on Hawthorne's own criticism of *Fanshawe,* see James R. Mellow, *Nathaniel Hawthorne in His Times* (Baltimore: Johns Hopkins Press, 1998), 41–44.

18. Hawthorne, *Fanshawe,* 112.

19. "Indifference," *Magenta* [Harvard], 1 (February 7, 1873): 15. The first college novels to appear after *Fanshawe* include Charles Bailey, *The Reclaimed Student: A Tale of College Life* (1844); Harry Hazel [Justin Jones], *The Belle of Boston; or, The Rival Students of Cambridge* (1844); Tim Whippoorwill [pseud.], *Nelly Brown; or, The Trials, Temptations and Pleasures of College Life* (1845); and John Denison Vose, *Yale College "Scrapes"* (1852). In addition to the novels by Bede and Brown, English college novels in the first half of the nineteenth century include John Gibson Lockhart, *Reginald Dalton* (1823); Joseph Hewlett, *Peter Priggins, the College Scout* (1841), *College Life; or, The Proctor's Notebook* (1843), and *Great Tom of Oxford* (1846); Francis Smedley, *Frank Fairlegh* (1849–50); Frederick William Farrar, *Julian Home: A Tale of College Life* (1859); Frederick Arnold, *Christ Church Days. An Oxford Story* (1867); Charles Lister, *The College Chums* (1845). While not a college novel, William Makepeace Thackeray's *The History of Pendennis* (1849–50) has several episodes at "Oxbridge" that set a precedent for scenes of student misconduct in later narratives.

20. Hawthorne, *Fanshawe,* 76–77; Bourdieu, *Distinction,* 54, on Plato's sense of the playful seriousness of culture; "Advocate Bards and Crimson Reviewers," *Crimson* (November 26, 1875): 54.

21. Bourdieu quotes the line but does not attribute it (*Distinction,* 331). The edition's translator credits it to the French politician Edouard Herriot.

22. Bourdieu, *Distinction,* 331 and 330; Hawthorne, *Fanshawe,* 11, 18, 5.

23. Geiger, ed., *American College,* 1–16; Leon Jackson, "The Rights of Man and the Rites of Youth," in *American College,* ed. Geiger, 78. See also Steven J. Novak, *The Rights of Youth: American Colleges and Student Revolt, 1798–1815* (Cambridge, MA: Harvard University Press, 1977). "Letters," *Amherst Collegiate Magazine: Conducted by Students at Amherst College* 1, no. 1 (October 1853): 17.

24. Roger Geiger, "Introduction: New Themes in the History of Nineteenth-Century Colleges," in *American College*, ed. Geiger, 10.

25. "Nostalgia for the Present" is a chapter title in Fredric Jameson, *Postmodernism; or, The Cultural Logic of Late Capitalism* (Durham, NC: Duke University Press, 1995).

26. Hawthorne, *Fanshawe*, 11; see Sheldon Rothblatt, "The Student Sub-culture and the Examination System in Early Nineteenth-Century Oxbridge," in *The University in Society*, vol. 1, *Oxford and Cambridge from the Fourteenth to the Early Nineteenth Century*, ed. Lawrence Stone (Princeton, NJ: Princeton University Press, 1974), 247–303. The quote appears on 247.

27. From Bliss Perry, *The Amateur Spirit* (1904), as cited in *The Origins of Literary Studies in America: A Documentary Anthology*, ed. Gerald Graff and Michael Warner (New York: Routledge, 1989), 107; Jameson, *Postmodernism*, 279.

28. Hall, *College Words and Customs*. In the 1856 edition, cited here, the English derivations of American college slang are taken from Charles Astor Bristed's *Five Years in an English University*, a memoir of his years at Cambridge, published in New York in 1852.

29. William Thompson Peters, *The College Experience of Ichabod Academicus*, illustrated by William T. Peters, and dedicated to their brother collegians by the editors, H.F.P. & G.M. (1849); George Henry Tripp, *Student-Life at Harvard* (Boston: Lockwood, Brooks & Co., 1876), 69 and 76. William Tucker Washburn's Wentworth becomes "somewhat blasé" in *Fair Harvard: A Story of American College Life* (New York: G. P. Putnam, 1869), 51. The definitions of slang I take again from Hall (*College Words and Customs*), but also James Buchanan Henry and Christian Scharff, *College as It Is; or, The Collegian's Manual in 1853* (ed. J. Jefferson Looney [Princeton, NJ: Princeton University Libraries, 1996]).

30. "The Senior's Soliloquy," *Harvard Lampoon* 2, no. 1 (October 12, 1976): 9. See Lyman Bagg, *Four Years at Yale* (New Haven, CT: Charles C. Chatfield, 1871), as quoted in Graff, *Professing Literature*, 25–26. Kirkland is quoted in Alexander Young, *A Discourse on the Life and Character of the Reverend John Thornton Kirkland, Formerly Pastor of the Church on Church Green, Boston, and Late President of Harvard University, Delivered in the Church on Church Green, May 3, 1840* (Boston: Charles C. Little & James Brown, 1840), 25. For more on cheating in college, see Helen Lefkowitz Horowitz, *Campus Life: Undergraduate Cultures from the End of the Eighteenth Century to the Present* (Chicago: University of Chicago Press, 1987), 32–33.

31. "On Dress," *Crimson*, September 30, 1875; James Russell Lowell, "A Great Public Character" (1867), in *My Study Windows* (New York: Houghton, Mifflin, & Co., 1882), 109.

32. "Genius in College," *Williams Quarterly Magazine* 6, no. 1 (August 1858): 66; "Editorial," *Magenta* 2 (July 9, 1874): 85.

33. T. S. Eliot, "Hamlet" (1919), in *Selected Prose of T. S. Eliot*, ed. Frank Kermode (New York: Farrar, Straus & Giroux, 1975), 49; William Shakespeare, *Hamlet*, ed. Philip Edwards (Cambridge: Cambridge University Press, 1985), 1.2.133–34.

34. "The Harvard Bible," *Advocate* 20, no. 3 (October 22, 1875): 33–34; "An Evolutionist's Idea of Harvard," *Advocate* 20, no. 5 (November 19, 1875): 53–55; "The Culture of Our Students," *Advocate* 20, no. 6 (December 3, 1875): 65–67; "The Reviewer Reviewed," *Crimson* (October 29, 1875); "Indifference Again," *Crimson* (November 12, 1875); "Harvard Pluck," *Crimson* (November 12, 1875); untitled item in the *Crimson* (November 26, 1875); "An Evolutionist Again," *Crimson* (November 26, 1875); "Advocate Bards and Crimson Reviewers," *Crimson* (November 26, 1875).

35. "Politics in College," *Williams Quarterly Magazine* 8, no. 3 (March 1861): 196.

36. "Indifference Again," *Crimson*, 41; Hale, *Lowell*, 22.

37. "American Politics," *Harvard Magazine* 6, no. 5 (March 1860): 187.

38. Graff, *Professing Literature,* 44–46; "A Glance at Some of the Peculiar Modes of College Existence," *Williams Quarterly Magazine* 1, no. 1 (July 1853): 15.

39. "Editor's Table," *Union College Magazine* 2, no. 3 (June 1862): 155; "Editorial Department," *Rutgers College Quarterly* 3, no. 4 (April 1861): 195.

40. "Otium Cum Dignitate," *Harvard Magazine* (November 1859); "A Glance," *Williams Quarterly Magazine,* 16; Simpson, *Romanticism,* 171; T. S. Eliot, "In Memory of Henry James," *Egoist* 5, no. 1 (January 1918), 1–2. Eliot on James is also cited in Simpson, *Romanticism,* 175.

41. "Indifference Again," *Crimson,* 41.

42. Ibid.

43. Simpson, *Romanticism,* 4; Irving Babbitt, "Literature and the American College: Essays in the Defense of the Humanities" (1908), in *Origins of Literary Studies,* 119. T. S. Eliot describes Babbitt's lecture style this way: "Superficially, his lectures were almost without method. He would enter the room with a pile of books, papers, and notes, which he shifted and shuffled throughout the hour; beginning to talk before he sat down, beginning anywhere and ending anywhere, he gave us the impression that a life-time was too short for telling us all that he wanted to say" (*Irving Babbitt: Man and Teacher,* ed. Frederick Manchester and Odell Shepard [New York: G. P. Putnam's Sons, 1941], 102).

44. "Indifference Again," *Crimson,* 41; "Extempore Speaking," *Harvard Magazine* (November 1859); Tocqueville, *Democracy in America,* 2:69.

45. Adams, *Education,* 175; Simpson, *Romanticism,* 27–28, 19; Babbitt, "Literature and the American College," 112. Stefan Collini's recent book about the "*question* of intellectuals" in twentieth-century Britain argues that such "long-established truisms" are false, exaggerated, or not particular to Britain; still, "what *has* been true is that the idea of British exceptionalism in these matters has flourished in the past two centuries (as, in each of the other countries one might discuss, has the idea of *that* country's exceptionalism)" (*Absent Minds: Intellectuals in Britain* [New York: Oxford University Press, 2006], 6). He cites, for example, Bulwer Lytton, writing in the 1830s about the "unintellectual English": "Our general indifference to political theories; our quiet and respectable adherence to things that are . . . this propensity has for centuries assuredly distinguished us; we have been very little alive to all speculative innovations in morals and politics" (70).

46. Anderson, *English Questions,* 57; Trilling, *Sincerity and Authenticity,* 113; Emerson, *English Traits,* 929, 903, 811, 899, 931–32, 786.

47. Adams, *Education,* 205; John Locke, *An Essay concerning Human Understanding,* ed. Peter N. Nidditch (Oxford: Clarendon Press, 1979), 104.

48. Adams, *Education,* 205, 213.

49. Emerson, *English Traits,* 830–31, 827; Trilling, *Sincerity and Authenticity,* 115, 113; Tocqueville, *Democracy in America,* 2:77; Lowell, "The Function of the Poet," 22; Grund, *Aristocracy in America,* 205; Adams, *Education,* 176.

50. Said, *Orientalism,* 70; see, for example, "English and Englishmen," *Williams Quarterly Magazine* (March 1858): 193–204; and "English Traits," *Harvard Magazine* (September 1856): 297

51. Trilling, *Sincerity and Authenticity,* 81; R. W. B. Lewis, *The American Adam: Innocence, Tragedy and Tradition in the Nineteenth Century* (1955; reprint, Chicago: University of Chicago Press, 1984).

52. George S. Hillard, *Life, Letters and Journals of George Ticknor,* 2 vols. (Boston: James R. Osgood & Co., 1876), 1:96–99.

53. Theodor Adorno, *Minima Moralia,* 189. For a good historical discussion of the difference between "humanities" in the English-speaking world and the humanities in Germany, see Samuel Weber, "Ambivalence: The Humanities and the Study of Literature," in *Institution and Interpretation* (Stanford, CA: Stanford University Press, 2001), 132–52.

54. Charles Leland Balch, "Cambridge University, England," in *The University Quarterly [The Undergraduate]: Conducted by an Association of Collegiate and Professional Students, in the United States and Europe* (New Haven, CT: July 1861): 1.

55. Franklin E. Court, *The Scottish Connection: The Rise of English Literary Study in Early America* (Syracuse, NY: Syracuse University Press, 2001); "The Scholar's Helps and Hindrances," *Williams Quarterly Magazine* 4, no. 1 (August 1856): 55; Young, *Kirkland,* 47.

56. Young, *Kirkland,* 47–48.

57. Lowell, *Essays, Poems, and Letters,* xxii.

58. Even aesthetic formalists such as I. A. Richards, who were often critically aligned with belletristic humanists against German-influenced modes of historicism and philology, could be attacked on these grounds. Writing mainly of Richards and Cleanth Brooks, for example, John Guillory argues that the New Critics "concede a very great deal to the epistemological tyranny of science . . . but only because that concession is strategic, because scientific truth has already been stigmatized as the origin of our dissociated modernity" (*Cultural Capital: The Problem of Literary Canon Formation* [Chicago: University of Chicago Press, 1993], 159). He suggests that the New Critical project to articulate the specific "difficulty" of literary language—and to codify a set of reading practices that "[redefined] the social space of literary culture as necessarily *institutional*"—reflects at once the growing marginalization of literature in twentieth-century mass culture and, also, the need of literary academics to compete with the increasing prestige of fields (in both the

sciences and social sciences) defined around specialized languages and techniques (165). In a more polemic vein, several of the essays in the recent anthology *Theory's Empire* assert an even stronger link between the rise of literary theory in the 1970s and 1980s and a culture of professionalization in the humanities derived in part from the example of the New Critics. See, especially, Daphne Patai and Will H. Corral's introduction (1–18), John M. Ellis's "Is Theory to Blame?" (92–108), and Morris Dickstein's "The Rise and Fall of 'Practical Criticism'" (60–77) (in *Theory's Empire: An Anthology of Dissent*, ed. Daphne Patai and Will H. Corral [New York: Columbia University Press, 2005]). Dickstein observes a powerful connection between the way New Critics such as I. A. Richards "[eschew] belletristic continuity, preferring the appearance of a scientific analysis" and the interpretive methodologies of Barthes and other poststructuralists, who "virtually [jettison] the human element in literature" in favor of a "self-conscious emphasis on mechanics, on formal engineering at the expense of theme and emotion" (72, 74). Ellis claims that the contemporary turn to theory and its abstract, quasi-scientific language "serves as a protective device in that its remoteness from ordinary speech camouflages triviality or absurdity" (105). These debates about the place of literary culture in the modern corporate-research university not only revisit many of the contested terms from nineteenth-century accounts of Harvard and elsewhere but also testify to similar anxieties about the usefulness of literary criticism.

59. Lionel Trilling, *The Moral Obligation to Be Intelligent: Selected Essays*, ed. Leon Wieseltier (New York: Farrar, Straus, & Giroux, 2000), xiii.

60. Lowell, "At Sea" (1854), in *Essays, Poems, Letters*, 45; Everett, as cited in Young, *Kirkland*, 71.

61. Lowell, "Books and Libraries" (1885), in *Literary and Political Addresses*, 98; Lowell, "Function of the Poet," 55.

62. Emerson, "Experience," 472–83, passim.

63. Ibid., 476–83, passim.

64. B. L. Packer, *Emerson's Fall: A New Interpretation of the Major Essays* (New York: Continuum, 1982), 172–73.

65. Emerson, "Montaigne; or, The Skeptic," in *Representative Men*, ed. Joel Porte (New York: Library of America, 1983), 708–9, 704, 700, 699, 694; Emerson, "Experience," 480–81.

66. Howard Mumford Jones, ed., *English Traits* by Ralph Waldo Emerson (Cambridge, MA: Harvard University Press, 1966), ix.

67. Emerson, *English Traits*, 929–32.

68. Emerson, "Experience," 477–81; Emerson, "Montaigne," 90. On genius as "common sense," see "Experience," 482.

69. William Wordsworth, "Essay, Supplementary to the Preface," in *Literary Criticism of William Wordsworth* (Lincoln: University of Nebraska Press, 1966), 182. On genius in the essay, and ideas of genius in the Romantic period more generally, see Martha Woodmansee, *The Author, Art, and the Marketplace: Rereading the History of Aesthetics* (New York: Columbia University Press, 1994), 35–55.

70. Emerson, "Shakespeare," in *Representative Men,* 710, 716, 711, 716. In "Quotation and Originality," Emerson writes, "And what is Originality? It is being, being one's self, and reporting accurately what we see and are" (in *Letters and Social Aims* [Boston: James R. Osgood & Co., 1876], 178).

71. John Keats to George and Tom Keats, December 21, 29, 1817, in *Letters of John Keats,* ed. Robert Gittings (Oxford: Oxford University Press, 1988), 43; Keats to J. H. Reynolds, February 19, 1818, in *Letters,* 67.

72. Emerson, "Shakespeare," 715, 723, 722, 724; George Henry Calvert, *Shakespeare: A Biographic Aesthetic Study* (Boston: Lee & Shepard, 1879), 12.

73. Henry Hudson, *Lectures on Shakespeare* (New York: Baker & Scribner, 1848), 50, 117, 120, 149.

74. "Shakspeare versus Sand," *American Whig Review* 5, no. 5 (March 1847): 471, 472; Lowell, *Essays, Poems, and Letters,* xliii.

75. "Plagiarism: An Apology for the Last Comer," *American Whig Review* 10, no. 29 (August 1849): 139; "Shakspeare's Sonnets," *American Whig Review* 6, no. 3 (September 1847): 306; "Whipple's Essays and Reviews," *American Whig Review* 9, no. 14 (February 1849): 151.

76. James Russell Lowell, "Shakespeare Once More" (1868), in *Among My Books* (Boston: Houghton, Mifflin, 1893), 152, 159, 171, 182, 156; Emerson, "Shakespeare," 724.

77. "Plagiarism," *Bowdoin Port-Folio* 1, no. 5 (September 1839): 131; "Recipes for Making a Composition," *The Dartmouth: Conducted by Students of Dartmouth College* 3 (October 1842): 76–77; "Originality," *The Classic, or College Monthly* [Middletown, CT] 1, no. 1 (July 1840): 27–28.

78. Bliss Perry, "The Amateur Spirit" (1904), in *Origins of Literary Studies,* ed. Graff and Warner, 104.

79. Santayana, *The Middle Span,* 155–57; Emerson, "Experience," 482; "Superficial Knowledge," *Magenta* (May 16, 1873): 98.

80. Bourdieu, *Distinction,* 92.

81. Richard Grant White, *Words and Their Uses, Past and Present: A Study of the English Language* (New York: Sheldon & Co., 1871), 57.

82. Ibid., 62; "The Anglo-American," *Magenta* (May 7, 1875): 70; Andrew Peabody, *Conversation: Its Faults and Its Graces* (Boston: James Monroe & Co., 1855), 4; J. A. Cummings, *The Pronouncing Spelling Book, Adapted to Walker's Critical Pronouncing Dictionary* (Worcester: Dorr & Howland, 1831), reverse of title page.

83. Review of *Lectures Read to Seniors in Harvard College,* by Edward T. Channing, *North American Review* (January 1857): 34–48.

84. See Story, *Forging,* 112; Edward T. Channing, *Lectures Read to the Seniors in Harvard College,* introduction by Richard Henry Dana, Jr. (Boston: Ticknor & Fields, 1856), xiii, 50; Hale, *James Russell Lowell,* 19.

85. Dana, introduction to *Lectures Read to the Seniors,* by Channing, xiii. For a discussion of Channing's lectures on rhetoric, see Dorothy C. Broaddus, *Genteel*

Rhetoric: Writing High Culture in Nineteenth-Century Boston (Columbia: University of South Carolina Press, 1999), 9–10, 29–36.

86. Howells, *Literary Friends*, 198.

87. Review of *An American Dictionary of the English Language*, by Noah Webster (1859) and *A Dictionary of the English Language*, by Joseph E. Worcester (1860), *Atlantic Monthly* 5 (May 1860): 631–37, as cited in Dennis E. Baron, *Grammar and Good Taste: Reforming the American Language* (New Haven, CT: Yale University Press, 1982), 33; "Letter from Noah Webster," *The Classic, or College Monthly* [Middletown, CT], 2, no. 9 (March 1842): 420; Goold Brown, *The Grammar of English Grammars*, 10th ed. (New York: William Wood & Co., 1851), 26, 31.

88. As cited in Barron, *Grammar*, 33.

89. Henry Alford, *The Queen's English* (New York: A. Strahan, 1869), 131. Henry Alford, dean of Canterbury, was popular in the United States, as was the American, George Washington Moon, whose response to Alford, *The Dean's English*, criticized his usage. See Baron, *Grammar and Good Taste*, 190–97, for the citations.

90. White, *Words and Their Uses*, 203, 5.

91. Edward T. Channing, "Elocution: A Study," in *Lectures Read to the Seniors*, 47.

92. "The Anglo-American," *Magenta* (May 7, 1875): 70.

93. "Our English Cousins," *Harvard Lampoon* (October 12, 1876): 5.

94. Cartoon, *Harvard Lampoon* (March 23, 1876): 42.

95. "College Dialect," *Harvard Magazine* (May 1858).

96. Channing, "Elocution: A Study," 47 and 71; Walter Prichard Eaton, "Here's to the Harvard Accent" (1936), in *The Harvard Book: Selections from Three Centuries*, ed. William Bentinck-Smith (Cambridge, MA: Harvard University Press, 1953), 29.

97. "The Centennial Ball," *Harvard Lampoon* (March 9, 1876): 32.

98. Henry James, *The Question of Our Speech* (Boston: Houghton Mifflin, 1905), 12, 16, 22, 35, 20.

99. Brown, *Grammar of English Grammars*, 133; James, *Question*, 39.

100. Ebenezer Porter, *The Rhetorical Reader; Consisting of Instructions for Regulating the Voice, with a Rhetorical Notation, Illustrating Inflection, Emphasis, and Modulation; and a Course of Rhetorical Exercises Designed for the Use of Academies and High-Schools* (Andover: Gould & Newman, 1840), 14.

101. Channing, "Elocution," 50; Brown, *Grammar of English Grammars*, 810.

102. Dana, introduction to *Lectures*, by Channing, xii–xiii; Lowell, "Shakespeare Once More," 152.

103. White, *Words and Their Uses*, 182, 162; Peabody, *Conversation*, 6; Oliver Bunce, *Don't: A Manual of Mistakes and Improprieties More or Less Prevalent in Conduct and Speech* (New York: D. Appleton, 1883), 65, 91

104. White, *Words and Their Uses*, 219; Royall Tyler, *The Contrast*, in *Early American Drama*, ed. Jeffrey H. Richards (New York: Penguin, 1997), 19; "Vacation Strollings of Geoffrey La-Touche," in *The Collegian* (Cambridge, MA: Hilliard & Brown, 1830): 116–17; "Dialogue at an English University," *The University Quarterly*

[The Undergraduate]: Conducted by an Association of Collegiate and Professional Students, in the United States and Europe (New Haven, CT: January 1860): 47.

105. "Indifference Again," *Crimson,* 42.

106. See Jackson's wonderful essay, "Rights of Man."

107. Novak, *Rights of Youth,* 25; see also Horowitz, *Campus Life,* 23–55.

108. See Frederick Rudolph, *The American College and University: A History* (New York: Alfred A. Knopf, 1962), 136–55; see also Thomas S. Harding, *College Literary Societies: Their Contribution to Higher Education in the United States, 1815–1876* (New York: Pageant Press, 1971).

109. Hall, *College Words and Customs,* 20 and 41–46; Henry and Scharff, *College as It Is,* 27, 157, and throughout, on undergraduate pranks at Princeton.

110. "The Society Spirit," *Magenta* (January 30, 1874): 112.

111. Both Guillory and Readings, from different vantage points, describe the place of the humanities as especially fragile in the context of the modern university, or the "university of excellence" as Readings puts it. See John Guillory, *Cultural Capital: The Problem of Literary Canon Formation* (Chicago: University of Chicago Press, 1993); and Bill Readings, *The University in Ruins* (Cambridge, MA: Harvard University Press, 1996).

112. Claude Lévi-Strauss, *The Savage Mind* (Chicago: University of Chicago Press, 1966), 25.

113. Charles Astor Bristed, *Five Years in an English University* (New York: G. P. Putnam, 1852); Thomas Hughes, *School Days at Rugby* (Boston: Ticknor & Fields, 1857); Thomas Hughes, *Tom Brown at Oxford* (Boston: Ticknor & Fields, 1861). See the review of *School Days at Rugby* in *Virginia University Magazine* (November 1859): 73. Tom Brown shows up at Harvard in a 1926 film directed by Jack Conway, *Brown at Harvard.* A review is reprinted in Richard Bissell, *You Can Always Tell a Harvard Man* (New York: McGraw-Hill, 1962), 19.

114. "Arnold of Rugby," review of *The Life and Correspondence of Thomas Arnold, Late Head-Master of Rugby School and Regis Professor of Modern History in the University of Oxford,* in *Williams Quarterly Magazine* (June 1859): 293.

115. See Baucom, *Out of Place,* 137–45.

116. "School Days at Rugby," *Virginia University Magazine,* 73; the president of Amherst, as cited in Frederick Rudolph, *The American College and University: A History* (New York: Alfred A. Knopf, 1962), 139; Lytton Strachey, *Eminent Victorians* (1918; reprint, New York: Penguin Books, 1986), 188.

117. Emerson, *English Traits,* 903; Trilling, *Sincerity and Authenticity,* 114.

118. "Editor's Table," *Williams Quarterly Magazine* 4, no. 3 (March 1857): 283–84; Tripp, *Student-Life at Harvard,* 466.

119. Benjamin Homer Hall, "Freshmen Servitude," 213–25; "Manners," on "outward observances of respect," 301–4; "Tutoring Freshmen," 468–69, all in *College Words and Customs,* by Hall. On "servitude" and "tutoring," see also Richard Waldron, "Freshman Guide" (1735); and Frederick West Holland, "A Freshman Hazing" (1827), both in *The Harvard Book,* ed. Bentinck-Smith, 145–46 and 146–48, respectively.

120. On alumni, see Story, *Forging of an Aristocracy,* 153–59; Grace Greenwood as quoted in Hall, *College Words and Customs,* 73.

121. "Religion at Harvard," *Magenta* (April 18, 1873): 75. For more on secularism and antisecularism at Harvard, see, for example, Daniel Walker Howe, *The Unitarian Conscience: Harvard Moral Philosophy, 1805–1861* (Middletown, CT: Wesleyan University Press, 1988).

122. Hall, "Academicals," in *College Words and Customs;* Anderson, *English Questions,* 31.

123. Everett, as described by Grace Greenwood on Class Day in Hall, *College Words and Customs,* 73. In *Harvard College by an Oxonian,* George Birkbeck Hill writes: "The need of ceremony is gradually becoming felt. On Commencement Day . . . the gown has for some while been commonly worn by 'the Graduating Class.' On this great day, and on this alone, the President and the Professors wear their gowns." Hill provides the following anecdote about the inherited use of gowns from Oxford before academic dress was standardized in the United States in the 1890s: "Some fifty or sixty years ago, Professor Ticknor—so the story runs—brought back from Oxford, where he had received an honorary degree, a gown which was, he said, that of a Doctor of Civil Law. This he wore at Harvard on solemn occasions. On resigning his professorship, he bequeathed it to Longfellow, who succeeded him in his chair, who in his turn wore it, and in his turn, on his resignation, bequeathed it to his successor Lowell" ([New York: Macmillan & Co., 1894], 155–56).

124. "My Chum," *Virginia University Magazine* (November 1859); Adams, *Education,* 66; "The Lesser Evils of Life," *Harvard Magazine* (July 1857): 246–47; Howells, *Literary Friends,* 190.

125. Fitzgerald, *This Side of Paradise,* 29; Herman Melville, "The Paradise of Bachelors and the Tartarus of Maids," in *Great Short Works,* ed. Berthoff, 322; "In Bed," *Harvard Magazine* (December 1858): 412–18. This college fraternal culture anticipates and reproduces many features of the fraternal organizations that Dana D. Nelson powerfully describes in *National Manhood: Capitalist Citizenship and the Imagined Fraternity of White Men* (Durham, NC: Duke University Press, 1998). See especially her chapter titled "The Melancholy of White Manhood; or, Democracy's Privileged Spot," where she argues that "fraternal ritual offered to provide men a formally and emotionally focused time during which they could experience themselves as part of a controlled male body" (185). In the context of an increasingly competitive and anonymous democratic society, the middle-class men who joined the Freemasons, Odd Fellows, and similar organizations experienced "a kind of narcotic for conflicts faced outside the lodges," as well as a space where "ritual enactments" of emotion and affection shaped bonds between men that courted a language of homosocial feeling but only to channel it toward what Nelson terms a "civic imaginary" (186–87). It is possible to observe a similar channeling of social energies in U.S. colleges of the period as the rise of institutionally sanctioned sociality came to replace older strictures of institutional discipline and rule; and of course, the solicitation of same-sex feeling is pronounced in college culture of the period.

126. "Editor's Table," *Harvard Magazine* (October 1857): 352; "Editor's Table," *Virginia University Magazine* (June 1859): 538.

127. René Girard, *Deceit, Desire, and the Novel: Self and Other in Literary Structure,* trans. Yvonne Freccero (Baltimore: Johns Hopkins University Press, 1976), 10; "College Prejudices," *Union College Magazine* (June 1870): 42 and 45.

128. Trilling, *Sincerity and Authenticity,* 115.

129. David Bjelajac, *Washington Allston, Secret Societies, and the Alchemy of Anglo-American Painting* (New York: Cambridge University Press, 1997), 14–20, passim. See also Jared B. Flagg, *The Life and Letters of Washington Allston* (New York: Charles Scribner's Sons, 1892), 59–66.

130. See Steven C. Bullock, *Revolutionary Brotherhood: Freemasonry and the Transformation of the American Social Order, 1730–1840* (Chapel Hill: University of North Carolina Press, 1996), 139–41.

131. Naomi Schor, *Reading in Detail: Aesthetics and the Feminine* (New York: Methuen, 1987), 24–28.

132. The quote is taken from Emerson's journal entry for February 26, 1822, *Emerson in His Journals,* ed. Joel Porte (Cambridge, MA: Harvard University Press, Belknap Press, 1982), 11–12.

133. Graff and Warner, eds., *Origins of Literary Studies,* 7–8.

134. Hall, "Class Day," in *College Words and Customs.*

135. On the history of the yard, see Samuel F. Batchelder, *Bits of Harvard History* (Cambridge, MA: Harvard University Press, 1924), 79–153; and Bainbridge Bunting, *Harvard: An Architectural History,* ed. Margaret Henderson Floyd (Cambridge: Belknap Press of Harvard University Press, 1985); also Story, *Forging of an Aristocracy,* 116.

136. On "adopted sons" and "classical shades," see definitions in Hall, *College Words and Customs.* "Editor's Table," *Williams Quarterly Magazine* (October 1853): 185; "College Life," *Harvard Magazine* (January 1863); "In the Buildings," *Harvard Magazine* (January 1858): 14; "Editor's Table," *Virginia University Magazine* (June 1860): 533. The views of Harvard are from Hamilton Vaughan Bail, *Views of Harvard: A Pictorial Record to 1860,* foreword by Samuel Eliot Morison (Cambridge, MA: Harvard University Press, 1949).

137. "In the Buildings," *Harvard Magazine* (January 1858); Raymond Williams, *The Country and the City* (New York: Oxford University Press, 1975), 139, 140.

138. Henry James, *The American Scene,* ed. John F. Sears (New York: Penguin, 1994), 45–50, passim.

139. See Staiti, *Morse,* 207–15 and 135–37. On Morse's nativism, see Samuel F. B. Morse, *Imminent Dangers to the Free Institutions of the United States through Foreign Immigration* (New York: Clayton, 1835); and Morse, *Foreign Conspiracy against the Liberties of the United States* (New York: Leavitt, Lord & Co., 1835).

140. In an ambitious book on admissions since 1900, Jerome Karabel argues that the selection process emphasized "character" over academic performance as a way of screening out "scholastically brilliant boys" who were ethnically "undesir-

able" (*The Chosen: The Hidden History of Admission and Exclusion at Harvard, Yale, and Princeton* [Boston: Houghton Mifflin, 2005], 131). He associates the Anglophilia of Harvard president Abbott Lawrence Lowell, for example, with the belief that immigrants posed a threat to democracy and that colleges should cultivate an elite and socially cohesive citizenry. From a different perspective, Jonathan Freedman provocatively argues that Trilling and other Jewish intellectuals pursued Anglophilic interests as a means of erasing their ethnicity and class through their literary achievements. See *The Temple of Culture: Assimilation and Anti-Semitism in Literary Anglo-America* (New York: Oxford University Press, 2000).

141. James Russell Lowell, *Fireside Travels* (Boston: Houghton, Mifflin & Co., 1904), 17; for more on emblematic English gardens and pastoral conventions, see Ronald Paulson, *Emblem and Expression: Meaning in English Art of the Eighteenth Century* (London: Thames & Hudson, 1975).

142. Lowell, *Letters*, 1:25.

143. Longfellow to George W. Greene, May 21, 1837, in *Life of Henry Wadsworth Longfellow*, ed. S. Longfellow, 253.

144. Trilling, "On the Teaching of Modern Languages," in *The Moral Obligation to Be Intelligent*, 383.

Index